Coleridge'

Barry Hough was formerly Professor in English Law at Bournemouth University and is now at the University of Buckingham. He is the author of numerous articles in the field of Constitutional and Administrative law and Employment law. He is author of the leading monograph *Street Trading and Markets and Fairs* (Boston, UK, Earlsgate Press, 1994) a contributor to four editions of J. Alder, *Constitutional and Administrative Law* (Basingstoke and New York, Palgrave Macmillan, and a contributor to William Blake Odgers (ed.), *High Court Pleading & Practice* (London: Sweet & Maxwell, 1991).

Howard Davis is Reader in Public Law at Bournemouth University. As well as law and literature his other research and teaching interests relate to constitutional law and human rights, in particular the reception of European human rights law through the Human Rights Act 1998. His textbook, *Human Rights Law Directions* (Oxford: Oxford University Press, 2009) is now in its second edition.

Michael John Kooy is Associate Professor at the Department of English and Comparative Literary Studies at Warwick University. His main research interests lie in British and European Romanticism, especially Coleridge, and in the relationship between philosophy and literature. Kooy is the author of *Coleridge, Schiller and Aesthetic Education* (Basingstoke and New York: Palgrave Macmillan, 2002) and he is currently completing a book called *Coleridge and War*, which assesses Coleridge's wartime activities as a journalist and poet in relation to his political theology.

Lydia Davis took her degree in Latin and Ancient History at Edinburgh University. Her PhD on *British Travellers and the Rediscovery of Sicily, 16th-19th Centuries* was awarded in 2006. She has lived and studied in Rome and Sicily. She currently works for Hansard at the House of Commons.

Samuel Taylor Coleridge (1819) drawn by C. R. Leslie, engraved by H. Meyer, published 1st April 1819 by Henry Colburn.

Barry Hough and Howard Davis

With an Introduction by Michael John Kooy

Coleridge's Laws
A Study of Coleridge in Malta

Translations by Lydia Davis

Cambridge
OpenBook
Publishers
2010

OpenBook
Publishers

40 Devonshire Road, Cambridge, CB1 2BL, United Kingdom
http://www.openbookpublishers.com

As with all Open Book Publishers titles, digital material and resources associated with this volume are available from our website:
http://www.openbookpublishers.com

ISBN Hardback: 978-1-906924-13-3
ISBN Paperback: 978-1-906924-12-6
ISBN Digital (pdf): 978-1-906924-14-0

Acknowledgement is made to the National Library of Malta for generously permitting use of material in their possession and for allowing the reproduction of the 'Bandi' and 'Avvisi' in this volume.

All paper used by Open Book Publishers is SFI (Sustainable Forestry Initiative), and PEFC (Programme for the Endorsement of Forest Certification Schemes) Certified.

Printed in the United Kingdom and United States by
Lightning Source for Open Book Publishers

To Mary and to Stella

Acknowledgements

We would like to express our gratitude to the British Academy without whose financial support this book would not have been possible. Dr Elinor Shaffer's keen interest in the project not only saw it through its early gestation but it also continued to guide, enrich and challenge our work as it progressed. Dr Michael Kooy's interest, advice and enthusiasm have also been great encouragement to us. We are particularly delighted that he accepted an invitation to write the Introduction to this book. The staff of the National Library of Malta, Valletta, and the National Archive of Malta, Rabat, have also shown us kindness and tireless assistance in locating sources. Dr Maroma Camillieri, Dr Charles Farrugia, and Dr Joseph Amodio have each provided us with tireless and valuable assistance. Richard Ireland and Robert Ireland each of the University of Wales, Aberystwyth also provided their scholarly expertise in interpreting some of the obscure Latin used in some of the witness statements. Our thanks are also due to Craig Willox of the Department of Law, Bournemouth University, for his assistance with the manuscript.

Contents

Illustrations

Cover and 5.: Aquatint bearing the inscription: "To the R.t Hon. ble. Lord Viscount Nelson, K.B. Duke of Bronte &c. &c. &c., This Print of the commencement of the gallant defence, made by His Majesty's Sloop Arrow of 23 Guns & 132 Men, Richard Budd Vincent Esq.r Commander; and His Maj: Bomb Vessel Acheron of 8 Guns and & 57 Men, Arthur Farquhar Esq.r Com.r against the French Frigate, L'Hortense and L'Incorruptible of 44 Guns & 550 Men each, including troops of the Line, which took place on the Morning of the 4.th of Feb.y 1805, off Cape Palos; for the preservation of a Valuable Convoy Is (by Permission most humbly Dedicated by his most obliged humble Servant, George Andrews. [&] To the R.t Hon.ble. Lord Viscount Nelson, K.B. Duke of Bronte &c. &c. &c.," Painted by F. Sartorius. Engraved by J. Jeakes. Published Oct. 21. 1805, by G. Andrews, No. 7, Charing Cross [private collection].

Frontispiece: Samuel Taylor Coleridge (1819) drawn by C. R. Leslie, engraved by H. Meyer, published 1st April 1819 by Henry Colburn [private collection].

1. A view of Valletta from South Street with the Marsamxett or Quarantine Harbour on the left [B. Hough, 2007].   27

2. San Antonio Palace, now the official residence of the President of Malta, at St Anton, Attard. During the Maltese uprising 1799-1800 Captain Ball used it as his residence. He returned when he became Civil Commissioner in 1802. Coleridge spent much of his time there [B. Hough, 2006].   28

3. The interior of the President's Palace, Valletta. It would not have been less opulent when Coleridge resided there [B. Hough, 2007].   35

Abbreviations

CL: Griggs, E.L., *Collected Letters of Samuel Taylor Coleridge*, 6 vols., Oxford: Clarendon Press, 1956-71

CN: Coburn, K., *The Notebooks of Samuel Taylor Coleridge 1804-1808*, New York: Bollingen, 1961

EOT: Erdman D. V. (ed.), *Essays on His Times in 'The Morning Post' and 'The Courier'*, in *The Collected Works of Samuel Taylor Coleridge,* volumes, 3: 1-3 (General Editor: Kathleen Coburn), London: Routledge and Kegan Paul, 1978

Kew: British National Archive, Kew

NAM: National Archive of Malta, Rabat, Malta

NLM: National Library of Malta, Valletta, Malta

Foreword

"I have the public Memorials to write & worse than all constant matters of Arbitration"[1]

Coleridge's Bandi (Proclamations) and Avvisi (Public Notices)[2] appear to be of a minor, regulatory character dealing with such matters as licensing, cartwheels, mooring ropes, foreigners and excise duties. In fact, these legal and administrative texts reveal how Coleridge used and controlled government information to advance the dominant strategic purpose of British rule. They were intended not only to alter behaviour, but also to influence public opinion and secure the legitimacy of British rule.

As we shall discover, the British in Malta were explicitly directed by the British imperial government to achieve popularity with the Maltese and to ensure the stability of the islands as a British possession. A series of policies and decisions, whether ill-advised in conception or operation, some resulting from the incompetence of administrators, or the deliberate hoodwinking of the British by the Maltese, led to a temporary, but profound, decline in British popularity. Confidence in the British and, in particular, in the Civil Commissioner, Sir Alexander Ball, whose autocratic constitutional authority made him the embodiment of British purposes and values, was at a dangerously low ebb by the spring of 1805. Coleridge was compelled, not least in the laws and public notices, to mount a propaganda offensive to "re-engage" with the Maltese public. He had to portray a selfless, benign administration that, according to Coleridge's narrative, prioritised Maltese interests, and acted merely to ensure the well-being of the local population.

In fact, Malta, at that time, exposed the difficulties administrators faced when confronted with the inherent conflict of interest in the colonial project. In many instances, British imperial goals were not invariably

---

1   To Mrs S. T. Coleridge, 21 July 1805 in *Collected Letters of Samuel Taylor Coleridge*, ed. E.L. Griggs, 6 vols. (Oxford: Clarendon Press, 1956-71), 2, 1169-70. Hereafter referred to as *CL*.
2   "Bando" and "avviso" in the singular.

congruent with Maltese interests. The de-stabilising tensions, springing from this divided colonial relationship, had to be managed because, as the British knew, a disaffected Maltese population could be capable of violent insurrection. They had responded to a call to arms as recently as 1798 to evict the unpopular French occupiers from their islands. A decline in popular support threatened continued British possession. In securing the long-term strategic goals of British rule, Coleridge was required to assume a weighty burden of responsibility. The evidence of depression, stress, over-work and addiction shown in his *Notebooks* attest to his struggle to fulfil the demanding expectations of him in his public office as well as overcoming the well-known problems in his private life.

Preface

In 1804-1805 the English poet and philosopher Samuel Taylor Coleridge stayed in Malta. He had travelled to Malta in pursuit of a cure for his drug addiction. He might have hoped for a petty colonial sinecure to defray the expenses of his travels. When, in January 1805, he became the acting Public Secretary under the Civil Commissioner, Sir Alexander Ball, he found himself burdened with a significant public role at the heart of government. Donald Sultana, in his major work *Samuel Taylor Coleridge in Malta and Italy*,[1] has written the fullest and most detailed general account of Coleridge's life on the Island. This book, though indebted to Sultana's study, has a more modest focus. It is a study of the Malta period predominantly from a legal and constitutional perspective. Its concern and focus is upon the "laws", the legal instruments (Bandi and Avvisi), that were drafted and promulgated by Coleridge in his official capacity. Sultana deals with a selection of these, but this book aims to be a comprehensive study. These instruments ("Coleridge's Laws") are given full descriptions and analyses, both critical and contextual. Their content is considered in the context of Maltese politics, economy and society and also of the British imperial ambition for the Island. This is done against the background of the Maltese constitution and the expectations of the rule of law that British rule might have brought.

The approach has been to go to the original sources relating to these laws, both in Malta (at the National Library, Valletta and the National Archive, Rabat) and in Britain (at the National Archive). Assistance for the Malta part of the enquiry was given by grants from the British Academy, which the authors are pleased to acknowledge. Similarly, the assistance of the staff at the National Library and National Archive in Malta was of very great help, not only in identifying the texts of Coleridge's laws but, also, in bringing to the authors' attention material from the relevant period from which some extremely interesting evidence was obtained (see, in particular,

1   D. Sultana, *Samuel Taylor Coleridge in Malta and Italy* (Oxford: Blackwell, 1969).

Chapter 5: public order and crime theme).

As we shall see, the British centralised model for the government in Malta vested supreme legislative, executive and judicial powers in the Civil Commissioner. The Public Secretary, whose role Coleridge assumed, served as the head of the Executive, and implemented the Civil Commissioner's policies. The Public Secretary represented the authority of the Civil Commissioner in the day to day administration. The office (which had formally been merged with that of Treasurer in 1803) had burdensome and wide ranging responsibilities involving such matters as the supervision and direction of policy in a dozen government departments (which the Public Secretary also had to audit), the administration of oaths, the arbitration of disputes, the issue of passports, some advocacy in the Court of Vice-Admiralty, as well as drafting the complex laws and public information notices which are the concern of this book. As we shall see, these instruments were not only used to create new law or bring some matter of importance to public attention but as a wider political engagement with the Maltese people, intended to manipulate and alter public opinion and behaviour.

Coleridge found himself in office at a critical time for the British, whose popularity underwent a decline as public expectations were disappointed, and poorly conceived policies failed. Sir Alexander Ball's government had to arrest this decline or risk not achieving its primary objective – securing the "attachment" of the Maltese to British rule. Government information – propaganda – became critical to the public standing of the British administration and, ultimately, to the future British presence on the Island. How government information was communicated by Coleridge and how he used it to serve the dominant strategic goals of British imperial policy is an important matter which this book considers. As a corollary, we shall also explore the limited freedom Coleridge had to pursue the constitutional and rule of law values he had advocated in his journalism. We shall also see how his conceptions of political morality subordinated to British policies for securing Malta as a politically-stable military base. Falling outside the compass of this book is the fundamental question: how did Coleridge's troubled experiences of government inform and enrich his later literary and philosophical work? It is, however, hoped that this book together with the first comprehensive translations into English of the Bandi and Avvisi will be of value to scholars in this respect.

Barry Hough and Howard Davis   *January 2010*

Introduction
Coleridge and the Rule of Law

by Michael John Kooy

Coleridge and law? Of all the professions Coleridge had dealings with during the course of his life – poetry, divinity, journalism, education, medicine – he had least patience with law. Though, as a young man, he once contemplated taking up law,[1] and later regretted not having done so,[2] he tended to regard law as a profession driven by an anti-metaphysical bias,[3] a prejudice that acquaintances like the jurists James Mackintosh and John Stoddart probably did little to dispel (Henry Crabb Robinson, friend of the German Romantics and later a lawyer, was a notable exception). Coleridge did of course study law, but on his own. There are references throughout his work to Manu, Montesquieu, Blackstone, among others, some as early as 1794,[4] and he even had a copy of the *Code Napoléon* (which he annotated). Coleridge read law as an autodidact, and often in relation to his other interests such as theology, in the case of Warburton's *Divine Legation of Moses*, or politics, in relation to the several versions of the French constitution he liked to comment on.

What is consistently characteristic of Coleridge's relation to law is his suspicion of the kind of people who write laws. A stout defender of the constitution and so far as we know a law-abiding subject, he nonetheless made it a point relentlessly to harangue British legislators, both during his

---

1   *CL* 1, 131.
2   *CL* 3, 470.
3   *CL* 2, 703, 861.
4   *CL* 1, 251.

radical years, when such actions risked indictment, and later, when his respectability allowed him to get away with it. Here he is in 1814, in a letter to his friend and *Courier* editor Daniel Stuart:

> ... our Parliament at home, or the faction of Landholders, are mad or id*EOT*ic. The Corn Law Debates are more disgraceful than even the Bullion – I again affirm, what I have often affirmed, that take away from the Legislature the Merchants & Manufacturers, & I will stand on Blackfriars or Westminster Bridge, & take the first 800 decently drest men that pass over, & would pledge my life for more intellect, more real knowledge, than is congregated in the two Houses.[5]

Like most of Coleridge's *jeux d'espirit*, this comment carries with it a complex subtext not entirely denied by the irony of its tone: beneath the healthy intolerance of corruption and parliamentarians' self-interest lies a cynicism about the whole process by which statute law comes into being. Part of Coleridge really does believe that a handful of arbitrarily chosen ordinary men would make better legislators than the ones currently in post.

It's one of the ironies of biography that this fanciful selection of legislators from among Westminster Bridge pedestrians describes, fairly nearly, what had happened to him ten years earlier in Malta. Landing at the port in Valletta on the morning of 18 May 1804, Coleridge, decently dressed and English, was picked up and introduced to the Civil Commissioner, Sir Alexander Ball. Hampered by a vacancy high in his administration, Ball promptly appointed him to his administration. Within a few months of his arrival on the Island Coleridge was drafting and then promulgating statute law for the native inhabitants. It's hard to imagine a more unlikely candidate for the post, or one whose prejudices so clearly pointed against such a task. And yet he stuck with it for nine difficult months.

How successfully he carried out that work is the subject of this remarkable book. Parts of the Malta story have been told before, notably by Donald Sultana in his detailed study *Coleridge in Malta and Italy*, but never quite like this. The story Hough and Davis tell makes for some disturbing reading. There is goodwill in the governor's palace, but also political *naiveté*, administrative incompetence, and a fairly persistent disregard for the rule of law. Hough and Davis's work will change how we understand Coleridge's politics and how we read his *oeuvre*. It will also contribute to how historians understand the early period of British rule in Malta.

---

5 *CL* 3, 497.

Reading Coleridge's Laws

But first, why has it taken until now for this story to come to light? There are two reasons. One is that Coleridge's work in Malta has never yet been analysed from the perspective of legal and constitutional history. No doubt such a perspective seemed to promise little: Coleridge became a law-maker by chance rather than choice, and anyway had many other things on his mind during his Malta years. The assumption has been that he carried out his duties with the moderate competency of any other well-meaning senior administrator in the colonial civil service, within the severe limitations such a post entailed. Yet, as Hough and Davis point out, he was no ordinary civil servant. He came to the job with an uncommon knowledge of British legal norms, picked up in his earlier work as a leader-writer for *The Morning Post*. Also, unusually for a man in his position, he enjoyed the full confidence of his superior. And, given the complexity of the political and constitutional situation in Malta in 1805, as well as its geographical distance from London, the path taken by the Ball administration was by no means a foregone conclusion. On the contrary, Ball and Coleridge enjoyed considerable room for exercising independent judgement. Taking a legal and constitutional interest in Coleridge's work thus opens up new territory.

The other reason for the originality of this research has to do with the nature of the archive. Hough and Davis base their work on six *Bandi* and fifteen *Avvisi* that were published, in Italian, under Coleridge's signature as Public Secretary to the Royal Commission between 29 January 1805 and 2 September 1805 . *Bandi* were proclamations having the force of law (i.e. new statutes) while *Avvisi* were public notices that clarified or applied already existing laws or administrative arrangements. The existence of these public documents has been no secret. Their titles are listed as an appendix in the second volume of Coleridge's *Notebooks*, edited by Kathleen Coburn and published in 1961, and are commented upon both there and, at somewhat greater length, by Donald Sultana in *Coleridge in Malta and Italy*. The documents have always been readily available in the National Library of Malta. That they are now published for the first time in translation – see Appendix 1 to this book – is a great boon for further researchers. What stood in the way of making any sense of these documents has been the presumed absence of an archival context, the supporting material necessary for scholars to place these documents in a political and socio-historical context. Famously, many of Coleridge's own letters, notes and drafts never made it back to England: they were unluckily caught up in the plague-infested effects of his friend Major Adye, and destroyed.[6] Some important policy papers written by Coleridge were preserved, such as the imperialistic *Observations on Egypt* (they are now in the British Library and the Victoria College Library, and are published in the Bollingen edition of *Essays on his Times*) but these do not touch upon Coleridge's role in helping to govern Malta. Did any relevant papers remain on Malta? Perhaps, but parts of Valletta had been damaged during the Second World War and scholars working upon this material in the immediate post-war period tended to assume that nothing of significance remained. There was only the well-known official government correspondence, preserved at the National Archives at Kew. Without additional, detailed archival material, Coleridge's *Bandi* and *Avvisi* remained stubbornly unrevealing at best, and at worst parochial. With their concerns about wine taxes, prize money, criminal convictions and cartwheels, the *Bandi* and *Avvisi* seemed, to most scholars, embarrassingly far beneath the attention of Coleridgean genius.

The authors of *Coleridge's Laws* demonstrate that this is not the case, and they do so with the help of an immense amount of new material that has been scrupulously sifted from the archives in Malta and London, much of it identified here for the first time. What they have discovered is that, contrary to scholarly consensus, the archival record does indeed contain essential material, enough, indeed, to reconstruct government activity, almost on a week by week basis, during the early years of British rule in Malta. Further, it allows one to pinpoint, with considerable accuracy, Coleridge's hand in that activity. This is an extraordinary achievement. Coleridge's *Bandi* and *Avvisi* here come to life, each proclamation and notice a calculated intervention in the daily lives of the Maltese people with, alarmingly, an often destabilising impact upon the precarious political and constitutional arrangements that characterised early British rule in Malta.

Here we come to the sharp end of *Coleridge's Laws*. Coleridge and Ball's handling of a number of key domestic government issues was sometimes fair, far-sighted and in accordance with British legal norms. At other times, though, it was none of these. I won't repeat the details of the argument here, but I will summarise Hough and Davis's three main claims:

1805 was a year of crises. Hough and Davis show that the period in 1805 that Coleridge spent working with Ball coincided with a range of social, political and economic crises unanticipated by the administration, notably

---

6   *CL* 2, 159-60.

the severe strain upon the Island's public finances, social unrest (against foreigners and the resident Jewish population), and an increasingly vocal group of nationalists critical of Ball.

Poor administration. Tracing in minute detail the record of Ball's administration, as found in contemporary witness accounts, in Ball's own reports to Whitehall, and in the subsequent assessment by historians, Hough and Davis argue that a number of the most serious difficulties encountered by the administration arose from internal weaknesses. These include its own poor management structures, the problematic nature of its domestic policies and the absence of limitations on executive power. Specific shortcomings include the wilful disregard of the worsening public finances, wastage (through lack of accountability) in public projects, the use of patronage to curry favour with the local elite, and less than frank communication with Whitehall. In nearly all of these instances, Coleridge, as well as Ball, was implicated.

Exploiting the law for political purposes. By the terms of the Royal Instructions for the civil administration of Malta of 1801, the Civil Commissioner acquired extraordinary powers, the implicit understanding being that these would only be used in exceptional circumstances and only in the interests of the Maltese. In what is the most important part of their study, Hough and Davis argue that Ball – with the active support of Coleridge – routinely took advantage of these powers in order to increase the civil commissioner's own personal standing among the Maltese and to strengthen British strategic control of the Island (which, for Ball and Coleridge, amounted to the same thing). As evidence of this, Hough and Davis point to the promulgation of edicts that fail to uphold rule of law principles, notably the separation of executive and judicial powers and *nulla poena sine lege* ("no penalty without a law"). We learn that Ball interfered in court judgements, and that, through Coleridge, he issued edicts that lacked legal clarity and sometimes manipulated the law to favour British strategic interests. In other words, Ball's governing of the Island, not just generally but also specifically during the period when Coleridge worked for him, was at times autocratic and arbitrary.

While these three claims are interrelated, the last, regarding the disregard for rule of law principles, is most significant, and it is this point that will, accordingly, remain my focus in the rest of this Introduction.

Judging Coleridge

What is the Rule of Law? Conventionally, the Rule of Law holds that legal judgements should be made according to known laws and principles rather than arbitrary ones. In his classic work on the subject, the English constitutional historian and theorist A. V. Dicey wrote that the Rule of Law consisted of three main principles: equality before the law; no punishment except in cases where the law is breached; no set of laws above the jurisdiction of the court.[7] Though Dicey first wrote in 1885, the principles he described were certainly found in the previous century, notably the view that the executive is not above the law and should itself not interfere in judicial processes, and the legal maxim *nulla poena sine lege*. As Hough and Davis point out, even in pre-Reform Britain these fundamental aspects of the Rule of Law had the status of broadly recognised legal norms.

The evidence that Ball's administration, during Coleridge's tenure of office, acted in ways that contravened these norms seems to me compelling: edicts were sometimes plainly used for political, rather than straightforwardly legal, purposes; Ball clearly interfered in the business of the courts; laws were promulgated in a haphazard fashion, sometimes with what can only be a deliberate attempt to create confusion, or to bolster the image of the Civil Commissioner. I find little to dispute in the evidence that Hough and Davis assemble. Yet one does feel, at times, that their standard is very high. If the Rule of Law was fragile in British-controlled Malta in 1805, how much more so in Napoleonic France, imperial Russia or even Great Britain itself. Accorded the level of scrutiny here given to Ball and Coleridge, few in office anywhere in Europe in 1805 would escape censure. But that is not quite the point. Ball's administration is measured against the British legal norms of the day (not contemporary practice), and by this measure its actions were clearly found wanting. It also seems clear to me, from the evidence, that one cannot exempt Coleridge from implication in at least some of these actions, given the responsibilities of his post and his personal proximity to Ball. Indeed, perhaps even more so, as Coleridge came to the job with the instincts of a civilian intact, and fresh from front-line parliamentary reporting in London. Coleridge stands exposed to the judgement of history in a way he never had been until now.

Defenders of Coleridge have a great deal of circumstantial material to draw upon, furnished by the research of Hough and Davis. I'll mention

---

7 *Introduction to the Study of the Law of the Constitution*, 6th Ed. (London: Macmillan, 1902).

what seem to me the most important points. Firstly, the British "continuity" policy in Malta. According to this policy, the British administration in Malta would continue to observe the laws and customs of the Maltese as they had developed under the 250-year long rule of the Knights of St John. That sounds liberal and enlightened, and indeed Ball did not depart from this policy. But the policy had unintended consequences. The Knights of St John had reserved to themselves, and notably to the Grand Master, sweeping despotic powers. Ball, in agreeing to preserve local constitutional arrangements, found he had inherited the powers of a feudal lord. On a sympathetic reading, it looks like Ball, and Coleridge with him, was caught in a catch-22: observe the local laws and customs (as promised to the Maltese in 1801) at the cost of acquiring despotic powers, or renounce or simply suspend those powers at the cost of abandoning commitments to maintaining local constitutional arrangements. From this perspective, the weak Rule of Law in Malta under Ball's administration seems to have systemic origins and was only secondarily affected by the personalities involved.

Secondly, the absence of international recognition of British rule in Malta. The failure of Britain to secure international recognition of its occupation of Malta, even though it occurred with the consent of the Maltese, was deeply problematic not only internationally (it led, after all, to the breaking of the Peace of Amiens and ushered in 12 more years of war) but locally. Ball, though he ruled by royal proclamation in the name of George III (see Chapter 2), nonetheless felt the insecurity of his position. Never fully backed by Whitehall on the one hand, nor by the Maltese on the other, his administration not only lacked legitimacy, it lacked the means by which it might gain legitimacy. Attempts on his and Coleridge's part to foster an image of benevolent paternalism, albeit by tampering with legal instruments, was the only way to maintain the appearance of legitimacy given the closure by war of all normal means. Without that appearance of legitimacy, the British hold upon Malta would weaken, and, with it, its strategic interests during wartime. It's unlikely Ball or Coleridge could have come up with a better response in the circumstances.

Thirdly, Coleridge's own unpreparedness for power. The argument here is that Coleridge, having left poetry and *The Morning Post* for the corridors of power, found himself confronted with tasks that were far beyond his level of competency and experience. He could not fully master technical matters and, more problematically, could not adjust appropriately to the real world of politics, where everyday one must trade off principles against real, if limited, material benefits. At the same time, he was under immense perceived pressure from his supervisors (both Ball and Whitehall) to keep the Maltese friendly, for British strategic reasons, during a period of rapid French imperial expansion. In his *naiveté*, and distracted by ill health, he abandoned too much for too little in return. Ultimately, his own latent respect for the Rule of Law resurfaced, and he managed to get himself released from a disagreeable post. Part of the disgust he later expressed, about the way British affairs were conducted abroad,[8] might have been directed at himself, unwittingly caught up in a political snare not of his own making.

These are important points. Indeed, the first two were implicitly made by the 1812 Royal Commission which, following Ball's death in 1809, attempted to place the Island on a proper legal and commercial footing. (The Royal Commission praised Ball and his successor for making the best of a difficult constitutional situation.) But each point has its weakness. Detractors will point out, regarding the first, that if Ball inherited arbitrary power from the outgoing Knights of St John, he needn't have exercised it – and yet, clearly, he did. Regarding the second point, it is true that the international situation was beyond anyone's control. And yet establishing legitimacy while maintaining Rule of Law might still have been possible. A wiser governor than Ball might have attempted constitutional reform, for instance by establishing a form of national assembly (the *Consiglio Popolare*). Ball and Coleridge might also have communicated the problem about legitimacy more clearly to Whitehall, seeking guidance instead of taking the matter into their own hands.

Finally, regarding Coleridge's own unpreparedness for office. This is indisputable, and indeed one might say that it's remarkable that he achieved so much considering how temperamentally unsuited he was to the job. But temperament and training don't really weigh very much in what is, after all, an ethical issue. Coleridge was in a position to draft laws within the norms of the Rule of Law and it seems that he occasionally used that position to do the reverse. The claim that he didn't know what he was doing doesn't convince: if Coleridge could bend the law for political purposes, he was certainly capable of refusing to do so. The harder issue is that he felt compelled by the gravity of the circumstances to do so. Coleridge helped to manipulate Maltese law because Britain's strategic war

---

8   *CL* 2, 1178.

aims in the Mediterranean required stable government on the Island, at whatever short-term cost to the local constitution and the Rule of Law. This reasoning is based upon a distinction between the ethical and the political that is sanctioned by so-called "realist" schools of political thought. It seems, however, out of keeping with the broadly Platonist orientation of Coleridge's own political philosophy. Taken together with occasional expressions of jingoism and militant imperialism at this time, Coleridge's willingness to assist in weakening the Rule of Law on Malta, for whatever perceived higher good, constitutes a disturbing departure from the liberal idealism he espoused both before and after.

Placing Malta in Coleridge's Career

But what kind of departure? This brings us to the question of how Hough and Davis's findings impact upon our understanding of Coleridge's career and, more broadly, early nineteenth-century British colonial policy and practice.

Regarding the former, the Malta period must, surely, now be taken much more seriously than hitherto. Coleridge called it one of the most instructive periods of his life,[9] but commentators have tended to regard that as an overstatement. That, now, appears to have been a mistake. We may not share Coleridge's assessment of this period (the sympathetic "Life of Ball' in *The Friend* appears to be even more of a projected fiction given Hough and Davis's research) but we must share his sense of its significance.

Part of that significance relates, straightforwardly, to political commitment. The new details offered to us by *Coleridge's Laws*, in particular Coleridge's willingness to subordinate Rule of Law to British strategic interests show that his conservatorism could and did take an authoritarian form. The gradualism and nationalism of the first edition of *The Friend* (1809-1810) and of the *Courier* journalism (1809-1817) have their roots not only in Coleridge's liberal critique of revolution in the 1798-1799 *Morning Post* essays, as many commentators suggest, but also in the authoritarism that first expressed itself in Malta in 1805. This may also sharpen the charge of apostasy.

Historically, questions about Coleridge's integrity have focused upon his opium addiction, plagiarism and political apostasy. These debates have

---

9   *The Friend*, ed. Barbara Rooke, 2 vols. (Princeton: Princeton University Press, 1969), 1, 533. Hereafter referred to as *The Friend*.

now largely played themselves out and moral opprobrium has diminished accordingly. Opium addition is now generally regarded as a medical rather than moral issue; plagiarism, now that originality is no longer regarded as a Romantic virtue, is no longer as ethically suspect as it once was; apostasy is less transparently disreputable. These debates reveal more about the culture that sponsored them than about Coleridge's integrity per se. Does our early twenty–first-century disappointment in his poor handling of Maltese legal and constitutional issues reveal, in the end, more about our own democratic aspirations than about Coleridge's personal integrity?

Elsewhere I have critiqued the narrowness of reading Coleridge only in terms of the politics of left and right, as well as the commonplace insistence upon a narrative of political apostasy, which I have argued is both reductive and self-righteous.[10] A richer understanding of Coleridge's Malta experience requires a broader historical view. I'd like to suggest one such view regarding the Rule of Law.

The Rule of Law is, conventionally, held up as a protection against arbitrary government. In a legal system where all citizens are equal before the law, and can be punished only when the law is broken, the scope for arbitrary rule is severely limited. Such a formalist conception of the Rule of Law says nothing, however, about the justice of the laws themselves. Strictly speaking, an unjust law protects against arbitrary government as well as a just one, the only requirement being that it be scrupulously administered by the authorities. The Rule of Law, thus formally conceived, is, in fact, compatible with the worst forms of state oppression, indeed, can be a necessary condition of that oppression, and an amplifier of it. For this reason, Rule of Law theorists have often referred to the supplementary need for institutions to review and, if necessary, modify laws, guided by constitutional tradition and natural justice.[11] In cases where these institutions are absent, not functioning, or themselves suspect, the appeal to justice may take place explicitly outside the Rule of Law. Thus, both the secular radical tradition, from Marx to Mao, as well as religious traditions, such as Protestant antinomianism (drawing upon Calvin's thoughts on rebellion against unjust rulers in his *Institutes*) and, more recently, Catholic political theology, reserve to themselves the right to reject the Rule of Law,

10 'Coleridge as Editor: *The Watchman* and *The Friend*', *The Oxford Handbook of Samuel Taylor Coleridge*, ed. Frederick Burwick (Oxford: Oxford University Press, 2009), 144-64.
11 Paul Craig, "Formal and Substantive Conceptions of the Rule of Law: An Analytical Framework', *Public Law*, 33 (1997), 467–87.

in order to achieve justice where the Rule of Law denies it.

The severing of justice from the Rule of Law is something that worried Coleridge throughout his career. It emerges clearly in his work as a radical journalist and lecturer, when he complained in the *Watchman* that simply to speak on certain subjects, such as imagining the king's death, was actionable under new treason laws. But also later, in his life-long cynicism regarding the self-interested workings of the British parliament, referred to at the start of this essay. Perhaps most characteristically, it comes out in his suspicion that the equitable application of statute law was no protection from injustice. The case of the young Irish nationalist and radical Robert Emmett, tried for treason and executed in September 1803, was particularly revealing for Coleridge in this regard. Emmett was, for Coleridge, an image of his younger radical self and hardly deserved to pay for his radicalism with his life.[12] He wrote to his friends the Beaumonts in October 1803: "poor young Emmett! O if our Ministers had saved him, had taken his Oath & word of honor, to have remained in America or some of our Colonies for the next 10 years of his Life, we *might* have had in him a sublimely great man".[13] In the case of Emmett, justice would have been served precisely by *not* applying equitably the full measure of the law. Sometimes the blind application of the law brings injustice.

Another example is Coleridge's response to the Corn Laws of 1815, which aimed to protect domestic agricultural production in the face of cheaper grain imports. Coleridge suspected – rightly, as it turned out – that the underlying causes of the economic distress were deeper than a single statute law ever could amend, and disparaged the attempt as an "elixir".[14] An example of legislation Coleridge supported suggests the same point. Robert Peel's 1819 *Act for the Regulation of Cotton Mills and Factories* prohibited children under the age of nine years from work, and restricted those over that age to working 12 hours per day. Coleridge supported it on moral grounds, and because its modest economic and social goals were achievable by law.[15] More ambitious improvements in social, political and economic conditions could only come about through gradual alterations in the vast terrain of collective ethical and religious life that statute law,

---

12 See Timothy Webb, 'Coleridge and Robert Emmet: Reading the Text of Irish Revolution', *Irish Studies Review*, 8: 3 (2000), 304-24.

13 *CL* 2, 1002-3.

14 *CL* 4, 565.

15 The pamphlets are reprinted in *S. T. Coleridge, Shorter Works and Fragments*, ed. H. J. Jackson and J. R. de J. Jackson, 2 vols. (Princeton: Princeton University Press, 1995).

because it is written by human beings touched by original sin (here is Coleridge's Augustinianism), cannot, and, therefore, ought not, interfere with directly.

To the extent that Coleridge had a philosophy of law, it lies here, in his minimalist conception of statute law as a necessary but blunt instrument to contain the worst of human behaviour rather than as a favoured means of engineering social or ethical improvement. An 1814 letter to Daniel Stuart, perhaps Coleridge's clearest statement of his view on normative jurisprudence, is worth quoting at length:

> The view, which our Laws take of robbery and even murder, not as *Guilt* of which God alone is presumed to be the Judge, but as *Crimes,* depriving the *King* of one of *his* Subjects, rendering dangerous and abating the value of the *King's High*-ways, &c, may suggest some notion of my meaning. Jack, Tom, and Harry have no existence in the eye of Law, except as included in some form or other of the *permanent Property* of the Realm — just as on the other Hand Religion has nothing to do with ranks, estates, or offices; but exerts itself wholly on what is *personal* — viz. our Souls, Consciences, and the *morality* of our actions as opposed to mere *Legality.* ... *Human* Jurisprudence wisely aware of it's own weakness & sensible how incommensurate it's powers are with so vast an object, as the Well-being of Individuals as Individuals ... knows nothing of Persons other than as Proprietors, Officiaries, Subjects. ... Guided by this spirit our ancestors repealed the Puritan Law, by which Adultery was to be punished with Death, & brought it back to a civil Damage — So too, actions for Seduction. — Not that the Judge or Legislator did not feel the guilt of such crimes; but that the *Law* knows nothing about Guilt —. So in the Exchequer common Debts are sued for on the plea, that the Creditor is less able to pay our Lord the King — &c &c —. Now contrast with this the Preamble to the first French Constitution, and I think, my meaning will become more intelligible — that the pretence of considering Persons not States, Happiness not Property, always has ended & always will end in making a new *State* or Corporation infinitely more oppressive than the former — and in which the real freedom of Persons is as much less, as the things interfered with are more numerous & more minute.[16]

This is a conservative position. But, complexly, it is a conservatism that retains an allegiance to early Christian anarchism. The law's relation to society is to act upon its margins, leaving untouched, at the centre, a self-regulating collective. Coherent with this position is Coleridge's defence of the Anglican settlement. The Church, in the widest sense of the term (lay members, clergy, tradition), was a institution expressive of that collective,

---

16   *CL* 3, 537-38.

a view Coleridge defended in a letter to his brother in 1802[17] and in remarkably similar terms in his 1829 *On the Constitution of Church and State*. The Church can have progressive social influence precisely because it is national by virtue of the constitution, and not by favour of the government.

What happened in Malta was a betrayal of this concept of jurisprudence. Coleridge was probably right in thinking that the Rule of Law on the Island had already been deeply compromised by the legacy of the Knights of St John (as he implied in *The Friend*). But he was wrong to correct the situation by taking matters into his own hands. He helped extend the arbitrary powers of his patron and manipulated statute law to achieve desired political and social ends, in both cases anticipating Carl Schmitt's grim *aperçu* that sovereignty in a state lies with the one who can suspend the normal functioning of law. But as my comments have tried to suggest, Coleridge's Malta experience was a betrayal not so much of the formalist conception of the Rule of Law, but, more profoundly, of his own conservative conception of the power and self-regulating potential of people acting and living collectively. That Coleridge later in life became, in spite of his Malta experience, an influential articulator of the constitutional tradition is the longer-lasting mark of his genius and the better test of his moral integrity.

There are other ways that this book will have an impact upon our conception of Coleridge's work as well as topics wider afield. While constitutional and political matters are, probably, of the first significance, we will want to consider the relationship of his legal work to the writing of poetry, to the fluctuations in health (Hough and Davis make interesting forays into both these areas), and to the other, more widely recognised, aspect of the Malta period, Coleridge's first-hand discovery of the art and literature of southern Europe.

There is also the contribution to British colonial studies. The book's analysis makes plain the fundamental antinomy of the colonial encounter. Colonisers occupy territory out of their own interests, and yet the appearance of a contiguity of interests must continually be maintained, such that both parties believe in it. This is no less the case in territories held by formal consent, such as Malta. Early Maltese history has, sometimes, been held back by the lack of detailed, archive-based studies. It is now enriched by this book's lavish attention to detail, much of it seeing light for the first time.

---

17   CL 2, 806.

1. The Battle of Self [1]

Introduction

In 1809, when Coleridge was prompted to write about Malta, by the death of Sir Alexander Ball, the Civil Commissioner whom he so much admired, he concluded that he regarded his stay on the Island "in many respects, the most memorable and instructive period of [his] life".[2] This assessment, no doubt, justified the hazards that he had ventured in making this difficult expedition, especially when its primary purpose – the pursuit of a cure for his addiction – seemed publicly to have failed. Sultana, who regarded Coleridge as distracted in public office and overly introspective, articulated the kind of criticism that perhaps Coleridge wished to pre-empt.[3] But, Coleridge's decision to make the journey poses important questions. Why did he choose to make an extended visit to Malta of more than a year? The decision to remove himself, travelling alone, to such a distant place, far from his family, his friends, and his Lake District residence, needs to be explained.

This chapter fulfils three aims. First, we shall trace the labyrinthine complexities in his family life and career in order to understand what led him to seek this self-imposed exile abroad; secondly, we shall touch upon aspects of his authorial career, most notably his political journalism, to

1   K. Coburn, *The Notebooks of Samuel Taylor Coleridge 1804-1808* (New York: Bollingen, 1961), 2, 1992. Hereafter referred to as *CN*. Coleridge grimly recorded some epitaphs of deceased soldiers after reaching Portsmouth at the end of March 1804. The voyage to Valletta would commence as soon as the adverse wind altered direction. This epitaph recorded that the "Battle of Self in the conquest of sin" was the "hardest engagement that [the deceased] was ever in".

2   S. T. Coleridge, 'The Friend', in *The Collected Works of Samuel Taylor Coleridge*, general editor Kathleen Coburn, London: Routledge & Kegan Paul, Bollingen Series, 1969, vol 1, 533. Hereafter *The Friend*. Comments made whilst still in public office were, however, less enthusiastic: see e.g. To Daniel Stuart, 1 May 1805, Griggs, E.L., *Collected Letters of Samuel Taylor Coleridge*, 6 vols., Oxford: Clarendon Press, 1956- 71, vol 2, 1167. Hereafter *CL* 2.

3   See Sultana, xviii-x.

indicate the views he expressed on constitutional principle and political morality before taking office. This background is important in assessing what Coleridge would bring to public office and helps us to understand his achievement. Finally, we shall explore his public roles in Malta, first as Under-Secretary, and, subsequently, as Public Secretary in the administration of Sir Alexander Ball.

The Journey to Valletta

"[P]erfect Tranquillity in a genial Climate".[4]

The background to Coleridge's Malta period is poignant. Loss of self-esteem as a poet, a problematic, asymmetric relationship with his collaborator, William Wordsworth, marital disharmony, declining health and an alarming drug addiction led him, at the age of thirty-one, to seek either death or renaissance abroad. Should he have recovered his health – for which the defeat of addiction was a *sine qua non* – he could return to England to pursue a literary career: if he failed, he could expire, almost unnoticed, amidst strangers on a distant Island, veiled in obscurity and far from public scrutiny. His reputation, and the good name of his family, might then be largely untarnished. Of these two possible outcomes, Coleridge may have hoped for the former, but he certainly expected the latter.[5] The decision to leave England may have been dominated by his desire to pursue a cure, but this expedition was, perhaps, only possible because of the complexity and dilemmas associated with his close personal and professional relationships.

Seditionist

Coleridge's early reputation had been earned as a political firebrand who interested himself, somewhat dangerously, in radical politics. The French Revolution had destroyed France's former political and social order, replacing it with entirely pristine structures that even extended to the calendar. All social and political institutions were to be re-fashioned, as if no trace of the *ancien regime* deserved to be continued. Coleridge's political and economic thought was stimulated by the reactionary forces all around him.

---

4   To Matthew Coates, postmark 8 December 1803, *CL* 2, 1021.
5   To William Sotheby, 27 March 1804, *CL* 2, 1106; see also to Mrs S. T. Coleridge, 1 April 1804, *CL* 2, 1115.

The philosophical energy underpinning the Revolution was responsible for a new conception of liberty based upon a vision of society in which all would be equal and where freedom was created and protected by the laws. According to this view, individual freedom flowed from, and was defined by, the state. Behind the ensuing war with France, from 1793, was the British determination to protect its rival conception of liberty, rooted in property and commerce, in which the main task of the state was to ensure peace and social stability. Individual freedom was comprised in all that which the law had not prohibited and not what the State cared to bestow.

This contest of ideas immediately divided English intellectual opinion. In his *Reflections on the Revolution in France* (1790) Edmond Burke denounced the Revolution. He advocated a co-operative relationship between groups in society – the political élites and the less advantaged – in the belief that sudden constitutional upheaval risked destroying much of what was valued. It was an argument for continuity.

Thomas Paine's response, *The Rights of Man* (1791-1792), was founded upon the argument that it is the right of each generation to establish its own forms of government. Far from establishing peace and good order, governments that used force to perpetuate an unequal social and political system often destroyed it. He argued for equal political rights for all persons, since this was the natural state of all men, and a programme of social reform to address the plight of the poor.

Joseph Priestley, a scientist, Unitarian and philosopher, published similar arguments advocating political reform[6] – only he took the further, and dangerous step, of establishing a "Constitution Society", in Birmingham, to advocate the reform of Parliament.[7] Its inaugural dinner, held somewhat auspiciously on Bastille Day 1791, attracted a mob of "anti-Jacobins" who pelted the diners with mud and stones. The windows in the hotel were then smashed.[8] Urged on by local Tories, comprising local justices of the peace, clergy and local landlords, the mob attacked and burned Priestley's house, destroying his laboratory, his books and manuscripts and forcing him to flee, first to London but, ultimately, to the United States. The wave of organised violence resulted in the destruction of twenty-seven

6   *A Political Dialogue on the General Principles of Government*, 1791.
7   Coleridge had paid a fulsome tribute to Priestley ("patriot and saint and sage") in his major poem *Religious Musings*, lines 371-6. Priestly (sic) was also the subject of a sonnet first published in the *Morning Chronicle* in December 1794. At one point, it seemed possible that Priestley might join Coleridge and his fellow Pantisocrats in America: see letter to Robert Southey, 1 September 1794, *CL* 1, 98.
8   Uglow, 440-1.

properties – all belonging to like-minded local intellectuals and reformers. Its slogan, chalked on the walls of Birmingham, was resounding: "No philosophers-Church and King For Ever". According to Uglow, polemics and empirical science alike were tainted: "This, " she wrote, " was a riot against intellectualism, and its abiding image is of book burning".[9] Inexorably, reform and revolution came to be seen as synonymous. And the Establishment was ready to fight back. The Edinburgh lawyer, Thomas Muir was sentenced to fourteen years transportation simply for advocating parliamentary reform. As far as the authorities were concerned, this was just the beginning.

This was the turbulent context to Coleridge's undergraduate years at Cambridge University. Together with Robert Southey – another progressive undergraduate – he considered removing himself from a conservative, reactionary Britain. With others, they would emigrate to America to form an ideal self-governing commune of "Pantisocrats", sharing property and labour. The scheme eventually foundered but, whilst the possibilities of an ideal society were still under discussion, Coleridge left his University to undertake a walking tour of Wales. It was on this tour that he was exposed to the fervent, popular denunciation of political radicals. He was witnessing a flux of British public opinion toward conservatism.[10] At one inn, as a response to Coleridge's "preaching of Pantisocracy and Asphetrism" a perplexed, burly, Welshman "called for a large Glass of Brandy, and drank off ….his own Toast-God save the King". Coleridge with unabashed revolutionary sentiment wrote to Southey: "..may he be the Last"![11] Elsewhere on his travels, Coleridge was patronised as a "open-hearted honest-speaking Fellow, tho'…a bit of a Democrat".[12] This reference to his politics suggested to him that, as far as his audiences were concerned, his opinions had fewer endearing qualities than his openness and honesty.

Another enriching experience, for a young poet fresh from University, exposed him to the true state of the less privileged. Whilst he was about to dine at an inn, a young mother, bearing a "half-famished sickly baby", intruded upon his meal by begging for food. Coleridge, rather pompously, claimed to have been annoyed by the intrusion, but he fully understood that what was on trial was not the conduct of the individual but the unequal social and political system that led, for so many, to paupery and starvation.

---

9   Uglow, 448.
10   *CL* 1, 40; Holmes (1989) 44.
11   To Southey, 13 July 1794, *CL* 1, 85.
12   To Southey, ibid. at 98.

Coleridge's response to a similarly bifurcated society, on Malta, will be considered in the ensuing chapters.

One of his most powerful interventions was the delivery of three controversial lectures on political and religious themes, at Bristol, in 1795. In these, whilst renouncing, on moral and religious grounds, the violence practised in France, he associated himself with the democratic cause, and, particularly, with well-known radicals some of whom were tried for treason for their reformist principles. The public lectures took place at a time when the authorities had no scruples about seizing and detaining articulate political opponents. Such advocates of Parliamentary reform as Thomas Hardy, John Horne Tooke, John Thelwall[13], Bonney, Joyce, Kyd, and Holcroft[14] were each arrested and detained for high treason. Coleridge's courageous campaign for social and political renewal was far from being risk free; indeed, after receiving death threats, he seems to have abandoned the lecture series.[15] By then he had made his stand, but in doing so he had acquired the reputation as a young man "shamefully hot with Democratic rage as regards politics".[16]

In Malta, it would be a different story as Coleridge supported the Civil Commissioner in criminal trials arising from anti-Semitic disturbances. Even before Coleridge held public office on Malta, his commitment to popular suffrage had undoubtedly cooled as his political leaders, written for *The Morning Post,* revealed.[17]

"Fire, Famine and Slaughter"

In January 1798 he published, pseudonymously, in *The Morning Post,* the poem *Fire, Famine and Slaughter* in which the three personifications of the poem explain that they have been sent to do work of misery by an individual

---

13   John Thelwall was, of course, known and respected by Coleridge. He was a guest at Nether Stowey in July 1797. Fruitless efforts were made to find a cottage that he might rent in the vicinity.
14   Holcroft seems to have known Coleridge: see Holmes (1989), 84.
15   He was forced to publish the first lecture as a pamphlet in order to demonstrate that there was nothing treasonable about its contents: Letter to George Dyer. *CL* 1, 152. A fourth lecture appears to have been planned, but threats to his life prevented him from delivering it: ibid.
16   Sandford,*Thomas Poole and His Friends,* quoted in Lefebure (1977), 137.
17   See e.g., D. V. Erdman (ed.), *Essays on His Times in 'The Morning Post' and 'The Courier',* in *The Collected Works of Samuel Taylor Coleridge,* volumes, 3: 1-3 (General Editor: Kathleen Coburn) (London: Routledge and Kegan Paul, 1978), 1, 32, 7, December 1799. Hereafter referred to as *EOT.*

whose name is unspeakable. Somewhat dangerously, given the nervous political climate, Coleridge's personifications of fire, famine and slaughter, each confide that "Letters four do form his name". It was, of course, open to the readers to infer that the architect of the catastrophic evils, depicted in the poem, was none other than the Prime Minister, William Pitt the younger. This was all the more likely since Coleridge's public position on the subject, Pitt, was already well-known: he had contributed a "vehement" sonnet on the Prime Minister to the Morning Chronicle in 1794.

In his maturity, Coleridge was to distance himself from some of the more inflammatory interpretations of this work. When, in 1817, in *Sibylline Leaves*, he republished the poem he did so with an explanation by way of an "Apologetic Preface". His argument was that a passionate protagonist may be a passive one and that vivid poetic imagery provided for the venting of the passions by acting as a safety valve to release excess. Imagining Pitt's death, he argued, virtually precluded realising Pitt's demise. Danger, he thought, lay in cold-blooded reasoning, not heated utterances. [18]

The Wordsworths and the "Dear Gutter of Stowey"[19]

Coleridge's friendship with the Wordsworths was, at first, mutually fulfilling and supportive. In time, the bonds between them attenuated. The weakening bond played its role in Coleridge's willingness to travel alone to Malta.

Coleridge and Wordsworth had met briefly, and had begun to notice each others' work, in Bristol in late 1795. Coleridge soon concluded that Wordsworth was "the best poet of the age".[20] However, the unsatisfactory dynamic of the Coleridge/Wordsworth friendship and collaboration ultimately exerted a detrimental influence both upon Coleridge's creative capacity, and his sense of identity as a poet.

Following his alarming experiences in Bristol, Coleridge now sought a more secluded life in which he could devote himself to poetry. At the close of 1796, he settled with his family in a damp, mice-plagued, cottage

---

18 See Barrell, Fire, Famine and Slaughter is discussed as an epilogue. However, as Barrell explains the argument depends entirely on Coleridge's conception of the imagination.

19 To T. Poole 29 [28] May 1796, *CL* 1, 217, "Dear Gutter of Stowey (sic)! Were I transported to Italian Plains, and lay by the side of a streamlet which murmured thro' an orange grove, I would think of thee, dear Gutter of Stowy, and wish that I were poring on thee!"

20 To John Thelwall, 13 May 1796, *CL* 1, 215-6.

in the main street of Nether Stowey, Somerset, by which time Wordsworth and his sister, Dorothy, were living, rent-free, at Racedown Lodge, Dorset. A visit by Coleridge to Racedown the following June, was a profoundly significant moment in the lives of each of them.

Coleridge remained with the Wordsworths for more than a fortnight, reading and discussing their respective poetry and dramatic works. Each of the poets had a profound effect upon the other; and Coleridge regarded Dorothy as "exquisite". He wrote to Joseph Cottle, his publisher, that "her taste (is) a perfect electrometer – it bends, protrudes, and draws in at subtlest beauties and most recondite faults".[21] She was a woman true to the romantic *beau ideal* of the child of nature. Dorothy would describe Coleridge as fluent, intelligent and sensitive to his surroundings. She proclaimed that he had a "conversation that teems with soul, mind and spirit...he is so benevolent, so good tempered and cheerful".[22]

Coleridge heaped critical praise upon Wordsworth's work. The chemistry of the relationship at this early stage had a deep, energising effect upon Coleridge's imaginative life. A bond of mutual enchantment was formed that each poet wished to continue. Coleridge drove the Wordsworths back to his cottage in Stowey, where they remained for a fortnight. They impulsively determined to give up Racedown – Dorothy never returned to it. Thomas Poole, the "democrat" tanner whose yard was adjacent to the cottage, and who had assisted the Coleridges find their cottage, now did the same for the Wordsworths. Within a couple of weeks of their arrival in the area they were settled at Alfoxden House (now Alfoxton Park Hotel), near Holford, just three miles from Coleridge's cottage.

Coleridge and the Wordsworths enjoyed a nonpareil summer, out of doors, walking the Quantock Hills, gazing down, from the hill-tops, upon the sea, taking pleasure in the white sails of the ships that made their passage up and down the Channel from Bristol. Whether entertaining such political radicals as John Thelwall,[23] wandering at night under the moon with the Wordsworths or dining in the open air under the broad-leafed trees of Alfoxden Park, Coleridge's poetic imagination fed upon observations and endless, inquiring conversations. He experienced a heightened response

---

21   To Joseph Cottle, circa 3 July 1797, *CL* 1, 195.
22   To Mary Hutchinson (?) June 1797, De Selincourt, 188-9.
23   Thelwall arrived on 17 July 1797 after having walked from London. Earlier he had been arrested and tried under the Treasonable Practices Act 1794, but was acquitted at trial. With the intention of retreating from London and retiring from active political life he briefly considered settling with his family near Coleridge.

to the landscape: the Quantocks, for example, supplied the topography for *"This Lime Tree Bower"*. Critics have commented upon how the shared experience of the three writers enriched their work. Coleridge's imagery may, for example, have benefited from what they witnessed on their walks. The "restless gossameres" of *The Rime of the Ancient Mariner* may have been discovered together, and possibly found an alternative imaginative interpretation in Dorothy's journal.[24] Similarly, the "(t)he one red leaf, the last of its clan" that appeared in *Christabel* might have resulted from the joys of shared observation.[25] Livingstone Lowes described these as "moments of exalted perception" from which each drew pleasure and inspiration.[26]

Coleridge's wife, Sara Coleridge, stood apart from these new friendships. She was left to take charge of Hartley, the Coleridge's first-born child, and had to bear the brunt of menial and arduous house work. She began to tire of the Wordsworths and the manner in which they treated her.[27] Sara's reaction to being left at home when pregnant with Berkeley, the Coleridge's second child, is easily imagined.

Coleridge's best known works, *Khubla Khan* and *The Rime of the Ancient Mariner*, were composed at this productive time. *The Ancient Mariner* was originally conceived as a collaborative work between the two poets. Although Wordsworth is likely to have suggested some of the imagery, he soon removed himself from the project on the grounds of artistic differences, leaving Coleridge to complete the poem early in 1798. As we shall see, Wordsworth's response to Coleridge's *tour de force* was, subsequently, to contribute to Coleridge's loss of self-assurance and declining morale.

Nevertheless, all this lay in the future. Coleridge continued to ride the wave of his *annus mirabilis*. The great collaborative volume of the *Lyrical Ballads*, written with Wordsworth, appeared in 1798. On the whole, the poems were well-received, but, in an anonymous attack in the *Critical Review*, Southey (Coleridge's brother in law) was highly dismissive of the *Ancient Mariner*. He condemned it as a poem of little merit. The real damage

---

24   The "surface (of the heath) restless and glittering with the motion of the scattered piles of withered grass and the waving of the spiders' threads". Knight, (ed.), Wordsworth, 8.
25   D. Wordsworth, ibid. recorded on 7 March 1798: "One only leaf upon the top of a tree-the sole remaining leaf-danced round and round like a rag blown by the wind". Cf. Christabel, I, 49.
26   Livingstone Lowes, 191.
27   De Quincey, Works II, 64-5. It seems that Dorothy Wordsworth, when her own clothes were soaked after walking in the rain, would simply borrow Sara's without asking her permission.

inflicted by Southey would emerge two years later when the second edition was in preparation.

Germany

Coleridge had long entertained an ambition to study at a German University, and the opportunity to do so arose following the offer of a life-time annuity by the Wedgewood brothers, Josiah and Thomas. His plan was to study German literature and write a life of Lessing. The Wordsworths agreed to accompany Coleridge on this adventure, although the party eventually separated when William and Dorothy chose to winter in Goslar. Sara Coleridge, who was by now nursing Berkley, was again excluded and remained in England on practical grounds. It was, however, suggested that she might join the party later, once it was established in Germany, if it could be afforded, and when the baby was old enough to make the journey.

During Coleridge's absence, first at Ratzeburg and, subsequently, at Göttingen University, Sara endured a miserable time: she fell ill and then had to nurse her children through illness. Worse was to come. In February 1799, Berkeley died. Such was her grief that Sara's hair fell out, and she was obliged to wear a wig for the remainder of her life.

Their family friend and neighbour, Tom Poole, persuaded Sara that Coleridge should, so far as possible, be prevented from receiving bad news as it would distract him from his studies. This injunction further isolated the grieving woman. Eventually, she succumbed to her instinctive need to communicate news of their bereavement to her husband. On 24 March 1799, she wrote Coleridge a long, grief-stricken letter. It sought Coleridge's return to his family: "Hartley…talks of his father every day….if you will try to come to us soon".

But Coleridge did not return immediately; indeed, for reasons that are not altogether clear, he seems to have procrastinated by taking a walking tour in the Harz mountains. Sara came to regard this behaviour with some bitterness. He remained in Germany for several more months; and when he eventually returned to Nether Stowey, in July 1799, husband and wife were soon in conflict.[28] His health also deteriorated.[29]

Coleridge's closest and most important professional relationship also came under strain at this period. During their stay in Germany, the

---

28 To Southey, 29 July 1799, *CL* 1, 523.
29 Ibid.

Wordsworths, who suffered from powerful homesickness, began to think of returning to their native country in the North of England.[30] When they landed in England they went to stay with relatives at Gallow Hill, Sockburn-on-Tees, rather than returning, with Coleridge, to Somerset.

The Lake District

Once back in the small family home in Nether Stowey, Coleridge appears to have been restless and unable to settle. In September, the household was disrupted, and, worse still, stank of sulphur when Hartley was thought to have succumbed to scabies, then known as the "Itch".[31] Sara was forced to work herself to exhaustion fumigating, washing and scrubbing. Her emotional state only drew adverse comments from Coleridge, who reported her "hypersuperlative Grief".[32] Meanwhile, he withdrew from the furore, leaving her, it seems, to cope without the aid of a servant on her own. He wrote of himself, apparently without shame, "I however, sunk in Spinoza, remain as undisturbed as a Toad on a rock". [33]

Despite his ostensible tranquillity, Coleridge soon removed himself from Stowey. He pretended to Sara, no doubt to reconcile her to yet another absence, that he would travel to Bristol to locate his luggage because this had not yet reached him from Germany. This pretext probably disguised his ultimate purpose of visiting the Wordsworths. Sara did not hear directly from Coleridge that he had travelled from Bristol to join them in the North; indeed she did not hear from him for six weeks.

Coleridge's visit was propitious: he met Sara Hutchinson – soon to become "Asra"– with whom he was, subsequently, to fall in love; and he witnessed for the first time, whilst on a walking tour with Wordsworth, the impressive tarns, fells and Lakes of Cumbria. It was on this tour that Wordsworth discovered "Dove Cottage", Town End, Grasmere. Shortly afterwards, in December 1799, he and Dorothy moved in and settled there. Some of Wordsworth's finest poetry would be written whilst he resided in the cottage (until 1808); and it was here that Dorothy wrote her sensitive "Grasmere Journals". If the literary partnership with Coleridge was to continue, it would only do so in the North. Wordsworth had finally bid his

---

30   DW *CL* 1, 105.
31   To Southey, 30 September 1799, *CL* 1, 534. Coleridge also reported that this diagnosis was probably inaccurate.
32   To Southey, 25 September 1799, *CL* 1, 530.
33   Ibid at 533.

farewell to the West Country.

Coleridge now planned to move with his family to live in the Lake District in order to be close to the Wordsworths. Mrs Coleridge was, at first, reluctant to relocate so far from the support of her family and friends, most notably their stalwart neighbour, Thomas Poole, whose practical assistance had been of real value, especially whilst Coleridge had been abroad.[34] She must also have been cautious about going so far to reside near to the Wordsworths whom she now regarded with some hostility. The decision to move away must have been another gritty and aggravating difference between the couple.

Special Parliamentary Correspondent and Commentator

After this first visit to the Lakes, Coleridge committed himself to earning money as a political leader-writer, special parliamentary correspondent[35] and critic for *The Morning Post* – a paper generally unsympathetic to ministerial policies. In his parliamentary role, he seems to have been given the freedom to report upon that which intrigued him as significant and newsworthy. But this was only a part of his duties. In a five month period, between December 1799 and April 1800, he penned some forty leading articles, verses and other miscellaneous materials at a time when one of the major national policy dilemmas was whether to continue the hostilities against France.[36]

Overtures inviting negotiation had been received from the French: but the British government summarily rejected this initiative. Ministers were then compelled to give a public explanation of their reasons for continuing the struggle. In a series of incisive articles, Coleridge mounted a persuasive case that the Government's arguments were flawed.[37] The French Government, acting under the new constitution may have been a "Usurpation", "Despotism" and "Tyranny",[38] but it was no longer a

---

34 See e.g., Sara to George Coleridge, 10 September 1800, quoted in Lefebure (1986), 127.

35 See D. Erdman cited in Hesell. Coleridge, who is thought to have been given a greater freedom than others by his editor, was arguably more faithful to the original than some of his rivals who focused on more "newsworthy" material, selected according to idiosyncratic political prejudices.

36 Lefebure (1977), 305.

37 *EOT*, 1, 64, 69, 73, 2-4 January 1800.

38 Ibid., 4 January 1800, 73.

threat to neighbouring States. The "French principles" of liberty, equality, and democracy had lost their allure in an England that had witnessed the regicide, blood-letting and tyranny in France. In short, France could not now de-stabilise the British legal, political and constitutional order. Powerful, reasoned and effective journalism of this kind must have added to the widespread clamour to hold the British government to account for its rejection of the French overtures – all the more so as Coleridge portrayed these two French approaches as patient, dignified and respectful in the face of British ministerial obstinacy and reproach.[39]

The widespread dismay aroused by the uncompromising rejections eventually forced Pitt to come to Parliament to offer an account of ministerial policy. He had to face Charles Fox who now returned to the Commons after having withdrawn from it in 1797 in protest at the war policies of the Government. Coleridge's treatment of this great set-piece confrontation is pre-eminent amongst his parliamentary reporting.[40] Material that other newspaper reporters (and editors) chose to excise concerned the second part of Pitt's speech in which he considered the implications of the new French constitution as well as Bonaparte's character. However, Coleridge prioritised this material as an important political statement rather than Pitt's reprise of the (well-known) origins of the war. Coleridge had clearly determined that appropriate British policy could only be established at a critical juncture in its history if France, its values, institutions and its leadership were properly understood. Later, when in public office in Malta, this acuity would be of value in his evaluation of the French intentions in the Mediterranean – a talent that no doubt contributed to the Civil Commissioner's desire to keep Coleridge in Valletta after he stood down as Acting Public Secretary.

Coleridge's understanding of constitutional doctrine is also revealed in a number of political leaders, on the proposed new French Constitution, published in *The Morning Post*.[41] Coleridge subjected the new Constitution to a sustained attack in which one of his most damaging broadsides was intended to reveal that the proposed settlement failed to respect the doctrine of the separation of powers.[42] Coleridge also condemned it's over-elaborate

---

39   E.g. ibid, 8 January 1800, 84.
40   This eventually took place on 3 February 1800.
41   This was the Constitution establishing the Consulate which placed military and political power in the hands of Napoleon Bonaparte. It was formally adopted on 24 December 1799. His articles appeared on 7, 26, 27 and 31 December, 1799: *EOT*, 1, 31-57.
42   This doctrine is particularly associated with the French writer Montesquieu

design. It was, he argued, "complex almost to entanglement" in its system of checks and balances.[43] Despite this, the Constitution singularly failed to provide appropriate curbs upon the powers of the new Chief Consul, Napoleon Bonaparte.[44] He was particularly concerned that France had created an oligarchy that would survive only with the use of military force – and that military was placed exclusively in the hands of the Chief Consul. In summary, Coleridge concluded that the reform was a failure that would not last ten years.[45]

When the British, somewhat conveniently from their point of view, exercised autocratic powers under the Maltese Constitution, which lacked similar curbs upon governmental and authoritarian power, Coleridge expressed no criticism, and indeed, devoted much of *The Friend* (as we shall see below) to eulogising the way in which the Civil Commissioner exercised power. This contrast is illuminating.

In this journalism, Coleridge also disclosed how far he had shifted from his earlier radicalism. Although it was a remark made in the context of French politics, he revealingly disclosed his view that Jacobinism was a "raving madness".[46]

From his pen, there also emerged both a treatment of Bonaparte[47] and a highly critical profile of Pitt.[48] In the case of the former, he acknowledged the dictatorial powers that Bonaparte exercised: but he portrayed his conduct, in seeking to end the war, as sincere and dignified, in contrast to that of British ministry whose public behaviour was "stupid". Whereas Bonaparte and the French ministry behaved with scrupulous respect and restraint, the British response to their invitation to negotiate was carping and recriminatory. [49]

---

whose work *L'esprit des lois*, 1748, asserted that the three functions of government (legislative, executive and judicial) should be performed by separate bodies. Misgovernment, or tyranny, would result if any two of those functions were performed by one body. Ironically Montesquieu, who was an admiring visitor to Britain, wrongly concluded that the British constitution exemplified these enlightened principles. Amongst its many controversial arrangements, the legislature in Britain is dominated by the Executive. As we shall see, under the Maltese constitution under which Coleridge worked whilst in office all legislative, executive and ultimate judicial authority was vested in the British civil commissioner.

43   *EOT*, 1, 46-7, 26 December 1799.
44   Ibid at 47.
45   *EOT*, 1, 49, 26 December 1799.
46   *EOT*, 1, 282, 3 December 1801.
47   *EOT*, 1, 211-14: 11, 13 and 15 March 1800.
48   19th March 1800, ibid. 219.
49   See e.g., *EOT*, 1, 211, 13 March 1800. Note, however, that once war with France

In the profile of Pitt, he castigated the Prime Minister as "a being who had had no feelings connected with man or nature, no spontaneous impulses, no unbiased and desultory studies, no genuine science, nothing that constitutes individuality in intellect..." Pitt was portrayed as lacking a coherent response to the relationship with France, when the *realpolitik* of 1800 was very different from that at the outset of war in 1793. In effect, Pitt personified the illiberal and repressive policies, in stamping out mature political debate in England, which had also attracted Coleridge's fire.[50]

This opinion-forming and influential journalism was professional experience that he would be able to put to valuable effect on Malta when writing the Bandi and Avvisi (Proclamations and Public Notices). As we shall see, it was in the political use of government information that, from the British point of view, Coleridge was arguably most successful in public office. Also valuable in his later office was his recognition of the central relevance and importance of constitutional principles. This would also be put to the test on Malta – although, arguably, with less success.

Lirycal Ballads, 1800

As stated, in July 1800 Coleridge moved his family to Greta Hall, Keswick. Greta Hall house stood then, as now, upon a low hill by the River Greta. When the Coleridges resided there, it commanded excellent views of Derwentwater, Bassenthwaite, Borrowdale, the Coledale Fells and Skiddaw. Coleridge was much enthused by this landscape. The cloudscapes, storms and moonlight on the lakes, richly inspired his writing, especially in the private *Notebooks*. Proximity to his fellow poet was also, Coleridge argued, a "priceless Value".[51]

The first edition of the *Lyrical Ballads* had been a success and now a second edition was projected. In this venture, however, Coleridge may have been over-willing to accommodate Wordsworth. Gradually, the latter began to assert himself as the dominant party in their literary relationship, and this contributed to Coleridge's subsequent loss of confidence in his

had resumed, Coleridge offered his support for possible British military action even if this included the annexation of territory belonging to a foreign power: see below. Note also Coleridge's essay on International Law in *The Friend* which argues for the legitimacy of an assertive foreign policy which might include the anticipatory use of force – *The Friend*, I, 298 et seq. It's also of interest that Coleridge had enlisted in, and briefly served with the dragoons in 1794.

50   See also 'Fire, Famine and Slaughter', *The Morning Post*, 8 January 1798.

51   To T. Poole, 21 March 1800, *CL* 1, 582.

imagination. His loss of self-esteem as an artist is a significant feature of the traumatic years that lay ahead.

First Wordsworth proposed, and Coleridge agreed, that the second edition of the *Lyrical Ballads* should be published under Wordsworth's name only. Despite this, Coleridge retained his commitment to the project and struggled to move forward with the second part of his important poem, *Christabel,* that was planned for inclusion in the second volume of the new edition.

On 29 August 1800 Coleridge walked across the mountains, including traversing Helvellyn in moonlight, carrying a draft of Part II of *Christabel* to show Wordsworth. However, despite the "increasing pleasure" that the Wordsworths derived from the poem, by 6 October 1800 it had been decided that Christabel would be excluded from the *Lyrical Ballads*. This was ostensibly on the grounds that it was not consistent with the literary aims of the project. But that was not all. Coleridge's major work, the *Ancient Mariner*, had attracted most of the criticism levelled at the first edition of the poems. Wordsworth decided to publish an apology for the inclusion of the poem in the second edition.[52] It is possible that Coleridge may neither have seen nor approved of this prior to its publication.[53] In it Wordsworth wrote: "The Poem of my Friend has indeed great defects...",[54] and he publicly acknowledged the criticism that the poem had attracted. Nonetheless he had, he stated, decided to publish it because its merits "gave to the poem a value which is not often possessed by *better Poems*". (Emphasis added).

Early in October 1800, Humphrey Davey received a letter from Coleridge. This broached the subject of the second edition and appeared to show that Coleridge had accepted Wordsworth's actions with equanimity.[55] But this may merely have been Coleridge's public mask. In fact, the rejection of two of his major works by a poet whose achievement he considered not to have been surpassed since Milton profoundly undermined Coleridge's confidence and self-esteem.[56] Coleridge subsequently wrote to Thelwall: "As to Poetry, I have altogether abandoned it, being convinced that I never had the essential poetic Genius".[57] A letter to Francis Wrangham also

---

52   *Lyrical Ballads*, vol 1, unnumbered page after the text, quoted in Livingstone Lowes, 475.
53   Lefebure (1977), 325-6.
54   Quoted in Lefebure (1977), 326.
55   To Davey, 9 October 1800, *CL* 1, 631. Coleridge thought that Christabel would subsequently be published with Wordworth's *The Pedlar*.
56   To Thomas Poole, 21 March 1800, *CL* 1, 582.
57   To Thelwall, 17 December 1800, *CL* 1, 656.

revealed what are likely to have been his true feelings: "As to our literary occupations, they are still more distant than our residences – He is a great, true poet – I am only a kind of Metaphysician".[58]

When, in 1818, Coleridge revisited this subject, he referred to the Wordsworths' "cold praise and effective discouragement of every attempt of mine to roll onward in a distinct current of my own". He continued, "[They] *admitted* that the Ancient Mariner [and] the Christabel…were not without merit, but they were abundantly anxious to acquit their judgements of any blindness to the very numerous defects".[59] Coleridge paid a high price for the Wordsworths' ruthless intellectual integrity. Their damaging attitude can also be seen as influential in Coleridge's eventual decision to spend an extended period away from their collaborations and friendship.

Addiction

During the stormy winter of 1800-1801 Coleridge's health deteriorated. Fever and rheumatic symptoms predominated. He was confined to bed for long periods and resorted to opiates, which was the primary remedy within the limited pharmacopoeia of the period. Coleridge had previously resorted to it as laudanum which was easily procured as a palliative. He appears to have used opium throughout the previous decade.[60] This undermines his subsequent argument that he became "seduced" into addiction. He claimed that he had read, in borrowed medical journals, of a case similar to his own that was successfully treated by these means. This possibility has been contested.[61] However, it seems beyond doubt that, by 1801, Coleridge was addicted.

Medical science did not, at this time, appreciate the nature of addiction. Neither Coleridge nor those of his friends who took it upon themselves to warn him about excessive opium consumption, realised that he could not withdraw from the drug merely by determined abstention. Withdrawal symptoms would occur each time he attempted it. Over the next three years, Coleridge came to realise that he was hopelessly, irredeemably, hooked on opium. But this understanding would only be reached after long struggles with the drug. Each failed attempt to give it up was succeeded by the unremitting cycle of an unpleasant withdrawal symptoms, followed

---

58 To Revd. Francis Wrangham, 19 December 1800, *CL* 1, 658.
59 MS New York Public Library, quoted in Griggs, *CL* 1, 631.
60 Lefebure (1977), 338.
61 ibid., 333 et seq.

by renewed dosing. Then he had to steel himself for yet another attempt at renunciation. Somehow he had to break the cycle of withdrawal and renewed consumption.

Morning Post

An early strategy was to remove himself from both his wife and the rigours of a Lake District winter. In the autumn of 1801, he returned to London to resume journalism for *The Morning Post*. Hard work, discipline and a drier climate would, he believed, serve him well. Nonetheless, his hopes of renouncing opium were dashed by severe withdrawal symptoms, which he confidently brushed aside as food poisoning.[62]

Even so, he was effective and industrious. He provided a sustained critique of the new Ministry and, in particular, Addington, the recently appointed Prime Minister.[63] He was acutely aware that in time of war or other emergency, the power of the Executive increases leading to the introduction of laws that are inimical to civil liberties and the rule of law – a problem he would encounter in Malta, where his support for the Civil Commissioner would be contentious and morally complex. Most controversial in Britain at this time were questions surrounding the moral and constitutional legitimacy of the *Habeas Corpus* Suspension Acts.

The writ of *Habeas Corpus* is one of the principal bulwarks of civil liberty. It is a writ issued by a court requiring the state to justify in law the arrest or detention of a subject. If the court is satisfied that the detention is unlawful, it will order the prisoner's release. *Habeas Corpus* thus prevents arbitrary arrest and imprisonment without trial. In the words of Erskine May, "It brings to light the cause of every imprisonment, approves its lawfulness, or liberates the prisoner".[64] In other words, it underpins the right, conferred by Magna Carta in 1215, that an individual should be free from imprisonment until properly convicted. It further provides the foundation of the right to a fair trial and judgement by peers.

Legislation "suspending" the writ was first introduced in 1794 and this was renewed annually until the legislation expired in 1802. The Suspension Acts had serious consequences for civil liberties. For example, one individual

---

62   To Thomas Poole, 19 February 1802, *CL* 1, 787.
63   March 1801. Pitt had resigned over the question of Catholic Emancipation, but would subsequently return to Prime Ministerial Office in 1804.
64   Vol. III, Chapter XI, 10-24.

was held for six years without trial and others for three years. [65]

The influence of demagogues, during the Revolution in France, encouraged the British government to fear the small but articulate minority of individuals who sought constitutional reform in England.[66] Imprisonment, upon mere suspicion of guilt, became possible and, after suspension of the writ, there would be no means of testing the credibility of any evidence underlying a detention order. Detainees would not, necessarily, know who had accused them, nor upon what evidence they had been detained. They had no right to demand a trial. This is why Coleridge's political lectures risked him being seized and imprisoned during the anti-democratic hysteria of 1795.

Political discourse advocating social and constitutional reform was, in the government's view, high treason. The harsh treatment of a number of its prominent political opponents revealed the lengths to which it was prepared to go to suppress free discussion of democratic reform. Nonetheless, the prosecutions failed as the juries had found the state's evidence of a public emergency to be inadequate.

Shortly after taking office, in March 1801, Addington had released political prisoners, but, to Coleridge's chagrin, soon effected a *volte face* by re-suspending *Habeas Corpus*. Addington's defence of this apparent inconsistency relied upon undisclosed "evidence" that had been presented to "Committees of Secrecy" in both Houses of Parliament, which (according to Coleridge) Addington accepted uncritically. Notoriously, these Committees, which comprised Government loyalists, excluded even senior members of the Opposition. Coleridge's central thrust attacked Addington's moral weakness in this affair. [67] Practices such as these forced him to conclude that, Addington was "beneath mediocrity".[68]

Thus, the Acts of Suspension were renewed until the end of 1801. But this

---

65   Erskine May, 16. The Government deployed the familiar assertion that officials accused of having acted unlawfully could not defend themselves without disclosing secret information or the sources of intelligence.

66   There were, however, advocates of reform in the House of Commons, most notably Francis Burdett, who held the rotten borough of Boroughbridge after 1797. He was elected the Member for Middlesex in 1802.

67   *EOT*, 1, 282-4, 3 December 1801.

68   *EOT*, 1, 308. Within a week of coming to power, Addington's administration opened negotiations with France to end the war. Its eagerness to end hostilities persuaded it to it agree to evacuate Malta on unfavourable terms. Had this occurred, the outcome could easily have been highly damaging to British interests. In the end, Malta was neither evacuated by British forces nor returned to its pre-British government. The war resumed in May 1803 with Malta as the *casus bellum*.

was not all because Addington's Ministry also secured the passage through Parliament of the Act of Indemnity 1801. This was a measure intended to protect, from liability, any official who had authorised detention since the passing of the *Habeas Corpus* Suspension Act 1794. The former measure put beyond doubt that there could be no accountability to the law for the arbitrary detentions.

The passage of the Indemnity Bill 1801 was a matter of heated political debate, and drew fierce criticism from Coleridge's pen. He used it to develop a conception of the Constitution that essentially rejected positivist theories of legitimacy. For Coleridge, a law could not be legitimate merely because Parliament had been persuaded to enact it and place it on the Statute Book; indeed, enacted law could actually be "unconstitutional" – an idea that was inimical to a system that lacked a written constitution. Coleridge's argument was, however, consistent with Natural Law theorists according to whom man-made norms are only valid if they conform to a morally and legally superior law. The latter system is not, however, enshrined in the English legal system. According to constitutional orthodoxy in Britain, Parliament is a legislature having unlimited law-making powers, so anything that is enacted becomes "law" and thus legitimate. Validity does not depend upon conformity to some higher moral order, which is the basis of legal authority.

Undeterred by this, Coleridge repeatedly argued that the British Constitution is founded upon certain fundamental moral principles, including principles designed to protect the individual from the unlawful predations of Government.[69] Laws that undermined those entrenched moral principles could, properly, be condemned as violating the Constitution. This was particularly so in the case of both the Suspension and Indemnity Acts. The latter, for example, would deny victims of arbitrary arrest and imprisonment (i.e. the victims of the Suspension Acts) a remedy in damages in the courts. Coleridge's use of language in describing the consequences of this reveal his idea of a hierarchy of laws within the constitutional system. He stated that the Indemnity Act was a "barrier between the individual and the law" (and thus not law itself).[70] This discloses his idea the "law" is something permanent and inviolable that lies beyond even the powers of (an inferior) Parliament to amend.

His further concern about these controversial measures also revealed

---

69   *EOT*, 1, 272, 27 November 1801; ibid., 282, 3 December 1801; ibid 287, 11 December 1801.
70   *EOT*, 1, 284, 3 December 1801.

an emerging constitutional conservatism.[71] The danger in violating fundamental political freedoms, he argued, was that it established a precedent that would make it easier for future governments to pursue similar repression. When this future conduct established its own precedent, the repressive measures could harden into accepted constitutional practices, destroying, by degrees, the fundamental principles of the British Constitution.[72]

He was acutely aware that repressive measures such as the Suspension and Indemnity Acts each violated the principle of the rule of law, which was one of the bulwark principles of the British Constitution. In summary, he warned that these measures were a fundamental erosion of the nation's constitutional morality, weakening the very foundations of a stable society.[73] His principled approach invoking natural law, as opposed to positivist legal theory, once more revealed his ability to locate contemporary political controversy within the framework of fundamental constitutional doctrine.

However, in 1802, Coleridge's political journalism had not yet been enriched by that significant engagement with practical politicians that would occur in Malta. He had not yet experienced at first hand the need for prudent rather than principled governmental decision-making. Whether the public good could be mediated only through principled action would force Coleridge to consider a doctrine that made it permissible for government to override principles of the constitutional, legal or political order to achieve general welfare. In his official capacity, Coleridge would have to confront the need to manipulate Maltese public opinion to gain consent to legislation that overwhelmingly served Imperial interests. He could not avoid the problem that the legitimacy of British rule was questionable in the absence of a congruence between governmental policies and Maltese sympathies. In drafting such measures, promulgating them above his signature, and in offering a highly partial and incomplete public account of their purposes, Coleridge was complicit, and his actions sparked questions of legitimacy that he could not avoid.[74] But that was in the future. He had yet to experience the moral dilemmas of power.[75]

---

71   Although, it can be argued that Coleridge had to invoke natural law theory to defend what saw as the "true" Constitution, this theory was actually foreign to it. Thus, Coleridge's "conservatism" is of a particular kind which emphasises morality – as an inherent and unchanging guiding value-over historical and legal precedent.

72   *EOT*, 1, 281, 3 December 1801; ibid., 295, 11 December 1801.

73   See *EOT*, 1, 295, 11 December 1801.

74   To Daniel Stuart, 22 August 1806, *CL* 2, 1178.

75   In *The Friend* he also described how Ball's naval vessels, prompted by the threat

Notwithstanding this, Coleridge's second period on *The Morning Post* must be regarded as unenhanced by his later experiences of governmental power in action; his high reputation as a political commentator and journalist was now assured.

"Asra"

Coleridge's relationship with his wife, which had been under strain since their Stowey days, was now becoming increasingly traumatic. Withdrawal from an uncongenial marriage would also have attracted him to overseas travel. He complained to Tom Wedgewood of Sara's "ill tempered Speeches…my friends received with freezing looks, the least opposition or contradiction occasioning screams of passion".[76]

Coleridge's deepening fascination for Sarah Hutchinson (Asra), which was not concealed from Sara Coleridge, broke open another fissure in their marital relationship. Sara demanded loyalty; Coleridge refused to renounce what he endeavoured to pass off as simply a virtuous friendship. Sara, (his wife) he argued, was the cause of his unhappiness. Friends whom he kept abreast of his domestic troubles advocated separation, and it is possible that the advice was first offered at about this time.[77]

By the summer of 1802, Coleridge reluctantly summoned the courage to broach the subject to his wife. Her reaction appears to have been an incandescent blend of anger, alarm and betrayal. Coleridge, who later wrote of this episode to Tom Wedgewood,[78] recoiled with "stomach spasms" and may have had some kind of seizure, which shocked and frightened his wife. They then resolved to talk about their difficulties and agreed to attempt reconciliation.[79] Coleridge's efforts to restore his marriage conspicuously fell short of renouncing Asra whom he continued to visit.

Wordsworth had, by the spring of 1802 embarked upon one of his greatest creative periods. In contrast, Coleridge who had written little, felt a deepening sense of failure. In late March, the Wordsworths came to stay

---

of mutinous revolt amongst the allied army, threatened force against Sicilian merchants who refused to relinquish grain that was needed do badly on Malta. Ball was eulogised for not using his legal authority to punish the starving mutineers as much as for breaching established legal order in his adopted means of securing the grain from a friendly power: *The Friend*, I, 558-60. See also Chapter 5.9: Passports.

76   To Thomas Wedgewood, 20 October 1802, *CL* 2, 876.
77   To George Coleridge, 2 April 1806 [1807], *CL* 3, 7.
78   To Thomas Wedgewood, 20 October 1802, *CL* 2, 875.
79   To Robert Southey, 29 July 1802, *CL* 2, 830-3.

at Greta Hall. Wordsworth brought with him examples of his recent work including part of the *Intimations of Immortality*. On the evening of 4 April 1802, Coleridge retreated to his study and began to pen the first version of the *"Dejection"* Ode. This was first composed as the highly confessional *"Letter to Asra"*. Its autobiographical themes are the unattainable Asra and the failure of his marriage.

In the summer of 1802, the Wordsworths took advantage of the temporary peace established after the Treaty of Amiens which we shall consider later (see Appendix 2). They travelled to France to meet Annette Vallon, who had born William a child, Caroline, almost ten years earlier. The purpose of the visit was to prepare for William's impending marriage to Mary Hutchinson and, doubtless, to make other arrangements for Caroline.

During their absence the Coleridges' marriage unexpectedly thrived: "Love and Concord" were rediscovered at Greta Hall. [80] Moreover, Coleridge enjoyed himself in other ways, not least by making the first recorded ascent of Scafell.

Further Struggles with Addiction

The return of the Lakeland autumn, in 1802, heralded the onset of the wild weather which Coleridge blamed for his poor health and increased opium consumption. He now planned to escape abroad with Tom Wedgewood. In the event, they ventured no further than South Wales and the West Country. Even so, it meant leaving Sara who was now heavily pregnant – a decision that must have put their marriage under further strain. His visit to Asra, *en route*, aggravated her further. An important exchange of letters between husband and wife ensued. Although Sara's letters have not survived, those sent to her by Coleridge reveal a mixture of assertiveness, contrition and apology. Their future depended, he proclaimed, on "your (Sara's) loving those whom I love" (i.e. Asra).[81] This condition clearly verged on a repudiation of their marriage, but Coleridge's tone was in other respects more accommodating. He repeated his commitment to the marriage, and told her that it was difficult to be apart from her.[82] He even apologised for his own faults, not least his quick-tempered outbursts against her.[83] Eventually, Sara seems to have been willing to pursue renewed

---

80   Ibid at 832.
81   To Mrs Coleridge, 13 December 1802, *CL* 2, 894.
82   To Mrs Coleridge, 4 December 1802, *CL* 2, 889.
83   To Mrs Coleridge, 5 January 1803, *CL* 2, 908.

reconciliation. Coleridge persuaded Wedgewood to travel to the Lakes so that Coleridge could rejoin his wife at the birth of their child. Needless to add, he was too late; Coleridge learned at Grasmere of the birth of his daughter (also called Sara).

Unable to travel abroad, Coleridge's health declined once more when he fell ill with rheumatic fever. This probably resulted in an increased consumption of opium. Fearful nightmares, which awakened him screaming at night were but one of the unpleasant symptoms of addiction. It was at this period that Coleridge at last may have begun to admit to himself that he had hitherto misunderstood cause and effect. Many of his ailments, for which he took opium, were in fact caused by it. His private *Notebooks* eventually revealed this.[84] However, at this period, he stoically insisted, to those who had begun to suspect the true nature of his problem, that nothing he consumed was habit forming.[85] Nevertheless, he made a will and took out a life assurance policy to provide his wife with £1000 in the event of his death.

There were renewed plans to go abroad. He planned either to take up an invitation to stay in Malta, with a John Stoddart, a school friend from his Christ's Hospital days,[86] or to visit Madeira.[87] Stoddart, a prominent journalist and literary critic, who had just been appointed Kings and Admiralty Advocate in Malta, visited Coleridge in October 1803[88] and may have then issued an invitation to stay with him. Stoddart was eventually to become a Chief Justice of Malta.

The Walking Tour of 1803

Meanwhile, Coleridge and the Wordsworths had decided to set off for a tour of Scotland. If this was an attempt to rekindle their exciting and halcyon days of Stowey/Alfoxden it was a dismal failure. Coleridge

84   *CN* 2, 2990.
85   To Robert Southey, 16 April 1804, *CL* 2, 1129.
86   Stoddart was a literary critic who reviewed Scott's work in the *Edinburgh Review*, No. II, January 1803, "Minstrelsy of the Scottish Border". Earlier he had published *Remarks on the Local Scenery and Manners in Scotland* during the years 1799 and 1800 (1801). He was political editor for the *London Times* from 1812-1816. He was eventually to serve as Chief Justice of the Vice-Admiralty court, Malta from 1826. His sister married William Hazlitt.
87   To Sir George and Lady Beaumont, 12 August 1803, *CL* 2, 965.
88   Coleridge wrote that John Stoddart had visited him on "Monday past", that is, Monday, 27 October, 1800: *CL* 1, 643. Coleridge and Stoddart had travelled together to Keswick on 23 October 1800: Purton, V., 49.

seemed, to Wordsworth, to be in bad spirits. For his part, Coleridge resented Dorothy's fondness for reciting William's verses aloud. The group of friends eventually separated. Coleridge left the Wordsworths at Loch Lomond and marched alone across the Highlands with a renewed sense of purpose and vigour. This was not the end of their friendship, but it signals a rupture whose origins lie, perhaps, in the second edition of the *Lyrical Ballads* and, in particular, the suppression of *Christabel* and the apology for Coleridge's *Ancient Mariner*. Coleridge saw little of them after his return to Greta Hall.[89]

Once free to pursue his own goals, Coleridge sought physical renewal in almost obsessive exercise. He appears to have believed that he might achieve a cure by driving the illness to the extremities of his body. In pursuit of this desperate and hopeless strategy, he covered 263 miles in 8 days on foot – as he proudly told his friends once back at Greta Hall.[90] However, his addiction simply refused to yield. Letters that resound with his physical prowess on the Scottish tour also reveal acute nocturnal struggles. Coleridge wrote to Thomas Wedgewood the "Night is my Hell, Sleep my tormenting Angel".[91] "Night-screams", he reported, "have almost made me a nuisance in my own House".[92] He nevertheless vowed to take up armed resistance if the apparently imminent French invasion took place. If the country were in danger he would fight the enemy.[93] This assertion of loyalty and patriotism is interesting because it reveals his willingness to use armed force to defend a country whose social, economic and political system he had earlier identified as oppressive. It is an early expression of his jingoism, which allows us to contextualise understanding of his complex responses to the behaviour of the British administration on Malta.

Preparing to Sail

At this time, his brother in law, Southey, had been bereaved by the loss of his only daughter. He came with his wife, Edith, and her sister Mary[94] to stay with the Coleridges at Greta Hall. Their visit eventually became permanent. Coleridge, whose health continued to be in a "distressful state"

89   To Thomas Poole, *CL* 2, 1012, 14 October 1803.
90   To Sir George and Lady Beaumont, 22 September 1803, *CL* 2, 993; also to George Coleridge, 2 October 1803 *CL* 2, 1005, and to T. Poole, 3 October 1803, *CL* 2, 1009.
91   To Tom Wedgewood, 16 September 1803, *CL* 2, 991.
92   To Thomas Poole, 3 October 1803, *CL* 2, 1010.
93   To Sir George Beaumont, 17 October 1803, *CL* 2, 1017.
94   I.e. Sara Coleridge's sisters.

throughout the autumn, could now travel abroad knowing that Sara and the children would be cared for by close family. He determined to leave the Lake District hoping that he could recover his health in a warmer climate.[95] He claimed that his departure was "a choice of Evils": to remain in England was to court death; the fulfilment of his desire for transcendence in the warm South was his final hope.[96]

Madeira or Malta?[97] Each seemed likely possibilities, although he seemed to favour the former.[98] Coleridge would only make up his mind, to accept Stoddart's invitation to travel to Malta, on 31 January 1804.[99] Even then he had no plan to spend much time there since he regarded Malta as merely a staging post for Sicily, to which he was attracted by the possibility of an ascent of Etna.[100]

As the day of his departure drew near his letters acquired a valedictory tone. His health and morale had deteriorated once more: and he recognised that his resting place was likely to be some corner of a foreign field:[101] "..if I return, we shall be Friends: if I die, as I believe I shall, you will remember me".[102] "Death...", he wrote to Sir George Beaumont, "will only be a Voyage – a Voyage not *from* but to our native Country".[103]

"Bear up and sail large"[104]

Coleridge arrived in Portsmouth on the morning of the 28 March 1804, ready to board his ship, the fast 130-ton merchant brig, *Speedwell*. The ship's voyage from London had been delayed by adverse winds and it had not

---

95 To Matthew Coates, 5 December 1803, *CL* 2, 1021; also to Robert Southey, 13 January 1804, *CL* 2, 1029.

96 To John Rickman, 13 March 1804, *CL* 2, 1089.

97 To John Thelwall, 26 November, 1803, *CL* 2, 1019. By January Catania was added to the list of potential destinations: to Sir George Beaumont, 30 January 1804, *CL* 2, 1049.

98 To Richard Sharp, 15 January 1804, *CL* 2, 1035.

99 To George Bellas Greenough, 31 January 1804, *CL* 2, 1050, but his procrastination was not fully conquered by his apparent resolve: see To the Wordsworths, 16 February 1804, *CL* 2, 1065.

100 He seems to have made two ascents of the volcano: to Mrs S. T. Coleridge, 12 December 1804, *CL* 2, 1157.

101 To J. G. Rideout, 23 March 1804, *CL* 2, 1098; see also to John Rickman, 26 March 1804, *CL* 2, 1098.

102 To William Sotheby, 27 March 1804, *CL* 2, 1106.; see also to Mrs S. T. Coleridge, 1 April 1804, *CL* 2, 1115.

103 *CL* 2, 1123.

104 *CN* 2, 2016, 6 April 1804.

yet arrived.[105] It was only on 9 April, after yet more contrary winds, that *Speedwell* weighed anchor and set sail in a convoy, which was to be escorted as far as Gibraltar by the *Leviathan*.[106] Coleridge carried with him letters of introduction to Major-General Villettes, the commander of the British army on Malta, and Sir Alexander Ball, the Civil Commissioner.[107]

The novelty of the journey, the talk of sailors, the idiosyncrasies of his fellow travellers, the routines of the convoy and the sight of ships in convoy under sail intrigued Coleridge. Seated upon the duck coop with the ducks quacking at his feet, and using the rudder case as a desk, Coleridge noted all that he saw and learned. He listened to the sounds of the ship, noting the "creaking of (the) Main top irons, & squeak of the rudder rope";[108] he learned that in certain winds the ship would travel faster with less sail;[109] he recorded the latitude of the ship and regularly noted its speed; he looked forward to his first glimpse of Cape Ortegal.[110]

Portugal sighted, he flung on his greatcoat and hurried shoeless on to the deck to observe it and the fishing boats laying off each side of the ship.[111] He marvelled at the apparently magical progress of the *Leviathan* in contrast to the laboured rolling of his own vessel. This powerful ship-of-the-line was, he wrote, "upright, motionless, as a church with its Steeple – as tho' it moved by its own will, as tho' its speed were spiritual-the being and essence without the body of motion".[112]

But the excitement was not to last. For the greater part of the journey between Gibraltar and Malta, as the weather deteriorated, he became seriously unwell. Lying in his bunk he returned to opium as the ship was alternately storm-blasted or becalmed. In adverse weather, the ship drifted backwards; when becalmed there hung the danger of attack from pirate

---

105   The passage, which Coleridge arranged on 12 March 1804, was, he judged, expensive. It cost 35 guineas, with Coleridge having to purchase his mattress, three sheets, two blankets a pillow and pillow case as well as his own wine and spirits to the cost of a further £7 or £8; but Captain Findlay, the Commander of the ship, furnished everything else required for the journey.
106   She was a 74 gun ship of the line that was to become the third ship after Victory to pass through the enemy line at the Battle of Trafalgar. On the Gibraltar-Valletta leg of the journey the convoy was escorted by the Frigate Maidstone which was also shortly to see action against French ships off Hyères near Toulon, where the French fleet was blockaded by Nelson.
107   To William Sotheby, 13 March 1804, *CL* 2, 1086.
108   *CN* 2, 1996.
109   *CN* 2, 2003.
110   *CN* 2, 2002.
111   *CN* 2, 2014.
112   To Robert Southey, 16 April 1804, *CL* 2, 1127.

1. A view of Valletta from South Street with the Marsamxett or Quarantine Harbour on the left

vessels using oar rather than sail.[113] These could dart into the convoy when even the most heavily armed escort ship would be powerless to help them.

He drifted into opium saturated reveries unable to return to the deck. At last, his body fell victim to the effects of opium; his bowels would not function. Tormented by self-disgust and guilt he suffered until finally the Captain of the *Speedwell* called upon the services of a surgeon. The remedy was humiliating and painful.

Malta

When *Speedwell* reached Malta, on 18 May 1804, Coleridge fled the ship. Leaving his baggage aboard, he went ashore and went directly to Stoddart's house in Valletta, the Casa di San Poix, (a former auberge of the Knights of St John) where he was warmly received and given rooms. (fig. 1) Two days later he called upon Major-General William Villettes[114] and Sir Alexander Ball, the Civil Commissioner, who was universally, albeit unofficially, known as

113   To Mrs Coleridge, 5 June 1804, *CL* 2, 1136.
114   Major-General Villettes had been appointed commander in chief of the British troops in Malta in 1801.

2. San Antonio Palace, now the official residence of the President of Malta, at St Anton, Attard. During the Maltese uprising of 1799-1800 Captain Ball used it as his residence. He returned when he became Civil Commissioner in 1802. Coleridge spent much of his time there.

the "Governor" of the Island.[115] Coleridge recorded of the meeting with Ball that it was unlikely to lead to his appointment to a colonial post.[116] This was a disappointment since Coleridge had thought it possible some small post might be offered by which he could defray the expenses of the voyage.[117] Fortunately for Coleridge, this unaccommodating first meeting was not to remain Ball's final position. The following day, Ball invited Coleridge to the country palace at San Antonio (now St Anton, fig. 2).[118] Riding back to Valletta, Ball posed the question whether fortune favours fools. Coleridge's

---

115   The Crown may have withheld the title of "Governor" as the status of Malta was unresolved, although an alternative possibility is ventured in Chapter 4. Normally, the use of the title might signal internationally that Britain would be unwilling to give up sovereignty over the island and Britain was reluctant to give offence, especially to Russia. Coleridge was later to point to other, more conspiratorial reasons touching upon inter-service rivalry between the army (Major-General Villettes) and the navy (the Civil Commissioner). Villettes was not subordinate to Ball in matters outside the civil administration. See *The Friend*, I, 544 n. and later *Table Talk*, I, 475, April 1834. The first Governor, properly so called, was appointed in 1813 at a time when British sovereignty would not be disputed.

116   *CN* 2, 2101.

117   To William Sotheby, 13 March 1804, *CL* 2, 1086.

118   The Palace lies about one hundred metres from the Valletta to Rabat road.

articulate response, on the subject of chance and superstition, clearly impressed Ball and a friendship was firmly established.[119] Coleridge was to write that this was "one of the most delightful mornings I ever passed".[120]

Sir Alexander Ball

As early as 1804, but most notably after Ball's death in 1809, Coleridge presented Ball as "the abstract Idea of a wise & good Governor".[121] In a Notebook written whilst he was acting Public Secretary on Malta, he recorded that Ball was "a great man",[122] and he subsequently eulogised Ball, in *The Friend*, as "[a] truly great man, (the best and greatest public character that I had ever the opportunity of making myself acquainted with)".[123] Ball's prudence, he wrote, resembled wisdom; "his Intellect (was) "so clear and comprehensive".[124] This unity of wisdom and prudence allowed Coleridge to present Ball as the essence of morally-legitimate political authority. In the Civil Commissioner, Coleridge thus considered that wisdom governed the inherent fallibility of acting prudently. This idea was developed and emerged as a major theme of *The Friend* in 1809-1810.

Coleridge's accounts have left us with important evidence as to how government in Malta operated. The qualities of the Civil Commissioner to which Coleridge drew the most attention were his willingness to consult and his open mindedness, evidenced by his readiness to seek the opinion even of those who might have very different opinions from his own.[125] Had Ball pursued his naval career, Coleridge considered that he would, like Nelson, have had a "band of brothers", a team of fellow officers, whose opinions he could trust and upon whose initiative he could rely. Coleridge arrived at this conclusion because, it seems, that was Ball's *modus operandi* in conducting the civil government of the Island.

Importantly, Coleridge also described Ball as a good listener who would make time to invite all opinion, even from those whose judgement would, it seems, not carry much weight. Coleridge made it clear that Ball was "zealous in collecting the opinions of the well-informed"; although, once he had consulted he would be careful to make up his own mind and

---

119   *The Friend*, II, 250-3 (1809).
120   *The Friend*, I, 533.
121   To William Sotheby, 5 July 1804, *CL* 2, 1141.
122   *CN* 2, 2438.
123   *The Friend*, I, 169.
124   *CN* 2, 2438. Coleridge privately referred to Ball as Sophosophron: *CN* 2, 2439.
125   *The Friend*, I, 552.

not slavishly follow what he might perceive to be the wishes of authority. Coleridge also described Ball's passion for fully reasoned, reflective decision-making. The impression that Coleridge was careful to leave is of an independent, evidence-led decision-maker concerned to gather all relevant information and opinion before reaching a decision.[126] And, Coleridge carefully emphasised that Ball was guided by principles of morality and justice. As Kooy describes, this is an idealised expression of "pure politics". It is Coleridge's deployment of conscience as the necessary means of subjecting politics to Reason.[127]

Coleridge provided direct evidence that he was amongst those whose formal, written opinion Ball invited. He also celebrated Ball's openness by revealing to us the latter's pleasure in finding that Coleridge had identified a wider range of argument than Ball had at first appreciated.

However, it would be wrong to assume that their relationship was always harmonious. As a surviving un-dated note from Ball to Coleridge[128] reveals, the two men seem to have held implacably opposed views upon certain political subjects, although the nature of these is not disclosed. Even so, the disagreement was such that Ball would not again raise the subject with Coleridge. Moreover, Ball was prepared to reprimand Coleridge quite severely for critical views that the latter had indiscreetly expressed. This may suggest that Coleridge had difficulty in accepting the strictures of collective cabinet responsibility, although this is but one possibility. Coleridge's irritated claim, in letters home, that Ball frustrated his attempts to return, also suggests that the two men were not always in harmony.[129]

Whilst on Malta, Coleridge became troubled by the political morality of those in power, which can only be a judgement upon Ball's conduct in office. Whilst still on the Island he had confided to Stuart: "But the Promises of men in office are what everyone knows them to be...".[130] This was a reference to Ball apparently breaking a promise that he had made to Coleridge himself, specifically that Coleridge should receive the whole salary of the combined offices of Treasurer and Public Secretary (although he did not act as Treasurer). He lamented the "heart-depraving Habits & Temptations of men in power, as Governors....is to make *instruments* of their

126 *The Friend*, I, 552-4.
127 Kooy (1999), 102-8.
128 The Wordsworth Trust, Grasmere, manuscript WLMS A/ Ball, Alexander, Sir/4 Ball to Coleridge.
129 To Mrs S. T. Coleridge, 21 August 1805, *CL* 2, 1170.
130 To Daniel Stuart, 1 May 1805, *CL* 2, 1166. He added that, in other ways, Ball treated him kindly.

fellow creatures-& the moment they find a man of Honor & Talents, instead of loving and esteeming him, they wish to *use* him".[131] More damning still was his conclusion that the public office entailed "intrigue".[132] He even confided to Stuart that he now knew "by heart the awkward & wicked machinery, by which all our affairs *abroad* are carried on".[133] The truth is that Coleridge's eulogy of Ball, in *The Friend,* almost certainly conceals from the public the limitations of the man and his government.

Other, perhaps more objective, evidence of Ball's competence as an administrator reveals that Ball's second period of office had only qualified success, especially during the difficult years of 1805-1806. As we shall see, in Chapter 2, the policies pursued by the administration were structurally flawed and the administration was, in some respects, ineffective. An over-arching complaint would be that the oversight of the complex system of government was completely inadequate. For example, amongst the proliferating problems, it seems that the system of financial control was particularly weak, resulting in a waste of British taxpayers' money.[134]

Other Members of the Civil Establishment

Apart from the Civil Commissioner, the dramatis personae of the British Civil Establishment, in Malta in 1804, included the Public Secretary *and* Treasurer, Alexander Macaulay, (at Ball's suggestion the offices had been combined in 1803). Although Coleridge regarded Macaulay as intelligent, honest and amiable[135] he was, at about eighty years of age, perhaps no longer effective in his role. Ball reported to Lord Windham that, even by 1802, it was a Mr Eton who was taking "the most active part in the administration of the civil Government".[136] Eton, who had left the Island sometime in September 1802 (but who retained his appointment), was to cause much trouble for Ball, both locally and in London.

Prior to Coleridge's appointment, Edmond Chapman, the Under-

---

131 *CN* 2, 2271, Friday, 23 November 1804. The Royal Commissioners, who report-ed in 1812, also found that the Civil Commissioners had legally "despotic" powers: see, British National Archive, Kew, CO 158/19 (hereafter referred to as Kew). This is discussed further in Chapter 3.
132 To Daniel Stuart, 22 August 1806, *CL* 2, 1178.
133 To Daniel Stuart, ibid.
134 Kew, CO 158/19.
135 *CN* 2, 2430.
136 Ball to Windham, 28 February 1807, Kew, CO 158/13/19.

Secretary,[137] and Giuseppe Nicolo Zammit, the "Maltese Secretary", probably bore the brunt of the Public Secretary's work. The archives reveal that whilst some of the written instructions to the departments of government were still being issued under Macaulay's signature, most were issued under Zammit's.[138] The frailty of the Public Secretary can clearly be seen in his markedly deteriorating handwriting during the latter part of 1804. At this period Ball was arranging for Macaulay's permanent successor to be appointed

The British staff also included the Reverend Francis Laing (who, at this time, acted as the private secretary to Ball[139]) and Edmond Chapman, the Under-Secretary.

Ball had to confront significant staffing shortages when Coleridge reached Malta. Chapman was absent from the Island pursuing an important official mission to the Black Sea region to secure corn supplies.[140] Laing, who also acted as tutor to Ball's only child, Keith, was going on leave to Scotland with the boy and one Anthony Sucheareau was intended as a temporary replacement for him.[141] Given the staffing problems, Ball made Coleridge the offer of Chapman's post as Under-Secretary during the

---

137   Edmond Chapman did not remain long as an active Public Secretary following his return from the Black Sea in September 1805. Ball informed Windham, the Secretary of State that Chapman had been given six months' leave on the grounds of ill health and that Laing had been appointed as acting Public Secretary: Ball to Windham, Kew, 4 June 1806, CO, 158/12/17. The illness might possibly have been a diplomatic convenience since the corn mission, for which Chapman had been partly responsible, had recently failed. Ball may have wished to be rid of him: see further Chapter 2.

138   National Archive of Malta, Rabat, Malta LIBR A22 PS01/1. Hereafter referred to as NAM.

139   Laing, who had been appointed as Acting Public Secretary during Chapman's medical leave eventually took over the latter's post. Laing was Public Secretary from 1807-1813 whereupon the office became that of the Chief Secretary. He held this post until 1814.

140   See Kew, CO 158/10. As we shall see, the Island was unable to produce sufficient foodstuffs for its own needs. By a peace treaty between France and Naples of 1801, the weak Neapolitan king had been forced to impose an embargo on corn supplies to Malta, thus cutting off food supplies from the customary source. Finding an alternative source, safe from French control, resulted in the corn mission to the Black Sea area. Coleridge was subsequently nominated for one of these missions (see below). Chapman's expedition was only partly successful: see further Chapter 2.

141   It was planned that, en route to Glasgow, they would stay with Mrs Coleridge and Southey at Greta Hall. Laing had been below Southey at Balliol College, Oxford University: To Mrs S. T. Coleridge, 5 July 1804, *CL* 2, 1142.

latter's absence.[142] After an assurance that the work would be "nominal" Coleridge accepted because the salary would defray the expenses of his planned journey to Sicily. Coleridge's contribution must have been most welcome, if not absolutely necessary. Coleridge thus began his official tasks as *Under-Secretary* to Ball.

Under-Secretary

In 1804 Ball was seeking to persuade British policymakers not only of the case for the permanent retention of Malta but also, more generally, to influence British political and military strategy in the Mediterranean. He decided to use Coleridge's talent and experience, as a political leader-writer, to help him with these tasks and to make the case that the Island should be permanently occupied by the British.

Coleridge was soon drafting a series of substantial memoranda on such issues as "future British policy and war aims' and "the intentions of the French".[143] Foreign policy in relation to Egypt, Sicily, and the North African coastal states were all subjects of papers from his pen.[144] In them, Coleridge was willing to advocate the aggressive assertion of the British national interest even if this meant annexing sovereign territory, as he argued in the case of Egypt. These papers were passed either directly to Granville Penn, an official in the office of the Secretary of State for War in London, or to Nelson who was then commanding the British Mediterranean fleet blockading the French at Toulon. In order to inform and influence opinion at home, Coleridge discreetly "leaked" material advocating the importance of Malta to Daniel Stuart of the *Courier*, directing him to use the material, but to avoid quoting him.[145]

---

142   With the salary of the Under-Secretary during Chapman's absence. To William Sotheby, 5 July 1804, *CL* 2, 1142, In this letter Coleridge mistakenly refers to himself as Ball's private secretary.

143   Note *CN* 2, 2143. It was important inter alia to deny French trading opportunities in the Levant.

144   *A Political Sketch on the Views of the French in the Mediterranean*, originally drafted by the Civil Commissioner but edited and polished by Coleridge; *Insults and Abuses which Great Britain Received from the Government of Algiers During the Period of 18 Years from 1785-1803*; a further paper on the retention of Malta by the British; also *Observations on Egypt* and a paper on Sicily in November 1804: see *The Friend*, I, 168-78; 382-4;. See further letter To Robert Southey, 2 February 1805, *CL* 2, 1164; also the Coleridge Collection at the Victoria University library, Toronto. This material reveals the extent to which Coleridge was committed to Imperial expansion.

145   To Daniel Stuart, 6 July 1804, *CL* 2, 1146.

Coleridge, notoriously, became as willing as Ball to advocate selfish British national interests, even if this meant abandoning principles (such as public international law). This was so, for example, in Coleridge's advocacy of the annexation of Egypt, simply to frustrate French ambitions – an aggressive policy that would appear to make Britain imperially ambitious and little better than France had been in its annexation of sovereign territories.[146]

Such was the contribution Coleridge was making that Ball's confidence in him grew and by early July he was given "cool & commanding Rooms"[147] in the Governor's Palace. (figs. 3 and 4). His success at this work, and his new regime – which included swimming before sunrise – dramatically lifted his spirits and improved his health.

In late November, Ball informed the Earl of Camden that Coleridge was to be sent, with Captain Leake, on the signally important mission to the Black Sea to purchase corn.[148] The success of this mission was critical to the maintenance of the Island's population who, as we shall see in Chapter 2, were highly dependent upon imported grain. According to Ball's plan, should Captain Leake be called away from the region, Coleridge would have been empowered to act as his substitute. In that event, he would have had sole responsibility for the success of this strategic mission, the funds for which amounted to £98,680.[149] Coleridge now seemed to be on the verge of building a career in the colonial service. Privately, however, he was reluctant to go. As matters turned out, he was not actually called upon to do so.

Coleridge, the Most Illustrious Lord, The Public Secretary

"..Like a mouse in a Cathedral on a Fair or Market Day".[150]

On 18 January 1805 Alexander Macaulay died in his sleep. Ball, thereupon,

---

146   See *Observations on Egypt* and Kooy (1999).
147   To William Sotheby, 5 July 1804, *CL* 2, 1140.
148   Ball to Camden, 26 November 1804, Kew, CO 158/9/52.
149   Ibid. And see Ball to Cooke, 1 February 1806, Kew, CO 158/11/9 in which a financial statement concerning the corn mission was enclosed. Ball was later rebuked for appointing Leake without the prior consent of the Secretary of State: Camden to Ball, 12 February 1805, Kew, CO 159/3/153.
150   To Mrs S. T. Coleridge, 21 August 1805, *CL* 2, 1170 (Figs. 3 and 4).

3. The interior of the President's Palace, Valletta. It would not have been less opulent when Coleridge resided there.

4. The Governor's [Civil Commissioner's] Palace with the Treasury Building in the background (now the Casino Maltese). Coleridge moved from the Civil Commissioner's Palace in Valletta to the Treasury in late 1804.

appointed Coleridge as acting Public Secretary.[151] Coleridge declined to serve as Treasurer and, eventually, drew only half the salary. Even so, the decision to assume, even temporarily, the Public Secretary's responsibilities was one that Coleridge later regretted.[152]

As Coleridge's *Notebooks* make clear, his appointment as the effective head of the civil service was "pro tempore of Mr Chapman's Absence"[153] and that Chapman would have the permanent appointment upon his return from the Black Sea region. The previous British government had earlier approved Chapman's appointment, so there was no question of Coleridge taking over permanently.[154] Moreover, Ball expected Chapman's return "almost daily" from Smyrna, so Coleridge's new position was expected to be particularly short-lived. The day following Macaulay's death Coleridge confirmed to the Wordsworths that he was still planning to leave the Island no later than at the end of March 1805.[155]

The Public Secretary played a key role in the administration. As we shall see in Chapters 2 and 3, the British plan for the government of Malta was that legislative, executive and judicial power would be placed in the hands of the Civil Commissioner. That ultimate authority was co-ordinated and managed through the office of the Public Secretary, who served as head of the executive. The office-holder represented the authority of the Civil Commissioner in the day to day administration of the islands. As such, he was centrally important in the government of Malta and was placed second in civil dignity to the "Governor".

The scope of the role was, legally, undefined when Coleridge held office, but its usual demands placed Coleridge in charge of a number of civil servants.[156] It gave him a place in Ball's cabinet, as well as in the *Segnatura* or

---

151   He declined the Treasurership, which meant that he received only half the salary otherwise due to the combined offices (i.e. £500). The roles had been combined since 1802: see Hobart to Ball, Kew, CO 159/3/108. It is likely that the role of Treasurer was not performed until Chapman's return to the Island in September 1805.

152   To Daniel Stuart, 1 May 1805, *CL* 2, 1167.

153   *CN* 2, 2408 see also 2430; also to Robert Southey, 2 February 1805, *CL* 2, 1163; and to Daniel Stuart, 30 April 1805, *CL* 2, 1165.

154   Ball to Camden, 30 January 1805, Kew, CO 158/10/1. Ball informed his superior of the death of Mr Macaulay and l continued, "I expect Mr Chapman daily from Constantinople, whom I shall put into the office of Public Secretary and Treasurer in conformity to the Orders sent me by the Earl of Buckinghamshire". These had been dated 9 January 1804. His lordship replied to Ball confirming the appointment of Mr Chapman on 24 March 1805: Kew, CO 158/10/26. See also *CN* 2, 2430.

155   To the Wordsworths, 19 January 1805, *CL* 2, 1160; to Robert Southey, 2 February 1805, *CL* 2, 1163.

156   By 1814 there were twenty-one staff in the Public Secretary's office. There

Council. The office-holder would normally have been required to oversee[157] about a dozen government departments, administer oaths and affidavits and arbitrate disputes between merchants – a constant task that Coleridge dreaded above all.[158] He had also to issue passports,[159] attend the Court of Vice-Admiralty,[160] and draft the Bandi and Avvisi.[161] Records of these had to be maintained locally, and, in some instances, copies had to be sent to England. The Public Secretary also held a magisterial appointment.[162] There is also evidence that Ball felt unable to take on the audit function and, thus, relied heavily upon the Public Secretary to perform it.[163]

The departments whose work Coleridge had to oversee[164] included the Public Treasury, the Lazaretto and Quarantine department; the Custom House; the harbour;[165] the Grand Almoner's Office for the Maintenance of the Poor; the Government Printing Office; the Tribunals; Two hospitals;[166] the Foundling and Invalids Hospital; and the Post Office.

Additionally, there was the Università, the function of which had become central to Ball's policies for the Island. This important issue is more fully

---

would not have been significantly fewer in Coleridge's time: Kew, CO 158/25/233.

157   *CN* 2, 2552.

158   To Mrs S. T. Coleridge, 21 July 1805, *CL* 2, 1170.

159   Passports other than those to serving military officers were to be issued under the authority of the Civil Commissioner and be signed by the "Secretary of Government": Kew, CO 158/1/209.

160   Coleridge, who may have been required to attend the Court regularly, provided advocacy in a wig and gown: see to Robert Southey, 2 February 1805, *CL* 2, 1163.

161   See below Chapter 4 and Sultana, 270-1.

162   Sultana, 149-50.

163   Ball to Edward Cooke 30 November 1807 Kew, CO 158/13/463.

164   Ball to Cooke 30 November 1807, Kew, CO 158/13/463at 465: "The superintendence, indeed, of the public departments more immediately devolves on the joint office of Public Secretary and Treasurer; but the various duties attached to that situation must necessarily prevent the investigation of accounts which requires exclusive and undivided attention". A list of the public departments was enclosed and can be found at Kew, CO 158/13/469. See also Ball to Shee, 12 May 1807, Kew, CO 158/13/ 315.

165   He received Harbour Reports: see e.g., *CN* 2, 2446 and *CN* 2, 2583; also the Avviso of 9 March 1805 concerning the shallow water in the Grand Harbour.

166   Ball had reported that the hospitals, one for men and another for women, were a principal expense of government. There had been spending abuses therein and he thought that it was possible to reduce the cost of maintaining them by about half: Ball to Dundas, 26 December 1800, Kew, CO 158/1/12-25. Cameron was directed to investigate, reform and to impose strict controls: see his Instructions of 14 May 1801. By 1805 one of the hospitals had been taken over for military purposes, although Coleridge retained a responsibility to conduct inspections: see *CN* 2, 2420 and Sultana, 277.

considered in Chapter 2 together with an account of the other departments of state.

A significant burden upon Coleridge's time, and a duty Coleridge found particularly disagreeable, was the arbitration and the settlement of disputes involving British merchants.[167] These disputes, ostensibly, fell within the jurisdiction of the Maltese Court, the *Consolato del Mare*. In his instructions, Charles Cameron (the first British Civil Commissioner, 1801-1802) had been ordered to abolish it, but it continued to function through Coleridge's period in office. However, the proceedings in this court were lengthy and complicated and the court did not win the confidence of the British mercantile class who, much to the chagrin of Maltese lawyers, (and the Public Secretary) preferred arbitration to expensive litigation.[168] Coleridge described himself (with reference to the requirement that he provide advocacy in the Court of Vice-Admiralty) as a "jack-of-all-trades".[169]

Soon after his appointment Coleridge reported that he was employed from 8am until 5pm on official business. This included writing "public letters and memorials',[170] – i.e. the laws and public notices with which we are presently concerned. He described this as a most anxious duty. He was also engaged, from time to time, in writing despatches.[171] It seems that this work would not normally have fallen to his Office but, according to Coleridge, his talents were such that this work was *assigned* to him.[172] Burdened as he was by persistent ill-health, by drug addiction, by poor morale, and the eclectic cacophony of his diverse governmental responsibilities it would be a *tour de force* if Coleridge entirely succeeded as a draftsman of Maltese law.

By Easter, Coleridge was complaining that he had "for months past ...incessantly employed in official tasks, subscribing, examining, administering oaths, auditing, etc".[173] For the first time he found that he had no time to write to his friends and family in England.[174] He complained

---

167   To Mrs S. T. Coleridge, 21 July 1805, *CL* 2, 1169 & 1170; *CN* 2, 2451 (Notes), 15 February 1805 and see also Sultana, 347.
168   The Royal Commission of 1812 was to recommend its abolition: Kew, CO 158/19.
169   To Southey, 2 February 1805, *CL* 2, 1164.
170   He usually referred to the Bandi and Avvisi as public memorials: see Sultana, 271. His role in their production is discussed in Chapter 4.
171   See e.g., Ball to Camden, 4 August 1804, Kew, CO 158/9/42.
172   To Robert Southey, 2 February 1805, *CL* 2, 1160; to Daniel Stuart, 30 April 1805, *CL* 2, 1165.
173   *CN* 2, 2552.
174   To Robert Southey, 2 February 1805, *CL* 2, 1160; to Daniel Stuart, 30 April 1805, *CL* 2, 1165.

that the work left him so tired, and his spirits so "exhausted" that he was almost unable to undress himself at night.[175] He regarded his official duties not only as excessive, but also stressful.[176] The role may simply have been too multi-faceted, requiring a range of skills that any office-holder, no matter how talented, would find difficult to discharge.

Coleridge's decision to decline the office of Treasurer was perhaps a judicious one. As we shall see in Chapter 2, the policy of introducing inexperienced Maltese into the civil service had disastrous consequences for accounting, auditing and record-keeping and there were insuperable problems with the national finances. At the same time, Ball's Administration was embarking upon a disastrous financial speculation in the purchase of corn resulting in significant losses affecting the public finances

There was, eventually, to be some recognition that the spread of responsibility was too great. Ball was later to seek permission from London to appoint an auditor or comptroller-general to take over some of the responsibilities of the Public Secretary, since even that part of the role demanded "exclusive and individual attention".[177] This was something of a *volte face* on his part, for it was Ball who had initiated the overloading of the Public Secretary/Treasurer by securing the agreement of his superiors, in 1803, that one office-holder perform the combined roles.[178] This blunder, which suggests the limited nature of Ball's understanding, may have contributed to some of the serious structural failings of the British Administration. In an official acknowledgement that the workload of the combined Offices was too onerous, the roles were split in 1811.

Zammit and Coleridge's role

There is strong evidence that Coleridge did not perform some of the key duties associated with the office of Public Secretary. There was, in effect, a gulf between what might be described as the informal, customary job description – the responsibilities and duties placed upon the office-holder – and those that Coleridge actually performed. However much Coleridge complained of overwork, it is likely that he did less than might otherwise have been expected. Leaving aside concerns about his health, and the effect

---

175 To Daniel Stuart, 1 May 1805, *CL* 2, 1166.
176 Ibid.
177 Ball to Cooke, 30 November 1807, Kew, CO 158/13/465, and also Ball to Shee, 12 May 1807, Kew, CO 158/13/463; also ibid 315-6.
178 Sullivan to Ball, 31 December 1803, NAM Libr 531 18.

that might have had on his effectiveness, he was not fully proficient in Italian, and not at all familiar with the unique system of administration on Malta. It is, therefore, unsurprising that others assisted him. We know that Coleridge worked closely with Zammit, the Maltese Secretary, a fellow member of the *Segnatura* and chief legal adviser to the government. Surviving records reveal that, after Macaulay's death, Zammit's role was enhanced. Despite his age, Zammit retained considerable energy: not only did he discharge a considerable workload, but he managed to do so until standing down on 15 June 1814.

Records reveal that there were at least two areas of responsibility in which Coleridge was not engaged. The first concerns the Università, the supervision of which, as we have described, normally fell to the Public Secretary. Before Coleridge took office the greater number of letters from the Jurats (directors of the Università) were addressed to Macaulay, although some were addressed to Zammit or even to Ball himself.[179] But after Macaulay's death, when Coleridge took over, letters from the Jurats were never addressed to him. Instead the Jurats communicated either with Ball or Zammit. Once Coleridge quit Malta, and Chapman took office, the Jurats communicated with him as well as to Zammit.[180] This raises the question about the extent to which the acting Public Secretary was fulfilling his responsibility of supervising the Università.

But this is not all, because a further important function of the Public Secretary's office was the issuing of formal written instructions ('ordini') to the departments of government and other officials such as, for example, the Luogotenente or civil magistrates of the villages (casals).[181] A similar pattern to that observed in the case of the Università emerges here. In 1804, whilst most ordini were issued in Zammit's name, others were issued by Macaulay, as Public Secretary. After Macaulay's death, no instructions are recorded as having been issued by Coleridge. Much of the work was undertaken by

179   See National Library of Malta, Valletta, Malta, Univ 42 (hereafter referred to as NAM). Letters from the Jurats to Macaulay in 1804 are dated 27 June, 10 July, 4 September and 26 October.

180   E.g., NLM Univ 425, 16 May 1806.

181   The functions of the Luogotenenti were defined in a Bando of 14th December 1801: NAM LIBR/MS 430 Bandi 1805 AL 1814. This was to keep the peace, safeguard of weights and measures in their districts as well as general responsibilities to look after the welfare of the local population, including particular responsibilities in relation to the poor and also to represent in their community the authority of the Civil Commissioner: see Galea (1949). Coleridge visited Giuseppe Abdillo, the Luogotenente of Casal Safi and his family on 27 March 1805. Coleridge considered him a "good" official: *CN*, 2 2506.

Zammit, although Ball issued all instructions to the Treasury.[182] Chapman, upon assuming office, after Coleridge's departure, issued his first instruction on 4 October 1805 and continued to do so regularly thereafter. Thus, a gap emerges. In cases where it might have been expected that Coleridge would have issued instructions, none are recorded under his signature. He seems to have been entirely inactive in this respect.

Despite this evidence, Coleridge was stretched by the volume of the work. Even in the early days of his tenure of office his desk already laboured under a "cumulus" of hospital and harbour reports – an irritation that he seems to have resolved by using them to light his candle, an act of destruction only committed with a "trembling" conscience.[183] References to the workload, and its effect upon him, occur more frequently from April 1805. He reported that official work had kept him "incessantly employed",[184] working "from morn to night".[185] There was undoubted stress, which left him unable to sleep. In late April he recorded: "So hard have I worked lately, & to so little effect in consequence of my Health, so many calls and claims – & such agitation and anxiety in consequence that this morning (awaking) very early – a little after 2 – mistaking the light of the Lamp... for the Dawn, my Heart sunk within me".[186] The nightmares and nocturnal screaming had not left him.[187] References to deteriorating health, in April 1805, become apparent in his letters home.[188] When the letters and papers he had sent home (documents that he had entrusted to the Captain in his capacity as Public Secretary) were thrown overboard from the *Arrow* when she was attacked by French frigates (figs. 5 and 6) he felt exasperated at

---

182   An illustrative list of these receiving formal written instructions in 1805 and their source appears in NAM LIBR A22 PS01/2. These would include the Universita della Valletta, 52 (Ball); Concessione del Ballo di Marmuscetto (Zammit), 52; Presidente della Gran Corte della Valletta 53 (Ball); Presidente della Gran Corte della Valletta 57 (Zammit); Amministratori de Bene Publiche 59 (Zammit); Giurati della Valletta, 60 (Zammit); Commissari di Sanità, 61 (Zammit); Intendente di Polizia, 67(Zammit); Circolare alli Luogotenenti di Campagna, 90 (Zammit); Presidenti degli Ospedali, 91 (Zammit); Tesoreria del Goveno (Ball); Luogotenente di casal Attard, 97 (Zammit) and Casal Zebbug, 102 (Zammit); Capitan di Verga, 108 (Zammit); Giurati della Valletta, 108 (Ball); Luogotenente in Birchircarà, 111 (Zammit).
183   *CN* 2, 2446.
184   *CN* 2, 2552.
185   *CN* 2, 2557.
186   *CN* 2, 2560.
187   *CN* 2, 2468.
188   E.g. to Daniel Stuart, 1 May 1805, *CL* 2, 1166 ; to the Wordsworths of the same date, *CL* 2, 1168; to Mrs S. T. Coleridge, 21 July 1805, *CL* 2, 1169.

5. Aquatint bearing the inscription: "To the R.t Hon.ble. Lord Viscount Nelson, K.B. Duke of Bronte &c. &c. &c., This Print of the commencement of the gallant defence, made by His Majesty's Sloop Arrow of 23 Guns & 132 Men, Richard Budd Vincent Esq.r Commander; and His Maj: Bomb Vessel Acheron of 8 Guns and & 57 Men, Arthur Farquhar Esq.r Com.r against the French Frigate, L'Hortense and L'Incorruptible of 44 Guns & 550 Men each, including troops of the Line, which took place on the Morning of the 4.th of Feb.y 1805, off Cape Palos; for the preservation of a Valuable Convoy Is (by Permission most humbly Dedicated by his most obliged humble Servant, George Andrews. [&] To the R.t Hon.ble. Lord Viscount Nelson, K.B. Duke of Bronte &c. &c. &c.," Painted by F. Sartorius. Engraved by J. Jeakes. Published Oct. 21. 1805, by G. Andrews, No. 7, Charing Cross

what he described as "an evil destiny".[189]

The work Coleridge encountered was onerous. This is so not only in its volume but also in its significance, for Coleridge found himself at the heart of government with responsibilities for its successful administration as well as financial rectitude. As we shall see, some of the public action he was required either to take or, at least, to support was of questionable morality. Such conduct does not cohere well either with the idea of the rule of law or the separation of powers. But it does fit with expectations of the role. When the Revd Francis Laing subsequently took over the role, an independent observer noted that the role of Public Secretary "certainly requires the

---

189   To Daniel Stuart, 30 April 1805, *CL* 2, 1165. In the same letter Coleridge described how, prior to the Arrow incident, a further, large, set of papers had been burnt. He had entrusted them to a Major Adye who had died of plague in Gibraltar. It was standard practice to burn the effects of the deceased for fear of contagion.

6. Coloured aquatint of the sinking of His Majesty's Sloop Arrow. Painted by F. Sartorius. Engraved by J. Jeakes. Published Oct. 21. 1805, by G. Andrews, No. 7, Charing Cross

exercise of talents not very compatible with the clerical character".[190] This speaks volumes about the hard-edged nature of Coleridge's new role, which was entirely subservient to the overriding British strategic goals.

The somewhat tainting experience of raw political action prompted Coleridge towards an intellectual response that strove to subject practical politics to Reason and principle. This struggle began within days of his appointment as Acting Public Secretary. He posed a question for himself in his private *Notebooks*: "Wherein is Prudence *distinguishable* from Goodness (or Virtue) – and how are they both nevertheless one and *indivisible*".[191] *The Friend* is a sustained engagement with this project. Indeed, it concludes, "Nothing is to be deemed rightful in civil society, or to be tolerated as such, but what is capable of being demonstrated out of the laws of pure Reason".[192]

His experience of public office, and reflections upon it, eventually led him to reject a utilitarian conception of political morality. Governmental action should not merely be concerned with the consequences of a political decision but the impulses that directed and motivated it. A concern with actions and consequences should not make government indifferent to

---

190   A' Court, William to Bunbury, 10 November 1812, Kew, CO 158/18.
191   *CN* 2, 2412, 23 January 1805.
192   *The Friend*, I, 167.

considerations of morality. Coleridge concluded that these "inward" motives contributed the essence of morality to the outward expression of public policy.[193] This meant that governmental action, that might appear to be justified after a purely empirical analysis, might nevertheless fall short of the appropriate standard for public action. He later offered, as an example, the terms under which the British concluded the Treaty of Amiens in 1802. Whilst the Treaty ended hostilities with France, Malta had been forced by the British to accept the return of the despotic Order of St John which would fall under French influence and expose the Maltese (who had rebelled against their former French occupiers) to the risk of reprisals.[194] We can surmise that it was his disappointment with the ethical standards of colonial administration that led him, upon his return to England, to express such powerful condemnations of the "wickedness" of colonial government.[195]

Our names, and but our names can meet[196]

He gradually sank into renewed opium consumption that confined him to his room for substantial periods. He thought that he appeared efficient in his public role. Ruminating in his *Notebooks* over Christmas 1804 he concluded that, in Malta, he was seen as a "quiet well meaning man, rather dull indeed".[197] At weekends he seems to have withdrawn to his books and opium. Notebook entries, sometimes barely coherent, were scribbled in the small hours of the night. Unable to free himself from his addiction, his thoughts rambled from homesickness[198] to suicide.[199] Privately, especially when Chapman did not appear as expected, Coleridge was struggling with despair.[200] He began to wonder whether he would survive to see his family and friends.[201] He was glad when one convoy was delayed – it might mean that he could return in it, for he could not endure the possibility it

193   *The Friend*, I, 314. It is revealing that in his Notebook Coleridge had interested himself in the relationship between positive law and "the dictates of right reason= inter Jus et aequitatem". CNB 2413 21.578.
194   Coleridge regarded the Treaty as disregarding British national honour: *The Friend*, I, 571. See Appendix 2.
195   To Daniel Stuart, 22 August 1806, CL 2, 1177.
196   From *An Exile* thought to have been composed by Coleridge whilst on Malta.
197   CN 2, 2372.
198   To Mrs S. T. Coleridge, 21 July 1805, CL 2, 1169.
199   CN 2, 2510; CN 2, 2527; CN 2, 2557.
200   CN 2, 2486, Sunday, 17 March 1805.
201   CN 2, 2560.

should depart without him. But he was also at a loss to know where to go.[202] He had clearly decided not to return to Greta Hall, and had resolved to separate from his wife.[203]

His early enchantment with Malta left him. He grumbled about the incessant noise of life in Valletta.[204] The Easter festivities, which involved the firing of guns and letting off of fireworks – behaviour that remains to this day a feature of the many Catholic festivals of the Island – seemed particularly irksome.[205] Even the "torture" of reveillée and the parade drums of the English garrison eventually grated upon him.[206] He bewailed the other denizens of street life: the courtship of Maltese cats, the pigs (which yelled rather than grunted) and "revival and playfulness" after sunset of the noisy packs of dogs, and, worse still, their night-long combat with the pigs.[207] He lamented the street cries, and the priests; even the Maltese advocates were a noisy and an abrasive profession.[208]

The intense summer heat caused prickly heat on his body, although without unpleasant sensations.[209] Performing his many tasks in the extreme heat must have been debilitating. He awaited Chapman's return with almost desperate, homesick, eagerness.[210] He wrote to his wife, in August, that he could leave once he had completed "six public letters and examined into the Law forms of the Island' – a commitment that would not burden him for more than a week.[211] It is not at all clear what work Coleridge meant by the "Law forms of the Island". Following this letter, only one further proclamation (Bando) was issued under his signature; and there are no further surviving Public Notices (Avvisi).

His health was not as robust as he would have wished. For this he blamed the lack of exercise caused by his duties. His departure still depended,

---

202   *CN* 2, 2536.
203   *CN* 2, 2536. But letters to her were reassuring. For example on 21 August 1805 he wrote to his wife: "My dear Sara! May God bless you be assured, (sic) I shall never, never cease to do every thing that can make you happy". *CL* 2, 1172.
204   *CN* 2, 2614.
205   *CN* 2, 2547.
206   *CN* 2, 2614.
207   *CN* 2, 2635; *CN* 2, 2641.
208   *CN* 2, 2614.
209   To Mrs S. T. Coleridge, 21 August 1805, *CL* 2, 1170.
210   Notwithstanding his claim that he missed his friends and family in England he extended his travels in Italy thereby delaying his return to England until August 1806. He separated from his wife following his eventual return to the Lake District, Holmes (1998), 77-80.
211   To Mrs S. T. Coleridge, 21 August 1805, *CL* 2, 1170.

however, upon Chapman's much delayed return to Malta; and, when this eventually occurred, on 6 September 1805, the Notebook exudes relief. An Avviso, signed by Ball, was issued on 21 September 1805 announcing that Chapman had been appointed to the office of Public Secretary. Coleridge recorded, in his Notebook, that he quit Malta on Monday, 23 September, 1805.[212] He was never to return.

An Assessment

Although questions can be posed about Coleridge's effectiveness in office (see Chapter 6), it seems that he continued to enjoy the Civil Commissioner's trust and confidence. Coleridge even claimed, in August 1805, that Ball had "contrived" to keep him on the Island and prevent his return.[213] Some corroborating evidence for this assertion survives. On 18 September 1805, Ball wrote to Granville Penn, assuring him that Coleridge had fulfilled the duties of Public Secretary to Ball's "satisfaction".[214] Significantly, Ball proposed that Coleridge should be offered William Eton's post at a salary of three hundred pounds a year.[215] Because the Superintendency of the Lazaretto and Quarantine Department would not over-extend him, Ball felt that Coleridge could continue to assist Ball's Government. He particularly wanted to exploit Coleridge's experience as a political journalist in so far as Coleridge should work with Barzoni, the editor of the *Malta Gazette*, to make that newspaper an effective propaganda tool for advocating British policy. However, the letter makes clear that wider, perhaps *ad hoc*, responsibilities were also envisaged. Ball's emphasis that Coleridge's appointment would serve an important public interest itself suggests an intention to keep Coleridge on the pay roll at the heart of Government.[216]

Whilst Ball was genuinely keen to retain Coleridge's services, we must also acknowledge the possibility of some mixed motives. Ball had powerful reasons for wishing to be rid of Eton. The appointment of Coleridge in his place would achieve this. Eton was a conspiratorial political opponent who

---

212   Coleridge, mistakenly, dated the Monday as 21 September 1805: *CN* 2, 2673.
213   To Mrs S. T. Coleridge, 21 August 1805, *CL* 2, 1170.
214   A draft letter in which Ball recommended Coleridge's "talents and good moral character" to his brother also survives: Wordsworth Trust, Grasmere, manuscript WLMS A/ Ball, Alexander, Sir/2.
215   If this proposal had been accepted, Ball would also have rid himself of a bitter political enemy.
216   Wordsworth Trust, Grasmere, manuscript WLMS A/ Ball, Alexander, Sir/2.

would agitate for many years to alter British policy and undermine Ball's authority.[217] This dangerous political enemy was eventually discredited and dismissed from office. Regrettably, from Ball's perspective, this only occurred after Ball's premature death in 1809.

Nothing came of Ball's proposal to retain Coleridge. After spending the winter of 1805-1806 in Italy, Coleridge eventually returned to England in August 1806. His opium addiction was unresolved, and his health and morale actually seemed to have deteriorated during his absence. When the moment had come to sail he described himself as exhausted. The prospect of his homecoming offered little joy.[218]

Dorothy Wordsworth was deeply moved at their reunion when he eventually returned to the North: "..never, never did I feel such a shock as at first sight of him".[219] She was convinced that he was ailing: "..but that he is ill I am well assured; and must sink if he does not grow more happy. His fatness has quite changed him-it is more like the flesh of a person in a dropsy than one in health; his eyes are lost in it".[220]

She offered a vivid description of a man in decline: "He is utterly changed; and yet sometimes, when he was animated in conversation concerning things removed from him, I saw something of his former self. But never when we were alone with him. He then scarcely ever spoke of anything that concerned him, or us, or our common friends nearly, except we forced him to it; and immediately he changed the conversation to Malta, Sir Alexander Ball, the corruption of government, anything but what we were yearning after". Dorothy portrayed a man who was distant and abstracted, ill and unhappy.[221] Such comments invite the conclusion that he might have failed in his primary goal in travelling to the Mediterranean, and sunk further into addiction and illness, without worthwhile gain.

Coleridge refuted this assessment; and powerful advocates would support him. Shaffer, for example, has demonstrated how Coleridge's

217 See further Chapter 2. His book *Materials for an Authentic History of Malta* which was made ready for printing in 1805 but not published until 1807 was highly critical of the administration on Malta.
218 Suicidal thoughts were expressed in verse: see, for example, his fragmentary "Come, come thou bleak December wind" composed at Leghorn on 7 June 1806.
219 Dorothy Wordsworth to Catherine Clarkson, 6 November 1806, De Selincourt, 277; See also Gittings, and Manton, 157.
220 Ibid.
221 Coleridge found it impossible to return to live permanently with his wife, but his children remained a joy: see e.g., the lines written to Hartley at about the time of his return from Malta: "Could you stand upon Skiddaw, you would not from its whole ridge/ See a man who so loves you as your fond S. T. Coleridge".

period in the Mediterranean contributed to his understandings and ideas on art, art criticism and philosophy.[222] And Kooy has shown how, when Coleridge was forced to confront the grim, pragmatic compromises of practical politics, it forced him to renew his endeavours in political theory to advance the case for a "purer" politics founded in reason and principle.[223] This engagement first emerged in *The Friend*. When Coleridge offered an account of Malta he was unequivocal: his administrative experience, in particular his close association with Sir Alexander Ball, had been an instructive and valuable experience. He had seen how government worked, had experienced at first hand the vigorous pursuit of national self-interest; he had witnessed the careful and, arguably misleading, manoeuvrings of a Civil Commissioner determined to retain Malta; he had even lent his pen to these projects. He had exercised governmental power in his own right, drafting Proclamations and Public Notices, for the good government of Malta, that could entail the severest punishment of those who committed ostensibly trivial crimes.[224] He had even indulged in manipulative "spin", having been prepared to exploit the well-known Maltese dislike of foreigners in order to secure public support for otherwise unpopular taxation.[225] He could, in future, write with the authoritative knowledge, of how politics worked, that his earlier works necessarily lacked.

'Let Eagles Bid the Tortoise Sunward Soar'[226]

Sadly for Coleridge, the hoped-for cure for his addiction had been chimeric. The decade after his return was plagued by separation from his wife and children, fitful literary achievement, unsuccessful quackery and opium collapses. Only when he went to live with Dr Gillman in Highgate, in 1816, did he receive appropriate and (by the standards of the time) successful treatment. His condition stabilised and, whilst remaining a controversial

---

222   Shaffer (1989).

223   Kooy (1999).

224   E.g., the punishment of mandatory exile was extended to those who let lodgings to unregistered foreigners. A landlord who was deceived-for example, by the production of false papers- had no defence. He may also have approved of the decision to exile a boy of 12 years of age for spreading malicious rumours: see Chapter 5: Public Order and Crime.

225   See Bando 8 March 1805, NAM LIBR/MS 430 2/2 Bandi 1805 AL 1814 f.2. The official line inferring that foreigners were somehow less deserving than the Maltese might have had unfortunate consequences given the uprising against the local Jewish community a few weeks later.

226   *CN* 2, 2932 (October-November 1806).

figure, he largely re-established his position in the pantheon of the English Romantic movement. It is a testament to the skill with which Gillman treated him that a long-term heart condition rather than the toxic effects of opium caused his premature death at Highgate on 25 July 1834. He was just sixty-one years of age.

2. Coleridge's Malta

Introduction

When Coleridge assumed the role of Public Secretary he was, as we have seen, acting as head of the Executive. He exercised a role that required him to implement the policies of the Civil Commissioner, Sir Alexander Ball, who had the ultimate administrative, legislative and judicial authority. Coleridge was required to understand the nature and function of the Maltese institutions, the legal system, and to assimilate the detail of the political, economic, social and legal policies that Ball was either required or authorised to implement by the British Secretary of State. As we shall describe, the British decided to continue and to exploit the constitutional arrangements of the former ruler – the Order of St John of Jerusalem. A consequence of this policy was that British provincial administrators, such as Coleridge, were required to administer a territory within a legal and political framework very different from their own.[1] Chapter 3 provides an evaluation of the system, chosen by the British for Malta, based upon indirect rule, together with the Civil Commissioner's constitutional powers, his accountability to the law, and the nature of the constitutional relationship between the Maltese administration and the Metropolitan territory.

The purpose of this chapter is to examine the wider Maltese context. In the first section, we shall survey the Maltese social, political and economic background together with the British strategy for the government of the islands before turning, in the second section, to a brief evaluation of the important Maltese institutions, including the legal system. In the final section, we will address the public reputation and standing of Ball's administration in order to explain why Coleridge's laws represented a crucially important political engagement with the Maltese people that transcended mere law making. It will be also be helpful to note the political

---

1 For a general introduction to the geopolitical context see M. Rapport, *Nineteenth-Century Europe*, (Basingstoke: Palgrave Macmillan, 2005).

and military events surrounding the British conquest and its aftermath, not least because these events provided some of the early causes of friction between the British and the Maltese, and thus contributed to the problems that Coleridge inherited in public office.

2.1. Maltese Social Political and Economic Context

Preliminary Remarks: The Maltese Islands

The Maltese archipelago comprising Malta, Gozo and Comino, lies at the crossroads of the Mediterranean, between the Islamic states of North Africa and Europe. The territory of the islands is small, extending little beyond one hundred and twenty square miles. At the time of Coleridge's stay on the Island, the Maltese population numbered about 100,000. [2]

Since 1530, Malta had been in the possession of the Knights Hospitaller of the Order of St John of Jerusalem who had acted as a regional military power. The resistance of the knights to the westward expansion of the Turkish empire culminated in the "Great Siege" of 1565. The Order, under the leadership of the Grandmaster la Valette, successfully resisted this epic Turkish assault mounted by some thirty thousand Ottoman troops. The attempted invasion eventually suffered defeat at the hands of a mere six thousand defenders and some six hundred knights. The halt of the Ottoman expansion in the western Mediterranean emphasised the strategic value and defensive strength of Malta, which was further improved by the subsequent construction of the city of Valletta with its massive fortifications.

Valletta's two vast, natural harbours, Marsamxett Harbour and Great Harbour, were formidable natural assets. From these, the Order's navy formally engaged the Turkish fleet, as well as the shipping of the Barbary States.[3] The harbours gave Malta its strategic importance for the British

---

2   *The Friend*, I, 577. The population increased rapidly during the period of prosperity, 1805-1812 to reach about 120,000 by the latter date. This population growth caused the many frictional and macro-economic effects outlined by the Royal Commission in 1812: Kew, CO 158/19.

3   The "Barbary States" referred to the territory between seaports of Tangiers and Tripoli. Britain and other nations trading in the Mediterranean, including France,

after it was won from the French in 1800.

Valletta (often called "La Valette" by the British) became, and remains today, the capital city. The city was purpose-built as a walled fortress that held a strong defensive position on a peninsula between Marsamxett Harbour and Great Harbour. The foundation stone was laid in 1566, a year after the withdrawal of the Turkish invaders. Its design included many fine churches, a baroque cathedral and palaces as well as gardens for recreational use. These gardens were turned over to military use by the British after 1800.

Valletta's suburb, Floriana, lay outside the city walls; the neighbouring "three cities" of Senglea, Vittoriosa and Cospicua[4] lay on the far (eastern) side of Grand Harbour away from Valletta. Collectively, Valletta and the three cities were administered as "the magistracy of the four cities".

The more heavily populated region of Malta comprised the eastern portion of the Island including the capital, Valletta, and the other cities. In the countryside, there were twenty-one "casals" or villages[5] each of which was administered by a Luogotenente or civil magistrate. To the north and west lay a more sparsely inhabited area which, nonetheless, included some dozen smaller "casals".[6] The reason for the concentration of population originated in the fear of raids by Barbary corsairs, which had once made those residing in the "uninhabited" region vulnerable to capture as slaves. Historically, this area had been under-developed, but by Coleridge's time, the threat to increased settlement had been removed: the British had maritime supremacy and they had concluded a Treaty with the Dey of Algiers,[7] guaranteeing the security of Maltese inhabitants from the predations of his corsairs. Since its climate and soil were indistinguishable

paid the Dey of Algiers a tribute of money and other goods in order to ensure the safe passage of their vessels. The corsairs of the Dey raided the ships of other nations, including those of the recently independent United States. This resulted in the Tripolitan War, 1801-1805, although this conflict did not finally resolve the problem of piracy and tribute.

4   These cities were renamed after the siege. Bormla became Cospicua; Birgu was re-named Vittoriosa; and L'Isla became Senglea. The cities are still occasionally referred to by their former names. The "Cottonera" is a reference to the Cottonera defensive lines – landward fortifications enclosing the three cities. These were constructed under the auspices of the Grandmaster Nicolas Cottonera in the 1670's.

5   Ball to Dundas, 26 December 1800, Kew, CO 158/1/12-25. The memorandum is unsigned but has been attributed to Ball: see Royal Instructions from Hobart to Cameron, Hardman 350 et. seq.

6   Ibid.

7   Treaty of 19 March 1801: see Hardman 349-50.

7. The Porte des Bombes, a gateway into Floriana and thus into Valletta from the countryside of Malta. Lith. By C. de Brocktorff [1838].

from the more cultivated parts of the Island, this area represented a realisable opportunity for both habitation and agricultural development. Coleridge recorded that the gradual enclosure of the uncultivated part of the Island was under way by the time of his arrival.[8]

The British Conquest and its Aftermath – The British Soldier and "Unhealthy" Posts[9]

The French had conquered Malta in 1798 whilst its forces, led by Napoleon, were *en route* to the planned campaign in Egypt. After a popular Maltese uprising, aided by the armed forces of Britain and other nations, the occupying French garrison in Valletta was forced, in September 1800, to capitulate. The successful military strategy had been characterised by a two-year siege of Valletta and a blockade of the islands by the Royal Navy. By the time that Valletta fell, the French garrison had been reduced to starvation, and little remained on the Island to feed the population.

Moreover, the events surrounding the British conquest and its aftermath are also important because they contributed to the declining confidence in Ball's administration. Amongst the early causes of friction was the, highly

---

8   *The Friend*, I, 570.
9   Ball to Dundas, (undated 1801), Kew, CO 158/1, 3.

controversial, negotiation of the French surrender.[10] The British had agreed the capitulation with the French commanders without consulting the Maltese, who felt slighted because, in their view, the British merely aided the Maltese military struggle with troops whose bravery and commitment was open to question, even by their own commanders.[11] This resentment, compounded by unsatisfactory terms, exacerbated social and economic problems for Ball's second administration (1802-1809). But that was not all. The absence of any public acknowledgement that the Maltese had, in law, become British subjects, after 1800, helped to create a divided society in which the British were seen as a dominant and foreign ruling class. The Maltese had purported to place themselves under British rule in 1802, but the apparent unwillingness of the British to accept their request, and make an unambiguous declaration that Malta formed a part of the British Empire, sent a signal that the fulfilment of their wishes was not Britain's dominant pre-occupation.

After the capture of Valletta, prize money had been promised to the Maltese who had taken part in the conflict; but the British, in an unwise *volte face*, angered and frustrated the Maltese who soon felt aggrieved and betrayed. Further Maltese dismay was caused by the Treaty of Amiens, under which Britain showed itself willing to sacrifice Maltese interests by restoring the islands to the unpopular and despotic Order of St John.[12] The refusal to respect Maltese wishes also undermined trust and confidence in the British administration.

The Siege and Depression 1800-1805: "The Plaintive Tones of Mendicancy"[13]

The lengthy blockade and siege of Valletta had profound consequences for both the economy and the administration of the Island. Battle and other damage associated with both neglect and military operations was extensive. Un-repaired highways, smashed buildings and other damaged parts of the infrastructure were problems that the new British administration, after 1800, had to address. Valletta, wrote Ball, was as if storm-swept: many houses had been damaged or destroyed; the shops had been plundered and emptied

---

10   Bonnici. The controversy is also discussed by Staines (2008).
11   'Humble Representation of the Deputies of Malta and Gozo' in October 1801, English translation, with annotated alterations: Kew, CO158/2; see also Hardman, 410-15 and See Ball to Sir Henry Dundas, (undated,1801), Kew, CO 158/1, 3.
12   Cameron to Hobart, 13 November 1801, Kew, CO 158/2/16.
13   *The Friend*, I, 567.

of stock, and the inhabitants "reduced to misery";[14] indeed, they were close to starvation. Coleridge described how the economic depression was so severe that large numbers of the poor could only survive by begging on the streets. Many would congregate along a thoroughfare in Valletta called the "*Nix Mangiare Stairs*", named after the cry of the supplicants who had nothing to eat.[15] The French had looted the assets of the islands, including the Università and the Monte di Pietà (below) leaving the Island short of capital for reconstruction. Raising additional revenue by levying further taxation posed Constitutional problems that Coleridge was required to address.

Naturally, during the blockade, international trade had ceased altogether. The collapse of the cotton trade, in which many of the Maltese were, in some way, connected, further reduced the Island's revenue and contributed to the economic problems faced by the British.

The maritime fleet had also been destroyed after the besieged French had broken up Maltese vessels, in the harbours, for firewood. This crippled the merchant capacity of the Island and impeded efforts to re-establish international commerce.[16]

But the loss of those vessels also created a more pressing problem. The lack of grain in Valletta, at the time of the surrender, compelled Ball to rely upon foreign-owned vessels to import supplies. As we shall see, he, controversially, granted passports to the foreign owners on the grounds that these vessels would be crewed by Maltese. This caused continuing embarrassment for the British. In 1805 Coleridge would be required to issue a public notice to prevent further abuses.[17] He grasped the opportunity to exculpate Ball (who had breached international law and brought Britain to the brink of war with the Dey of Algiers) by explaining that a public good can and ought to be furnished even if the government was compelled to act outside of a normative framework.

The Order of St John of Jerusalem: "Beings of a Different Race"[18]

The policy of the British ministers, and, therefore, of the administration

---

14 Ball to Cooke, 21 July 1805, Kew, CO 158/10/187-8.
15 *The Friend*, I, 567.
16 Ball to Cooke, 21 July 1805, Kew, CO 158/10/187.
17 See Chapter 5.9: Passports.
18 *The Friend*, I, 536.

on Malta, was to continue, so far as possible, the legal, constitutional and political structures of the *ancien regime* of the Knights of the Order of St John, as it had applied in 1798. The Knights and their paternalistic system of government are, therefore, of central importance to any account of Malta and, indeed, of Coleridge's role on the Island. What follows here are some brief introductory remarks about the Order and its policies.

Prior to their withdrawal from Malta following the French invasion, the Order had been drawn from aristocratic European families and comprised a lay and an ecclesiastical elite. The most important feature of their administration was that all legislative, executive and administrative authority was vested in the Grandmaster under an autocratic system. The Order refused to share power with the Maltese, which meant that there was no popular assembly with legislative powers. The Maltese were a subjugated people.

As part of their founding charitable and military mission, the Order had pursued the expensive welfare and health care policies that Britain eventually agreed to continue. These policies may have had unintended consequences because the Maltese were inclined to look to government to provide benefits for them. This culture of reliance was later to influence British policy and create significant burdens for the Administration.[19]

The regime of the Order of St John fell into a rapid decline during and, in particular, at the close of, the eighteenth century. Coleridge clearly held them in contempt.[20] According to him, the Knights had been "useless idlers" who were "generally illiterate". Coleridge explained that, as a celibate order, they had laid aside any pretence of adhering to their vows of chastity by openly preying upon the Maltese population to acquire mistresses; often, it seems, this was achieved by forceful seduction.[21] Each family amongst the more affluent classes of the Maltese had one of the Knights as a patron to whom a daughter or sister was, as Coleridge put it, "sacrificed".[22] With not

---

19   As we shall see in Chapter 5.4: Public Order and Crime, there were frictions between the entrepreneurially effective Jewish community and the inhabitants.

20   *The Friend*, I, 536.

21   Hardman describes how the husbands of attractive women might find themselves banished; similarly fathers of daughters who caught the eye of the Knights. Their predations seem to have fallen in particular upon urban families; and in Valletta there may not have been a single family unaffected by it. See Hardman, Chapter 1.

22   *The Friend*, I, 536; and *Table Talk*, I, 475, 16 April 1834. The latter records that, in Coleridge's opinion, moral corruption was not confined to the Knights of the Order at the time of the capitulation in 1800. Ball's task in addressing it was a considerable one.

8. St John's Cathedral, Valletta. Lithograph by C. de Brocktorff [1838]

inconsiderable irony, given the British strategy for government, Coleridge further added that, as "aliens", they regarded themselves as a privileged social and governing class, who absolutely refused to share power with the Maltese. He regarded their government as a contagion, "a perpetual influenza" – an indictment that invites the conclusion that their rule was almost without worthwhile achievement.[23]

Coleridge seems to have given the Order little credit for the creation of charitable institutions and the welfare policies of the government that clearly benefited the disadvantaged members of the Maltese population. The provision of abundant and affordable food, as well as health care and welfare payments for the destitute, were achievements that deserved recognition. He also omitted to mention publicly the significant architectural, artistic and cultural achievements (not the least of which is the magnificent Cathedral of St John in Valletta) which he recorded in his contemporary *Notebooks*.[24] It seems that the passage of time had hardened his views.

From the British point of view, continuing the Constitution of the Order created unforeseen problems that exposed the difficult tensions between modernity and tradition. The consequence of the Order's unpopularity

---

23 *The Friend*, I, 536 et seq.
24 "Of the Maltese/ my first impression, their ingratitude to the Order to whom they owe everything, those splendid Towers of Balsan": *CN* 2. 2567.

with the Maltese seems particularly to have been overlooked. When, in
1802, the British proposed to restore the Order as governors of the Island,
there was popular outrage that the despotic rulers could return.[25] What
the British did not appreciate was that by continuing the constitutional
system created by the Order (with the Civil Commissioner exercising the
powers of the former Grandmaster) they had perpetuated a system which
was not universally popular. Thus, the key strategic goal of stability – and
the "attachment" of the Maltese inhabitants to British rule – was threatened
by the British decision to adopt a constitutional and political system that
placed it at risk.

2.2. The Maltese Economy

Finances

The financial state of the Island was to became a pressing and intractable
concern for the British administrators. The central tenet of British policy
was to continue the institutions and policies of the Order, but acquiring the
revenue to sustain this policy became problematic.

   During the time of the Order, the islands' revenue had been derived
from various sources, including excise duties, the profits the Order derived
from commissioning privateers as well as rents from property on Malta
owned by the Order. More important than any of these, were the revenues
arising from each individual Knight's European estates. However, this
revenue was reduced by three quarters[26] after the French confiscated the
assets of the Order in France in 1792.[27] From the point of view of both the
inhabitants and the Order the confiscation had been calamitous because
the government's finances were plunged into a grave and irredeemable
deficit.[28]

---

25   Cameron to Hobart, Kew, CO 158/1/335, 23 October 1801.

26   See Hardman, 548. The immediate loss of revenue as a result of the actions of
the French Republic was about £50,000 per annum. In 1788 the Island's revenue was
£136,417, but by 1798 this was reported to have declined to a mere £34,663 14s 2d.
See also Ball to Dundas, 26 December 1800, above n. 5.

27   It has been estimated that the Knights spent circa £180,000 p.a. in Malta from
their overseas revenues: see Bartolo.

28   In 1796, this was £34, 249.

During the final days of the Order, local discontent at the failure of its welfare policies threatened political instability. The Order became desperate to secure the fragile foundation of its government by negotiating to place itself under the protection of Russia. The French, who disapproved of this development, had responded by mounting an invasion in 1798.

When Britain took over, and prepared a report upon the financial state of the Island, these structural economic weaknesses were entirely omitted from it. Captain Ball, (later, Sir Alexander Ball), represented to London, in December 1800,[29] that the expenses of government would be minimal. This puzzling misrepresentation was to have very serious consequences for him when he returned to office, in 1802-1809, because the Secretary of State in London ordered him, in effect, to deliver the welfare policies and a balanced budget. These were incommensurate policy goals.

Food and "the Casualties of Ordinary Commerce'[30]

One of the Island's major strategic problems was its inability to produce sufficient food to nourish the population. Even in the most productive years, there was barely sufficient grain to meet one third of local needs. Often it was less.[31] The Island was, thus, dependent upon imported food supplies, notably grain, which were traditionally imported from Sicily. Because this food source became unavailable after 1801, a primary task of the early British administration, as we shall see, was to secure alternative supplies. The system for acquiring and subsidising basic foodstuffs is considered below, suffice it to note that Coleridge became acting Public Secretary after the death of Macaulay because the latter's appointed successor, Mr Chapman, was absent from Malta purchasing corn in the Black Sea region.

Agriculture[32]

The landscape of Malta was well-described by Coleridge himself: "... it is a barren Rock ... the Sky, the Sea, the Bays, the Buildings are all beautiful but

---

29   Ball to Dundas, above n. 5.
30   *The Friend*, I, 570.
31   Ball's Memorandum to Dundas, 26 December 1800, above n. 5, recorded that corn production was only sufficient for three months' supply in any one year. Coleridge was aware of this: *The Friend*, I, 577. The annual consumption was about 50,000 quarters: Ball to Cooke 3rd February 1805, Kew, CO 158/10/ 19.
32   For a general account of agricultural practices in the late eighteenth century immediately prior to the British conquest see, Debono (1988).

no Rivers, no brooks, no Hedges, no green fields, almost no Trees & the few that are unlovely".[33]

Similar comments had been made by Ball who had reported, in 1801, that Malta was "a naked rock, where the hand of Industry has not covered it with soil".[34] The majority of the Maltese population pursued subsistence agriculture on thin, barely adequate loam. Much of the cultivated part of the Island had been divided into small fields, which Coleridge noted were little larger than English cottage gardens, enclosed with robust stone walls and arranged in terraces.[35] Many of these can still be seen.

The 1812 Royal Commission recorded how the Maltese had created the soil upon which their livelihoods depended, by importing it, in some cases from Sicily. Their historical struggle to wring crops from this otherwise barren and largely unproductive Island was recognised by the Royal Commissioners who thought little more could be done to make the soil more productive.[36]

Agricultural practices were highly conservative: the Maltese preferred to adhere to the customary practices of their ancestors, rather than experiment with new farming methods. This suggests that, in their role as newcomers, the British had not persuaded the Maltese that they had any superior skill or knowledge to impart. Even the potato, which the British had introduced to the Island,[37] had not been widely cultivated by the time Coleridge held office.

Ball had firm views upon agricultural improvements, including the creation of "gardens" in each of the casals. The establishment of gardens for the Luogotenente (village magistrates) was another flagship policy designed both to promote horticulture, to diversify the economy and to supplement the food supply.[38] It was Ball's brainchild and he committed significant sums of public money to their construction. Not the least reason why much would have been expected of this project was its cost. Moreover, it also served a need, given the precarious state of the food supply. After

---

33   To Mrs S. T. Coleridge, 21 August 1805, *CL* 2, 1171.
34   Ball to Dundas, 26 December 1800, above n. 5.
35   *The Friend*, I, 561. See also *CN* 2, 2508.
36   This was another implied criticism of Ball's failed attempt to construct the "gardens" in the casals.
37   By the time of Ball's *Memorandum* of 26 December 1800, above n. 5, the potato was already under cultivation. His confident expectation that this "will prove of great advantage to the inhabitants" had not been realised by 1812: see *Report of the Royal Commission*, Kew, CO 158/19.
38   Hardman, 346-7.

1800 the Island was facing increased immigration, reduced emigration and, thus, increased demand for food.

The benefits of the horticultural project were, however, negligible;[39] indeed, it is surprising that Ball appears to have pressed on with the policy notwithstanding the uncomfortable dissonance between its cost and its benefit. The initiative resulted in little more than a waste of public funds.[40] It is just one of many instances where, having introduced a project or initiated a reform, he lost interest in monitoring its implementation. This general characteristic of his government led to many problems in the administration including the squandering of resources – a particular problem in the Università and the hospitals, despite Ball's reform of the latter (1804).

The absence of shade and running water meant that soldiers who deserted from the army in the summer of 1805 must have been recaptured unless they had assistance. As we shall see, this is contrary to the narrative that Coleridge constructed in several instruments, and this is a further testimony to his manipulative use of government information.

Economic Policies: Employment, and Public Works

"...the multitude and low wages of the laborers in Malta"[41]

To address the hardships of the economic slump, which lasted until 1805, the British organised public works projects, some of which were intended not only to generate employment opportunities but also to create long term infrastructure or other benefits for the Maltese people. Some convicts and prisoners of war were also employed upon public works.[42] Thus, large numbers of unemployed Maltese were heavily dependent upon government-funded employment schemes until the economy of the Island began to improve as a result of increased maritime trade. An unwillingness to share in the merging prosperity may have been a contributory factor in the racial tensions of 1805 that we describe below.[43]

Examples of the public projects undertaken included a botanical garden,

---

39   Kew, CO 158/19.
40   Royal Commission of 1812, Kew, CO 158/19.
41   *The Friend*, I, 570.
42   See Bando, 29 January 1805, NLM LIBR/MS 430 1/2; Bandi 1790 AL 1805, 356; also 22 March 1805 NLM LIBR/MS 430 2/2 Bandi 1805 AL 1814, 4.
43   Chapter 5.4: Public Order and Crime, and note Ball to Camden, 19 April 1805, Kew, CO 158/10/123-45 at 134.

which was intended to be self-financing. It would also allow local people to enjoy the shaded walks that had been lost when other open areas of Valletta were given over to military use.[44] Another project for recreational, or perhaps health, purposes was the construction of bathing facilities.[45] Ball also ordered the construction of a fish market;[46] and he repaired the wharf – the Pietà.[47] Workhouses were also built, operated and regulated by the State, to provide employment.[48]

Effort was also invested in the re-construction and repair of roads.[49] Work of this kind was still continuing when Coleridge was in office. His important Bando of 29 January 1805[50] revealed that the government wished to reduce further wear upon the roads by regulating types of wheels. But this was not all because, in Coleridge's Bando of 8 March 1805, Ball re-imposed certain excise duties to raise further funds in order to finance the construction of new public buildings.

Ball also devoted his attention to the maritime economy. A fishery was created off the southern coast of Sicily, not only to increase wealth but also to make fishing serve as a training ground for another generation of Maltese seafarers. These benefited from boats supplied by the administration.[51] This subsidy was, of course, necessary given the destruction by the French of the Maltese vessels during the siege and the very limited capital available on the Island after the surrender.[52]

Cotton[53]

Growing grain instead of cotton "would leave half of the inhabitants without employment".[54]

44   Ball reported in 1804 that the garden was finished: Ball to Penn, 4 July 1804, Kew, CO 158/9/23.
45   Cost £250: Ball to Penn, ibid.
46   Cost £200: ibid.
47   Cost £7,000: ibid.
48   See e.g. Macaulay to Ball, 10 September 1804, Kew, CO 158/9/51-2.
49   See Memorandum of 26 December 1800, above n. 5, and CO 158/13/123.
50   NLM/LIBR /MS 430 1/2 Bandi 1790 AL 1805, 356.
51   Pirotta, 49; see also Ball to Penn, 4 July 1804, Kew, CO 158/9/13 to whom Ball reported that the fishery was still in the process of being established.
52   Ball to Cooke, 21 July 1805, Kew, CO 158/10/187-8.
53   See generally Vella; Debono (1988), 1, 27-50, and the Report of the Chamber of Commerce on the Economic Condition of the Island 1776: NLM, Lib. 1020, item 20, no folio reference. The text of this document (in Italian) is incorporated in Debono (1988).
54   *The Friend*, I, 577.

The major addition to subsistence farming was the extensive cotton industry, which served to clothe the inhabitants. According to Coleridge's observations, Maltese cotton was "naturally of a deep buff, or dusky orange color (sic)" capable of producing the most hard-wearing cloth.[55] Cotton had also provided a lucrative source of foreign revenue during the *ancien regime* and foreign cotton imports were, generally, prohibited in order to protect domestic producers.[56] The export of raw cotton was also forbidden in order to ensure the employment of (mainly) women in spinning,[57] thus, cotton had to be spun on the Island before export.

In 1776 the Grandmaster de Rohan had revived the Chamber of Commerce (previously abolished in 1741) as a recognition of the vital importance of this trade and the need to promote it. His initiative had two primary goals: firstly, he wished to ensure that both farmer and spinner obtained the best possible prices for the commodity; secondly, he sought to increase capacity by increasing the number of persons engaged in the production and manufacture of cotton.

The revived Chamber pursued the expansion of the export markets with some success. Cotton exports increased from an average of 500 *quintali* per month in 1776 to 800 *quintali* per month in 1798. Whereas, exports had once been destined for Lisbon, the principal market eventually shifted to Spain because the British had encouraged the Portuguese to import cotton from the West Indies. Thus, in the years after 1743, Maltese vessels traded primarily with Barcelona, although a subsidiary market, accessed via Marseille, existed in northern Italy and South-East France. Maltese exports had, of course, been interrupted during the blockade between 1798 and 1800, and the Spanish market was lost once hostilities with Spain broke out in 1804.

The impact of the loss of the export trade after 1804 proved to be a grave economic crisis because the cotton trade, had in one way or another, benefited most of the workers on the Island. Coleridge suggested that about half of the inhabitants were, in one way or another, employed in

---

55   Ibid.
56   At different times, various Proclamations were enacted forbidding the importation of foreign cotton: see, e.g., the Bando of 7 May 1757: NLM, Libr. 429, Bandi 1756-1765, 7. Some importation seems to have been permitted under Proclamations of 1796 and 1797: see Debono above n. 53.
57   Coleridge recorded with approval that Maltese women were normally not required to do hard work out of doors. "...[T]hey were almost exclusively employed in spinning and management of the House". *CN* 2, 2650.

this industry.[58] Debono, who described the state of the industry, in the eighteenth century, observed:

> Capitalists, small savers who could dispose of a few scudi[59] for lending, merchants who bought and sold the seed and the cotton yarn, middlemen who helped to bring farmer and merchants together, spinners who spun their cottons at home, sea captains who owned ships and transported the product overseas, all had a share in the thriving cotton industry.[60]

Ball had reported, in December 1800, that exports of *spun* cotton thread had produced half a million pounds sterling per annum.[61] Cotton seed was also used as cattle fodder, but, as Coleridge observed, this foodstuff altered the quality of the meat.[62]

Government employment schemes to alleviate poverty had also thrived upon the back of the cotton trade. For example, under the *ancien regime,* the invalids' hostels had been constructed, in Floriana, in which the poor of both sexes could be employed as cotton spinners. In Coleridge's time, the chief centre of production was at Città Vecchia, the operation of which had a charitable, as well as a commercial, purpose, since it provided employment for "several hundred indigent females" as well as others.[63]

By 1805 the Maltese had begun to weave the cotton into cloth. The wartime conditions meant that they were forced to rely, only, upon sales of their products to occupying troops and others within their home market.[64] Some were tempted to breach regulations governing quality and this attracted the intervention of the British authorities. In March 1805 Coleridge was compelled to issue an Avviso, or Public Notice, reminding the population that it was forbidden to make cotton which was not spun either with seeds or with wool.[65]

---

58   *The Friend,* I, 577.
59   The denominations of Maltese currency were "scudi, "tari" and "grains". Twenty grains made one tari; twelve tari one scudo. The exchange rate in late 1800 was ten scudi to one pound: Ball to Dundas, 26 December 1800, above n. 5.
60   Debono (1988), 27, 32.
61   Ball to Dundas, above n. 5.
62   Above, n. 58.
63   Blaquière, 275-7.
64   By 1807 the number of looms present on the Island increased from 1945 to 2986: Ball to Windham, 28 February 1807, Kew, CO 158/13/51.
65   Avviso of 22 March 1805, NLM LIBR/MS 430 2/2 Bandi 1805 AL 1814, 5, discussed below.

2.3. British Model of Government on Malta: the "Continuation" Strategy[66]

Stability not Reform

When the British military first intervened in the struggle of the Maltese to liberate themselves from the French, they did not do so with any desire to acquire the Island for themselves; they respected the sovereignty of the King of the Two Sicilies. The principal British objective was to oust the French army from an island where its forces could threaten British interests in Egypt and the Levant. At that time, neither British commanders nor policy-makers fully understood the military importance of the Island, Nelson having expressed the opinion that it was of less value than Minorca.[67]

Following the surrender of the French garrison, Ball unwaveringly advocated the case for the permanent retention of Malta. He had set out, as early as December 1800, to convince the Secretary of State in London of the military value of the Island, its harbours and impregnable fortifications. A central thrust of his argument was that the Island enjoyed a strategic value superior to that of Minorca.[68] Nevertheless, in 1804-1805, Malta's status within the British Empire had not been fully resolved.

During the blockade, Ball learnt that the resentment and dissatisfaction of the Maltese, with the Order of St John, had been exacerbated when the Order was no longer sufficiently resourced to continue its expensive welfare policies.[69] Even before the French invasion, the Maltese had begun to conspire against the Order because it could not provide for them.

Ball understood that, from a Maltese perspective, the legitimacy of British rule would depend, in part, upon a congruence between its values and those of the wider community. The French had prompted a disastrous social legitimation crisis by plundering the churches and taxing the population. Ball had to achieve legitimacy by convincing the Maltese of a harmony between their interests and those of the British. He understood the need to avoid policies likely to provoke public animosity.

---

66 See Pirotta, 45-6.
67 See Randon, 354.
68 Ball to Dundas, above n. 5.
69 There had been little assimilation of the knights as rulers into Maltese society. As a celibate order, assimilation by marriage was obviously precluded. The Order refused to share power with the Maltese and was thus perceived as despotic, arrogant and elitist. In this sense Malta was a divided society: see Hardman; also Pirotta.

His preferred strategy, designed to win popularity with the inhabitants, was to continue operation of all the institutions of the government of the Order of St John. He believed that it was necessary to give the Maltese a material benefit from continued British possession of the Island, which meant not only re-establishing the legal and political order of the *ancien regime* but also pursuing the policy of benign paternalism that characterised its administration. It was a policy of reassurance and stability.

He proposed, to his political superiors in London, that the constitutional, political, legal and administrative order of the *ancien regime* should be continued.[70] In particular, the policies and institutions of the Order should be sustained with only minor changes. The rationale of this policy was to preserve the structure of Maltese political and economic life to avoid the Maltese being required to make a sudden adjustment to an unfamiliar legal, political, administrative or social structure. It was also consonant with the view that the Island's ultimate future would only be resolved once the war had ended. Ministers would, naturally, wish to avoid fundamental change within the institutions of government in case British possession proved to be one enjoyed merely for the duration of hostilities.

Ball's plan was also consistent with the general principles of the British constitution as well as the lessons the British had learned from the somewhat difficult experiences in other colonies during the latter part of the eighteenth century.[71] It appeared to be a coherent, rational and constitutionally-appropriate policy that was consonant with both domestic and international law. In embracing the constitutional and administrative architecture of the Order, the British would, apparently, be sending a reassuring public signal about the synonymity of Maltese and British values and, thereby, making a powerful claim for the legitimacy of British rule. However, the policy, whilst capable of pacifying anxieties that might have arisen when the alien British first assumed government, nonetheless also created a potential problem of ossification. To what extent could the Administration initiate reforms that would improve the lives of the inhabitants? What scope was there for a reforming mission, for "modernity", in this territory? And how far should a modernising project extend? "Continuity" thus posed important questions about the meaning of justice within a colonial context. This was to pose significant problems for Coleridge when in office.

---

70   Ball wrote: "It has consistently been my uniform system to abstain from every kind of change except in case of absolute necessity". Ball to Windham, 28 February 1807, Kew, CO 158/13/45.

71   See Chapter 3.

Nevertheless, British ministers in Whitehall ratified the continuity model and established it as the guiding principle of government after 1801.[72]

Accordingly, the first proclamation of a British Civil Commissioner (Cameron) of 15 July 1801[73] informed the Maltese of the guiding principles of British rule. This Declaration, which has been described as "the Magna Carta" of the Maltese people,[74] undertook that the British would respect the "dearest rights" of the Maltese. These rights were enumerated in an order which was, perhaps, not coincidental: their churches, holy religion, persons, and property.[75]

When Ball was sent back to the Island, his Instructions included a further and significant obligation. This explicitly required him to ensure the "attachment" of the Maltese to the British so as to avoid Malta falling under the influence of a rival foreign power once the Order of St John was restored to the Island.[76] British government of the Island had to be popular. The restoration of the Order did not, of course, take place.

Problems with the Continuity Strategy

The principal difficulty was that the British were assuming substantial financial and political burdens. Expectations amongst the Maltese were

---

72   As the Instructions of 14 May 1801 make clear: Kew, CO 158/1/ff 53 et seq; Hardman 350, 355. They are a vindication of Ball's position. However, the political support for this plan rested somewhat shakily on the information that Ball supplied to London. Continuity was also a requirement of the Law of Nations, see de Vattel, 389, section 201 – relating to the conqueror of a hostile sovereign. Where, as in Malta, the population was not hostile, the sovereign had a duty to maintain the existing laws-for how long is not made clear.

73   NLM LIBR/MS 430 1/2; Bandi 1790 AL 1805, 204. Cameron seems to have played a minor role in the affairs of government, preferring instead to leave many of his responsibilities to a William Eton in whose abilities he had complete confidence. William Eton (later knighted) was a private citizen with, it seems, considerable experience of effecting quarantine regulations. The British government appointed him Superintendent of the Lazaretto and Quarantine Department in 1801. Cameron seems to have left many of his responsibilities to William Eton in whose abilities he had complete confidence. Eton seems to have been the de facto civil commissioner. Eton may have expected to have succeeded Cameron (see e.g., Ball to Windham, 28 February 1807, Kew CO 158/13/20) and disappointment may explain why he became such an implacable opponent of Cameron's successor, Sir Alexander Ball. As we shall see, Eton stimulated dissent and agitated for Ball's downfall.

74   Galea.

75   Hardman, 342. There is further discussion of the status of these Instructions in Chapter 3.

76   Downing St to Ball, 9 June 1802, Kew, FO 49/3/51.

raised,[77] which it would be dangerous to frustrate. Pressing questions were posed concerning how the policies were to be funded, given the loss of much of the Island's revenue after 1792. This, eventually, forced Ball to raise funds by way of taxation – a risky strategy given the promises to uphold a Maltese system in which regular taxation was unknown. [78]

A further political risk lay within the structure of government. The absence of a popular representative assembly under the Order of St John meant that the burden of securing the compliance of the Maltese inhabitants rested entirely upon the administration. In continuing this system, the British had assumed an exclusive responsibility to deliver. There would be no possibility that the Civil Commissioner might escape blame for any failure of policy by using an inept local assembly as a convenient scapegoat.

But this was not all because the continuity strategy also rested upon an assumption that the autocratic constitution, embracing the despotic powers of the Grandmaster (which the Civil Commissioner would assume and exercise), was politically acceptable to the Maltese population. This was not necessarily the case. Particularly irksome was the refusal of their governors (whether British or the Knights) to share power. There is little evidence that the British properly understood this problem and assessed its risks. The way in which Ball exercised these extensive governmental powers exacerbated tensions with the Maltese inhabitants and created grave political problems which, during his time in office, fell to Coleridge to address.

In a Memorandum of December 1800, in which Ball proposed continuity, he had also raised political expectations in London. These did not always cohere well with the need to maintain popularity with the Maltese. On the one hand, Ball had led the Secretary of State to believe that the islands would not be a continuing drain upon the British Treasury. On the other, the Maltese had been encouraged to believe that the expensive welfare policies would be maintained. This latter commitment meant that some unpalatable measures would have to be imposed to raise revenue to meet the expense of civil government. How this was done without alienating Maltese public opinion was deeply problematic. Coleridge, as acting Public

---

77   There were a number of formal, public declarations to the Maltese intended to reassure them. For example a Proclamation issued by Pigot on 19 February 1801 which included the following: "...every possible means shall be used to make you contented and happy". He referred to the restoration of peace and liberty following the armed resistance of the Maltese people and their allies before adding, "It shall be my constant care to ensure the continuance of this well-being". Hardman, 341-42.
78   See Chapter 5.3: Taxation.

Secretary, would be confronted with dilemmas of this kind when drafting of several of his Bandi and Avvisi.[79] Moreover, this first-hand experience might well have prompted his deep disillusionment with what he soon condemned as "corrupt" government.[80]

Although it had superficial merit, the continuation policy was fractured by structural weaknesses both in its conception and in its implementation. Some of these difficulties derived from the rather elusive and problematic state of the Island's finances; others from the tensions surrounding the priority to be accorded to British interests in a relationship that the British wished to present as benign and protective towards Maltese interests. But, at an operational level, there were problems. For example financial and administrative accountability seems to have been weak. Proper scrutiny was part of the expected role of the Public Secretary, yet the evidence suggests that Coleridge may have only partly fulfilled this expectation.[81] This not only reveals something of Coleridge's success as an administrator, but it also exposes an important lacuna lying within the heart of government in 1805.

2.4. Maltese Institutions

After the capitulation of the French garrison, Ball began to re-instate the political and legal institutions that existed under the Order, and it is to these that we must now turn.

The Law and the Maltese Courts

The Maltese constitution did not embody any conception of the independence of the judiciary,[82] the separation of powers, nor of the rule of law.[83] All legislative, executive and even ultimate judicial authority was,

---

79 E.g. the Bando of 8 March 1805, NLM LIBR/MS 430 2/2 Bandi 1805 AL 1814, 2 (above) and see generally the introduction to the Bandi and Avvisi in Chapter 4.

80 To Catherine Clarkson, 6 November 1806, DW Letters 1806-1811, letter 277.

81 Hough and Davis (2007).

82 The Act of Settlement 1700 guaranteed judicial independence in Britain in so far as judicial salaries were thereafter protected by law. For the modern statutory guarantee against ministerial interference in the judicial process in the United Kingdom, see the Constitutional Reform Act 2005, s.3.

83 In contrast, the requirement that Executive action had to conform to the stric-

constitutionally, concentrated in the hands of the Grandmaster. But it is a mistake to ignore the extent to which there was a fully functioning legal system enforcing the ordinary civil and criminal law. The fact that there was no effective public law able to restrain the exercise of executive power did not mean that reasonable protection for private rights did not exist.

The Code de Rohan

The basic law, restored by the British, was the Code of Rohan.[84] The administration of law, and the status of the Code, as well as its application was to prove highly controversial because, as we shall see, the Civil Commissioner, in suppressing public disorder, chose to impose criminal punishments beyond the maximum permitted by the Code – actions that Coleridge supported.

The Code was effected in 1784 by Grandmaster Emmanuel de Rohan-Polduc (1725-1797), in office 1775-1797. Matters not covered by the Code, or where the law was unclear, were resolved, in normal civilian fashion, by reference to Roman law and the collected opinions of authoritative jurists, predominantly from Italy.[85] The Code was supplemented by the issue of Proclamations – the Bandi – a power also enjoyed by the Civil Commissioners under British rule in which, of course, Coleridge was closely involved.[86]

The Code de Rohan continued much that was in an earlier codification, the Code de Vilhenha,[87] subject to some important differences. William Eton, the Superintendant of Quarantine, who was one of Ball's English critics, thought that continuing the Code de Rohan rather than returning to the original Code de Vilhenha involved a political choice, made by Ball, designed to strengthen the grip of the British Civil Commissioner over the affairs of Malta. The earlier Code, he claimed, gave fuller recognition to the privileges of the Maltese people privileges which were limited or subordinated in the Code de Rohan.[88] Nationalists, such as Mitrovich, are

---

tures of the positive law had been laid down in England in Entick v Carrington (1765), 19, *Howell's State Trials*, 1029.

84 *Del Diritto Municipale di Malta Nuova Compilazione con diverse altre costituzioni*, Malta, Stamperia di Palazzo, 1784.

85 *Code de Rohan*; see also Royal Commission of 1812, Kew, CO 158/19/17 and 30.

86 Eton, 134.

87 Grandmaster 1722-1736.

88 Eton, 144.

said to have "detested" the Code on these grounds.[89] This view, however, needs to be understood, first, in terms of Eton's general support for traditional nationalism as expressed, in particular, through the argument for a restoration of the *Consiglio Popolare*, and, secondly, in the context of his general thesis that the laws of Malta were perfectly adequate and that the Island's problems stemmed from the fact that the laws were not properly enforced by an autocratic Civil Commissioner.[90]

The Code and its contents were described by Eton (writing between 1802 and 1807):

> The Code is divided into eight books, containing 434 pages of small folio-large and open print. The greater part of the matter regards the military and naval regulations of the Order-and bulls of the pope-and many other things, which have no relation to the present state of the island.[91]

It had significant provisions regarding judicial offices (Book 1) and criminal procedure, including torture, and sentences (Book 2); Book 5 defined a range of crimes and their punishments including those relating to public order. As we shall see, the public order provisions of the Code were, from Ball's standpoint, inadequate. When the anti-Semitic disturbances arose, in 1805, Coleridge issued Avvisi (Public Notices) which extended the criminal law. As indicated, when convictions were obtained, Ball dictated the sentences which were not always those prescribed under the Code.

Through British eyes, in 1812, the laws were, with the exception of commercial law, "well founded on just and equitable principles".[92] The Code, subject to some additions and amendments to suit local conditions, was based upon Roman law and, thus, located the Maltese legal system within a legal tradition common to much of continental Europe. The decisions of foreign courts and tribunals which applied Roman law were accepted as precedents, as were the opinions of eminent jurists on occasions when the Code needed interpretation.

---

89   Frendo, 66; cf. Mizzi, 32. The Code "In fact, it took into consideration local customs and traditions and included improvements made in Italy and Franc in legal enactments and procedures".

90   This general view was broadly endorsed by the Royal Commission of 1812.

91   Eton, 153.

92   Royal Commission of 1812, above n. 37, 9. Commercial law, administered by the Commercial Court (the Consolato del Mare) and based on traditional civilian principles, needed, according to the Civil Commissioners, root and branch reform if it was to meet the needs of Malta as a hub of imperial trade.

The Maltese Judges

The judicial system on Malta was characterised by a lack of security of tenure of the judges and, hence, their lack of independence from the executive. The judges were appointed by the executive (the Civil Commissioner) who also had the power to dismiss them at his pleasure; that is to say, without reason and irrespective of their own behaviour or performance in the role. It must have been an anxiety for members of the judiciary, who might have been tempted to act independently, that judges held only annual appointments and were, thus, subject to annual scrutiny.[93]

In practice, judges seem to have been removed only infrequently. More usually, they were transferred to other courts.[94] In a despatch to Hobart, Ball justified this interference as an "ancient usage" and, thus, in line with the principle of continuity. An additional comment suggests that Ball realised the practice needed justification and that this lay in its political utility:

> This [usage] I have thought it necessary to conform to, since it operates as an incitement to the faithful discharge of their duty, and at the same time affords the Government a powerful check over a body of men who have the greatest influence in the Island.[95]

The Civil Commissioner was not required to give reasons for any decision relating to the power of appointment or removal, nor was he formally accountable for its exercise. There was not even the appearance of judicial independence and judges wishing to stay in office, therefore, had a powerful incentive not to offend the executive by their decisions.

The Courts

The law was administered through a court system that was, largely, effective though subject, as we shall see, to some severe criticisms. Grandmaster Rohan, as well as re-codifying the law, had also restructured the courts. Ball, in his first administration, reversed some of those changes. He was responding to the concerns, in the Royal Instructions,[96] about the effects

---

93   Royal Commission of 1812, above n. 37, 20.
94   Ibid.
95   Ball to Hobart, 15 November 1803, Kew, CO 158/7/437, 440.
96   Hardman, 350-7. The Royal Instructions identified the basic principles (such as the continuation strategy discussed above) and some particular policies (such as the possible reforms of the courts mentioned here) which the British administration was to promote. They are discussed further in Chapter 3.

upon the administration of justice of the fact that the judges were paid out of court fees. This matter is discussed below. In particular, Ball reduced the number of judges. The resulting changes created the court structure that existed in Coleridge's time.[97] Ball's reforms were part of a broader strategy to reinvigorate Maltese institutions after the French departure[98] and seemed to have been successful. However, as the Royal Commission noted, from a British perspective, serious problems remained, which are outlined below.

The court structure during Coleridge's time can be discerned from various sources.[99] The High Court of Valletta was composed of a President or *Castellano* (a knight), a criminal judge, two civil judges, a procurator fiscal and deputy fiscal; advocate fiscal, a pro-advocate for the poor; a protector of prisoners (a knight), two notaries, actuaries and writers, and captains or officers of police, with their assistants.[100]

Criminal cases

Criminal cases[101] were to play a significant part in Coleridge's workload. He used Avvisi to notify the inhabitants of politically significant or noteworthy convictions, not least for its deterrent effect. The trials were usually held in the Grand Criminal Court (*Sale Criminali della Gran Court della Valletta*[102]), a part of the High Court. As well as a President, whose role was formal, there was a specialist criminal judge.[103] The jurisdiction of the court included all criminal cases which were based upon the Code de Rohan. The Code differentiated the criminal law into "public" crimes (which included not only crimes against the state, such as treason, but also murder and other offences that disturbed the public peace) and "private" crimes. Private crimes may border closely with what, in the common law system, are torts. The former were proceeded against by the authorities upon their own motion, the latter only upon the complaint of the victim.[104] Robberies, of which there were a rising number at this period, and which were part of a wider crime wave that was politically damaging to Ball, were pursued by the fiscal upon receipt of a complaint from the victim. Procedure was

---

97   Eton, 131; Laferla, 53.
98   Pirotta, 53.
99   Royal Commission of 1812, Kew, above n.37.
100   Eton, 131-2.
101   See further, Royal Commission of 1812, above n. 37, 15-20.
102   Laferla, 54, fn 1.
103   Royal Commission of 1812, above n. 37.
104   Book 2 Chapter 1 #19 of Eton's translation, in Eton, 153 passim.

summary; no jury[105] and the judge decided issues of fact and law. Minor cases involved an oral hearing, but more serious cases seem to have been decided mainly upon the basis of written submissions. Evidence gathering was a judicial process with witnesses being examined by the judge with the fiscal, scribes and others present to assist.[106] Though the court process was non-adversarial, the law asserted the need to "confront" the witness, to cross-examine and to test the evidence.[107] Surviving testimony, in relation to the public disorder of May 1805, gives some insight into the nature of the process, and this is considered further below.[108]

From a British perspective, the most controversial provision was the legal requirement of detaining the accused in prison if an initial investigation confirmed a "well grounded suspicion of guilt".[109] Those suspects (described as "criminals" in the law) could, it seems, stay in prison awaiting the pleasure of the judge and other court officials. There appears not to have been an independent judicial remedy to order release, though release could have been obtained at the discretion of the Civil Commissioner by way of a petition to the *Segnatura*.[110]

The Code referred, in general terms, to protecting the rights of the defence though, from a British perspective, the absence of a right to silence, and, thereby, a full presumption of innocence, was troubling.[111] Torture was still occasionally used notwithstanding that the Code suggested its abolition in time to come. An accused person who had confessed to treason could be tortured in order to obtain the names of accomplices.[112]

---

105   The lack of a criminal jury was a matter of concern to the 1812 Commission, who viewed fairness through British common law eyes. However, they did not recommend its introduction because, at that time, it was likely to be unpopular. The first juries were found in the new Court of Piracy (1815) but it was not until 1829 that a more extensive scheme was introduced, see Cremona (1964). Similarly, Major General Pigot, as part of his objection to allowing British soldiers to be tried by Maltese courts, cited the lack of the jury system: Pigot to Cameron, Kew, 16 August 1801, CO 158/2/81, the matter is discussed below.

106   This procedure was laid down in the Code de Rohan, Book 2, Chapter 3, #11 of Eton's translation; in Eton, 141.

107   "The criminal cannot require a note of the names and Christian names of the witnesses; but after the examination, in every case, the criminal and witnesses are to be confronted". *Code de Rohan*, Chapter 11, ibid.

108   See Chapters 5.4: Public Order and Crime, and Chapter 6.

109   Book 2, Chapter 1 #19 of Eton's translation, in Eton.

110   See further below****.

111   Silence in the face of serious offences would result in convictions and a threat of an equivalent punishment for the less serious offences, ibid #33 and # 34.

112   *The Code* had significant provisions dealing with the methods of torture and the rights of the accused, ibid #27.The main method suggested is "the corda" by

However, one of the grievances raised by the Maltese against Ball was the use of torture in other cases.[113] Formally, the maximum punishment that the Grand Criminal Court could impose was life on the Galleys, but this punishment was entirely obsolete by 1805.[114]

There was a range of other punishments including banishment, fines and the requirement to undertake public works. Capital punishment was allowed, in the Code, for murder.[115] Capital cases could be heard by the Grand Criminal Court but only the Supreme Court of Appeal could pronounce sentence. In the British view, expressed in the Royal Commission, some penalties were over-severe. The death sentence was rarely pronounced and, in the Commission's view (speaking, of course, from a United Kingdom which used the death penalty extensively in ways that still awaited Parliamentary reform), punishments were, sometimes, out of proportion to the seriousness of the offence.[116]

Appeal was to the Supreme Tribunal of Appeal (*Supremo Tribunale di Appello*).[117] There were three judges, after Ball's reorganisation. One of these was also one of the two judges in the civil court. This tribunal acted upon its own procedure and at its own time. The appeal judges needed to be different from the judge at first instance. There was a right of further appeal, within the Tribunal, to two new judges nominated by the Executive.[118] Two confirmations of the initial sentence (i.e. three pronouncements of guilt or innocence) were generally considered final and binding with no further appeal.

Civil Cases[119]

Apart from prize cases in the Court of Vice-Admiralty, civil suits did not

which the suspect is suspended by ropes and then dropped. Eton alleged that a market inspector, Sateriano, had been tortured by being imprisoned with live rats and thereby forced to confess. His conviction resulted in banishment to Tripoli: Eton to Windham, 11 October 1806, Kew, CO 158/12/ no folio reference.

113   Ibid. and *Memorial and Petition of the Maltese* [unsigned and undated], Kew, CO158/10/151.

114   According to the Commission the maximum sentence was, by 1812, no more than 10 years in the galleys. The Code clearly allows for a life sentence in the galleys such as for abusing and injuring parents or "senior relatives", *Code de Rohan*, unpublished translation by Dr Lydia Davis (*Code de Rohan*), Book 5, Chapter 3, #4.

115   *Code de Rohan*, Book 5, Chapter 4, #1.

116   Royal Commission of 1812, above n. 37, 79.

117   *Code de Rohan*, Book 5, Chapter 4, #1.

118   Royal Commission of 1812 above n. 37, 19.

119   See Royal Commission of 1812, ibid., 29-34.

feature in Coleridge's duties and so the Maltese system is noted here only briefly.

Civil cases were heard in the Grand Civil Court (*Tribunale Civile della Gran Corte della Valletta*). The jurisdiction of the Court extended to all civil matters except those pertaining to state property (heard by the Court of Administration and Public Property) and commercial cases (heard by the Commercial Court, the *Consolato del Mare*). There was also a small claims, summary, process for sums under fifty *scudi*.[120] There were two judges nominated to the *Tribunale Civile*. Cases were heard, at first instance, by one judge sitting alone; the other judge sat in the appeal court, the Supreme Tribunal of Appeal. As with the criminal court, the civil procedure was, predominantly, based upon the papers, although the judge could examine the parties after a statement of facts and issues had been agreed. Appeal was to the Supreme Court of Appeal (*Supremo Tribunale di Appello*) (Supreme Tribunal). Characteristically of civilian systems, this was a process of confirmation, necessary to give the first instance decision its authority, rather than an "appeal" based upon specific grounds. The initial confirmation, in the Supreme Tribunal, was by one of the three appeal judges nominated to the Supreme Tribunal. Further confirmation or appeal, within the Supreme Tribunal, was to different Supreme Tribunal judges including the judge who sat in the Grand Civil Court but who had not heard the case. Three confirming judgements were normally considered final. If the judgement was not confirmed (i.e. the judges were divided) there was the opportunity for a fourth or even a fifth hearing before a Supreme Tribunal judge and also two other judges nominated by the government.[121] There was no formal provision for further appeal after the fifth hearing.

There were also civil and criminal courts in Città Vecchia and Gozo with ultimate appeals to the *Gran Corte* in Valletta. Fortunata Tagliana, for example, about whose case Coleridge issued an important Avviso, was tried and convicted in the criminal court, the Corte Capitanale, of Città Vecchia.[122]

Disputes involving state property were heard by the Court of Administration and Public Property (which, by 1812, was conducting little business). The Commercial Court dealt with matters of trade and commerce, such as disputes over commercial contracts, bankruptcy, bills of exchange and insurance. It was the court that was likely to involve British

---

120   Royal Commission of 1812, ibid., 34.
121   Royal Commission of 1812, ibid., 32.
122   This case is discussed below in Chapter 5.

inhabitants and it came in for considerable scrutiny and criticism (for being slow and over formal) by the 1812 Royal Commission which suggested major reforms.

Two other courts, neither of which was directly part of the Maltese legal system, should be noted in the context of Coleridge as a public servant in Malta. Courts of Vice-Admiralty were established under the Royal Prerogative throughout the British Empire, including in Malta early in British rule. Their jurisdiction was the settlement of maritime disputes between seamen and merchants which related to events on the high seas. Coleridge's duties included advocacy in this court dressed in wig and gown.[123] The experience may not have been a pleasant one, for he privately lamented that the Court was a forum for the "world's squabbles".[124]

There were also three ecclesiastical courts in Valletta, Città Vecchia and Gozo. Their jurisdiction was over ecclesiastical matters but upon issues which also affected public order (such as immorality or blasphemy) their jurisdiction, sometimes, traded close to the state courts. Appeal from these religious courts was to the Metropolitan Court in Palermo or the Holy See. The 1812 Royal Commission suggested no change to their position. It was, however, concerned with the abuse of sanctuary, an issue that clearly existed in Coleridge's time. Sanctuary interfered with the authority of the criminal courts and gave rise to a potential for conflicts between the Holy See (to whom a person removed from sanctuary could appeal) and the state. It was, clearly, a complicated matter and raised issues upon which petitions to the Civil Commissioner could be grounded. One such involved an alleged murderer (Grazio Fenech) who had sought sanctuary after escaping from custody but who had then been returned to prison at the request of the court. He was willing to trade his (disputed) right to sanctuary for exile, which the Civil Commissioner could order. The right to sanctuary depended upon issues such as the seriousness of the offence and the nature of the defendant (in another case sanctuary was refused, by the bishop, to deserters).[125] The particular concern of the 1812 Royal Commission was that "foreigners" (including British soldiers) were subject to attack by Maltese who then sought sanctuary. The British had little sympathy with immunity sought by perpetrators through sanctuary and the Royal Commission recommended careful steps, through consultation

123   To Robert Southey, 2 February 1805, *CL* 2, 1164.
124   *CN* 2, 2379.
125   Advice to Ball from the Corte Capitanale, 22 May 1805: NAM 92/04 1805 box 04.

with Rome, to bring the practice to an end.[126]

Failings of the Courts

The 1812 Royal Commission identified a number of serious failings of the Maltese courts and legal system which would have been prevalent in 1805 and are, to some extent, confirmed in a few of the Avvisi.[127] The most important flowed from the low wages paid to judges and their consequent reliance upon court fees and a proportion of criminal fines for their personal remuneration.[128] This may have caused corruption;[129] it certainly compromised the range of case management decisions, that judges needed to take, over issues such as the length of pre-trial detention, the timing of trials, of sentencing and confirmation hearings. Judges would tend to concentrate upon the higher fee cases (e.g. high value property cases), a consequence of which could be that criminal defendants might have stayed in pre-trial detention for much longer than they otherwise would[130] and poor litigants might have suffered longer delays. Some civil cases were heard in a judge's home creating at least the suspicion of corruption and private arrangements rather than the open administration of the law.[131] Delay in both civil and criminal justice became a major problem and a characteristic of the Maltese system.

It was not unusual, in a colonial context, for local judges to rely upon fees and for corruption and unfairness to be alleged.[132] Similarly, concerns about the administration of justice on Malta were not confined to the Maltese courts and the Maltese judiciary. In particular, allegations of corruption and other difficulties flowing from a fee-based remuneration system were also made, including in the House of Commons, in respect of the British Court of Vice-Admiralty in Malta.[133]

126   Royal Commission of 1812, above n. 37, 28.
127   Royal Commission, ibid.; see also an incident attempted bribery in Avviso of 14 June 1805, NLM LIBR/MS 430 2/2 Bandi 1805 AL 1814, 11.
128   Broadly speaking, the court fees amounted to about 90% of the salary of one of the judges in the High Court in Valletta who earned (in 1812) £20 p.a. salary and shared court fees to increase their incomes by about £300 p.a.: Royal Commission of 1812, above n. 37, 21.
129   Hinted at by the Royal Commission of 1812, ibid., 20 and 53.
130   Royal Commission of 1812, above, n. 37, 17.
131   Royal Commission of 1812, ibid., 31.
132   Manning, 115-19; also 153-4. Generally, the issue was exacerbated if the judges were not judicially trained; this was not a problem in Malta.
133   Cobbett's Parliamentary Debates Vol. 20, 1811, 464-70.

The problems with the Maltese judicial system, identified from the British perspective, were recognised early. The Royal Instructions of 1801 instructed Cameron (the first Civil Commissioner) to continue with the system of payment of fees but to regularise their application by producing and publishing a table of those fees. Furthermore, the Civil Commissioner was required to examine whether the system undermined the "pure and impartial administration of justice" and, if it did so, to take appropriate, regulatory, steps to remedy the problem and report these to London. Ball's reforms in 1803 (mentioned above) involved a reduction in the number of judges in order to reduce the burden of fees. This seems not to have been successful. Problems emanating from low judicial salaries were a major concern of the 1812 Royal Commission one of whose principal recommendations was for major increases aimed at a salaried remuneration equal to what was obtained under the fees approach.[134] None of these issues, however, seemed to trouble the Maltese during Coleridge's time in office. Their major grievance was the manner in which Ball used his constitutional powers to interfere in the judicial process in order to impose harsher sentences than the law otherwise allowed.[135] This highlighted problems with the scope of the powers vested in the Civil Commissioner

Interventions in the Judicial Process

After Coleridge left office, the role of the Civil Commissioner in the legal and judicial process was recognised as problematic. After all, it had been one of the central reasons why the Nationalist's complained that the Civil Commissioner held despotic powers.[136] These damaging complaints contributed, along with other causes of friction, to troubling public dissatisfaction with Ball, in 1805, and sparked the "propaganda offensive" in which Coleridge became engaged in the Bandi and Avvisi. The substance of the Nationalists' complaints about the role of the Civil Commissioner was, eventually, accepted by the 1812 Royal Commission, although without explicit criticism of the late Sir Alexander Ball. This marked a closing of ranks to maintain British prestige.

---

134   Large pay rises were put into effect by Maitland after he came to office as Governor: Maitland to Bathurst, 24 October 1814, Kew, CO 158/25/215; see enclosure 13, Kew, CO 158/25/284-5 for a table of wage increases.
135   See below and Chapter 5.
136   *Memorial and Petition of the Maltese* (unsigned and undated), Kew, CO 158/10/151. Considered below, and especially in Chapter 5.

The problem was that the Grandmaster (and hence the British Civil Commissioner) could intervene directly in a criminal trial after the judicial process of confirmation or appeal had been completed.[137] He could confirm, revise or annul the sentence of the court. The sentence could be varied even if there had been two confirmations of the original sentence.[138] The Civil Commissioner could also increase the sentence, or require the judge to refer up his proposed sentence for confirmation. Ball's exercise of these powers aroused strong dissent during Coleridge's period in office.[139] The Grandmaster (and Civil Commissioner) had, in effect, a dispensing power rather like, in English eyes, the power pretended by the Crown over domestic affairs. These had been made unlawful, domestically, by the Bill of Rights 1688 and it was this power that Lord Mansfield may have had in mind when he sought to limit the legislative power of the Crown in conquered and ceded colonies by reference to "fundamental principles".[140] For critics, such as Eton, this dispensing power was an important part of the argument that the country was ruled tyrannically. The formal complaints by the Maltese themselves were embarrassing and damaging for Ball and his senior advisers (including Coleridge).

According to the 1812 Royal Commission, the content of the laws was unobjectionable, but the power to dispense with them was obnoxious.[141] In fact, the dispensing power was not *necessarily* objectionable in practice in Malta since, as mentioned above, there were significant reasons to doubt the fairness of some of the judicial processes. They recommended the removal of the most important legislative and judicial powers.[142] But, during Coleridge's time, Sir Alexander Ball could and did, act in conformity with the Maltese constitution and the continuity principle, by exercising

---

137   For further discussion of the powers of the Grandmaster, see Chapter 3.

138   Eton, 132: "this Grandmaster [Pinto] ordered by his sign-manual, which constitutes a law, certain thieves to be hanged, who had been by three concurring sentences condemned to be banished to Sicily, and they were executed".

139   *Memorial and Petition of the Maltese* (unsigned and undated) Kew, CO158/10/151; see also Chapter 5: Public Order and Crime.

140   See the discussion of Mostyn v Fabrigas (1774), 1 Cowp. 160, below.

141   Eton, 143.

142   Although the prerogative of mercy would be retained as a prerogative of the executive authority, as it is under the English constitution. The power to prevent cases coming to court was also to be preserved but only in so far as it related to disputes over state property. The Royal Commission was concerned that there would otherwise be a flood of possible claims against the administration on this ground. Under the Royal Commission's proposal, the Civil Commissioner would have a duty to report any exercise of this power to Whitehall.

the arbitrary or, at least, despotic powers of the Grandmaster. Similarly, with respect to civil cases, after the (potentially extensive) process of confirmation and appeal had been completed, petitions were often made to the Civil Commissioner who could revise the order given or cause a re-hearing.

> The ultimate decisions of this Supreme Court ought to be final, but there are frequent instances upon record of case sent back and revised, and some even of a total and summary reversal of its decrees by the sole authority of the Grandmaster.[143]

Segnatura (Council of the Civil Commissioner)

The Civil Commissioner exercised significant powers through the *Segnatura*.[144] In his Public Notice of 1 March 1805, Coleridge reminded the population that they were at liberty to petition the Civil Commissioner with their grievances. Any person, whose interests were adversely affected by an administrative decision, had a further avenue of redress.

At the weekly meetings, the caseload was huge. On 17 May 1805, for example,[145] the *Segnatura* had to process seventy-five petitions.[146] Eton thought there was "scarcely" a limit upon the kinds of request that could come before this Council, and the surviving records substantiate this.[147] Coleridge, observing Ball's operation of the system, noted, rather unflatteringly, that the Maltese inhabitants consulted Ball's opinion with almost "child-like helplessness"[148] even upon matters that were, essentially, private matters. Claims concerning administrative decisions, injustice, delays, a pardon or a reduction in a fine or term of imprisonment, the rescission of banishment, or requests for political preferment or even charity are examples.[149]

---

143   Royal Commission of 1812, above n. 37, 47.
144   See e.g. Harding, 66-7.
145   A date selected at random: NAM LIBR 43/12 vol N- 10 May-11 September 1805.
146   Ibid.
147   Eton, 143; see also *Registro dei Memoriale e Decreti da Sua Excellenza il sig Cavalier Alessandro Ball Regio Commissionario Civile di Sua Maesta' Britannica*, NAM LIBR 43/11.
148   *The Friend*, I, 561.
149   The petitions for 1805 can be examined in NAM 92/04 1805. These petitions have been handwritten and various relevant parts have been underlined for emphasis (presumably by the responsible auditor). They relate to a wide variety of administrative and judicial matters. For example, some deal with "clemenza" of sentence;

The possibility of petitioning the Civil Commissioner meant that there was always the opportunity to persuade him to change or modify the outcomes of judicial or administrative processes. This had two consequences. First, it signified that the Civil Commissioner was the highest court of appeal. Secondly, it meant that legal and administrative problems needed not to be resolved according to published, impersonal legal norms but by the ethical responses, the political necessities, the self-interest or other expressions of the will of the Civil Commissioner. This resulted in uncertainty, if not in arbitrary rule. In summary, the *Segnatura* was the embodiment of the despotic power of the state because it combined executive, judicial and legislative functions in the unaccountable, unchallengeable and subjective discretions of the Civil Commissioner/Grandmaster. It embodied, in English eyes, a system without constitutional and legal guarantees of liberty and property.[150]

No reasons were given for the *Segnatura's* decision,[151] and neither, of course, was the Civil Commissioner accountable to the courts for those decisions. The Civil Commissioner was assisted by four *Uditori* who were salaried lawyers or ecclesiastics[152] serving as advisors.[153] They had an important role in receiving the petitions and subjecting them to an initial evaluation, highlighting the essence of each and summarising it for Ball's benefit. His Public Secretary and Treasurer was also present, thus Coleridge must have participated in the *Segnatura*.[154] The *Uditori* held office at the appointment and during the pleasure of the Civil Commissioner and, it seems, were often replaced.[155] There was no legal or constitutional principle that they should be broadly representative of society. In practice, they were thought to be the Civil Commissioner's creatures.[156]

---

others licence applications; others are appeals relating to the award of prize money. They are addressed "Eccelenza".

150   Eton, 136.
151   Above n. 144.
152   At the time of Ball's second administration, (1803-1809) there would appear to have been at least one lawyer present. He had reported to Dundas, 26 December 1800, above n. 5 (also Hardman 344-6), that only some of the appointees had to be legally qualified.
153   See Ball to Dundas, ibid.
154   Ball had combined the offices: see Sullivan to Ball 31 December 1803- Libr 531, 18.
155   Eton described the Uditori in Eton, 145 et seq.
156   The Grandmaster could consult with them, but under the normal procedure (certainly that followed in Ball's time) they would not venture an opinion on a matter unless asked to do so.

Ball's conduct in the *Segnatura* seemed to embody the despotism of the Grandmaster. According to Eton, petitioners who used "least freedom in remonstrating" were liable to punishment. Ball, it seems, continued this policy as a discouragement to critics of government policy.[157] There is evidence that in 1805 a petition had been made to the *Segnatura* for the "re-establishment" of the *Consiglio Popolare* (the allegedly traditional legislative assembly that the Maltese critics of British rule wanted restored). Ball punished the petitioner by summary banishment, a severe punishment *pour encourager les autres* who, by seeking an assembly, were challenging the Civil Commissioner's autocratic powers. This harsh response confirmed Ball's "despotic" reputation amongst the Maltese. His willingness to punish severely those who advocated reform also featured as one of the most serious complaints against his government made in the Petition to the Crown of 1805.[158]

The *Segnatura* could be used to moderate criminal sentences where the political context and British interests allowed for it. As we shall see, some of those convicted and exiled for anti-Semitic conduct, in May 1805, successfully petitioned for their sentences to be commuted. Some of them were restored to their families on Malta soon after the disturbances subsided. From the British point of view, this possibility was advantageous. The harsh crackdown had signalled that anti-Semitic conduct would not be permitted, but when that message had been conveyed and stability had returned, the unpopularity of the sentences was quietly addressed and moderated.

In the view of the Royal Commission, the right of petition to the *Segnatura* and its exercise in practice was wrong in principle, as setting the Executive above the law, which they saw as a dangerous doctrine amounting to a "despotism" with the "potential to cause injustice".[159] They also concluded that suspending the power to reverse or modify judicial decisions would be "very objectionable"[160] and repugnant to British ideas of the rule of law and constitutional government. Despite this, it concluded that the system was generally acceptable to the Maltese people.[161]

It is particularly revealing that the Royal Commission also concluded that, notwithstanding the unlimited scope of their powers, the Civil

---

157   Eton, 146.
158   See the undated *Memorial and Petition of the Maltese*, Kew, CO 158/10/151 (1805).
159   Ibid.
160   Royal Commission of 1812, above, n. 37.
161   Royal Commission of 1812, ibid., 82-3.

Commissioners' (including Ball's) behaviour was "exemplary".[162] Their, somewhat surprising, position was that Civil Commissioners were uncertain of their powers and, therefore, tended to exercise their considerable discretion with caution. Ball's arbitrary use of his powers to suppress possible political dissent and to deter threats to public order, suggest that this part of the Royal Commission's judgment was either not fully informed or perhaps reflects a desire to bolster British authority rather than uncover the truth about the exercise of governmental power during Coleridge's Malta period.

The Catholic Church and the "Catholic Superstition"[163]

From the very commencement of their administration the British were at pains to emphasise that they would respect the liberties of the Maltese in their religious beliefs.[164] The Maltese were devout Catholics, and many remain so to this day; their church plays an important part in their daily lives. Village society in Coleridge's time focused around the family, home and church.

British religious toleration was, of course, designedly central to the "attachment" of the Maltese to British rule. The new administration was fully aware that the *casus belli* of the insurrection against the French had been its treatment of the Catholic Church, especially its plundering of church property. The outbreak seems to have begun in Rabat where officials, responsible to the French, had been sent to seize property of the Church of Our Lady of Mount Carmel. Ball was determined that the British would do nothing to arouse similar hostility.

An overt demonstration of Ball's toleration policy was the recognition of the traditional religious festivities. He gave these his full support, subject only to regulations to preserve good order. Coleridge noted, during his period of office, how noisy public celebrations were.[165] Fireworks were tolerated and children seemed to let them off "every three yards".[166] Coleridge subsequently suggested that, in contrast to Sicilian festivals, the Maltese ones were subdued.[167] Even so, he had little time for the Catholic

162 Ibid.
163 *CN* 2, 2420, 28 January 1805.
164 Proclamation of 15 July 1801, NLM LIBR/MS 430 1/2; Bandi 1790 AL 1805, 204.
165 See e.g. the Easter celebrations 1805, *CN* 2, 2547.
166 *CN* 2, 2547. He noted the noise accompanied most forms of catholic ritual practised on the Island: *CN* 2, 2561.
167 *The Friend*, I, 566.

religion. After an early official visit, to the Maltese hospital, he also lamented the presence of religious iconography and complained of the "indefatigable ubiquitarian intrusia of the Catholic superstition".[168]

Ball may have tolerated religious expression but he drew the line at compensating the religious institutions for property looted during the French occupation. Private individuals fared better, as was made clear in one of Coleridge's most important Bandi dated 8 March 1805.[169] The religious institutions never succeeded in recovering their stolen property or its equivalent monetary value. This was a lingering controversy, which we will discuss below.[170]

Whilst Ball appreciated the valuable role the church played, he also recognised its potential threat. In 1800 he had thought it desirable "to keep a watchful eye" on the priests who had a substantial influence over the population.[171] There was always the possibility that disaffected priests could provide leadership and organise popular dissent, as some had done during the insurrection against the French. This implies that Ball's refusal to underwrite the Church's investments must have carried certain political risks. As we shall see, however, by 1805 any policy that aggravated the Island's financial deficit was even less appetising than the risk of political agitation from its priests.

The Maltese Administrative System

A complex administration had been developed under the Order, which had often been pre-occupied with funding the defence of the Island. Despite this priority, the Order had maintained a system of courts for the redress of disputes. It had minted coinage, enforced laws, run hospitals, and established and maintained an effective water supply.[172] It also operated the bulk purchase and supply of grain and other foodstuffs via the Università.[173] We shall now consider some of its principal institutions.

---

168   CN 2, 2420, 28 January 1805.
169   NLM LIBR/MS 430 2/2 Bandi 1805 AL 1814, 2.
170   See Chapter 5: taxation theme.
171   He had reported that it was necessary to treat the religious "prejudices" of the Maltese with "great indulgence": Ball to Dundas, above n. 5.
172   Water was scarce; drought often threatened: Pirotta, 21.
173   Ibid., 10.

Hospitals

> In [the Maltese] Hospital among the Venereal Convalescents I saw (in the
> same bed) a child of 12 years old, and an old man at least 70![174]

The care of the sick had been one of the main charitable objects for which
the Order of St John was originally founded, and it had continued this limb
of its mission on Malta. The British policy, inaugurated by Sir Alexander
Ball, was to continue the health provision of the Order. At around £10,000
per annum[175] the required expenditure was a significant part of the Island's
budget.

Ball fought for and won back, from the military authorities, the use of
the civil hospital (which Coleridge called the Maltese Hospital[176]) which,
during the French administration, had been appropriated for military use.
This was a key policy, for it was tangible evidence of the administration's
desire to win the favour of the local inhabitants by giving them the
assurances of funded public health provision.

Ball undertook a major re-organisation of the hospitals, in 1804, which,
notwithstanding the financial pressures upon his administration, included
salary incentives for senior management.[177] His aim was to ensure the
efficient and effective running of the hospitals and it augured well that he
was able to report that the costs of health provision declined sharply in
1805 as the reforms took hold. Thereafter, the hospitals apparently ceased
to claim much of Ball's attention. This was another example of the failure to
supervise and monitor the implementation of his important policies.

Such scrutiny as there was must have been ineffective. Large numbers
of the destitute were unnecessarily sheltered within the hospitals even
though they had no need of medical care.[178] This was another major cost
to government that was allowed to go unchecked. But that was not all.
Suspiciously, there were unexplained rises in costs, which drew the criticism

---

174   *CN* 2, 2420.
175   Pirotta, 31.
176   *CN* 2, 2420, 28 January 1805.
177   See e.g. Macaulay to Ball, 10 September 1804, Kew CO 158/9/51-2. Ball admitted that the salary of the President had been increased, to ensure his leadership in providing good management. He drew attention to "considerable reforms" including the merger of the Invalids and Foundlings Hospital. Costs were predicted to fall in 1805: Ball to Camden, 19 April 1805, Kew, CO 158/10/147-9.
178   Maitland to Permanent Committee of Management of the Charitable Institutions, 14 January 1816, Kew, CO 158/27/ no folio reference, where he referred to a "mass" of individuals in the hospitals who were not entitled to be there. He wrote that he had discovered "a place of resort for the idle".

of the 1812 Royal Commission. Governor Maitland, who discovered that the hospitals were still overstaffed and inefficient, reformed the system in 1816.[179]

Coleridge's official responsibilities embraced the inspection and supervision of the civilian hospitals. His *Notebooks* record that, when he visited them, he discovered care arrangements that provoked his severe criticism.[180] Despite this, he seems to have been unable to effect appropriate changes, for the problems remained in Maitland's time.[181] This is intriguing because Coleridge, when later travelling in Italy, professed a greater interest in the Pisan hospitals than he did in the leaning Tower, which he viewed in moonlight. The two Pisan hospitals, he discovered, were notable for the size of the rooms, the light and their "perfect cleanliness & good order".[182] If this inspired him to reflect upon what might have been achieved in Malta, it came too late.

Alms

The monthly distribution of alms also provided welfare support to those in need.[183] It was a function performed by the office of the Grand Almoner – an office that also came under the scrutiny of the Public Secretary. During the administration of the first British Civil Commissioner, we know that alms derived from the profits of the sale of wheat.[184] And the substance of this policy continued under Sir Alexander Ball. One of Coleridge's Public Notices, for example, reveals that judicially confiscated property could be sold and the proceeds distributed amongst the poor.[185] Coleridge lost no opportunity to emphasise this in order to enhance Ball's intended image as a kindly protector of the vulnerable.

Monte di Pietà e Redenzione

The Order had also created a pawn brokerage, known as the Monte di Pietà

179   Maitland to Permanent Committee, etc, ibid.
180   *CN* 2, 2420.
181   Maitland later found that the standard of care was characterised by a "filth and misery" which was "degrading to the government" and "disgraceful" to the inhabitants: Maitland above n. 178.
182   *CN* 2, 2856.
183   See, for example, the Bando of 8 March 1805, NLM LIBR/MS 430 2/2 Bandi 1805 AL 1814 2.
184   Cameron to Hobart, 24 February 1802, Kew, CO 158/3/16.
185   Avviso of 14 June 1805: NLM LIBR/MS 430 2/2 Bandi 1805 AL 1814, 11.

e Redenzione. This institution was to enable those who needed short-term finance to obtain it without having to sell their possessions to raise funds. It charged an interest rate of 6% per annum, which was below that demanded by private sector lenders.

The Monte di Pietà was a semi-autonomous facility which, it seems, was used by all classes of the population. According to Ball, three hundred pounds a year accrued to the revenues of the Island as a result of its lending activities during the time of the Order.[186]

Unfortunately, it had also fallen victim to French rapacity when all pledged assets were plundered. Ball considered that it required a capital investment of five thousand pounds to re-establish it.[187] In his Instructions to Cameron, Lord Hobart allowed the Civil Commissioner to determine who should manage it, but he explicitly required that the management be supervised so as to avoid fraud or abuse. [188]

Administrators of Public Property

The British Imperial government learned from Ball's Report, of December 1800, that various classes of property had formerly been vested in either the Order or the Grandmaster. After the French surrender, these properties became vested in the Crown. They included gardens, houses, warehouses; and Hobart ordered the Board of Administrators of Public Property, which fell under the scrutiny of the Public Secretary, should continue to manage them. Ball was, later, to use his power to appoint its members in order to promote broader political purposes. For example, the Marchese di Testaferrata was "demoted" from the office of a "Jurat" of the Università to the Board of Public Property once his nationalist sympathies had become known. He is likely to have been one of the anonymous authors of the 1805 Petition to the Crown, which made a series of damaging allegations against Ball's administration. We will consider this in Chapters 5 and 6.

The Università

"..a strange, yet valid, anomaly in the operations of political economy".[189]

The Università of Valletta[190] was a centrally important Maltese institution,

186 Ibid.
187 Ball to Dundas, above n. 5.
188 Instructions of 14 May 1801, Kew, CO 158/1/ff 53 et seq; Hardman, 350.
189 *The Friend*, I, 570.
190 More formally, of Valletta, Cospicua and Vittoriosa.

which handled far greater sums of money than even the Island's Treasury. It was to become a main bulwark in Ball's policy of continuity. As we shall see, Ball's policy in relation to the Università, leading to the distribution of bad bread, dealt a major blow to public confidence in his administration. Much of the resentment and ridicule was eventually targeted at Ball himself, which was a major crisis in confidence that Coleridge had to address.

Ball required the Università to succeed in two ways each of which was central to his continuation strategy. Firstly, he expected it to generate a financial surplus upon its activities. This was needed to replace the lost revenue of the Order. Without that revenue, Ball could not afford the welfare policies and subsidised food necessary to "attach" the Maltese to British rule. Secondly, the Università was pivotal in ensuring a regular and, above all, affordable food supply to an island that was largely dependent upon imported foodstuffs. Without cheap bread the poor would be especially vulnerable to starvation, especially in the years 1800-1806 when there as an international grain shortage. The success of the Università system was a *sine qua non* of the success of his administration.[191] Ball's difficulties in both acquiring cheap grain and balancing the budget were the central anxieties of the Administration whilst Coleridge held office. It is, thus, important to examine the Università in some detail.

The Role of the Università

The Università of Valletta was a municipal corporation, with local government functions, that formerly operated under the control of the Grandmasters who received monthly accounts of its transactions.[192] One of its primary functions, and the one with which we are presently concerned, was to control a *monopoly* upon the purchase and supply of grain, as well as other staple food items, including meat,[193] and oils. Traditionally, after the annual harvest, the Università would despatch buyers to neighbouring countries, principally Sicily, to purchase grain, which was placed in public granaries and sold at a fixed price. The grain was retailed to the Maltese population via designated shopkeepers. This system had come into existence

---

191   Funds derived from the importation and selling grain, whether as surplus on sales or on taxes derived on grain imports, provided a major source of government revenue until 1939: See Bartolo.
192   Bartolo, ibid, citing Muscat, 98. See also Thornton (1836).
193   After 1800, the Università began to trade in cattle to meet the demand from the increasing numbers of British military and other personnel on the Island: Thornton, ibid., 39-41.

because it was recognised that international mercantile trade would ensure that the grain needed to feed the Maltese would be sold in countries where better returns could be obtained. This would leave the Maltese population vulnerable to famine, unless they were able to pay the higher prices. As Ball reported, in 1800, this was a particular risk to the "labouring poor";[194] and in the words of the 1812 Royal Commission a "permanent abundance" of grain was absolutely necessary.[195] The government-controlled monopoly enabled the State to buy the required quantity, on the international market, and then control the retail price to ensure that the abundant supply of grain was marketed at an affordable price, in the domestic market.[196]

The Order had once been able to achieve a long-term balanced budget by retailing the grain at a higher price than the purchase price when this could be afforded. In other words, the cost of subsidy in some years was off-set by the surpluses in other years. However, there was a structural flaw in the way the system was organised. The Jurats fixed the prices at which grain could be *bought* whilst the government fixed the *sale* price.[197] This system meant that the government could not require a surplus to be achieved unless it gave clear directions as to the maximum purchase price to be paid. This division of responsibility was a fundamental weakness in the management of the Università.The Università had also operated as a public bank, receiving deposits in return for which it paid interest of three per cent per annum from the surpluses it made upon the grain monopoly. The deposits were used as capital with which to acquire the grain. But the private capital of the Island had other uses, too. For example, it was used by the Order for public works and defence. The problem for the British, after 1800, was that these deposits, belonging to perhaps one thousand depositors, had been plundered by the French during the occupation. The victims included many private individuals whose livelihoods depended upon the interest payments and whose impoverished circumstances was causing political embarrassment. Convents and other religious bodies

194   Ball's to Dundas, above, n. 5.
195   In 1822, British policy makers in the Colonial Office were finally persuaded by local commercial interests to abolish the monopoly. This was surprising if only because the Università had, by this time, become profitable and provided revenue to support the welfare schemes which the government that were implemented through the charitable institutions. Notwithstanding the consequences of the loss of revenue, the monopoly was dissolved, whereupon the supply of grain fell into the hands of a private cartel, which was highly damaging to the public interest. Eventually the monopoly had to be restored: see Pirotta, Chapter 5.
196   Thornton (1816).
197   Ibid.

also gained the majority of their revenue from accrued interest, and they, too, were now in difficulty.[198] Confidence in the Bank had collapsed and so British funds had to be used to underwrite the Bank as well as to fund the purchase of grain. As we shall discover, the confiscation and its consequences were to create significant problems for British administrators, including Coleridge.[199]

The difficulty facing the British administration (of which it does not appears to have been fully aware) was that, in the eighteenth century, the Università system had sunk into perpetual decline, incapable of achieving a long-term balanced budget. The Grandmasters of the Order had subsidised grain so heavily, since about 1740, that the Università was insolvent even before the French invasion.[200] In some years, the sale price of the grain had been only one quarter of the cost price.[201] The Order had also raided the capital deposited by the inhabitants rather than draw upon the Maltese Treasury, and this accelerated the Università's decline. For example, the Knights relied upon the deposits to shore up the funding of other institutions, and the welfare system.[202] Notwithstanding these fatal, structural problems, the Università system continued until the French invasion.

Thornton, the careful and authoritative official who became Auditor-General in Malta charged with the arrear-audit of every Maltese public institution, reported, in 1816, that the deficit was in excess of one million *scudi* (£100,000) by the time of the French invasion.[203] It is difficult to believe that Ball was not aware of these critical difficulties when he decided to revive the Università in 1800. But if he was, indeed, aware of the problems, his insistence, in despatches, that the Università had delivered an annual surplus, even in the later years of the Order, seems inexplicable.[204] It placed

198   Eton to Sullivan, 29 July 1801, Kew, CO 158/2/308.
199   See especially, the taxation theme in Chapter 5.
200   See generally the account of the Royal Commission of 1812, above n. 37, and Thornton (1816, 1836).
201   Grain was bought for 60 scudi and sold for 15 scudi: Royal Commission, above n. 37, or 16 scudi, per Thornton (1816). These losses, according to the Commission, went on increasing.
202   The value of loans made by the Università to the Exchequer exceeded £65,000: Bonnici, 128.
203   Thornton (1816), and further Bartolo, who comments on the reliability of Thornton's data. The assessment of the Royal Commissioners was that the deficit was about a million and a half scudi or about £150,000. Thornton thought that the deficit was about one million scudi by the date of the French invasion (June 1798). By September 1800, the Bank had debts "upwards of three and a half million scudi" (£350,000): Thornton, (1816), 5-7.
204   By 1801 Hobart had somehow come to believe that the Università "produces

his financial strategy for the Island upon the most precarious of footings because he committed himself to spending on popular projects without having the resources to fund them. This placed his administration in a straitjacket which he hoped to escape by speculation on the grain market. The project involved using British Treasury funds to purchase a year's worth of cheap grain from Russia and then selling it at a profit within Malta and elsewhere. The surplus would, he hoped, substantially remove the Island's deficit.

In the end, Ball miscalculated; the mission inflicted severe damage upon the Island's finances, and he fell back upon unpopular taxation and economies – the latter of which seem to have been only intermittently pursued. In this respect the guiding policies that his administration followed seem to have been ill-considered or, at least, poorly implemented.

The grain mission of 1804-5

"up the Black Sea to the mouth of the Dnieper"[205]

Ball's predictions, of a financial surplus to be realised from grain speculation, had hardened into a firm political expectation for which, as the Secretary of State made clear, Ball would be accountable. No further funds to support the Università would be forthcoming from the British Treasury. Politically, the venture was required to succeed in the manner that Ball had, unwisely, predicted that it would.[206] He now had to remove the Island's deficit and deliver upon the Report he had made to Dundas in 1800.

As it turned out, the grain mission was poorly executed, and the débacle was one for which the Jurats were made scapegoats and dismissed.[207] The wheat purchased by Chapman had been of a "soft" or "tender" variety that

---

considerable revenue". Hardman, 354. The erroneous impression that the Order had made a surplus on the grain monopoly still influenced the actions of the Secretary of State in 1805: see Cooke to Ball, 27 March 1805, Kew, CO 159/3/162.

205   To Mrs S. T. Coleridge, 12 December 1804, ^{CL} 2,1158.

206   Camden to Ball, 24 February 1804, Kew, CO 159/3/121-2.

207   According to Borg, the dismissals took place on 23 July 1806: Borg to Eton 23 July 1806, CO 158/12 (no folio reference). This is corroborated by NAM LIBR PS02/02, 138-9, 23 July 1806. On that date, Charles Livingstone was also appointed as a replacement Jurat. Ball regarded Borg as a "subversive" not least because Borg had openly advocated the establishment of "a congress to make laws for the Island". He had been deprived of his public office (as a Luogotenente) in 1804. Ball to Windham, 28 February 1807, Kew, CO 158/13/25; also Ball to Penn, July 1804, Kew, CO 158/9/7.

was liable to decompose when shipped and which, in any event, could not be stored longer than five or six months.[208] It was quite unsuitable given that the wheat was to safeguard the Island's needs for one year.[209] Ball ignored the Jurats' advice, that the newly arrived grain was only fit for animal fodder. They were ordered to release the wheat into the market.[210] The oversupply of decomposing grain meant that the market prices that it fetched were much lower than anticipated. The poor quality of bread, made from the bad wheat, caused political disquiet.[211] Most importantly, the evident failure of the mission damaged the administration's reputation and added to the financial problems of the Università and, thus, of the Island.[212]

Moreover, it is possible that Coleridge might have been partly responsible for what happened, since the Public Secretary's role included giving directions to the Jurats. Although Coleridge seems to have left the Island

208　See Ball to Windham, 28 February 1807, Kew, CO 158/13/78, also Livingstone to Ball, 25 February 1807, Kew, CO 158/13/203.
209　Ball had impressed upon Camden that this was the amount required, and the Secretary of State signalled his acquiescence: See E. Cooke to Ball 27 March 1805, Kew, CO 159/3/162.
210　See Eton to Windham 11 October 1806, Kew, CO 158/12/ (no folio reference).
211　E.g. Borg to Eton, 30 May 1806, Kew, CO 158/12 no folio reference. Borg lists a number of causes of popular displeasure with Ball, including "the bad quality of the bread". In his response to the Secretary of State, Ball flatly denied that there was dissatisfaction. He stated that the inhabitants were "extremely well satisfied" to purchase a staple food at low prices: Ball to Windham, 28 February 1807, Kew, CO 158/13/58-9.
212　Ball seems to have tried to cover up the disaster. At first, he reported to London that Chapman's consignment had generated a "saving to government" of £21,957: Ball to Cooke, 1 February 1806, Kew, CO 158/11/9. By 1807, Ball's language had subtly altered. He then reported that the profit stated to have been made by the Università in 1805-1806 was £12,033: Ball to Shee, 12 May 1807, Kew, CO 158/13/315. The true picture was very different. Thornton described it as a costly failure being "by far the greatest loss that [the Università] had then, or since, sustained". Thornton (1816). His investigation revealed a loss in excess of 805,000 scudi (about £80, 500) for the financial year 1805-1806. Thus, almost all of the British taxpayer's capital investment in the scheme was wasted. Ball's obfuscations may have succeeded and delayed the moment when Ministers became convinced of the truth. This is so because Chapman (conveniently sent home on sick leave in June 1806) was rewarded by the Secretary of State with a £1000 payment for his services. Had his negligence been understood such a generous reward would have been unlikely: Castlereagh to Ball, 8 May 1807, Kew, CO 159/3/227. Within Malta, the Jurats were publicly made scapegoats and Ball dismissed them en bloc: see Borg to Eton 23 July 1806, Kew, CO 158/12 (no folio reference): and further, n. 207 above. Coleridge's role in the affair remains somewhat unclear.

by the time the grain arrived,[213] he might have been expected to have begun planning for its arrival during 1805. This is so because, as early as February 1805, both he and Ball expected Chapman's imminent return.[214] Since the storage capacity of the Island could not be increased without significant advanced planning (especially given the occupation of the granaries by the troops destined for the planned expeditionary operation under Lieutenant-General Sir James Craig) it, perhaps, says something of Coleridge's period in office that nothing appears to have been done either by him or the pro-Seggretario, Giuseppe Zammit, to ensure that the imminently expected grain could be properly stored when it reached Valletta.

The Civil Service: Ball's Staffing Policies

The "wide-branching tree of patronage".[215]

Ball's staffing strategy altered, in a number of ways, the established principles of the Order. Appointments to government offices under the *ancien regime* had been a reward to the Knights for military valour but, as operations against the Turks declined, the system under the Order degenerated into one based upon intrigue and patronage.[216] Notoriously, their administration had excluded the Maltese from power.

Ball continued the principles of patronage, but, in contrast to the Order, he favoured appointing Maltese to public office. In particular, he wanted to use his patronage to reward loyalists[217] and to demonstrate to any influential

---

213   Allegations about the quality of bread and the diminution in the weight of a loaf referred to the entire period Coleridge held office: Borg to Eton, 30 May 1806, Kew, CO 158/12.

214   Ball to Camden, Kew, CO 158/10/1, 30 January 1805, in which Ball informed Camden of Mr Macaulay's death. He continued, "I expect Mr Chapman daily from Constantinople, whom I shall put into the office of Public Secretary and Treasurer in conformity to the Orders sent me by the Earl of Buckinghamshire". Coleridge wrote in similar terms to Robert Southey, 2 February 1805, ^{CL} 2, 1163.

215   *The Friend*, I, 568.

216   Hardman, Chapter 1.

217   The system of reward extended to any public office in Ball's grant. For example, upon its revival in October 1800, he appointed one of the leading insurrectionists, Canon Saverio Caruana, as Rector of the University. The dominant motive in this appointment seems to have been to reward a loyal individual rather than a desire to promote education. This is so because the University could not thrive without a system of popular education to underpin it and from which it could derive its students. Instead, private education was available for the few who could afford it. Ball took no steps to introduce a public system. See for Coleridge's views on the importance of mass education: *The Friend*, I, 540; also Debono (1996), 47-74. Caruana's appoint-

citizens, tempted to agitate against British rule, that loyalty carried notable benefits. Coleridge gave his support to this policy.[218]

Ball's insistence upon his right to make appointments produced tension with Whitehall, because British officials did not wish to relinquish their own powers of patronage.[219] Nevertheless, Ball pressed on; in fact, there is evidence that he must have moved quite rapidly to achieve his goals: Coleridge recorded, with approval, that by 1804-1805 each civil appointment, apart from the Public Secretary and the Civil Commissioner (both appointed by ministers in Whitehall), was held by a Maltese.[220] Subject to the exceptions mentioned, he inferred that both senior and junior posts had native Maltese office-holders by that date. However, he appears to have overlooked the fact that that there were a number of Englishmen who staffed Ball's private office.

Amongst a number of consequences, the already large Civil Service now grew further as Ball increased the staffing compliment by the appointment of local Maltese. This further increased the costs of government and with it the need to generate more revenue.

The new appointments also posed a number of questions about competence and effectiveness. One such question related to the depth of technical expertise and administrative experience in the new administration. The Heads of Department under the *ancien regime* had, largely, been recruited from the Knights. Most of these experienced administrators had left the Island in 1798, and those that remained were no longer in post. Ball's policy, in effect, replaced these experienced experts using criteria other than their lack of fitness for office. It was a policy that would reap sour rewards because, given new office-holders' lack of professionalism, the need for effective systems of scrutiny and systematic financial reporting was all the greater. The weakness in such systems was a cardinal failure of Ball's administration generally, and it was a problem which Coleridge seemed unable to resolve.

Ball's willingness to delegate important matters to the Maltese officials was not unqualified. One example of this emerges in Coleridge's important

---

ment is a revealing one that speaks volumes of Ball's real concerns. As we shall see, his policy implanted deep structural flaws into the Maltese administration.

218   *The Friend*, I, 569; see also Table Talk I, 475, 16 April 1834.
219   See Coleridge's discussion in *The Friend*, I, 568-9. Hobart to Ball, 2 December 1803, Kew, CO 158/7/443-7 reveals that Ball was ordered to find a suitable post for one M. Viale.
220   *The Friend*, I, 568.

Proclamation of 22 March 1805[221] which, as we shall see, was concerned with the regulation of spirits. It was, no doubt, intended to prevent disorder and drunkenness amongst the large number of British troops who had arrived on the Island in readiness for an impending attack upon Sicily. Whilst certain wholesalers were licensed by the President of the Grand Court of Valletta, the shopkeepers, pub owners and manufacturers all fell under the direct control of the Civil Commissioner. Clearly, trust in Maltese officials only went so far. Ball was under pressure from the military and needed to maintain a close supervision of the premises where soldiers could consume alcohol. He was right to be concerned because, as we shall see, alcohol-related violence between soldiers and civilians was to lead to at least one fatal stabbing in 1805.

A further problem was cultural. Coleridge informs us that the Maltese appointees of high social standing, most of whom seem to have been rewarded for loyalty, accepted public office as "honourable distinctions".[222] Certainly, the early British administrations brought into the civil service a number of individuals who were, subsequently, judged to be "too old, infirm or from other causes incompetent in their duties".[223] One Maltese complained that "(p)laces are given not to the honest or meritorious but through favour to the worst people".[224] Record-keeping and correspondence was neglected as letters not requiring an immediate response were thrown on the floor.[225] These criticisms suggest that some, perhaps many, of the appointees were either not interested in becoming active professional administrators or were ineffective for other reasons. Their lax approach to government business may furnish some explanation for both the lamentable state of the accounts,[226] and the poor record of financial accountability uncovered by the 1812 Royal Commission.

---

221 See the consumer protection theme in Chapter 5.
222 *The Friend*, I, 569.
223 Maitland to Bathurst, 24 October 1814, Kew, CO 158/ 25/210.
224 Borg to Eton, 30 May 1806, Kew, CO 158/12 no folio reference.
225 Mark, *At Sea with Nelson*, 125 quoted in Laferla, vol I, 48 and Pirotta, 65.
226 See Thornton (1816) at 9 who discovered that the only accounting record of the Jurats were the ledgers "supported by a journal and other auxiliary books". The ledger operated a double entry system, but when the book failed to balance the accountant failed to close the account or, alternatively, made fictitious entries to make the books appear to balance.

English Officials

The establishment, in 1803, of the Court of Vice-Admiralty, staffed by English lawyers, added to the small number of British office-holders who provided close assistance to Ball.[227] This group established a small, but influential, society of English expatriates which did not, it seems, mix socially with the Maltese. Curiously, there is some evidence that Ball may actually have been unenthusiastic about English officials forging social relationships with the inhabitants.[228] Borg reported to Eton that Ball "laboured to prevent friendships and acquaintance between Maltese and English". Certainly, Sultana has noted that Coleridge did not appear to have made a single friend amongst the Maltese during his year and a half stay on the Island. If Borg's somewhat surprising assertion is correct, the explanation may be that fraternisation was officially discouraged.

It would be surprising if Coleridge agreed with any such policy. He had noted, and strongly disapproved of, the habits of the English to reach hasty, irrational, judgements about the local population. He condemned the tendency to overlook the virtues in vices, and to show intolerance for different customs and lifestyle.[229] However, he lamented. in *The Friend* that, in general, the British behaved with *hauteur* showing insolence to and contempt for the local population – views that he also expressed in conversation with John Coleridge.[230] Blaquière also noted a "marked and mutual coldness" between natives and the British.[231] Mistrust of the British on the part of the Maltese may, of course, have had its origins in the Treaty of Amiens in which, according to Maltese opinion, Britain had revealed its willingness to sacrifice its wartime ally in order to further its own selfish interests. The marked coldness is also consistent with the rising unpopularity of the Administration in 1805. It is to that issue that we now return.

---

227   The key figures have been noted in Chapter 1.
228   Borg to Eton, 30 May 1806, Kew, CO 58/12/ no folio reference.
229   *The Friend*, I, 555-7. Whether Coleridge acted on this can be questioned, especially in his vitriolic reaction to the Catholic Church and its rituals.
230   Talker, 158-60, quoted in Holmes (1998), 247.
231   Blaquière.

2.5. The Public Reputation of the British Administration 1802-1806

"... the very clamors of the market-place were hushed at [Ball's] entrance".[232]

As we shall discover, Coleridge's Bandi and Avvisi served a number of political purposes which went far beyond law-making or drawing the attention of the public to some particular issue of public importance. Coleridge used these instruments as propaganda tools that were intended both to influence Maltese opinion and to change behaviour and attitudes. These instruments reveal a systematic political agenda to enhance the public reputation of the Civil Commissioner and to persuade the Maltese to accept otherwise unpalatable measures. How Coleridge achieved this is discussed in Chapters 5 and 6, but for present purposes it is important to outline why Ball's administration in 1805 was losing public confidence.

The orthodox account of this period in Maltese history is dominated by a narrative strongly influenced by the British establishment.[233] According to this account, complaints about Ball's government in 1805 were orchestrated by known agitators, organised and assisted by William Eton, the Superintendant of Quarantine.[234] Many of these individuals had grievances against Ball.

Although, at first, the complaints were taken seriously and investigated, (inflicting temporary damage to Ball's reputation) Ball's superiors in London eventually exonerated the Civil Commissioner. They satisfied themselves that Ball had presided over an effective and popular government. The substance of the complaints was thus dismissed as scurrilous and seditious.

First, it will be argued that this account is not supported by the wider historical record and secondly that, in any event, the conclusions reached, in 1808, contained a *non-sequitur*. It is true that many of the complaints were, as the British concluded, maliciously motivated, but it did not follow that they were, *ipso facto,* false. A more thorough investigation would have revealed that many of them could have been independently corroborated. Thus, it will be suggested that the William Eton's[235] known personal agenda,

---

232 *The Friend*, I, 566.
233 See Hardman and most recently Staines.
234 See n. 73 above.
235 Eton was eventually dismissed from his office as Superintendant of the Quarantine in Malta: Liverpool to Oakes, 18 September 1811, Hardman, 503. His allegations against the Ball's administration were then seen as "calumnies": Oakes to

in discrediting Ball, allowed Ball's superiors to marginalise the damaging allegations in order to re-establish the reputation of its government in Malta. In that way damage to Britain's standing as a colonial power was conveniently avoided. Thus, it was Eton, now regarded as "a most dangerous man",[236] who was eventually dismissed from public office, and not Ball.[237]

Coleridge's period in office took place during Ball's second administration. As a Royal Navy Captain, Ball, acting in the name of the Kingdom of the Two Sicilies, had administered the islands during the siege and blockade between 1799 and 1800. There is little doubt that in doing so, Ball won public support.[238] After having shared the privations of the long siege of Valletta the inhabitants had composed the Maltese national song in his honour.[239] In *The Friend* Coleridge went to some lengths to recount how fond a regard the Maltese had for "father Ball". In the poorest houses, he recorded that two pictures were inevitably found: the Virgin and Child together with a portrait of Ball.[240] According to Coleridge, the market place in Valletta fell into a reverential hush at Ball's passing. [241]

And the affection was not merely a personal admiration of one administrator. When Ball was replaced by Cameron in 1801 we learn that the latter was greeted by the inhabitants as a "Messiah". The British were at first warmly received as liberators from the tyranny of the Order of St John and the French.

Coleridge was convinced that during his second administration, following his recall to the islands in 1802, Ball had public confidence. He recorded that Ball had unlocked the fetters of political oppression which, of course, implied that the inhabitants, under Ball's regime, enjoyed a new political freedom.[242] As we shall discover, it is doubtful whether the Maltese shared this assessment.

A more convincing account is that, after the Treaty of Amiens, 1802, (which even Coleridge regarded as a "betrayal" of the Maltese[243]) the

---

Liverpool, 1 August 1811, Kew CO 158/17. See generally, Staines, Essay 06.

236   Oakes to Bunbury, 30 July 1811, Kew, CO 158/17.
237   Liverpool to Oakes, 18 September 1811, Hardman, 503.
238   Maltese officials sent numerous expressions of gratitude to Ball on his quitting office: see Hardman, 343-4.
239   *The Friend*, I, 566.
240   Ibid.
241   Ibid.
242   Ibid.
243   Ibid., 571.

political context became more challenging and called for a broader range of political skills than those previously required. Friction between the inhabitants and the Administration had increased.

The effect of the Treaty of Amiens upon the relationship between the governors and the governed cannot be over-stated. From the British point of view, the French offer to discontinue hostilities if Malta was returned to the Order of St John under the protection of Russia seemed attractive. However, this settlement was acutely unpopular in Malta. Cameron, the first British Civil Commissioner, reported to Lord Hobart that a mere rumour of the agreement "has occasioned most violent fermentation" locally.[244] The Maltese remonstrated that, as France had confiscated the French property of the Knights in 1792, in effect, France would have an indirect control of Malta.[245] They were also concerned about possible reprisals against their people.

These objections were swept aside because the benefit to Britain was thought to outweigh the concerns of the Maltese. In an attempt to force the British into a *volte face* the Maltese, on 15 June 1802, issued a Declaration of Rights[246] declaring that the "King of the United Kingdom of Great Britain and Ireland is our Sovereign Lord, and his lawful successors shall, in all times to come, be acknowledged as our lawful sovereign". The purpose of this was to try to prevent Britain renouncing possession of the islands.

As matters turned out, the Treaty was never implemented; Britain retained possession and, in response to the British refusal to evacuate, France resumed hostilities in May 1803. But the damage to Maltese public opinion had been done. The inhabitants had seen that Britain was capable of "sacrificing" Malta when its own interests demanded it.[247] To make matters worse, the British were dragging their heels over prize money that had been promised to the Maltese following the capture of Valletta, and were thought to have breached faith with the inhabitants who had served in the Maltese military. This was, eventually, to provide another administrative burden for Coleridge.[248] Complaints about the terms of the French surrender, under which it was alleged that Britain had not taken up an offer by the French commander to compensate those whose property

244   Cameron to Hobart, 23 October 1801, Kew, CO 158/1/335.
245   Hardman, 410-15.
246   Widely reproduced; see, for example, Cm 9657 Appendix F; Frendo.
247   Lord Hobart replied to the Maltese Deputies to London in a letter dated 20 April 1802 that the abandonment of Malta was "an indispensable sacrifice": Hardman, 412.
248   See Chapter 5.2: Distributions of the Prize.

had been looted, also formed a part of the context at this period.[249] A mutually cynical relationship seems to have evolved in which the Maltese took what they could from Britain until their conquerors should once again abandon them. [250]

The immediate consequence of the Treaty of Amiens was to stimulate an invigorated Nationalist campaign for political pluralism to gain some measure of self-determination. After 1802 the calls for the "restoration" by the British of the *Consiglio Popolare* – a popular council which the Maltese alleged had deliberative and legislative powers – became more evident. This campaign also included an assertion that the British had reneged upon their promise to restore the traditional constitution (which included, they argued, the *Consiglio*). The British emphatically rejected both arguments and steadfastly refused to share power with the Maltese.[251] These and other frustrations were undoubtedly coming to a head in the spring of 1805.

Crime remained high, most notably highway robbery and burglary in the countryside. The murder rate was also a concern, combined with low levels of detection and prosecution.[252] Moreover, the British had reversed a centuries old policy of prohibiting Jews from settling on Malta. Jewish immigrants had begun to arrive in late 1804 and, by 1805, many had set up in business as rivals to the Maltese. This was causing resentment amongst the small traders of Valletta who were afraid that competition might return them to poverty just as the economy lifted from depression. Underlying trade anxieties boiled over into violent public disorder in May 1805. As we shall discover, suspected Jews were stoned, and two thousand demonstrators poured down the main street in Valletta. The demonstration was, of course, heading to the seat of government, which signalled that the Maltese held the British responsible. The situation was, as Coleridge later admitted, a "difficult emergency".[253] We shall return to this in relation to public order and crime.

To restore order Ball directed the judiciary to impose more severe sentences than the Code de Rohan permitted – a controversial political intervention in the judicial process that caused consternation amongst the Islanders. The sentence of life-long exile that was imposed upon a twelve

---

249   See Appendix 2.
250   Corrupt practices were later identified: Maitland to Bathurst, 24 October 1814, CO 158/25/209, et seq.
251   Hardman, 498-9.
252   Borg to Eton, Kew, 30 May 1806, Kew, CO 158/12/ no folio reference.
253   *The Friend*, I, 544.

year old boy, who had been implicated in the disturbances, must have added to the accusations (albeit accusations from well-known political opponents) that Ball's government exercised "thundering vengeance" and despotic powers.

Moreover, serious problems in feeding the population were also emerging. As we have seen, Ball had staked much of the financial strategy upon the success of the grain mission. Following the decay of the imported wheat, the Maltese now grumbled about unfit bread.

There had also been a breach of faith when the British re-imposed the excise duty on wine and to initiate a further duty on liquor in March 1805. The potentially inflammatory *volte face* emanated directly from Ball's failure to grasp the financial condition of the islands in 1800. The repercussions were damaging. At about this time (March 1805) it appears that one of the Nationalists decided to petition the Civil Commissioner. Most likely, this sought political reform – a power-sharing between British and Maltese by means of a representative assembly – the *Consiglio Popolare*. Notwithstanding that the Maltese constitution allowed individual citizens to petition on *any* subject, a report reached London that Ball had summarily exiled the petitioner.[254] This uncompromising denial of structured political pluralism meant that the Maltese had no lawful avenue to pursue their political grievances; indeed, it was this ruthless crushing of political expression taken with the politically-motivated interventions in criminal trials held after the anti-Semitic uprising that eventually featured strongly in the flurry of complaints to the Secretary of State in London. Frustrated and angry Nationalists petitioned Lord Windham arguing that they should be able to by-pass Ball and send their grievances directly to the King.[255] Revealingly, the petition stated that, if this direct channel were permitted, those who sought to re-establish the *Consiglio Popolare* could make their

---

254 *Memorial and Petition of the Maltese* (unsigned and undated): Kew, CO 158/10/151 et seq. No record of it appears in the *Memoriali e Decreti of the Segnatura*. So the petition must have been made directly to the Civil Commissioner.

255   Ibid. The petition sought "some channel thro' which the Maltese might state (either in a body or individually) grievances without the risk of being banished to the Coast of Barbary, or otherwise punished if their petitions are intercepted". Other grievances included: (i) failure to establish the Consiglio Popolare; (ii) freedom from torture; (iii) that no-one should be punished without trial; (iv) the trial judge should be under no control other than the law-i.e. not subject to the direction of the Civil Commissioner; (v) that sentences should be mitigated, but not augmented by the Commissioner (pronounced in open court) and not first submitted to the Civil Commissioner.

argument for it *without the risk of banishment to the coast of Barbary.*[256] Moreover, the complainants argued for laws to be reformed so that no person could be punished without trial and that sentences should only be pronounced by the judge in open court, without the prior approval of the Civil Commissioner.

These and others complaints were legitimate grievances and not the fanciful inventions of disappointed individuals. Ball *did* interfere in the sentences of the criminal courts;[257] the corn mission *had* failed and, (according to the Jurats), the bread *was* bad;[258] crime rates *were* high and detection rates low (because of reluctant witnesses and community solidarity); the government was nervous about friction and resentments arising from the new tax burden. Moreover, disgruntled citizens flooded the *Segnatura* with a significant number of petitions complaining that they had been unjustly denied their share of the promised prize money. This volume of litigation disclosed grave policy misjudgements in encouraging and then frustrating Maltese expectations. Dissatisfaction also simmered over the collapse of the cotton markets; there were tensions over military enlistments, the hunting down of deserters from the Royal Regiment of Malta, the wasted expenditure, Ball's civil service staffing policy, and the diminution in the weight of bread.[259]

To make matters worse, Eton had (with some justification) written in the strongest possible terms to Windham (the Secretary of State) condemning Ball's "shameful speculation" on the grain market and, in effect, accusing him of abusing the unfettered powers of his Office. He called for Ball's immediate recall on grounds of incompetence and financial mismanagement.[260] By mid 1806 graffiti lampooning Ball and his administration appeared all over Valletta and one complainant, albeit a member of Eton's cabal, wrote:

"Country people have no faith in Ball. His bad conduct has produced this effect. No one shews (sic) him any respect in the streets, neither in town nor

---

256   Petition of the Maltese, ibid.
257   See Chapter 5.4: Public Order and Crime. The recommendation of the Royal Commission of 1812 that the Civil Commissioner should lose the power to interfere in the judicial process vindicates the complaints made in this respect: Kew, CO 158/19.
258   Ball denied the quality of the bread was poor, but the denial is unconvincing given that the wheat had deteriorated: Ball to Windham, 28 February 1807, Kew, CO 158/13.
259   Borg to Eton, 30 May 1806, Kew, CO 158/12. It is interesting to note the complaint that the Maltese had suffered bad bread for the previous thirty months.
260   Eton to Windham, 13 March 1806, Kew, CO 158/12/245.

country…[t]hey tremble at his despotic scourge".[261]

If this allegation is true then it is unsurprising, given the inevitable frictional effects of the policy failings described above. The suggestion that Ball's administration was competent and effective in the years 1805-1806 lacks credibility.

Thus, notwithstanding the eulogistic narrative of Ball's administration that Coleridge promoted in *The Friend*, the wider historical record bears witness to the mounting problems of unpopularity that Ball and Coleridge faced. Confidence in the British administration at this time was in a rapid and steep decline.

In fact, evidence of a damaging loss of public confidence in the administration is corroborated in Coleridge's official work. The emerging popular resentment and unpopularity of the Civil Commissioner explains why Coleridge, in the Bandi and Avvisi, undertook, as we shall see, an effective and systematic public relations offensive to boost Ball's image and to restore Ball's reputation and public standing. This is explored in Chapters 5 and 6.

Coleridge's later accounts suggest that this project continued after he left Malta. It seems that he still experienced a loyalty both to the Maltese colonial project and to his late colleague, the Civil Commissioner.

There is little doubt that Ball had once enjoyed, as Coleridge claimed, an excess of gratitude from the Maltese,[262] but this was likely to have been a legacy of days when he administered the Island during the struggle against the French (1799-1800). The British betrayal of Malta, in the Treaty of Amiens, had marked a change and the popular mood gradually became one of disillusionment and disappointment. Coleridge's period of office occurred at a time of crisis. As Public Secretary, it fell to him to frame the government's political message and to win back popular support whilst loyally implementing measures (such as re-imposed taxation) that were widely disliked. If Malta were to be retained as a British possession, the consent of the Maltese had to be maintained, so Coleridge's role was of strategic significance. Hitherto, this onerous burden of responsibility has not been fully understood. Nevertheless, it goes some way to explaining Coleridge's exhaustion whilst in office. Much was expected of him and he had to deliver.

During his time as Public Secretary Coleridge struggled to work within,

261   Borg to Eton, 30 May 1806, Kew, CO 158/12/ no folio reference.
262   *The Friend*, I, 566.

and make popular, ill-judged, counter-productive and contradictory politics: to maintain the welfare system, whilst avoiding taxation; to "attach" the Maltese to British rule whilst crushing political expression; to continue the Constitution whilst, in fact, breaching it; to pursue popularity whilst punishing opposition, even amongst children; and, in the face of these actions, to surround Ball with a propaganda myth of wise, benign and prelatic authority.

At this time the intractable conflict between liberty and empire that had been exposed in the American Revolution was far from resolved. The experience of the early British administrations on the Island revealed that the "continuity" model of government, both in conception and implementation, posed significant challenges to the provincial administration.

Coleridge's talent, as we shall see, was not in the skilful drafting of legal norms, but in sensitive, but crucial, political engagement with the Maltese people. In the Bandi and Avvisi the Administration spoke directly to them, and in this work Coleridge (from the British point of view) stood out as particularly talented.

Eventually, the damaging complaints,[263] from Eton and his fellow agitators forced Windham to demand Ball's formal response to the "serious charges" they alleged.[264] After Ball had, in 1807, provided his answer to the allegations,[265] the Secretary of State delayed forming an early opinion about the standard of public administration; Ball had to be content with a holding reply.[266] It seems that, in official eyes, Ball had been tarnished and his superiors were uncertain how to respond. However, no thorough investigation was stimulated by these complaints until after Ball's death. However, once it emerged that Eton was a vindictive troublemaker, his and the other complaints lost credibility. This presented a useful exit strategy for Ball's superiors. In 1808, almost a year after the holding reply, Ball was formally exonerated.[267] The Establishment had finally decided to close ranks.Ball's reputation in Malta was also to recover. Improved economic prosperity, political stability and improving government finances were,

---

263   Even Ball thought that he would be removed from office: Ball to Graham, 14 September 1806, NLM 441.
264   Windham to Ball, 6 January 1807, Kew, CO 159/3/220 at 223. For Ball's sustained rebuttal to the allegations made against him see Ball to Windham, 28 February 1807, CO 158/13/9 et seq. Investigations continued and Windham delayed offering a formal response: see Cooke to Ball, 4 May 1807, Kew, CO 159/3/226.
265   Ball to Windham, 28 February 1807, Kew, CO 158/13/9 et seq.
266   Cooke to Ball, 4 May 1807, above n. 264.
267   Cooke to Ball, 5 April 1808, Kew, CO 159/3.

perhaps, Ball's legacy after his early demise in October 1809.[268] Even concerns over Ball's intervention in the criminal process eventually faded, for the Maltese Deputies summarised Ball's achievement in government as "substituting *a just and paternal Government* in the place of a revolutionary regency (i.e. France)".[269] (Emphasis added). But this cannot disguise how difficult the years 1805-1806 had been; and this period coincided, very closely, with Coleridge's term of office, which meant that the burden of dealing with it fell upon his shoulders as well as upon Ball's. If this period of difficulty eventually proved to be a temporary crisis, it was, nonetheless, a grave one. There's no doubt that Coleridge is due some credit for the administration's success in the field of government communication, which must not only have played some part in re-building popular trust in the Civil Commissioner, but also in achieving stable government in Malta.

---

268   See comments of the Royal Commissioners of 1812, Kew, above n. 37.
269   Letter of the so called "Deputies of the Nation" to the acting Public Secretary, Chapman, 22 December 1809, Hardman, 508.

3. The Constitutional Position of the Civil Commissioner

Introduction

Coleridge occupied the office of Public Secretary, "Segretario Publico dell'Isole di Malta, Gozo e delle loro dipendenze'. This office was the channel through which all the civil administration of the islands and all the policies of the British Civil Commissioners were put into effect.[1] His legal authority to act in that office came from the authority of the Civil Commissioner, Sir Alexander Ball. Ball was a British official exercising, indirectly, upon authority from London, powers recognised under English law as flowing from the Royal Prerogative. Ball's authority also came from the considerable prerogatives of the Grandmaster whose powers the British officials took over after the British occupation began in 1800[2]. In these capacities it was Ball who exercised the legislative, law making power (formally and actually) in Malta. Coleridge advised, drafted and signed the instruments (the Bandi and Avvisi) but political and legal responsibility for these, and for actions taken under them, lay with Ball. In this chapter we will explore issues relating to the constitutional and legal position of Ball in his capacity as a British official albeit one exercising the powers of a Grandmaster. Those powers were, potentially, despotic and the general theme of this chapter is the nature and degree of the limits and controls imposed, not only politically, but also, and in particular, by the rule of law, on the exercise of these powers by a British official. There are actions by Ball in which Coleridge, if only by being Public Secretary, is implicated and which were politically, but also legally, problematic. Political accountability for such actions, under the new approach to colonial government that the

---

1 Caruana.
2 The role of the Grandmasters in areas such as welfare policies and the law is discussed in Chapter 2.

British had adopted, was not, it seems, very effective. Legal accountability, on the other hand, was, at least in principle, more rigorous. There could have been challenges to Ball's actions, not in the Maltese courts but in the courts in London, applying English law to the position of a Civil Commissioner. On a number of points, such as the way he sometimes intervened in the judicial process, Ball could have been vulnerable to such action. In fact, though, no such cases were brought.

3.1. Colonial Policy and the Civil Commissioner

Introduction

A Civil Commissioner was appointed in Malta in order to meet Maltese concerns about being subjected to military rule and, thereby, to try to confirm Maltese allegiance to the British Crown. Following the capitulation of the French garrison, in September 1800,[3] the British government considered the possession of Malta in predominantly military terms, as a base for the defence of British military and commercial interests in the Levant and, in particular, for blocking any renewed threat to Egypt. The military government, that had been established under Major-General Pigot, was, for a time, considered sufficient to meet these British aims and to provide a stable and effective government for the Maltese. For many Maltese, however, a military government was unsatisfactory. It might threaten those liberties that they had enjoyed in practice under the Grandmaster and, also, those that might be anticipated under British rule. From aboard his ship, Ball wrote to Dundas, in March 1801, that "(t)he inhabitants conceive their liberty insecure until the military and civil power be divided".[4] He added that the burden of a civil and military government would be excessive for one office-holder, and insisted that the Maltese were anxious lest their concerns were neglected. Ball's representations were clearly persuasive. The Secretary of State appointed Charles Cameron the

---

3   See Chapter 2 and Appendix 2.
4   Ball to Dundas, 26 December 1800, Kew, CO 158/1/1. Eton (a British political opponent of Ball's, see below) thought that any delay in establishing a civil government could lead to insurrection (Eton to Sullivan, 5 July 1801, Hardman, 496).

first Civil Commissioner, in May 1801.[5] Though, according to William Eton, the new Civil Commissioner was "received as a Messiah" by the people,[6] the Civil Commissioner's authority was to operate in parallel with the military and the issue of military and civil relations was left unresolved for a number of years.[7] In 1803 Cameron left Malta to become governor of the Bahamas and Sir Alexander Ball was appointed as Civil Commissioner.

The Absence of Legislative Assemblies

As with Cameron, Ball had to work within the context of British colonial policy and ambitions. The occupation, by the British, of Malta, in 1800, took place at a time of a gradual, and not completely conscious, shift in policy towards colonial government[8]. The former model of colonial government was decentralised and had at its centre a more or less complex relationship between a local legislative assembly and a Governor whose consent was required to enact legislation. The ideology of this "First" Empire had been one of assimilation. It had not been an empire of conquest but an "outpost of British norms', founded predominantly upon oceanic commerce and Protestantism and inhabited by metropolitan migrants.[9]

However, the British became increasingly disenchanted with having to govern through a legislative assembly. This disenchantment stemmed from areas of conflict (such as slavery) between London and different colonies and also difficulties, illustrated by the American experience, of subduing any spirit of independence amongst the colonial population. Difficulties meant that imperial policy had to be pursued by encouraging governors to use diplomatic and exhortatory means in order to avoid an assembly garnering popular support and becoming the focus for impasse or even revolt.[10] Even where an Assembly assumed powers at variance with a governor's Instructions, Secretaries of State might advise the governor to act with caution and discretion;[11] and a minister, in order to avoid direct confrontation, might provide the governor with some

---

5   Randon, 347-74.
6   Eton to Sullivan, 5 July 1801, Hardman, 496.
7   The issue is discussed in more detail below.
8   See generally, Manning, Part One.
9   Armitage, "The Ideological Origins of the British Empire', 3.
10   E.g. Manning, 140-2.
11   Hobart to Seaforth, 20 August 1801, Kew CO 29/29/1, where the Secretary of State reminded the governor of the importance of "Prudence and Discretion" in dealing with the Executive government of Barbados.

negotiating leeway by speaking to influential members to discover how far, in fact, the practices of the Assembly would be in conflict with "true Constitutional principle". Above all was the need to avoid an open breach, "open contest.... cannot be too cautiously avoided".[12] Thus, ministers were forced to adopt diplomatic means to secure imperial goals and to remind assemblies of the constitutional constraints that bound them.[13] There was the possibility of dissolving a recalcitrant legislative assembly. But, though governors might expect support from London[14], this was a course of action that raised delicate political questions and considerable risks. Following *Campbell v Hall*,[15] indeed, a dissolution in most cases would require an Act of Parliament, which could be difficult to achieve.[16]

The advent of the Revolutionary and Napoleonic Wars, changed the purposes underlying the acquisition of colonies and reinforced a tendency towards more centralised colonial governance that had its origins in the loss of the American colonies. Malta, in particular, was a colony acquired for an immediate military purpose and advantage in the context of war and it then achieved strategic importance. Issues of settlement for British people, which had been central in the "first" empire, were not a consideration. Changes in the purpose and nature of the British perspective on colonies and the pursuit of the national interest overseas led, often though not always, to a change in the general principles of colonial governance one of whose central features was a determination to govern independently of a local legislative assembly.[17]

12 Hobart to Seaforth, 6 January 1803, Kew, CO 29/29/25-6, quoted in Manning, 141.

13 Castlereagh seemed to prefer prorogation followed by a public relations campaign by the governor to win public support against the assembly was an alternative: Manning, 142. After 1815 ministers were more prepared to support governors anxious to adopt a firmer stance with assemblies: the governor was praised for dissolving the Bahamian assembly in 1817 after it ordered the imprisonment of the Attorney-General: Kew, CO 24/17 Bathhurst to Cameron, 30 April 1817, quoted in Manning, 147.

14 See Bathurst to Cameron, 31 April (sic), 1817, Kew, CO 24/17/64.

15 (1774), 1 Cowp. 204, 98 ER 1045.

16 In outline, Campbell v Hall held that once the Imperial government had allowed a legislative assembly to be set up it could not be dissolved other than by an Act of Parliament unless the Crown, when establishing the assembly, had reserved a power of dissolution.

17 See generally, Manning. The Quebec Act 1774 embodied the new approach that was based on the acceptance of the existing laws and institutions of the subject territory but the refusal to allow local legislatures with significant power to develop: Manning, 294-6. A contrary example is Britain's brief occupation of Sicily, 1806-1815: see Gregory.

For Malta, therefore, it was not surprising that the British consistently rejected the claim, by elements of the Maltese opposition, including William Eton,[18] to allow or restore a legislative assembly in Malta (the *Consiglio Popolare*) that, it was claimed, was customary in Malta but had been allowed to fall into disuse by the Knights. As discussed in Chapter 2, the British ruled by the principle of continuity with the constitution, laws and institutions of Malta as they were prior to the French invasion. It was important, from the British point of view, to demonstrate that, even if there had been a customary assembly in Malta, it had not enjoyed legislative powers.[19]

The Authority of the Civil Commissioner

The system that was imposed, in the early years of British rule, was, therefore, autocratic. The autocracy was based not simply upon the revised approach to colonial governance which the British had adopted. It also gained legitimacy from the continuity principle which mandated the British, through the Civil Commissioner, to take over the Maltese system, a system ultimately rooted in the autocracy of the Grandmasters. As shown in Chapter 2, the new system was established under the Proclamations of 19 February[20] and 15 July 1801[21] and the Royal Instructions of 14 May 1801.[22]

Indirect Rule under the Royal Prerogative

Cameron's and Ball's authority to govern, from the British perspective, was based upon the Royal Prerogative. Blackstone, writing of the eighteenth-century constitution, defined the Royal Prerogative as "that special pre-eminence which the King hath, over and above all other persons, and out of the ordinary course of the common law, in right of his regal dignity".[23]

18   Cameron was compelled to warn Eton not to encourage the Maltese to expect "restoration" of a Consiglio Popolare: Cameron to Eton, 22 May 1802, Kew, CO 158/4/43.
19   This was eventually established to British satisfaction by the Royal Commission of 1812: Kew, CO 158/19, although rejection of the Maltese claim was consistently done through Ball's period.
20   Hardman, 341-2; NLM LIBR/MS 430 1/2; Bandi 1790 AL 1805, 185.
21   Hardman, 358-359; NLM LIBR/MS 430 1/2; Bandi 1790 AL 1805, 204.
22   Hardman, 350-7. The Royal Instructions provided a policy framework for Commissioners to work within. The Royal Instructions for Malta are discussed below.
23   Blackstone, Book 1, Chapter 7, 232. No attempt is made here to discuss modern day issues about the scope of the Prerogative.

In effect, it meant that ministers, formally advising the Crown, could act and legislate for Malta independently of any need for authorisation by an Act of Parliament. The Royal Prerogative was used in London to create and authorise a local official (the Civil Commissioner) who would exercise the Crown's legislative and executive powers in the colony.

From London's point of view there were obvious practical advantages which this system had over any attempt at more direct rule. In particular, the presence of a locally-based official meant that necessary legislation could be identified and the resulting laws would be appropriate to local conditions. At the same time, the Imperial interest would not be threatened (as it might be by a local legislative assembly) because local legislation would be in the hands of a British official. Political direction and control could be retained in London. The Civil Commissioners would not be exercising some uncontrolled vice-regal authority but be subject to political limits upon their powers. The authority of the Commissioners derived from their Commission and from Royal Instructions which governed their appointment. Civil Commissioners, such as Ball, were subject to Royal Instructions, from the Secretary of State, which set out, albeit in general terms, the policy goals, and the powers delegated to them in order to achieve those goals.[24] These Instructions, along with the practical supervision of the Secretary of State and formal review by the Privy Council and its Committee for Trade, established a supervisory context within which Commissioners operated. The Instructions (14 May 1801) to the first Civil Commissioner for Malta, Charles Cameron, were explicitly stated to be "guidance", but they had the constitutional force of a Royal command.

Once the initial Instructions had been issued, ministers could and did provide further advice to the Civil Commissioners. Despatches supplemented, refined or even countermanded the initial instructions.[25] The traffic was clearly not all one way. Malta's Civil Commissioners were in regular communication with ministers, reporting upon the state of the Island's finances, the system of financial controls, proposals for the food supply, and all other major questions of policy. Such reports, then, assisted the ministers in London to advise the Civil Commissioners on the direction and execution of future policy.

Under this indirect system, the Civil Commissioner had a great deal

---

24 The Royal Instructions of 1801 for Malta are discussed below.
25 The despatches that followed Cameron's Instructions, for example, clarified and amended them in relation to the demarcation of responsibility between the civil and military authorities.

of local freedom. In particular, as in the case in Malta, he was not only the apparent but usually the real initiator of legislative proposals. Thus, in the case of "Coleridge's laws", all of the political initiatives, leading to their enactments, originated in Malta; subject to the exceptional case relating to passports.[26]

Powers and Discretion

The Commissioner's authority and powers derived from his Commission and the Instructions presupposed additional, general powers widely enjoyed by Governors and Commissioners[27] in the colonial context. These were implied powers which were assumed in the Instructions and would apply unless explicitly overridden.

Implied and ancillary powers were derived from interpretation of the Instructions and were those which were necessary or expedient in order to give effect to the Instructions. Such powers, in effect, would expand the scope of the express Instructions, but in a manner that was consistent with and supportive of them. However, their scope was unclear on issues such as whether and to what extent they could authorise coercive actions. In principle that was a matter of interpretation of the Instructions which, under a constitutional separation of powers, should have been done by the courts. In Malta, however, there was no effective procedure by which a judicial challenge to the exercise of his powers by the Commissioner could have been brought. This issue is discussed further, below.

An example of ancillary powers can be offered from the Instructions received by Charles Cameron in May 1801. Malta could not feed herself. By 1801, the corn supplies from Sicily, a traditional source, had become uncertain when Sicilian ports were closed to British vessels. The Instructions required the Civil Commissioner, as one of the most "essential" of his duties "to make yourself thoroughly acquainted with every circumstance

26   This was the Avviso of 25 June 1805 NLM LIBR/MS 430 2/2, Bandi 1805 AL 1814, 15. A copy of this instrument was transmitted to London: Kew, 158/10/195; see Chapter 5.9: Passports.

27   Nothing of significance, in terms of authority, turns on which of these offices is used: Roberts-Wray, 306. The Maltese experience suggests that "Governor" applies when British sovereignty was certain. The first "Governor" was Sir Thomas Maitland appointed in 1813; formal cession occurred in the Treaty of Paris 1814. In Sammut v Strickland [1938] AC 678, British courts accepted Malta as a ceded colony "not later than 1813" and left its status between 1800 and 1813 uncertain. The issue is discussed by Davis and Hough (2007).

relative to the purchase and sale of corn at Malta, of which you will transmit
to me (the Secretary of State) a full detailed account".[28] Nothing was said
about how this was to be done and Cameron could well have argued that,
if necessary, coercive powers to seize and inspect relevant documents (e.g.
from recalcitrant officials of the Università) were ancillary to this instruction.

Furthermore, the Civil Commissioner had other powers which were
inherent to his office. These were powers conferred by law as an incident
of the office, rather than by express or presumed terms of the Instructions.
Those powers were ill-defined and potentially controversial. The law
recognised two grounds for such inherent powers: custom and necessity. A
customary power was one usually exercised by the governor of the territory
in question.[29] Governors lacking express power to pass a particular law
would sometimes fall back upon an alleged custom that permitted their
action, but the custom relied upon could only be established in evidence
by reference to practice within the territory in question.[30] This would be
extremely valuable for Cameron and Ball in Malta given the wide, if not
unlimited, scope of customary authority of the Grandmasters. A "necessary"
power was one that the Governor or Commissioner required in order to be
able to perform his functions. Governors often claimed as "necessary" a
range of powers that the English courts refused to countenance. Suspending
the law in order to deal with serious threats to public order is as example.
Mostyn v Fabrigas[31] indicates that it was for the judges, in England, to
determine whether otherwise unlawful actions were justified on necessity
grounds. Most notable amongst these was the power to amend the law.
However, in *Cameron v Kyte*,[32] the Privy Council held that the legislative
power was not an inherent power of a governor. Although this case was
decided after Coleridge's departure from Malta, it is doubtful whether an
English court would have decided the issue differently in 1805. In practice,
this meant that if the instructions omitted to confer a law-making power
– or only conferred a restricted power – the courts would not allow Civil
Commissioners to by-pass these restrictions and act in any manner they
thought necessary under the banner of an inherent or necessary power.
The powers actually conferred upon the Civil Commissioners in Malta are

---

28   Chapman's absence from the Island on the Corn mission to the Black sea in
1805 was the immediate reason why Coleridge became Acting Public Secretary.
29   Cameron v Kyte (1835), 3 Knapp 332, 345-6.
30   Ibid.
31   (1774), 1 Cowp 161, 98 ER 1021.
32   Ibid.

considered below.

Grandmaster

From the position of the Maltese, it must be remembered, the British Civil Commissioner continued to exercise the authority of the Grandmaster. This followed from the principle of continuity upon which British government, in the early years, was based.

Once the Order of St John had assumed power in Malta the Grandmaster governed as an absolute ruler.[33] This absolutism explained the judgement of the 1812 Royal Commission that the Maltese Constitution placed the Civil Commissioner above the law.[34]

Legislative authority was vested exclusively in this office:[35] the Grandmasters could make new laws and repeal existing ones on any subject matter. No court or other person or body could question the validity of the laws so passed. The Bandi and the Avvisi under Coleridge's signature were, thus, immune from legal or constitutional review in the courts of Malta. Grandmasters and their British successors continued to deny, as discussed above, any nationalist claim to the traditional existence of a competing or complementary legislative assembly. As has been discussed, in Chapter 2, Grandmasters had important judicial powers and these Sir Alexander Ball was happy to continue with. He appointed and dismissed the judges and exercised a constitutionally unlimited power to punish, including banishment. His quasi-judicial role of hearing petitions through the *Segnatura* has also been considered in Chapter 2. A further significant power enjoyed by the Grandmasters was the power of patronage: they nominated persons to every public office. Ball regarded this as a key tool to reward loyalists and to cement the acceptance of British rule. The disastrous consequences of this policy – for which Coleridge expressed support in *The Friend* – have been considered in Chapter 2.

Whilst his legal or constitutional position was unlimited, the Grandmaster's authority was, nevertheless, constrained by circumstances, and by his own conception of customs and morality. In particular, he took

33 See Hardman, 6.
34 Royal Commission of 1812, Kew, CO 158/19.
35 Note, however, that legislative powers were, at different times, delegated. In some instances, this may have been necessary since the Order was itself not permitted to engage in commerce. For example, the first Chamber of Commerce, during its brief existence in the eighteenth century, was authorised to make laws for the better regulation of commerce: see, generally, Debono (1988).

an oath of office which included a promise not to raise general, permanent, taxes.[36] Because the Grandmaster had absolute power, this oath, if breached, would not be enforceable in the courts. One of the most controversial legislative acts of the Coleridge period was the introduction, by a Bando, of an excise duty on spirits. The legality of this is discussed in Chapter 5.

He would not act entirely by himself but would take advice. Ball, for instance, was usually advised by others, including Coleridge, though consultation was not, in any sense, a legal requirement. Ball was (appropriately) advised by Maltese law officers such as Dr Guiseppe Zammit, but not English law officers. He was also able, informally, to call upon the English legal expertise of the staff of the Court of Vice-Admiralty, after its establishment in 1803.[37]

As regards his public actions, the Grandmaster, like any sovereign, would be expected to act within the law but subject to two important qualifications. First, he had to follow the law as a matter of grace and not obligation. As indicated, his actions could not be directly tested in the Maltese courts. Secondly, the law itself granted wide discretionary powers to the Grandmaster, in particular he seems to have enjoyed an unchallengeable power to suspend laws. We shall see later in the chapter that for the Civil Commissioner, exercising these powers in his capacity as a British official, the situation was, at least in principle, different. In that capacity he was responsible under English law for the exercise of powers derived from the Royal Prerogative and the question of whether his actions, as actions of the Civil Commissioner, could be challenged in the English courts is discussed further below.

Contexts, Limits and Constraints

Coleridge's authority to draft and sign the Bandi and Avvisi derived from that of Sir Alexander Ball, the Civil Commissioner, and he, Ball, exercised the constitutionally-despotic powers of the Grandmaster but did so as the British official responsible to ministers in London whose own authority was that of the Crown exercising its Prerogatives. As such he was also subject to

36 I.e. taxes which were general and permanent rather than focused specifically on particular projects.
37 This included its judge, Dr Sewell, and senior advocates such as Dr Moncrieff and Dr Stoddart. The independence of such advice is challengeable because all four (and Coleridge) enjoyed a close social relationship. He did this in relation to criminal cases see Chapter 2 for a discussion of his powers, where the outcomes were conformed in all but one case: Ball to Windham, 28 February 1807, Kew, CO 158/13.

a range of constitutional, military, legal and political constraints upon the effective exercise of his powers.

The Royal Instructions in Malta, 1801-1805[38]

The Royal Instructions, given to Cameron in May 1801, adopted by Ball and, as mentioned above, subject to further instructions, advice and other pressures from London, created the general policy context within which the Civil Commissioner exercised his powers.

The Instructions, firstly, embodied the primary strategic policy: the continuation of the legal, constitutional and administrative order of the Knights, as it obtained in 1798[39]. They required the Civil Commissioner to acquaint himself with the laws, customs and privileges of Malta, under the Knights, as well as the financial state of the islands.[40]

> ...in substance at least, and so far as circumstances will admit in for also, no alteration should be made in the modes, laws and regulations according to which the civil affairs and the Revenue of the Island have been heretofore managed unless the same shall appear to the officer commanding HM forces to be required for the safety and defence of the Island, or to be evidently beneficial and desirable, as to leave no doubt of its expediency or of it being generally acceptable to the wishes, feelings and even prejudices of the inhabitants. You will therefore understand that the administration of justice and police is, as nearly as circumstances will permit, to continue to be exercised in conformity to the Laws, and Institutions of the antient (sic) Government of the Order of St John of Jerusalem, subject only to such directions as you may from time to time receive from this country, and to such deviations, in consequence of sudden and unforeseen emergencies, as may in the judgment of the Commander-in-Chief, render departure therefrom necessary and unavoidable, the occasion whereof, however, you will by the first opportunity report to me.

The important point to note is that any changes to the laws of Malta, such as those made under Coleridge's hand in 1805, had to fall within the exceptional categories outlined by the Secretary of State, Lord Hobart, in these Instructions.

The Instructions suggest a presumption in favour of continuity, both in "substance" and also in "form". Nevertheless, the *status quo* was subject to

---

38   Hardman, 350-7.
39   See Chapter 2.
40   On this he could rely on Ball's Memorandum of 26 December 1800, Ball to Dundas, Kew, CO 158/1/1.

any necessary changes caused by the new circumstances. There was a wide power to make general laws of any kind affecting "civil affairs and the Revenue" which were undoubtedly beneficial (in the Civil Commissioner's view) or generally acceptable to the inhabitants. There is no indication how either of these tests were to be established. No court was ever asked to rule upon the legitimacy of laws and policies pursued by the Civil Commissioners, including Ball, although the advice of Maltese jurists was certainly sought in 1895, over the validity of Coleridge's Bando imposing excise duties.[41] Nothing in the Instructions implied that the test for obvious expediency could, for a court, be based upon anything other than the Civil Commissioner's subjective judgement, at least in the absence of strong evidence pointing to corruption or bad faith. Similarly, the Instructions say nothing about how the wishes, feelings or prejudices of the Maltese were to be ascertained. Again, it is likely that any court would have felt bound to uphold the Civil Commissioner's judgement upon Maltese opinion. In particular, it must be remembered that there was a clear British intention not to allow a legislative assembly to develop. Thus, the Instructions gave the Civil Commissioners a wide discretion over changes to the law; and it is clear that their political judgement upon what was expedient or desirable for the local population could (and would) involve an overall political assessment in which the British imperial interest, partly reflecting policy instructions from London, was a major factor.

Nevertheless, the Instructions did not envisage an unlimited legislative power for the Civil Commissioner. There was only a limited power to alter the laws controlling the "administration of justice and the police" unless on the basis of directions from London or in the context of emergencies, as recognised by the military authorities. But this was more honoured in the reach than in its observance. As we shall discover, some of Coleridge's laws were passed without reference to the military authorities; although they would, nonetheless, have to be justified under the expediency clause.

The purport of the Royal Instructions was communicated to the Maltese in Cameron's Proclamation of 15 July 1801[42] which included the undertaking to respect the "dearest rights" of the Maltese: their churches, holy religion, persons and property.[43] The Proclamation promised that the laws would be upheld but there was no explicit promise not to alter Maltese law. A Public Notice (Avviso) of 23 July 1801, signed by Pigot and Cameron, indicated

41   See Chapter 5.3: Taxation. Coleridge's Bando was accepted as binding in law.
42   See Chapter 2.
43   Hardman, 342.

that it was His Majesty's intention to continue in force the existing laws and administration of justice until such time as *His Majesty* (emphasis added) should command. The Proclamation is interesting because it gave greater emphasis to the power and willingness of the British Crown to alter the law than was found in the Instructions. Moreover, it implied that alterations to the law would be initiated by the Crown, in London. What was not made explicit was the fact that local legislative and administrative authority, in reality, resided in the person and judgements of the Civil Commissioners, local British officials, rather than the benign paternalism of the British monarch.

The Instructions continued by requiring the public revenues to be maintained and administered, as under the Knights, subject to changes "obviously requisite" following the change to British rule. In particular, the various categories of the property of the Order, as identified by Sir Alexander Ball, were to be taken over by the Crown. Customs and Excise was to continue, subject to likely, future, reform; the system, directed by the Unversità, for feeding the population was to continue; the fees and expenses of government were to be identified and reformed if necessary; trade was to develop by making Valletta a free port with particular attention to maintaining effective quarantine through the lazaretto (with the advice and superintendence of William Eton).

Civil and Military Power

Underlying the Royal Instructions was one of the great constitutional tensions of the early British period – the relations between civil and military powers. Although much of the initial tension had evaporated by Coleridge's time, it remained an important part of the context, and basic assumptions, behind the exercise of the civil power in 1805. It indicates the kinds of issues that, though they have a military aspect to them, were within the jurisdiction of the Civil Commissioner (and so could be the subject of legal change); it also helps to explain why Coleridge's signature was required upon the Bandi and Avvisi.

The Instructions began with the doctrine that "direction and superintendence of the civil affairs and of the revenue of Malta should be separated from the duties of the commander of the forces in that Island...". Nevertheless, the Instructions did not give the Civil Commissioner any authority over military affairs but insisted that the control of the civil and revenue affairs should be "in concert" with the officer commanding British forces. Military matters were those concerned with the "safety and defence" of Malta but other than that, no attempt was made to differentiate between the civil and the military.[44] Furthermore, at the beginning, the commanding officer's "concurrence and approbation" and signature[45] were necessary for all legislative measures, whether civil or military, and the Commander claimed the right to propose legislation for safety and defence with no equivalent power of veto vested in the Civil Commissioner.[46] London swiftly realised that the suborning of the civil to the military power, even if real, should not be apparent to the population. A despatch of 21 May 1801 made it clear that, in the event of disagreement with the military commander, the Civil Commissioner was, nevertheless, to sign the instrument and communicate his reasons for dissent only to the commanding officer and the Secretary of State.[47] Pigot, the military commander, claimed a wide jurisdiction.[48] Disputes between Pigot and Cameron occurred over issues such as the admission of foreigners to the islands, the allocation of passports, the policing of the fortified towns and, in particular, the intractable issue of the jurisdiction of Maltese law and process over British soldiers accused of crimes against Maltese citizens.[49]

Cameron sought clarification on the issue from London. Lord Hobart's response of 2 September 1801 was of great significance.[50] The British Government remained unwilling to demarcate, precisely, the discrete civil and military jurisdictions. Rather, the need for co-operation, compromise and the maintenance of harmonious relations with the military was emphasised; though the Civil Commissioner's right to refer concerns to London was re-stated.

Nevertheless, Hobart's despatch clarified and expanded the civil jurisdiction at the expense of the military. Some of Pigot's specific claims were rejected. Immigration control, specifically the granting of passports

---

44   Hobart to Cameron, 2 September 1801, Kew, CO 158/1/207 suggests that this was unlikely to have been an oversight. The British Government's policy was evidently not to define the scope of these two jurisdictions.
45   Royal Instructions, Hobart to Cameron, 14 May 1801, Hardman, 357; Kew, CO 158/1/88.
46   Ibid.
47   Hobart to Cameron, 21 May 1801, Kew, CO 158/1/107.
48   Pigot to Cameron, 2 July 1801, Kew, CO 158/1/119.
49   Ibid., 114; also, Pigot to Cameron, Kew, 16 August 1801, CO 158/2/81.
50   Hobart to Cameron, 2 September 1801, Kew, CO 158/1/207 et seq. A copy of this despatch was sent with a copy to Pigot for the avoidance of future misunderstandings between them: see Kew, CO 159/3/40.

and admitting foreigners, was characterised as a civil matter within the Civil Commissioner's jurisdiction, and it was an issue in which Coleridge would become closely involved.[51] What is more, the reply stated that the Civil Commissioner would, henceforth, have an *exclusive* authority over civil matters.

> In all public acts relative to the civil administration the name of HM Civil Commissioner should *alone* appear and all such acts should be signed by you or by the Secretary of Government under your Authority.[52] (Emphasis added).

Thus, Coleridge's name eventually appeared at the foot of the Bandi and Avvisi issued by Ball's administration whilst Coleridge held office as public secretary.

Whilst Hobart's reply of 2 September 1801 was aimed at restricting military jurisdiction, it did not attempt to remove military authority over security matters. There was still scope for civil and military tensions over, for example, the extent to which military competence embraced not only the defence of the Island from external attack but also internal security. The precise distinction between civil and military jurisdictions was not resolved (as if it ever could be) and the practical business of government would depend upon achieving pragmatic co-operation between the military and civil authorities. Much would, therefore, depend upon the individual personalities and the relationship between the Civil Commissioner and the commanding officer. By 1805 military and civil relations seemed to have improved. Pigot had left the Island and had been replaced by Major-General Villettes, with whom Sir Alexander Ball seems to have had an effective working relationship.[53] Several of the instruments promulgated by Coleridge seem to have been influenced by representations from or co-operation with the military authorities.[54] Thus, the Proclamation (Bando) on spirits[55] partly emerged from discussions with the army chief physician

---

51 See Chapter 5. 9: Passports.
52 CO 158/1/207; A copy of this despatch was sent with a copy to Pigot for the avoidance of future misunderstandings between them: see CO 159/3/40.
53 Although there was at least one allegation that there was friction between Ball and Villettes: see statement by Borg, 30 May 1806, Kew, CO 158/12 (no folio reference). There may also have been some friction between Ball and Pigot, which may explain why Ball was not chosen as the first Civil Commissioner in May 1801 despite his popularity with the Maltese: see the address to Ball dated 11 February 1801, Hardman, 343.
54 See, generally, Chapter 5.
55 Bando of 22 March 1805, NLM LIBR/MS 430 2/2 Bandi 1805 AL 1814, 4.

and had the support of senior commanders; similarly, the Avviso and the Bando concerning the recapture of deserters and the Avviso relating to the dishonest taking of enlistment money, also suggest some high-level co-operation between the military and civil jurisdictions.[56]

Power to Change the Law in Malta

It is clear, therefore, that the Royal Instructions, whilst establishing the principle of continuity, nevertheless envisaged the British making changes to the laws of Malta from the beginning of the occupation. The limits of that legislative power, as written into the Instructions, were quite vague and uncertain and would be difficult to establish judicially. The question, therefore, is whether there were any other, overriding, constitutional and legal constraints upon the exercise of the legislative power which are properly thought of as implied or presumed limits to what could have been done by changing the law. Such limits would have applied to the Bandi and Avvisi promulgated by Ball and Coleridge and so, to the extent that they are recognised or ignored in the drafting, are part of the analysis and evaluation of those instruments.

Legislation and the Grandmaster

As discussed above, the Grandmaster, whose authority in Malta the Civil Commissioners adopted, had a legally unconstrained power to change the laws of Malta. The forms of this power were used by Ball, through Coleridge, in the drafting and signing of the Bandi and Avvisi. Whilst the Grandmaster was not subject to legal constraints there were, as suggested above, customary restraints upon his power such as restricting the introduction of new forms of general taxation. The view of the 1812 Royal Commission was that the Grandmasters were "practically if not legally despotic"[57], suggesting that any customary restraints were honoured in the

---

56 Deserters: Avviso of 15 July 1805, NLM LIBR/MS 430 2/2 Bandi 1805 AL 1814,17; Bando, 2 September 1805 NLM LIBR/MS 430 2/2 Bandi AL 1814,21; enlistment money: Avviso, 20 June 1805 NLM LIBR/MS 430 2/2 Bandi 1805 AL 1814, 12. These are discussed below, Chapter 5.
57 Kew, CO 158/19. During his administration, there were Maltese critics of Ball, such as Vincenzo Borg (the former leader of the Birkirkara battalion. Following his dismissal by Ball from the Board of Administrators of Public Property, and as part of a campaign to discredit, the Civil Commissioner, Borg described the Maltese as fearing Ball's "great despotism": Borg to Eton, 30th May 1806 Kew, CO 158/12/ no

breach. Indeed, critics of Ball, such as Eton, made the same point about his performance in the Grandmaster's role – it was not the lack of formal constitutional restraint that was the issue but, rather, the despotic practice of his discretion by the Commissioner.

Legislation under the Royal Prerogative

Other, more complicated, issues arose concerning the limits, if any, of a Civil Commissioner, as a British official, to change the law in a colony. There were two linked issues. First, the general power of the Crown to authorise and require changes to the law in a colony and, secondly, whether the Commissioner could exercise that Royal power himself, like a Viceroy, or whether his powers were always limited, in principle, even if the practical scope of the limits were hard to establish, by the specific grant of legislative authority from the Crown.

By the eighteenth century it was agreed, following the Case of Proclamations 1610,[58] that the scope of the Royal Prerogative was a matter of law to be determined by the courts in England and that the Crown had lost the power of independent legislation at home in normal times. The eventual result of the Civil Wars made it clear that any independent right of the Crown to legislate, tax or take other coercive actions in times of emergency (and who defined the emergency) was also lost. Changing the law required an Act of Parliament. However, the Crown retained an independent power to legislate for colonies, such as Malta, which were either conquered by the Crown or ceded to it.[59] This power could be exercised in one of two ways. The first way was by ministers themselves in the form of an Order in Council. Such Orders had the force of an Act of Parliament but, as *Campbell v Hall* (below) makes clear, could be overruled by a later Act of Parliament whose terms were clear and which applied to the colony in question (as discussed below, there were a few such Acts applying to Malta). The second way, used predominantly in Malta, was to use the Royal Prerogative to authorise an official with legislative powers. Since a delegate could not expand his own delegated powers, such authority would, at most, be restricted by any limits on the Crown's powers.

Following *Campbell v Hall*[60] a distinction was made between settled

folio reference
58 12 Co. Rep 74, 77 ER 1352
59 Campbell v Hall (1774), 1 Cowp. 204, 98 ER 1045, below.
60 (1774), 1 Cowp. 204; 98 ER 1045.

colonies and those which were conquered or ceded. Settled colonies were uninhabited or places where, from a European perspective, there were no established, working institutions of law and government. In such places, the English colonists brought with them, as it were, the domestic law of England.

Malta clearly did not come into the category of a settled colony; it was either "conquered" or "ceded". The Kingdom of the Two Sicilies had not formally ceded sovereignty following the French invasion and occupation. The British, at least at the beginning of the occupation, offered reassurances to Ferdinand's court despite the fact that the French surrender was accepted by Major-General Pigot exclusively under the British flag to the deliberate exclusion of Maltese, Sicilian and Russian representatives.[61] In respect of the view that Neapolitan sovereignty was not restored by the removal of the French but reverted to the Maltese people, it has been powerfully argued that Malta was informally ceded to Britain by the Maltese through the will of the people and, in particular, the *Declaration of Rights of the Inhabitants of the Islands of Malta and Gozo*.[62] In regards to this theory, the British would have been bound by the terms of the Declaration and this might have been seen as restricting the development of British interests. The British government's had a preference for conquest as the justifying theory for British rule in the early years[63]. In any event, conquered or ceded colonies have the same status in English law.[64]

Conquered or ceded colonies were Crown dominions. The local population became fully equal subjects of the Crown. The existing laws (e.g. the Code de Rohan in Malta) continued to apply,[65] but the Crown had, under English law, the legal authority to alter this law without needing

---

61   Laferla, XI. Napoleon had ceded sovereignty over Malta to the Czar shortly before the French were expelled; the Czar became Grandmaster.

62   15 June 1802. Widely reproduced, e.g., Cm 9657 Appendix F, Frendo; see Roberts-Wray, 685 (who accepts formal accession as an alternative).

63   The Foltina (1814), 1 Dods 450 suggests that military conquest itself transfers sovereignty. See also Penn, for a contemporaneous view. Deliberating retrospectively, in 1836, Lord Glenelg, the Secretary of State, endorsed the conquest thesis for the early period through his criticisms of the voluntary cession in the reports on the legal system by the Chief Justice, Stoddart: Kew, CO 158/91. Stoddart's Reports are bound as appendices.

64   For a discussion of the issues, which sides with the conquest theory, see Davis and Hough (2007).

65   This, by the end of the eighteenth century was also a principle of international law (Vattal, 389, section 201), at least where the quarrel is with the sovereign power rather than the peoples.

the consent of the United Kingdom Parliament. However, this power to legislate, with the authority of the Royal Prerogative alone, was subject to at least three caveats.

First, whilst it was within the scope of the Royal Prerogative to establish a colonial legislative assembly, once this occurred, it was the assembly and not the Crown, exercising its Royal Prerogatives, which could legislate. What was even more serious from a British ministerial point of view was that an assembly's power to legislate could only be revoked by an Act of Parliament. This was one reason why the British were unwilling to create an assembly, with legislative powers, on Malta. In a conquered or ceded colony, of course, such a move would, in any case, have been inconsistent with the principle of continuity.

Secondly, the Crown's power to legislate alone for a conquered or ceded colony was subject to the overriding authority of an Act of Parliament (one which extended to the colony or which limited the overseas exercise of the Royal Prerogative). In other words, Parliament could always pass laws applicable in Malta.

Thirdly, the extent of the content of the Crown's legislative power (outside Parliament) was unclear. *Campbell v Hall*[66] suggested that the Crown's legislative powers may have been restricted but just what those restrictions were appeared then, as now, elusive. Lord Mansfield, in words that have become notorious, said

> this legislation [the Crown's legislative power outside Parliament] being subordinate, that is subordinate to his own authority in Parliament, he cannot make any change contrary to fundamental principles: he cannot exempt an inhabitant from that particular dominion; as, for instance, from the laws of trade, or from the power of Parliament, or give him privileges exclusive of his other subjects; and so in many other instances that might be put.[67]

At least three possible meanings arise from these words. The first possibility was that Royal Prerogative legislation (including laws purportedly authorised by Ball and signed by Coleridge) must not be "repugnant" to (inconsistent with) an Act of Parliament extending to the colony. This would seem to be uncontroversial, since Parliament and not the Crown is the supreme law-making body. Secondly, Lord Mansfield may have meant that there were "fundamental principles" or an irreducible minimum of basic liberties, such as freedom from slavery, which could,

---

66 (1774), 1 Cowp. 204; 98 ER 1045.
67 (1774) 1 Cowp. 204, 209; 98 ER 1045, 1048.

as *lex non scripta*, restrain the Crown or the Civil Commissioner. Finally, the possibility that, as the context and examples suggest, the "pretended power" of the Crown to suspend the laws was not be used by the Crown in its overseas possessions.[68] If this had been correct, the King's legislative power did not extend, for example, to legal discrimination against members of the local population (such as punishing a person more severely than the law allowed) or giving particular legal privileges or exemptions.[69] If so, Ball may have contravened this in relation to the banishment of certain offenders convicted of rumour-mongering.[70]

Lord Mansfield's statement became notorious in the mid nineteenth century and led to legislative change. Under the Colonial Laws Validity Act 1865, the restraint upon the Crown's power to legislate for a colony was limited to matters repugnant to an Act of Parliament extending to the colony. In later years they were subject to little argument.[71] In the early British period in Malta, the statement stood in all its ambiguity.

The question about the limits to the Civil Commissioner's legislative powers will be returned to later in this chapter when the issue of civil and criminal liability is discussed.

Lord Mansfield also said, regarding conquered colonies, that the "articles of capitulation upon which the country is surrendered and the articles of peace by which it is ceded, are sacred and inviolable according to their true intent and meaning". It is unclear whether "sacred and inviolable" restrains the Crown exercising its Royal Prerogatives voluntarily or as a matter of law;[72] it is possible that it could restrict Parliament in regard to the way general words in an Act are interpreted but it is doubtful whether it could restrict the deliberate and expressed intention of an Act of the Crown in Parliament.

The Malta Articles of Capitulation[73] gave rise to few clear rights or duties with respect to the parties. They were mainly concerned with the disposition of French troops and the military take-over. Provisions reaching civilians included collaboration – the matter of whether a person could be punished for things said or done during the occupation (article 8) and the matter of freedom of movement and property. British acceptance of Article

---

68   The power ended, at least for domestic UK purposes, by the Bill of Rights 1688.
69   See the discussion in 2008 by Lord Hoffman in R (Bancoult) v Secretary of State for Foreign and Commonwealth Affairs [2008] UKHL 61, [90].
70   See Chapter 5.4: Public Order and Crime.
71   Lyanage v R [1967] 1 AC 259, 285.
72   Chitty is clear that this is a legal restraint on the King (Chitty, 29).
73   Hardman, 319-22.

8, dealing with collaboration, merely assured the population that that they would be treated with "justice and humanity, and shall enjoy the full protection of the laws". Article 9 proposed the right of French civilians to return to France with all their property, this was accepted by the British but, as with Article 8, with the weakening caveat that it was not an appropriate provision for military capitulation. Article 12 was the most controversial because it proposed a general right to the benefit of all property transactions undertaken by the French government and civilians. This seemed to ratify the French despoilment of the Island. The legal obligation upon the British was qualified since Article 12 was only accepted so far as the transactions were "just and lawful".

3.2. Legal Restraints on Power

Introduction

We have seen that Coleridge's authority was a reflection of that of the Civil Commissioner. The latter had, in effect, the powers of the Grandmaster. These were wide and despotic. Despotic, formally, because of the absence of a separation of powers and properly independent judiciary, and despotic in practice depending upon the personality of the incumbent. There were few legal constraints, powers were discretionary and limited by the personal conscience of the incumbent. But the Civil Commissioner was also a British official who was exercising authority stemming from the Royal Prerogative. This gave him wide executive and legislative powers including the right to change the law in Malta (a ceded or conquered colony). The scope of this right, as a power under the Royal Prerogative, was certainly wide but not, perhaps, thought to be unlimited in the early nineteenth century. The problem, in what follows, is to identify and discuss any general, legal or constitutionally-based constraints upon the exercise of these legislative and executive powers. The underlying issue is the lawfulness of particular actions and how these might have been challenged in the courts and the focus is upon the grounds a court might have had for holding an action, legislative or executive, to have been unlawful.

There were three general grounds upon which a Governor or Commissioner could have been brought before the courts. First, there was civil liability where the Commissioner or Governor could have been sued by a victim of his actions, secondly there was criminal liability where he could have been prosecuted by the Crown for criminal offences and, finally, the possibility that actions that were neither tortious (invoking civil liability) nor criminal could, nevertheless, have been unlawful because they were *ultra vires* being beyond the Commissioner's powers. The first two, civil and criminal liability, raised two important issues which will be discussed below: the issue of jurisdiction and the issue of justification.

By the early nineteenth century, English law was beginning to develop a somewhat ill-defined conception of accountable, constitutional government. Civil Commissioners operated within the normative framework of their office as it was being structured not just by ministers and Parliament but also by the courts reflecting English constitutional practice and conceptions of the rule of law. The nature and scope of this framework, the understanding of the constitutional and legal position of British administrators exercising official power overseas, was complex and developing as the scope and purposes of British rule changed.

Jurisdiction

Could Governors and Commissioners have been brought before the courts at all or were they, as Royal representatives, outside the jurisdiction of the courts altogether? English courts decided in *Mostyn v Fabrigas*[74] that Governors and, therefore, Civil Commissioners could be liable for exercising their powers in an unlawful way by committing crimes or civil wrongs in their official capacity. Briefly, the governor of Minorca had assaulted, imprisoned and then exiled to a foreign country, a political opponent whom he alleged was fermenting riot and disorder. The alleged actions had taken place on a part of the Island where the writ of the local courts did not run and the governor's powers where absolute or at least not justiciable in the Minorcan courts. The English courts accepted jurisdiction (by using a legal fiction that the assault had also taken place in London) and held that the governor was liable in tort.[75]

Mostyn is the authority for the view that the governor was like a Viceroy and so immune from civil or criminal action in the local courts (in relation, it seems, to alleged violation of either local or English law). In question,

---

74   (1774), 1 Cowp 161, 98 ER 1021.
75   He recovered £3,000 damages with £90 costs.

on one hand, was the scope and substance of Royal power and this was not within the competence of local courts to determine: "for no question concerning the seignory, can be tried within the seignory itself". On the other hand, it could not be lawful to abuse the Crown's commission without remedy. It was a "monstrous proposition" to claim that "...a governor acting by virtue of letters patent under the Great Seal, is accountable only to God, and his own conscience; that he is absolutely despotic, and can spoil, plunder, and affect His Majesty's subjects, both in their liberty and property, with impunity,..."[76] The matter, therefore, could be tried before the English courts.

In subsequent cases, the view that the legality of a Commissioner's actions could not be challenged in the local courts was said to be a mere *obiter dictum* and eventually set aside[77]. The point being that in Minorca the actions were, geographically, outside the jurisdiction of the local courts. In Malta, of course, there was, similarly, no procedure for bringing the Grandmaster before the Maltese courts and, under the principle of continuity, the Civil Commissioner enjoyed the same immunity. Thus, *Mostyn* does not address the situation where the local law *does* have procedures for questioning the actions of the Commissioner. In Sir Alexander Ball's time, the issue was uncertain but it can be speculated that it would not have been possible to act against him in the Maltese courts but the English courts *would* have had jurisdiction to hear complaints that he had acted in a criminal or tortious fashion. The cases of Borg, Hasciach and Bonello would have raised interesting possibilities here.[78]

Mostyn v Fabrigas illustrates the fact that a Civil Commissioner had personal civil liability, enforceable in English courts, at the suit of a person harmed by an unlawful, tortious act which was, nevertheless, done in the course of the Civil Commissioner's conception of his duty, in good faith and for the public interest.[79] As *Mostyn* illustrates, these tortious actions could include assault and battery, false imprisonment and torture. These were also criminal offences that might be prosecuted by the Crown. Criminal responsibility, of Governors and Civil Commissioners, was established under a series of statutes. Governors who oppressed their subjects, or who violated the laws of England or the laws of their colonies, were also liable

---

76   (1774), 1 Cowp 160, 175.
77   See Hill v Bigge (1841), 3 Moore PC 465, 481-2; 13 ER 189.
78   See Chapter 5.4: Public Order and Crime.
79   See also, for example, Dutton v Howell [1693] Shower PC 24; Comyn v Sabine (1738), cited in 1 Cowp, 169.

to be tried in England under a statute of 1700[80] and this was extended, by
the Criminal Jurisdiction Act 1802, to the effect that all persons who, in
the course of their responsibilities, whether civil or military, committed a
misdemeanour or offence whilst in the public service abroad, could be tried
in England.[81]

Justification

Any Commissioner or Governor brought before the English courts
would be entitled to defend an otherwise criminal or tortious action upon
the grounds of lawful justification, that the actions were within the scope
of his lawful powers. Thus, as mentioned above, English law recognised
implied powers to take necessary actions to maintain order and security.
Though justification would need to be determined by the English courts,
they would allow defences derived from the local law upon which
evidence could be taken. However, there could be a problem, not clearly
resolved in the early nineteenth century, if the actions in issue, though
lawful under the local law, were unlawful under English law. *Mostyn v
Fabrigas* suggests that a Commissioner would not, necessarily, have a legal
justification for actions that, if done in England, would have been unlawful
just because the actions (taken bona fide and in the public interest) were
lawful under local law. In the case, Governor Mostyn had been advised that
a Governor's powers, under Minorcan law at the time of British occupation,
allowed arrest, detention and exile. Lord de Grey, at first instance, took
the view that, even under the policy of continuity, local laws which were
offensive to fundamental principles recognised in English law, such as the
illegality of torture, ceased having legal validity once English authority
was established.[82]

But the issue was not decided at that time and had become increasingly
controversial by the mid nineteenth century. The question of the definition
and specification of what counted as a "fundamental principle" was too

---

80   11 William III c.12.
81   Unlike the Act of 1700 the 1802 Act did not extend to felonies.
82   "I suppose the old Minorquins thought fit to advise him [Governor Mostyn]
to this measure. But the governor knew that he could no more imprison him for a
twelvemonth, than he could inflict the torture; yet the torture, as well as the banishment, was the old law of Minorca, which fell of course when it came into our
possession", Fabrigas v Mostyn [1773] 2 Wm Bl 929; (1773), 20 St Tr 82, 181 De Grey
LCJ; quoted by Lord Rodger in R (Bancoult) Secretary of State for Foreign and Commonwealth Affairs [2008] UKHL 61 .

complex and discretionary to answer with adequate certainty. So, under the Colonial Laws Validity Act 1865, the limiting principle was redefined as inconsistency with a United Kingdom statute applying to the colony.[83]

In the early nineteenth century, however, the issue was clearly live as is indicated by the famous case of *R v Picton*.[84] The defendant, who had been governor of Trinidad, was accused of having personally authorised torture, as a technique of questioning, in a criminal investigation.[85] Under the procedures of the day he was convicted, then the conviction was set aside and a re-trial followed. The re-trial was suspended in 1812 but, it seems, Picton was never fully exonerated. [86]

Picton's defence was that torture, in order to question a defendant, was allowed for by the normal procedures of traditional Spanish law which applied in Trinidad at the time of British occupation. Much of the case involved an exploration of whether Spanish law did authorise torture and this was a question that an English jury, on the basis of expert evidence and judicial direction, had to decide. In the first trial the jury found that torture was not part of the law *status quo, ante* the British occupation, and so there was a conviction. The hearing to set that conviction aside, and the second trial, involved a challenge to that finding – the defence argued that torture was part of the applicable Spanish law and so (given that there was no evidence of bad faith or malice and that Picton had done nothing more than follow normal procedures) Picton should be acquitted. But the prosecution's point was that, even if it was allowed under Spanish law, and given the principle of continuity, torture was both illegal under the

---

83   Though the issue was to some extent revived in R (Bancoult) Secretary of State for Foreign and Commonwealth Affairs [2008] UKHL 61 where a majority of the House of Lords accepted that, at least after the enactment of the Colonial Laws Validity Act 1865, the Crown had the power to legislate to exile the local population of a colony. On this view even a local law upholding torture could not be set aside if it was not repugnant to a UK statute extending to the colony (per Lord Rodger, para 98) though in practice its enactment would not have been permitted.

84   (1812), 30 St Tr 225.

85   By "picketing" or using a wooden spike to pierce the foot under the weight of the victim's body which was suspended onto the spike from a pulley. The practice was used in the British army. In Picton the prosecution sought to distinguish this army practice from torture ("piqueting" from Pictoning) because the soldiers could, temporally, pull themselves off the spike.

86   The case report ends to the effect that it was thought by the Bar at the time that Picton would have been convicted but only lightly punished. It is noted that he fought with distinction in the Peninsular War and died an heroic death at Waterloo in 1815, leading a bayonet charge.

positive law of England[87] and was also contrary to fundamental principles which were the bases of and presumed by that positive law. Authorities cited included Blackstone, the leading authority on the eighteenth-century English Constitution, who considered that local laws contrary to the laws of God would not be continued[88], and his opinion reflects the Master of the Roll's memorandum, of 1722, that "until the conqueror gives them [the inhabitants of a conquered country] new laws, they are to be governed by their own laws, unless their laws are contrary to the laws of God or totally silent".[89] Similarly, the view of Lord de Grey, in *Mostyn,* was urged upon the court. In the end, the issue was never decided though it is clear, from the report, that the presiding judge, Lord Ellenborough, was sympathetic to the defence case. This might, contrary to the view of the Bar at the time, have led to him ordering an acquittal on the sufficient grounds that torture was lawful under the local law (if that was the finding). If so, he would have rejected the view that oppressive and unconscionable laws became unlawful with the arrival of the British flag.

The issue is important because the law, the Code de Rohan, permitted torture where the victim had been convicted of treason and the aim of torture was to identify accomplices. There were allegations that the authorities may have used it in at least one case.[90]

Ball may have violated Lord Mansfield's principles in other ways. As we shall see, in Chapter 5 (the public order and crime theme), Ball seems to have been prepared to go beyond his legal powers in order to exile individuals responsible for anti-Semitic violence.[91] In so far as this involved suspending the laws (the Grandmaster's powers in the criminal part of the Code de Rohan) he was, clearly, vulnerable to legal action based both on the grounds that executive suspension of the laws violated fundamental principles as did the power of exile itself. If the imposition of the exile, which Coleridge publicised in Public Notices, was, thus, contrary to "fundamental

87   Torture was, apparently, always illegal under common law; the Crown lost the Prerogative right to torture in 1640.

88   Blackstone, Introduction, section 4, 105. Blackstone cites Calvin's Case and so is vulnerable to Lord Mansfield's view in Campbell v Hall that the doctrine in anachronistic.

89   See Peere Williams's Reports Vol 2, case 15, 74, 1826, London: Butterworth.

90   Eton alleged that a market inspector, Sateriano, had been tortured by being imprisoned with live rats and thereby forced to confess. His conviction resulted in banishment to Tripoli: Eton to Windham, 11 October 1806, Kew, CO 158/12/ no folio reference. The facts have been disputed: see Staines, 226.

91   See the cases of Hasciach, Borg and Bonello discussed in Chapter 5.4: Public Order and Crime.

principles" in Lord Mansfield's sense, it raises the intriguing argument that some of the sentences of exile (which Coleridge publicised and appeared to approve) may have been unlawful and challengeable, at least in an English court. How sympathetic to Ball an English court would have been if Borg, Hasciach or Bonello (the subjects of Coleridge's Notice) had challenged their punishment is now a matter of speculation. However, it is not a foregone conclusion that the English judges in the early nineteenth century would have accepted that Ball's actions were lawful, merely because he acted in good faith, without malice, and on the grounds of security and public order.

Ultra Vires Actions

Mostyn v Fabrigas and *R v Picton* deal with a gubernatorial action which was unlawful in the sense that, had the actions been committed in England, they would, subject to any lawful justifications, have been crimes or torts. Governors and Commissioners were required to exercise their powers using lawful means. A different question relates to whether Governors or Commissioners were lawfully limited in the scope of the powers they had. In particular, whether there might be legal consequences if a governor or civil commissioner exceeded his powers, as expressed in the Royal Instructions, even though the actions taken where not otherwise unlawful – were neither criminal nor tortious? An example would be where an unauthorised tax was imposed. Could the courts restrain such acts? There were two general views. On one view, Commissioners or Governors were like Viceroys. In other words, they were, themselves, exercising the Royal Prerogative directly, in the eyes of the law. Whatever the Crown could do in its colonies so, too, could a Viceroy. No doubt, the Crown should use lawful means (though the Crown's judgement of what would be justified in the public interest would be hard to challenge) but a court could not, as a matter of law, limit the purposes and policies being pursued. According to the the other view, Commissioners or Governors were like Royal delegates governing on the basis of their Instructions. This interpretation would mean that actions taken outside those Instructions would lack legal validity.

At the time when Ball was Civil Commissioner, and Coleridge his Public Secretary, the position was unclear. In *Mostyn v Fabrigas,* Lord Mansfield had appeared to suggest that an otherwise lawful *ultra vires* act could be invalidated by a court (though, of course, only in England) but his formulation of the principle was decidedly ambiguous:

So that emphatically the governor must be tried in England, to see whether he has exercised the authority delegated to him by the letters patent legally and properly; or whether he has abused it in violation of the laws of England and the trust so reposed in him.[92]

This suggests both an *ultra vires* argument (in the first clause) but, in the second clause, an implication that an illegal and improper exercise of authority is confined to criminal or tortious actions. Furthermore, in *Mostyn*, Lord Mansfield had asserted that "it is truly said that the Governor is in the nature of a viceroy"[93] (and, therefore, is not subject to criminal or civil liability in local courts). This also implies that the Viceroy (having all the powers of the sovereign in the territory) could, in law, pursue otherwise-lawful administrative actions even if they went beyond the authority in the Instructions. In the absence of a crime or a tort, he could not be challenged in the courts either locally or in England. This meant that, at the time Coleridge was in office, it was probably, though not certainly, the case that actions not authorised by Royal Instructions would be valid and binding upon the local courts. In other words, the Instructions directed the Civil Commissioner but did not create mandatory, legally-enforceable, obligations. Only the Secretary of State, in London, would have the authority to require the recission of an unauthorised measure and the measure would be valid until rescission had taken place.[94]

The English courts only resolved the matter decades after Coleridge had resigned his office and left Malta. In *Cameron v Kyte*,[95] the Governor had issued an "instruction" purporting to reduce the commission of the local Vendue Master.[96] The power to make such a reduction could not be found in the Governor's Instructions and, though it was not directly a tort or a crime, the English court (upholding the local courts) allowed the Vendue Master's claim. The Governor's purported act was invalid and incapable of having legal effect, it was outside his Commission and Instructions. The idea that the Governor was like a Viceroy, with the "whole Royal power" delegated to him, was explicitly rejected in the judgement.[97] A further point about *Cameron v Kyte* is that, although final appeal was to the Privy Council

---

92   Mostyn v Fabrigas (1774), 1 Cowp 161, 173, 98 ER 1028, Lord Mansfield.
93   Mostyn v Fabrigas (1774), 1 Cowp 161 172, Lord Mansfield. See also Roberts-Wray, 147.
94   This represents academic opinion: see, generally, Swinfen.
95   (1835), 3 Knapp 332, 12 ER 678.
96   An official who sold, by public auction, property seized under the order of the court.
97   (1835), 3 Knapp 322, 344, 12 ER 678, 683

in London, the jurisdiction of the local courts (Supreme Court of Civil Justice in Demerara and Essequibo) to hear a dispute about the scope of a Governor's powers was not challenged.

International Law

Finally, it is worth observing that the law of nations was sufficiently developed to provide a normative framework within which policy, action affecting other states would have to be conducted and justified.[98] This had possible implications in Malta in the early British period. For example, the decision to feed a Maltese population which was, in January 1800, on the brink of starvation, by seizing, at gunpoint, grain supplies loaded onto ships in Sicilian ports, was a *prima facie* unlawful action. It was crucial that the Sicilian Crown later ratified this use of force against ships in a friendly port.[99] International law also influenced British ministers in repudiating Ball's adventurous and controversial policy of granting British passports to Sicilian and Neapolitan vessels.[100] As acting Public Secretary, Coleridge was required to re-structure the government's passport policy to ensure consonance with both the principles of international law and the political direction of British ministers.[101]

3.3. Political Constraints

Introduction

The legal analysis of the position of a Civil Commissioner, such as Sir Alexander Ball, suggests that there were, in legal principle, a number of areas within which he could be constrained by the courts. In practice, though, this was difficult to do (if only because of the need to bring an action in the courts in London) and, thus, it is true that Ball's actions were never challenged. Of greater practical significance were the conditions and

---

98   De Vattel's *The Law of Nations* was considered to be an important source book for diplomats by the end of the eighteenth century. Hinsley, 200-1.

99   Kew, CO 158/13/262.

100   Kew, CO 159/3/131.

101   See Avviso of 25 June 1805, NLM LIBR/MS 430 2/2 Bandi 1805 AL 1814, 15; and further, Chapter 5.9: Passports.

constraints upon a Commissioner's freedom of action based upon political procedures and power.

Political Accountability to London

Commissioners were subject to political supervision, guidance and instruction from London. This political control was exercised through letters and despatches between the Civil Commissioner and the Secretary of State. In these despatches, Civil Commissioners reported their decisions and actions to ministers and received further detailed instructions from them. A diligent Secretary of State could, thus, limit the Civil Commissioner's freedom of action to policies and decisions established within a framework prescribed in London.[102]

Civil Commissioners who took unauthorised action outside of their Instructions naturally courted political sanctions. Reprimand or removal from office could follow as a result of unauthorised conduct. These sanctions reflected political judgement rather than being the necessary consequence of legal wrongs and depended upon the judgement of the Secretary of State in London. Unlike a determination by a court, the political outcome was not governed by a legal normative framework. Indeed, an errant Civil Commissioner could escape all sanction because a minister could properly decide, upon political grounds, either to ratify the unauthorised conduct or, simply, to take no action. However, there were limits. Ratification could not make lawful an act which was unlawful in the sense of being a crime or a tort. In other cases, political considerations were usually overriding, and the preservation of the prestige and authority of British rule was an important consideration.

In Malta, for example, politics played a critical role in how the Secretary of State responded to the serious, and not altogether unfounded, criticism of Ball's administration in 1806. As we have seen in Chapter 2,[103] Ball had been invited responded to "*such serious Charges against your administration, as call for immediate Investigation*", but once he had done so, a formal decision

---

102   The constitutional doctrine was that the Secretary of State acted under the authority of the King in Council. It is doubtful whether the Secretary of State read every despatch; much was delegated to one of the two Under-Secretaries. Sir Alexander Ball, for example, often addressed despatches to E. Cooke: see Ball to Cooke, 3 February 1805, Kew CO 158/10/ 19; Ball to Cooke , 21 July 1805, Kew, CO 158/10/187-8; Ball to E. Cooke, 1 March 1806 Kew, CO 158/11 (no folio number) Ball to E. Cooke, 30 November 1807, Kew, CO 158/13/463.
103   Chapter 2 Section 3.

was delayed until 1808.[104] When the decision came Ball was formally (if not altogether convincingly) "acquitted", by his superiors, but the significant issue is that embarrassment had been avoided by a politically-convenient long delay. As we have argued in Chapter 2, the finding that the complaints were entirely baseless was not fully supported by the evidence and suggests a closing of ranks by the Establishment.

Accountability and Legislation

Under the old system of colonial governance, colonial legislation, emanating from provincial legislative assemblies, was submitted to the Secretary of State in London for review under the authority of the Privy Council (its Committee for Trade). Colonial statutes could be disallowed upon various grounds including interference with individual property and rights and general inexpediency. The Committee could act upon political advice from the Secretary of State and upon the advice of the Law Officers, who were alive to constitutional objections such as an improper encroachment upon the Royal Prerogative.[105]

Malta, was an early example of the new model of colonial governance, which, therefore, lacked a legislative assembly. Accordingly, the process of legislative scrutiny did not apply. Ball's/Coleridge's legislative acts were legally effective without the Secretary of State's prior approval. And they were not routinely ratified *ex post facto*. In other words, despite the continual stream of correspondence upon major policy issues, between London and Ball, there is no surviving evidence that texts of the Bandi and Avvisi were communicated to London either for approval or to keep the Secretary of State abreast of new developments in the legal system.

There were, however, a number of particular issues upon which the Instructions required that information, and proposals for regulation, be transmitted to London for His Majesty's approval. These included any "deviations", deemed necessary and unavoidable from the existing Maltese laws and practices, relating to justice and police. There was also an express requirement that any regulations deemed necessary, to deal with possible abuses in the courts and the judicial system (a particular concern in 1801 and discussed in Chapter 2), should be communicated to London prior to

---

104   See Windham to Ball, 6 January 1807, Kew, CO 159/3/220 at 223; Windham to Ball, 19 December 1806, Kew, CO 159/3/218 at 219. A formal resolution was not despatched. Ball to Windham, Kew, 28 February 1807, CO 58/13/9.
105   Manning, 75-81.

publication for approval. However, it should be noted that Ball chose to submit a copy of the Avviso of 25 June 1805 to the Secretary of State in order to demonstrate that he had fulfilled instructions in relation to passports.[106] This is, of course, a very different matter, from establishing a duty to submit each of the Bandi and Avvisi.

This is not necessarily surprising since, under the principle of continuity, there was an assumption that little legal and regulatory change would be necessary. This was a major weakness in the system of ensuring that the British administration on Malta was accountable. As Chapters 5 and 6 make clear, a number of the Bandi and Avvisi issued under Coleridge's signature contained provisions which were inconsistent with basic assumptions of the rule of law. They, sometimes, lacked comprehensibility, seemed to impose obligations upon the population of an uncertain nature or created criminal offences by notice rather than by proper legal procedure.[107] The lack of any reporting requirement meant that such defects in legislation, obvious to legal scrutiny, could not be picked up and remedied by Law Officers in London.

Other forms of direct political control from London were equally weak at this time.

Ministerial Responsibility to Parliament

Although the modern convention of ministerial responsibility had yet to evolve, a Secretary of State might, nonetheless, be called upon to explain and justify, to Parliament, his colonial policies, including those relating to Malta. In the case of the Crown's prerogative powers, however, ministerial accountability was more discretionary than for other national affairs.[108]

There were some Parliamentary debates relating to Malta in the period 1800-1806. These related to the negotiations on the Treaty of Amiens and the resumption of the war with France in 1803 – Malta having been the *casus belli*.[109] There were no debates dealing with the ordinary governance

106   See Chapter 5.
107   See, for example, the Avviso of 22 May 1805, NLM LIBR/MS 430 2/2 Bandi 1805 AL 1814, 8 which appeared to create criminal offences in a public notice and described those offences in such a vague, un-followable, way.
108   E.g., the Lord Chancellor refused to report on treaty negotiations with Russia in 1805, which involved the exercise of the crown's prerogative powers in relation to a foreign state, Cobbett's Parliamentary Debates Vol 5, 2-12.
109   See, famously, Lord Wyndham's intervention on the negotiations for the definitive treaty of peace, 1802 Cobbetts Parliamentary History, vol. 36, 565.

of Malta in this period.[110] This lack of Parliamentary concern and scrutiny can be contrasted with other areas of colonial activity in which Parliament did express a considerable and continuing interest, such as the affairs of India and the slave trade.[111]

The quiescence of the Parliament meant that colonial policy was dominated by Whitehall without serious parliamentary scrutiny.[112] A Minister could invite the Privy Council to enact an Order in Council – if he wished to pass a law that would be directly effective in a colonial territory. This was a comparatively rare occurrence. The system chosen for Malta emphasised bureaucratic rather than democratic controls over the Maltese. When Ball's administration passed laws in Malta, they did so under the political and legal authority of instructions from ministers in Whitehall under which Ball enjoyed considerable freedom of action.

Legislation

As discussed in this chapter, the British system for governing Malta, in the early period, was based upon indirect rule using the Royal Prerogative. A possible alternative, rule on the basis of powers conferred by an Act of Parliament, was avoided. The political costs and insecurities of securing Parliamentary consent for the details of colonial policy were too great. Nevertheless, where an objective was sought that could not be done under the Royal Prerogative, an Act of Parliament was necessary, and there were occasions, in the early nineteenth century, when ministers obtained Acts of Parliament which related to Malta. The aim of creating a free port in Malta, immune from certain taxes, was such a purpose and was pursued through

110   See Cobbett's Parliamentary History (until 1802) and Cobbett's Parliamentary Debates 1803, vols. 1-6. The first recorded debate specifically on Maltese affairs occurred in 1811 and involved allegations of extortion (by extracting unlawfully high fees) by the Court of Vice Admiralty, Parliamentary Debates, XL, 1077-9.

111   Cobbett's Parliamentary Debates vol. 2 has, for instance, debates on the India budget, Sierre Leone Company and compensation for the West Indies relating to proposals to abolish the slave trade; vol. 36 of Cobbett's *Parliamentary History* includes a debate on Trinidad and the slave trade.

112   In 1819 Joseph Hume attacked ministers on the grounds that governors and the secretary of state were conducting government in the conquered colonies without either being properly accountable. Criticism was particularly levelled at whether the Secretary of State, without reporting the matter to Parliament, should have control over significant expenditure in relation to the military establishments of the colonies. Worse still, Parliament had no knowledge of the revenue produced by the colonies. The absence of a colonial council meant that there were no checks on the governors.

the enactment of the Malta Act 1801.[113] Legislation was also enacted to provide for the payment of salaries of the Vice-Admiralty judges in the newly created Court of Vice-Admiralty in Malta in 1803.[114]

When problems arose about the mode of trial of a British soldier, Private John Allary, who was accused of murdering a Maltese civilian, the civil and military authorities disagreed as to the applicable law.[115] When the unresolved dispute was placed before the Law Officers of the Crown, they favoured the arguments of the Civil Commissioner that the local civil jurisdiction should apply. As this outcome was unsatisfactory to the military, the matter had to be resolved by the passing of legislation in Westminster.[116]

3.4. Conclusion

Sir Alexander Ball, under the continuity principle, exercised the wide and absolute powers of the Grandmaster, powers that were not effectively reviewable by the Maltese courts. They were autocratic powers in the sense that he controlled the legislative, executive and judicial functions. Nevertheless, Ball was also a British official operating the law of Malta. His authority derived from his Commission and Instructions, which were subject to little, if any, review by the courts.

The Crown, under English law, had the power to change the law in a conquered or ceded colony and, in the case of Malta, this legislative power would be exercised by the Civil Commissioner (using the forms of Maltese law). At least, as a matter of politics, if not law, Ball had to ensure that changes to Maltese law would need to be for the express, implied or ancillary purposes found in the Instructions. As we have seen, these purposes were very wide. Ball would have little difficulty in establishing that the laws promulgated under Coleridge's signature were (in the words of the Royal Instructions) "evidently beneficial and desirable, as to leave no doubt of [their] expediency". The task of persuading the Maltese of this was, in some instances, significantly more challenging. As we shall see in

---

113 41 Geo III c103, repealed by the Statute Law (Repeals) Act 1986 Ch 1 pt IX.

114 43 Geo III c160. The salaries were to be paid under the same conditions as laid down in the Act 39 Geo III c110.

115 Harding, 10 et seq; the issue is discussed above.

116 A clause was inserted into in the Articles of War, published annually under the authority of the Mutiny Act, exempting from civil jurisdiction members of the military accused of criminal offences in Malta.

Chapters 5 and 6, it fell to Coleridge to make the political case for each of the instruments, within the text of the laws and public notices.

Persons detrimentally affected by allegedly unlawful actions of the Civil Commissioner could pursue whatever domestic remedies were available. In the case of Malta, it seems that the law and its practice provided little by way of remedies against the Civil Commissioner. It was clear, from earlier cases, that if the Civil Commissioner committed a tort or a crime under English law he could be tried in England and English courts would determine any defences of lawful justification (based upon the local law) that might be argued. Any locally-lawful justifications, like torture in the context of treason, might be rejected, if they were deemed to be unlawful under English law, upon the grounds that, being unconscionable and against fundamental principles, they had ceased to be lawful following the British occupation. However, in Coleridge's time, such a view was only arguable, not settled. It might have been the case, as became settled later in the nineteenth century, that unlawful actions could be addressed in the local courts but, again, this was not clear at the time and, anyway, may have had little impact in Malta given the strength of the Civil Commissioner's position. Similarly, it is unclear whether an otherwise lawful action, outside the express or implied powers in the Instructions, could be challenged in the courts, local or English. In particular, any such act could, retrospectively, be validated by the Secretary of State in London.

No suit, whether civil or criminal, was ever brought in England challenging any of Sir Alexander Ball's actions as Civil Commissioner.[117] However, this is not to say that his decisions were always unambiguously within the law. The punishments that Coleridge notified to the Maltese public by an Avviso of 22 May 1805 are problematic.[118] In these cases, Ball inflicted severe punishments that, apparently, exceeded the maximum penalty available in Maltese criminal law. The punishments were a *prima facie* tort, under English law, and the question for the English courts would have been whether Ball's defence of justification would have succeeded. His actions were probably lawful under Maltese law (given the position of the Grandmaster) but this would not necessarily have satisfied the English

---

117   At least not in his life time. In 1895 a claim to compensation from Britain for losses caused by the French between 1798 and 1800 was rebutted by the British authorities by reference to Coleridge's Bando of 8 March 1805, LIBR/MS 430 2/2 Bandi 1805 AL 1814 f.2; the latter was treated as still valid law in 1895: see Chapter 5.3: Taxation.
118   See Chapter 5.4: Public Order and Crime.

court if they were outside the written law and also, perhaps, unconscionable.

Ultimately, the despotic powers of the Civil Commissioner meant that the liberties of the subject depended upon the conscience of the Civil Commissioner. The 1812 Royal Commission concluded that this was unsustainable. It recommended that constitutional reform, necessary to impose "some restraint", should be pursued. In this, some of the criticisms of the nationalists, particularly Eton, were implicitly accepted.[119] The Royal Commission recommended the ending of the Commissioner's suspending and dispensing powers, though it considered that the power of exile, by a simple warrant, should remain, albeit subject to greater checks than previously.[120] However, those reforms lay in the future, many years after Coleridge left Malta.

119   See Chapter 2.
120   Royal Commission of 1812, 236. At the same time, they steadfastly refused to recognise traditional existence of a legislative assembly or promote its establishment.

4. Coleridge's Proclamations and Public Notices

4.1. Coleridge's Role: the "Most Illustrious Lord, the Public Secretary" [1]

Coleridge's Authorship

Whilst he was Public Secretary, a number of instruments published in Italian, were promulgated under Coleridge's name. In some, but not all, of these, Dr. Guiseppe N. Zammit's name was also subscribed in his capacity as "Prosegretario" or Maltese Secretary.

The exact nature of Coleridge's responsibility for the instruments is not clear. There are numerous references, in his letters home, to his onerous responsibilities in writing official documents. Coleridge did not refer to the Bandi and Avvisi as such; nor did, he explicitly refer to the equivalent English terms, "Proclamations" and "Public Notices". The allusions in his letters reveal, however, that he was, probably, obliged to write three different types of official document during his Malta period: dispatches, Bandi and Avvisi respectively. And, it should be noted that he consistently refers to having to "write" these, rather than to supervise others in their authorship. His descriptions of this, as an "anxious duty",[2] are almost always intended to convey the sense of a heavy and stressful workload.

Coleridge's nomenclature for the different classes of document he dealt with are, on the one hand, "public Letters" and Memorials",[3] and, on the

---

1   To Mrs S. T. Coleridge, 21 August 1805, *CL* 2, 1172.
2   To Daniel Stuart, 30 April 1805, *CL* 2, 1165.
3   To Robert Southey, 2 February 1805, *CL* 2, 1160; to Daniel Stuart, ibid; to Daniel Stuart, 1 May 1805, *CL* 2, 1166; to Mrs S. T. Coleridge, 21 July 1805, *CL* 2, 1169; to Mrs S. T. Coleridge, 21 August 1805, *CL* 2, 1170 .

other, "public Memorials".[4] The question is: what did he mean by these terms? Does his idiosyncratic use of these terms mean that we can attribute the authorship of the Proclamations and Public Notices to him?

Before we investigate this question, it is important to remember that Coleridge, as Public Secretary, was, constitutionally, required to *sign* the Bandi and Avvisi.[5] We shall argue below that he also had a major role in drafting them, but even if he did not, he could not avoid the ultimate responsibility for ensuring their coherence and fairness.[6] Thus, Coleridge had *some* responsibility for what emerged under his signature. It is the nature and extent of that responsibility with which we are now concerned.

He seems to have used to term "memorial" (sometimes capitalised) in its conventional sense to mean a report comprising a statement of facts, as well as argument and conclusions derived from those facts. For example, he wrote to Southey:

> I could tell you how for the last nine months I have been working in memorials concerning Egypt Sicily and the Coast of Africa...[7]

These memorials were not identified as "*public* memorials" because, for obvious reasons, these were for government eyes only.

Similarly, he later described as a "well-reasoned Memorial"[8] an essay on Lampedusa written by a third party. This was not, it seems, to be published un-amended,[9] so it is unsurprising that he does not describe it as a "*public* Memorial". The latter term, ("public Memorial"), no doubt, had a different meaning.

We cannot be certain, but if he meant official statements of fact *placed before the public,* it is possible to conclude that Coleridge had the Avvisi or Public Notices in mind when he used the term "public Memorial". These Public Notices would fulfil an important public role because they invariably give the public factual information, such as, for example, the sentence imposed upon a named convicted criminal or the presence in Malta of counterfeit coinage. These and the other examples of his Avvisi are considered below. But did Coleridge also use the term "public Memorial"

4   To Mrs S. T. Coleridge, 21 July 1805, *CL* 2, 1169-70.
5   See Chapter 2.
6   Unless the requirement for signature was treated as a "rubber-stamp" exercise, although this can hardly have been intended by British ministers when they imposed it.
7   To Robert Southey, 2 February 1805, *CL* 2, 1164.
8   To Daniel Stuart, 30 April 1805, *CL* 2, 1165 at 1166.
9   Although he thought it might provide the foundation of a newspaper article, which is why it was sent to Daniel Stuart.

to embrace documents other than just the Avvisi?

Sultana seems to think so. He does not suggest that the term "public memorial" was confined only to the Avvisi. His conclusion is that, in his private correspondence, Coleridge did not distinguish between Bandi and Avvisi, (i.e. the Proclamations and Public Notices respectively) treating each alike and calling them, indifferently, "public Memorials".[10]

Sultana's point does not, necessarily, mean that Coleridge simply failed, in his nomenclature, to make significant distinctions. The ordinary meaning of the term "memorial" can include any communication containing significant information which the addressees are required to remember and act upon. If Coleridge used the term *"public Memorial"*, in this second sense, it could, as Sultana suggests, embrace all official public communications, which would include both the Bandi and the Avvisi – each of which was to be acted upon and the latter to be remembered and understood. "Public Letters", could then be taken to be Coleridge's terms for government correspondence – including the dispatches – an argument that is also supported by Sultana.[11]

This conclusion, which strongly points to Coleridge's authorship of the Bandi and Avvisi , is corroborated by a complaint that Coleridge made in a letter to Daniel Stuart, written in April 1805. In referring to his workload, he complained:

> .. having beside the most anxious duty of writing public Letters and Memorials *which belongs to my talents rather than my pro-tempore Office...*[12] (Emphasis added).

Assuming that "public" qualifies "Letters" and not "Memorials", Coleridge was here disclaiming formal, *ex officio*, responsibility for having to write both the public Letters (dispatches) *and* Memorials. This does not challenge our conclusion concerning his responsibility for the Bandi and Avvisi because he refers to these, it will be recalled, as *"public* Memorials". He could not have meant that the Bandi and Avvisi fell outside his role because the Secretary of State had ordered otherwise:[13] but he was complaining about the additional burden of having to write dispatches and reports.

---

10   Sultana, 270-1.
11   Sultana, 271.
12   To Daniel Stuart, 30 April 1805, *CL* 2, 1165.
13   By the Royal Instructions of 1801, and the dispatches succeeding them, the Public Secretary was required to sign all such measures: see Chapter 3. The case we are making here is that he also had a major role in drafting them.

Given the heavy burden of the Public Secretary's normal tasks, Coleridge was not acting unreasonably. It did not, usually, fall to the Public Secretary to write official reports, such as those Coleridge had once produced in his former role as Private Secretary to Ball (e.g., about Sicily and about Egypt). The Public Secretaries did not hold a "political" office, in the narrow sense of being officially involved in influencing the formation of British military and foreign policy. The Public Secretary's concern was the efficient administration of Malta. Thus, Coleridge had good cause to grumble.

There is also some internal evidence, in the Bandi and Avvisi, of his authorship. Coburn[14] and Sultana[15] have each detected features in the drafting of the Bando of 29 January 1805[16] that suggest Coleridge's early and inexperienced work. The practice of including justificatory material in the Bandi, whether signed by Coleridge or other office-holders, was not unique. A preamble explaining the factual context to new laws or administrative practices, explaining why they were needed, was sometimes adopted in instruments published before Coleridge took office.[17] Coleridge, subsequently, adopted this practice in Bandi, such as that of 8 March 1805,[18] (this concerned the politically sensitive excise duties), where the stated reasons for the legislation, included in the preamble, were detailed, extensive and served to make the political argument for their enactment. But Coleridge's first Bando is quite distinct from this later approach. This is shown by the nature of the material included and its location within the text.

Coleridge was anxious to demonstrate, scientifically, why enlightened self-interest favoured certain conduct that the government wished to promote. This reasoning, based upon scientific principles, was a last effort at persuasion. But its location within the structure of the Bando is also revealing. Rather than include it in the preamble, where the contextual and justificatory material was usually located, Coleridge inserted it into the final paragraph. Because, in later Bandi and Avvisi, Coleridge did not return to this structural technique, Coburn has, convincingly, argued that it is suggestive of the experimentation of the inexperienced draftsman.[19] Thus, the nature of the sustained argument that protruding nails act to

14   Coburn, 2, Appendix B.
15   Sultana, 278.
16   NLM LIBR/MS, Bandi 1790 AL 1805, 356.
17   See e.g., the Bando of 29 August 1801, NLM LIBR/MS 430 1/2; Bandi 1790 AL 1805, 213.
18   NLM LIBR/MS 430 2/2 Bandi 1805 AL 1814, 2.
19   Coburn, 2, Appendix B.

impede forward motion of a cart is at least suggestive of Coleridge's work in the Bando of 29 January 1805.

Some further internal evidence of Coleridge's authorship may also be detected in measures that reveal an inexperience and lack of familiarity with Maltese conditions: the narrative in the Avviso announcing the conviction, for anti-Semitic violence, of Fortunata Tagliana, in which Coleridge underscored the evil nature of her conduct by drawing upon her motive.[20] This feature of the Avviso is particularly interesting because no evidence of motive emerged from any of the extensive witness testimony. The reference to it may well have been an invented device to heighten further moral outrage and isolate other potential racists. Coleridge's superior skill in using information, to which Ball was to testify,[21] also suggests his very close involvement with the texts. This is more fully explored in Chapters 5 and 6.

There is also evidence of Coleridge's lack of familiarity with the Maltese social context, especially the attitudes of the less advantaged. As we shall see, there is persuasive evidence that the criminal justice system was weakened by a reluctance, on the part of the Maltese, to inform upon their neighbours. For example, the high crime rate but low conviction rate emerged as a complaint against the government in 1806;[22] many offenders "melted away" into a supportive local community. In the early days of his office, Coleridge may not have fully understood the significance of this "community solidarity". In an early Avviso, dated 22 March 1805,[23] Coleridge announced new punishments for offenders one of which required that those convicted of growing cotton, illegally, should hand over a proportion of the crop to an informant. Given the reluctance to inform, the prospect of the informant, personally, having to confront the offender, to demand the share of the crop, would seem to have been impracticable and unlikely to succeed in its purpose of providing an incentive for neighbours to give information to the authorities. Someone more experienced in Maltese conditions might not have entertained such unrealistic expectations.

There is a final, indirect, argument to suggest Coleridge's responsibility for the drafting of the Bandi and Avvisi (albeit in English). It is simply that, apart from the Bandi and Avvisi, there are no other known official documents issued to the public that could answer the description that

---

20   See Chapter 5.4: Public Order and Crime.
21   See Chapter 1, nn.
22   Borg to Eton, 30 May 1806, Kew, CO 158/12 (no folio reference).
23   NLM LIBR/MS 430 2/2 Bandi 1805 AL 1814, 5. LIBR/MS 430 2/2 Bandi 1805 AL 1814, 5.

Coleridge offered in his letters. The suggestion is, therefore, that Coleridge had a significant drafting responsibility, albeit that he most likely relied upon an official to translate his text into Italian. No doubt, he would also have sought advice from experienced civil servants, and, possibly, also from Ball himself, although no evidence has yet been found of this in the surviving archive.

There is no suggestion, however, that Coleridge had an exclusive responsibility for the final published text of these instruments.[24] He, almost certainly, had professional assistance of some kind, not least because these instruments were published in Italian. Indeed, the Italian used in the Bandi and Avvisi is of a stylised form, suggesting that Coleridge, with his limited command of the language, could not have had sole responsibility for the Italian text.[25] Sultana suggests that Coleridge may have drafted the Bandi in English, but gained the assistance of a translator, such as Millar, or, indeed, other assistants.[26] An alternative possibility is, of course, that the translator was none other than Dr. Zammit himself since such work also fell within his responsibilities.[27] His name was also subscribed upon some of the Bandi and Avvisi, which may also suggest his involvement in them.

As legal documents the issue arises of how effective they were, not only in achieving the substantive good, the general purpose they aimed at, but at embodying what might be called "rule of law" principles and general principles of good governance. We shall consider these questions in Chapters 5 and 6.

"Segretario Publico dell'Isole di Malta, Gozo e delle Loro Dipendenze"[28]

The Bandi and Avvisi, are signed: "Samuel T. Coleridge, Public Secretary to the *Royal Commissioner*".[29] (Emphasis added). This is an inaccurate

---

24   Nor, of course, for the substance of the laws enacted, since the law-making power was vested in Ball as Civil Commissioner, not Coleridge as acting Public Secretary. See further below, Chapter 3.

25   See Coburn, 2, Appendix A where she concludes that although Coleridge could converse in Italian by early 1805, his understanding was far from perfect.

26   Sultana, 278.

27   Zammit was required to transcribe official documents into Italian: see Caruana.

28   To Robert Southey, 2 February 1805, *CL* 2, 1163.

29   The alternative formula was, "S. T. Coleridge, Secretary to the Royal Commissioner". Ball was formally entitled, "His Majesty's Civil Commissioner for the

statement in so far as Sir Alexander Ball was the Civil Commissioner rather than the "Royal" Commissioner. Ball's decision to use an alternative is revealing.[30]

We know that Ball thought that his proper title was confusing to the Maltese. He also hinted, perhaps somewhat pompously, that he thought that it was not sufficiently commensurate with the dignity of his Office.[31] The *Bandi* and *Avvisi* suggest that, for local purposes, Ball used an alternative and more regal title, substituting "Royal" for "Civil". He presented a request to Lord Windham for permission to be called "Governor". Ministers refused to accede to this request,[32] although formally a decision in this matter was merely deferred.

Coleridge's Responsibility for Policy

In what follows, it is important to recall that, in accordance with the Maltese Constitution, and the Royal Instructions from the Secretary of State to the Civil Commissioner, the law-making power was, in a constitutional sense, vested in the Civil Commissioner, not in the Public Secretary. Coleridge, in describing governmental decision-making, recorded, in *The Friend,* that Ball was the *de facto,* as well as the *de jure,* decision maker.[33] Coleridge, it might be stated, was merely "his master's voice", in so far as he had, loyally, to introduce such Proclamations and Public Notices as Ball ordered. In other words, he was not responsible for (i) the decision to pass a Proclamation or issue a Public Notice; (ii) its subject matter; (iii) the policy it sought to advance.

However, Coleridge's primary intention, in describing in *The Friend* the

Island of Malta and its Dependencies and Minister Plenipotentiary to the Order of St John".

30   His adoption of this style appears elsewhere and seems to represent a general practice intended to association his office more closely with Royal dignity: see e.g., *Registro di memoriali decretati da sua Excellenza il Sig. Cavalier Alessandro Ball, Regio Commissionario Civile di Sua Maestà Britannica Incominciato li 14.9.05 sino li 24.12.1805.* NAM LIBR 43/13, volume "0".

31   Ball to Windham, 27 August 1806, Kew, CO 158/12/153, 157.

32   A possible reason for this rejection is that it coincided with rising ministerial concern about Ball's administration. Windham was about to demand of Ball that he respond immediately to the serious allegations made against him by Eton and others: see Windham to Ball, 6 January 1807, Kew, CO 159/3/220, 223. Ball's request for a change in his title was under consideration at the very time his reputation was impugned: see Windham to Ball, 19 December 1806, Kew, CO 169/3/ 218, 219.

33   *The Friend,* 1, 552-3.

processes of government, was to impress upon us that, before deciding any question, Ball consulted widely and, most significantly, that he consulted Coleridge. Thus, the Civil Commissioner was presented as an administrator who, according to Coleridge, enjoyed fully-reasoned and evidence-led decision making. But, Coleridge also makes clear, that the final decision as to what government did was Ball's. Thus, when we consider Coleridge's responsibility for the outcomes – the Bandi and Avvisi that he issued – we must bear this important *caveat* in mind.

This means that, where the substance of the law appears to the modern reader to be harsh or oppressive (as in the case of the banishment of minors for repeating false rumours), the responsibility for this action lies, predominantly, with Ball. We might hope and expect that in the extensive consultation that took place before such new measures were introduced Coleridge would have made arguments consistent with the ideas that had earlier been advocated, for example, in *The Morning Post*, which emphasised the need to observe the appropriate constitutional and moral standards.[34] But the contemporary documentary evidence, required to establish what advice Coleridge actually gave, has been lost. It is now only possible to conclude that, if Coleridge offered such advice (and Coleridge is clear that he was consulted) he did not always succeed in persuading the Civil Commissioner to adhere to these "constitutional" standards.[35]

This is not to say that Coleridge can always be distanced from controversial decision-making. For example, in *The Friend*, Coleridge expressed support for a number of administrative and criminal justice policies that we regard as problematic. For example, he supported the appointment of (unqualified) Maltese to important government posts, which is likely to have been a major cause of administrative inefficiency and even corruption.[36] Even more controversial is his *ex post facto* assessment that the measures taken to suppress the anti-Semitic disturbances were appropriate and even wise.[37] In this conclusion he must have accepted, for example, that the public interest could, sometimes, only be safeguarded where the judiciary acted upon the instructions of the government, and that the need to protect the Jewish community overrode constitutional

---

34   See Chapters 1 and 6.
35   Thus, Coleridge could only be held to account for the initiatives discussed below if it could be demonstrated that he had acted without instructions from Ball. Unsurprisingly, there is no surviving evidence that this ever happened.
36   *The Friend*, I, 569.
37   Ibid., 544.

orthodoxy. This expression of support does, of course, implicate him in the banishment of minors for rumour-mongering. It was a sentence dictated by the government; presumably Coleridge was consulted about it; and he expressed a general approval for the actions of government in relation to the disturbances in his later writing. This invites the conclusion that his earlier opinions on, for example, the emergency powers proposed by Addison's government in 1802, that Rule of Law values should be maintained even in times of emergency (see Chapter 6), had undergone some revision whilst he held public office.

Moreover, Coleridge was not merely a public functionary who lacked authority to exercise some independent professional judgement. Whilst the political, legal or administrative objectives of each instrument could be determined by Ball, Coleridge's judgement affected *how* the Bandi and Avvisi were drafted and what "extraneous" material went into them.[38] Coleridge, as we shall discover below[39], experimented with various techniques, either to win public support for the laws or for the British administration more generally. These techniques included: the promotion of Ball as a wise governor; arguments that compliance with the new law was in the self-interest of the inhabitants; or in other cases, somewhat controversial and even unpalatable experiments with propaganda. Sometimes, he even misled the population about why a particular measure had been adopted. Whether Coleridge discussed these techniques with other officials, or even with Ball himself (and if so, what advice he might have received) remains unclear. However, it must be assumed that Ball would have interested himself in the legislation that was critical to the success of his government. The Bando of 8 March 1805,[40] concerning excise duties, is pre-eminently such a measure. It can be assumed that the two men would have discussed how to persuade the Maltese to accept the new tax.

4.2. The Nature of Bandi and Avvisi

We are presently concerned with the Bandi and Avvisi, and we must now explain more fully what these instruments were.

---

38 By extraneous, it is meant material (often explanatory or justificatory) that was not strictly necessary to achieve the purposes of the measure.
39 See also Chapter 6.
40 NLM LIBR/MS 430 2/2 Bandi 1805 AL 1814, 2.

Definition of Bandi

A Bando, which was a form of regulation known since at least the middle ages, has been described by Leopardi as a Proclamation.[41] Accordingly, we use the term "Band" and "Proclamation" inter-changeably.

A Bando had the force of law. If this had ever been in doubt, from the English perspective, the matter was settled in a dispute that, as it happened, concerned Coleridge's Proclamation of 8 March 1805[42] – one of the most important instruments published under his name. The dispute concerned a claim for compensation made, in 1894-1895, by the Ecclesiastical Corporations on Malta. They argued that, in this Bando, the British had assumed a responsibility to compensate them for losses sustained after the French looted their capital, which had formerly been invested in the Bank of the Università. Their case was that a legally-enforceable promise had been made, which the British had reneged upon. The outcome turned upon whether the Bando of 8 March 1805 had the force of law and, if it had, whether an unambiguous undertaking to compensate them had been made within it.

The Maltese and British governments, who consulted the opinion of jurists and judges, were advised that a Bando was a binding legal instrument, which remained in force until repealed. However, Coleridge's text, when properly understood, had not created an unambiguous undertaking that the Ecclesiastical bodies would receive compensation. It merely stated: "As soon as he is able, His Excellency shall not neglect to give the necessary help to places of worship, and to religious foundations".

The payment of compensation was thus an aspiration, not a promise. This meant that the claim by the Ecclesiastical bodies failed upon its merits.

In fact, there could be few doubts about the constitutional authority of the British authorities to pass laws in Malta after 1800, so it is not surprising that a Bando was found to be a legislative instrument; but for our purposes the case of the religious foundations serves to remove any serious question about the legal status of Proclamations issued by the Civil Commissioner in 1805.

Characteristics of a Maltese Bando

There is an interesting distinction between an English statute and a Maltese

41   Leopardi, 186.
42   See Chapter 5: Taxation.

Bando of this period. English statutes express the commands of the Crown in Parliament; and they are enforced by the coercive powers of the State. Most significantly, the obligations created and imposed by this legislation are regarded as outcomes of the political process. The reasons that persuaded Parliament to enact the law are not incorporated or expressed within the instrument itself. They were made known to the public by means of newspaper reports of parliamentary debates of the kind that Coleridge had himself undertaken prior to his period in Malta. The debates that these reports stimulated would be a part of a wider public-political engagement .

This means that the reasons for legislation will have been explored and tested in the political process leading to the enactment of the statute. Once the legislators had been persuaded that a legislative enactment was either desirable or necessary, and it was placed upon the statute book, individuals were expected to obey it.[43]

Unlike English statutes, Maltese Bandi often commence with a recital or preamble as to why the introduction of the law was either necessary or desirable. This contextual material, appealing to the reason of the inhabitants, was no doubt intended to make the obligations imposed upon them more acceptable. Merely by having to justify its intervention in their lives, the state might be seen to respect the autonomy of individuals thereby affected. As his later accounts in *The Friend* revealed, Coleridge placed a significant emphasis upon the importance of fully-reasoned decision-making within Ball's cabinet. He associated this with what Coleridge described as Ball's love of justice which served to demonstrate the moral authority of the law.[44] Thus, for Coleridge, there would have been a close relationship between having sound reasons for introducing a Bando and communicating those reasons to the Maltese. As we have described, the Bando of 29 January 1805[45], about the regulation of cart wheels, is a pre-eminent example of his attempt to incorporate and communicate the reasons why legislation was being introduced. Other examples are considered in Chapter 5.

This is not to say that securing the consent of the inhabitants was legally or constitutionally necessary. The inhabitants lacked a legal veto over measures enacted by the Civil Commissioner. Ball was, in a constitutional sense, exclusively equipped to identify and implement policies beneficial to the wider community. There was not even the veneer of democratic legitimacy to measures introduced into law. Nevertheless, both the Civil

---

43   This was, of course, before the introduction of universal suffrage.
44   *The Friend*, I, 169-70.
45   See Chapter 5.1: Reconstruction.

Commissioner and Coleridge would have been aware that securing popular consent to an enactment was, politically, fundamental to Ball's continuation strategy; indeed the Instructions from the Secretary of State required him to ensure the continued support of the Maltese for British rule.[46] At the very least, unpopular laws would fan agitation for a representative, legislative assembly, such as the *Consiglio Popolare*. Confronted with unpopular laws that went against the grain of Maltese preferences, their leaders would demand influence, or even control, over new legislation. As we saw, in Chapter 2, this reaction occurred in 1805 and became a serious political issue for Ball after the first petition to the Crown was made by nationalists who (by-passing Ball) pressed the Secretary of State for fundamental political reform.[47]

In *The Friend*, Coleridge revealed his opinion that an engagement with the reason of the Maltese had a moral as well as a practical value. "No body of men (sic) can for any length of time be safely treated otherwise than as rational beings".[48] He intuitively understood that argument had to be ventured to persuade the inhabitants of the merits of British rule – "If there be any difference between a Government and a band of robbers, an act of consent must be supposed on the part of the people governed".[49] The Bandi and Avvisi reveal how Coleridge practised these political values.

Definition of Avvisi

Avvisi were also published, as official instruments, by the British administration. An Avviso has been described, by Paul Cassar and Albert Ganado,[50] as an "advertisement", although the nomenclature "Public Notice" would seem to be equally apposite. For present purposes the latter term, "Public Notice" is used interchangeably with "Avviso".

Ball ordered Coleridge to publish Avvisi to ensure public awareness of government action. The administration of the law provided one of their major subjects. For example, he used them to publicise the punishment meted out to offenders. Deterrence required the widest publicity, for which notification of the conviction and punishment would be a pre-requisite.

46   Downing Street to Ball, 9 June 1802, Kew, FO 49/3/51.
47   Memorial and Petition of the Maltese (unsigned and undated), 1805, Kew, CO 158/10/151.
48   *The Friend*, I, 540.
49   Ibid., 175.
50   P. Cassar and A. Ganado, 'Two more Documents of 1813 written on Wood during the Plague of Malta', *Melita Historica* (1979), VII/4: 356-62

These Avvisi also ensured the denunciation of the convicted criminal in order to effect a public shaming. But this is not all because Coleridge's Avvisi, in fact, served diverse bureaucratic purposes, such as, for example, announcing the revocation of passports[51] or ensuring that the population was made aware that armed deserters were roaming the countryside.[52]

One question concerns why public information notices were used, to convey this government information, rather than newspapers. This is of particular interest because the only printing press on Malta was under government control. The *Malta Gazette* was the government's propaganda organ which, by the time of Coleridge's sojourn on Malta, was edited by Vittorio Barzoni under the title of *Il Cartaginese*. This was used as a tool to counteract the effects of French propaganda.[53] Information about the sentences imposed upon miscreants might easily have been published in the Gazette rather than in a Public Notice.

The likely reason why *Il Cartaginese* was not used was that the poor literacy levels,[54] as well as the expense, probably limited its circulation. Moreover, the Avvisi could be deployed as a means by which the administration "connected" – which could not occur so effectively if the Maltese thought they received information through the prism of the editorial function – even if the paper was controlled by government. Addressing the Maltese directly, in a governmental capacity, contributed to the sense that their government was speaking to them, notwithstanding that the instruments were in Italian – a language with which most Maltese were unfamiliar. A Public Notice, which would be read aloud to a fanfare of drums in the villages and towns would be more likely to be effective in disseminating the information to a wider audience, especially where some educated person, most likely the local priest, was on hand to translate the instruments for the assembled crowd.

During the earliest days of their administration, the British had experimented by publishing new laws and public notices with a parallel English and Italian text. Presumably, the English text was of little interest to the Maltese since few spoke the language, and the practice was quickly abandoned.

---

51   Avviso, 25 June 1805, NLM LIBR/MS 430 2/2 Bandi 1805 AL 1814, 15.

52   Avviso, 15 July 1805, NLM LIBR/MS 430 2/2 Bandi 1805 AL 1814, 17.

53   See Sultana, 13.

54   The widespread illiteracy amongst the Maltese prompted Coleridge to remark in his private Notebook that the time spent by the priests in religious observance might have been better spent in teaching the poor to read. His further despairing comment was that ignorance served the interests of the Church: *CN* 2, 2484.

Coleridge knew how to give this information the heightened impact necessary in an effective public instrument of this kind. As we shall see, nowhere is this more clearly revealed than in some of the Avvisi relating to crime and punishment. Where widespread disorder occurred, Coleridge sought to maximise popular revulsion to reinforce the deterrent effect of the conviction. Instead of a dull record that a named individual had been convicted and sentenced for a serious offence, we sometimes discover a richly-informative narrative style to give an account of the horrifying events constituting the offences. It is in instruments such as these, rather than the legally rigorous Bandi, that Coleridge can be said to excel.

Avvisi were, therefore, more than mere advertisements or notices; and they were more useful to government than a controlled press. An Avviso allowed the government to directly control the tone and content of the message – to exploit its propaganda value, and to choose what information to reveal to, and what to conceal from, public consumption. They allowed Coleridge and Ball to speak directly to the Maltese people, creating a stronger relationship than would have been possible if they had used the medium of the press. Thus the Avvisi were, clearly, valuable tools of communication, especially in Coleridge's hands.

Avvisi as Legal Instruments

Some Avvisi also reveal a legal complexity that remains perplexing. There are two senses in which this was so: in the first, the Avviso indicated how existing legal power would be exercised in future; in the second the Avviso purported to change the law itself. In this second sense, their constitutional status was controversial.

An example of an Avviso indicating how power would, in future, be exercised is that of 22 March 1805.[55] It suggested that existing, but not specified, powers over health and consumer protection would be used to inspect wine shops and confiscate any wine of insufficient quality. It does not, however, state any legal authority for such a drastic sanction. The suggestion is that the Notice itself purported to create that authority.

A similar example concerns the Avviso of 12 June 1805 which brought to the attention of the Maltese the circulation of false currency. The text included a duty upon those receiving the coins to deliver them to the

---

55   NLM LIBR/MS 430 2/2 Bandi 1805 AL 1814, 6.

authorities.[56] It is unclear whether this merely expressed an existing obligation recognised by law or purported to impose a new one. If the latter, it would be constitutionally controversial whether a Notice could achieve this. It is to this issue in several of the Avvisi that we now turn.

Bando or Avviso: Choice of Instrument

A rigid distinction between a Bando and an Avviso was not always practised, which meant that an Avviso could, sometimes, be used where the Administration sought to amend the law or the punishment available to the courts for particular offences and where a Bando was more constitutionally appropriate. In an interesting dispatch, Ball reported to Lord Castlereagh that he had complied with instructions by issuing a "Proclamation". It is most revealing that he was actually referring to Coleridge's Avviso (Public Notice) relating to passports, dated 23 June 1805.[57] If Ball's report was not a mere lapse, this language may suggest that officials sometimes regarded Bandi and Avvisi alike as "Proclamations", each capable of altering Maltese law.

The problem, in Malta, was that executive and legislative power was fused in the office of the Civil Commissioner. Law reform depended, ultimately, upon Ball's discretion because, under the Maltese Constitution, he exercised unlimited powers. The difference between a Bando and an Avviso might have seemed to some officials – perhaps even to Coleridge himself – to be a trifling, bureaucratic formality especially when there appears to have been no substantive differences concerning the process of their promulgation.

However, the differences were fundamental and ought to have been recognised as such. The Maltese would have understood that a Bando altered the legal relationship between citizen and state. Thus, the adoption of an instrument officially entitled "Bando" communicated to the Maltese that their legal rights and entitlements were being altered. This was not obviously the case with an Avviso. Where the administration purported to reform the law by means of the latter, it risked confusing the Maltese and failed to meet the requirement, of the Rule of Law, that rules should be comprehensible. For example, the decision to criminalise those who

56   NLM LIBR/MS 430 2/2 Bandi 1805 AL 1814, 10. These coins resembled silver coins having a face value of one scudo bearing the mark of Grandmaster De Rohan.
57   NLM LIBR/MS 430 2/2 Bandi 1805 AL 1814, 15; also Ball to Cooke, 21 July 1805, Kew, CO 158/10/187.

repeated false rumours as well as those who were present when false rumours were spread, but who did nothing to "undeceive" other listeners, represented a clear extension of the Code de Rohan, which ought to have been achieved by a Bando rather than an Avviso.[58] Similarly, with the "severe" punishments for assisting deserters that the Administration purported to impose by the Avviso dated 15 July 1805.[59] And, in the Avviso of 22 March 1805,[60] regulating the cotton trade, the Civil Commissioner "ordered" new (and presumably more severe) punishments to be imposed upon those who used illegal means to produce inferior cotton.

The announcement of new punishments was also a breach of the principle of *nulle poena sine lege*, which requires that legitimate punishment can only be imposed in accordance with existing, publicly disclosed laws. A person should know, in advance, what is proscribed, and he or she should be able to alter their behaviour accordingly. Thus, the prior existence of a valid law that prescribes a penalty for the condemned behaviour is a requirement of the Rule of Law. This principle is, perhaps, the most important guarantee of civil liberty, for without it any conduct of which the administration disapproved could be subjected to punishment.

There is a suggestion that the authorities became aware of this problem (and thus understood that a Bando and not an Avviso ought to have been the legitimate means of altering Maltese law) because the "offences" that were supposed to have been created, by an Avviso of 15 July 1805,[61] were placed into a Bando, dated 2 September 1805.[62] This Bando would not have been required if the Notice of 15 July 1805[63] had been understood to be legally effective.

Bandi, Avvisi and Coleridge's Health: "Some Intrusions of Sickness"[64]

The Bandi and Avvisi were issued at irregular intervals. A flurry of activity, which might sometimes involve the issue of several instruments on a single day, could be followed by a significant lull. One interesting question is

---

58   Avviso, 15th July 1805, NLM LIBR/MS 430 2/2 Bandi 1805 AL 1814 17.
59   NLM LIBR/MS 430 2/2 Bandi 1805 AL 1814, 17.
60   NLM LIBR/MS 430 2/2 Bandi 1805 AL 1814, 5.
61   See n. 58 above.
62   NLM LIBR/MS 430 2/2 Bandi 1805 AL 1814, 21.
63   Ibid. 17.
64   To Daniel Stuart, 30 April 1805, *CL* 2, 1165 .

whether these irregular "pulses" of administrative and legislative action coincide with Coleridge's bouts of ill-health and remission, or whether the explanation was merely bureaucratic convenience – a requirement to focus upon other tasks? A further question is whether Coleridge's low morale, albeit originating in his addiction, also suffered because of the moral ambiguities of the work he was required to undertake. For example, did his relapses occur after the most controversial Bandi and Avvisi and were these collapses attributable to his responses to the work upon which he was engaged?

In the state of present knowledge, the task of establishing any detailed correlation between Coleridge's reports of his health and the dates upon which the Bandi and Avvisi were promulgated is problematical. A further problem is that Coleridge did not, explicitly, express a connection between the Bandi and Avvisi and his emotional or physical state whilst in office. If he felt distaste for some of his more controversial work, it may only have formed a part of an intricate array of causes for his physical and psychiatric suffering. Coleridge seems to have been acutely aware of this: "...did I not groan at my unworthiness, & be miserable at my state of Health, its effects, and effect-trebling causes?"[65]

If his own accounts of his condition are reliable, Coleridge suffered from the physical and psychiatric symptoms of his addiction throughout his period of office. Homesickness, the failure of communications with family and friends, and the unrelenting pressure of work associated with his public duties each affected him.[66] Sir Alexander Ball's insistence that he remain in post, against his will, was also likely to have been damaging to his morale and resilience.[67] Moreover, Coleridge had assumed the role of acting Public Secretary on the understanding that it would not last for more than a few weeks. The disappointment that Mr Chapman (his permanent replacement) was inexplicably delayed must have been particularly wearying when Coleridge's hopes of release were repeatedly frustrated.[68]

It is known that Coleridge reported a decline in his health from mid February 1805, barely a month into his tenure. The demands upon Coleridge were considerable even though he did not act as Treasurer and

---

65   *CN*, 2, 2453, 15-16 February 1805.
66   See e.g. To Mrs S. T. Coleridge, 21 July 1805, *CL* 2, 1169; also to Mrs S. T. Coleridge, 21 August 1805, *CL* 2, 1170.
67   "...my gloom has encreased (sic) at each disappointment". To Mrs S. T. Coleridge, 21 July 1805, *CL* 2, 1169.
68   To Robert Southey, 2 February 1805, *CL* 2, 1163.

some of the Public Secretary's work (such as directing the departments of State) was, apparently, delegated to Giuseppe Zammit. Despite these limits upon his workload, Coleridge's already-weakened health suffered an early deterioration. Almost as soon as the volume and complexity of his public role became apparent to him, he seemed to struggle, not least because of the volume and unfamiliarity of the work involved. In his correspondence to friends and family at this time, the onerous nature of his work and his sense of fatigue were described alongside various symptoms of ill-health. Privately, in his *Notebooks*, he added further information, most particularly his responses to his suffering and the depressing side-effects of his addiction.[69]

However, there was no hint, in his correspondence, that the moral complexities of his work affected his mood. In a revealing letter to Daniel Stuart, after having complained of his excessive workload, Coleridge proceeded to describe a recent illness followed by an inexhaustive list of its perceived causes, none of which referred to the political manipulation of governmental information.[70] However, his participation in what he later confessed was the "awkward & wicked machinery" of colonial government makes it difficult to dismiss the possibility that his experience of morally-complex policy-making did not have some influence upon his depression whilst in office.[71]

The period between late February and early March was, unquestionably, a stressful time because he was required to produce a critically-important Bando (the excise duties upon wine and spirits) and three Avvisi. As we have seen, it would not be an exaggeration to claim that Ball's financial and political strategy for the islands depended upon persuading the Maltese to accept the new duties notwithstanding a constitutional provision that precluded it. The political situation was all the more dangerous because the British had formally promised the Maltese to maintain the constitutional rights of the Maltese people. As we have seen, in Chapter 2, the risks presented by breaching these undertakings, and frustrating the very expectations that the British had encouraged, should not be under-estimated. The burden of deflecting Maltese hostility, and even winning Maltese support for the highly controversial measure – tasks that might have seemed all but impossible – fell upon an ailing Coleridge.

69   *CN* 2, 2453, 15-16 February 1805; *CN* 2, 2457, 18 February 1805 discloses re-morse and self-disgust, which implies a relapse.
70   To Daniel Stuart, 1 May 1805, *CL* 2, 1166.
71   To Daniel Stuart, 22 August 1806, *CL* 2, 1178.

Perhaps unsurprisingly, these burdens took their toll upon him. His coping strategy meant that he resorted to opium. By 21 February 1805 he was reflecting on possible ways of deterring his resort to the drug. He, stoically, considered writing and displaying warning memoranda wherever he might see them to stiffen his resolve to stay away from narcotics. This idea was gloomily put aside because the notes displayed would only remind him of his frailties.[72] He struggled on with symptoms that were already very familiar to him: bad bowels and nightmares.[73]

As soon as the Bando and the three Avvisi had been issued, Coleridge seems to have fallen back into despair and a further period of ill-health. On 8 March 1805 – the very day the Bando about the excise duties had been issued – Coleridge recalled lines from his poem *The Pains of Sleep* and then concluded, "Help Lord! Or I perish".[74] In an entry a few hours later, he verged upon "utter Despair".[75] There is no doubt that this was an expression of his wretched realisation that, after almost a year in Malta, he had not succeeded in liberating himself from dependency upon opiates. The web of propaganda that he had just created might well have had a further depressing influence upon him.

He was to issue three further instruments, on 22 March 1805, which meant that the immediately-preceding period must also have been busy. Sunday 17 March 1805 found him at a particularly low ebb. It was, he wrote, "A Day of Evil/wretch....O a groan deep and almost of moral despair!" His work at this time was suffering. The Bando about the regulation of spirits[76] lacked clarity in drafting. Even identifying which was the responsible licensing authority was far from clear. Moreover, there were indications of a lack of attention to detail. Similarly, Coleridge may have overlooked the fact that the Avviso governing wine inspections[77] (also dated 22 March 1805) should have been a Bando rather than an Avviso because it appears to have introduced a new penalty. These lapses suggest that his ability to comprehend and execute his complex new role may have been affected by his physical and mental condition.

A letter written to Daniel Stuart, on 1 May 1805, recorded that, from mid April, he had been very ill, much worse, indeed, than at any other

72   CN 2, 2489, 21 February 1805.
73   CN, 2, 2468, 5 March 1805. See also to T. Wedgewood, 16 September 1803, CL 2, 991.
74   CN 2, 2482.
75   CN 2, 2483.
76   NLM LIBR/MS 430 2/2 Bandi 1805 AL 1814, 4.
77   Ibid. 6.

period during his time on Malta.[78] After 22 March 1805, no further Bandi or Avvisi were promulgated for two months. Not until the emergency caused by the anti-Semitic uprising was Coleridge compelled to return to producing Avvisi. This substantial interval suggests either that there was no requirement to issue further instruments or that Coleridge was prevented from attending to that business. Although he seems to have been active in other ways during this interval, he could judge for himself that his effectiveness was in doubt. An undated Notebook entry of April 1805 is revealing: "So hard have I worked lately, & *to so little effect in consequence of my Health...*"[79] Despite his most industrious efforts, he seems to have understood that he was unproductive. This failure was, he claimed, causing him "agitation and anxiety".[80] Perhaps this is unsurprising when he was forced to confront his own decline, and most particularly, difficulties in work in which he should have excelled. Moreover, his description of an "anxiety" state is an under-statement. He had, very recently, contemplated suicide and feared that he would not survive to see his family.[81] Even so, there were still occasional moments of joy. The emerging spring blossoms and flowers were a particular delight.[82]

Six instruments were promulgated in the second half of June and a further (Avviso) on 15 July 1805. The effort this required also appears to have taken its toll upon him, for he reported in a letter to his wife, dated 21 July 1805,[83] that his health had recently been "very, very bad". The final quartet of official instruments emerged in August and early September by which time he reported that he was too busy to exercise.[84] He had once more sunk into a despondent frame of mind and seems to have found sleep difficult.[85] At the same time, there are signs of an impaired ability to produce coherent and fully considered law reform. The bizarrely drafted Bando of 5 August 1805, concerning unripened fruit, is an example of this.[86] Even more significant was that, on the very same day, he issued an Avviso containing the erroneous statement that a Proclamation of 1801 had criminalised sales of goods to soldiers (rather than purchases from soldiers). Was this a

---

78   To Daniel Stuart, 1 May 1805, *CL* 2, 1166.
79   *CN* 2, 2560.
80   Ibid.
81   *CN* 2, 2557, 21 April 1805 and *CN* 2, 2560.
82   E.g. *CN* 2, 2499, 2519, 2538 and 2565.
83   To Mrs S. T. Coleridge, 21 July 1805, *CL* 2, 1169.
84   To Mrs S. T. Coleridge, 21 August 1805, *CL* 2, 1170.
85   E.g. *CN* 2, 2638, 14 August 1805.
86   NLM LIBR/MS 430 2/2 Bandi 1805 AL 1814, 19.

careless error or a reckless intention to deceive – a decision, in other words, to gamble with the reputation of Ball's administration? Taken together, these instruments might well mark a further stage in the progressive disintegration in his effectiveness in public office.

The summer heat caused a boil on his arm and he became ever more irascible at the intrusive sounds of dogs, pigs, parade drums and reveille.[87] To make matters worse, on 24 August 1805, he sustained an injury to his left eye, which troubled him for several days. This occurred just after he had issued a second Avviso concerning the distribution of prize money. The injury, as well as his general condition, may have delayed the production of his final measure – the Bando criminalising the provision of support for the deserters from the Royal Regiment of Malta. The civil administration was under pressure from the military to assist in the apprehension of these men. The previously-unsuccessful intervention had been issued, on 15 July 1805. Given the urgent emphasis that the military authorities had placed upon locating and capturing these soldiers, it is, perhaps, surprising that the necessary Bando was delayed until 2 September 1805. The explanation for the likely postponement may lie in Coleridge's reduced capacity for work during the latter part of August 1805.

---

87   CN 2, 2614.

5. Thematic Analysis of the Proclamations and Public Notices

The Themes

In this chapter each of the twenty-one Proclamations (Bandi) and Public Notices (Avvisi) under Coleridge's signature will be contextualised and evaluated. For convenience, they are grouped into themes according to their ostensible subject matter, and these themes are set out in Table 1 below. This classification is not definitive in so far as the stated purpose of the measure may sometimes be different from its true motivation. Equally, some measures have more than one purpose. An example is the Bando of 22 March 1805,[1] which might, fairly, be seen as a measure concerned with the prevention of crime, or military discipline rather than consumer protection, which is its stated purpose. Similarly, the Avviso of 20 June 1805,[2] which is considered under the heading of "military discipline" might, fairly, be regarded as a measure to combat crime.

The themes are: (i) reconstruction; (ii) distribution of prize; (iii) taxation; (iv) public order and crime; (v) corruption; (vi) consumer protection; (vii) regulation of trade; (viii) the harbours; (ix) passports; (x) military discipline.

---

1   NLM LIBR/MS 430 2/2 Bandi 1805 AL 1814, 4.
2   NLM LIBR/MS 430 2/2 Bandi 1805 AL 1814, 12.

Table 1:
Proclamations (Bandi) and Public Notices (Avvisi) under Coleridge's signature

Date	Tyoe	Subject	Theme	Reference
29 January 1805	Bando	Roads	Reconstruction	LIBR/MS 430 1/2 Bandi 1790 AL 1805, 356; 431 II/3, 50
1March 1805	Avviso	Extortion	Public Order and Crime	LIBR/MS 430 2/2 Bandi 1805 AL 1814, 1
8 March 1805	Avviso	Prize Money	Distribution of Prize	LIBR/MS 430 2/2 Bandi 1805 AL 1814, 3
8 March 1805	Bando	Wine tax	Taxation	LIBR/MS 430 2/2 Bandi 1805 AL 1814, 2
9 March 1805	Avviso	Safe navigation	Harbours	LIBR/MS 431 2/3 Bandi 1804-1808, 97
22 March, 1805	Bando	Regulation of spirits	Consumer Protection	LIBR/MS 430 2/2 Bandi 1805 AL 1814, 4
22 March 1805	Avviso	Cotton	Regulation of Trade	LIBR/MS 430 2/2 Bandi 1805 AL 1814, 5
22 March 1805	Avviso	Inspections of wine	Consumer Protection	LIBR/MS 430 2/2 Bandi 1805 AL 1814, 6
22 May 1805	Avviso	Notice of conviction	Public Order and Crime	LIBR/MS 430 2/2 Bandi 1805 AL 1814, 8
25 May 1805	Avviso	Notice of conviction	Public Order and Crime	LIBR/MS 430 2/2 Bandi 1805 AL 1814, 9
12 June 1805	Avviso	Counterfeit coinage	Consumer Protection	LIBR/MS 430 2/2 Bandi 1805 AL 1814, 10
14 June 1805	Avviso	Attempted bribery	Corruption	LIBR/MS 430 2/2 Bandi 1805 AL 1814, 11
20 June 1805	Avviso	Enlistment	Military Discipline	LIBR/MS 430 2/2 Bandi 1805 AL 1814, 12
21 June 1805	Avviso	Ferryboat licensing	Harbours	LIBR/MS 430 2/2 Bandi 1805 AL 1814, 13
21 June 1805	Bando	Foreigners and Vehicles	Public Order and Crime	LIBR/MS 430 2/2 Bandi 1805 AL 1814, 14
25 June 1805	Avviso	Mediterranean Passports	Passports	LIBR/MS 430 2/2 Bandi 1805 AL 1814, 15
15 July 1805	Avviso	Deserters	Military Discipline	LIBR/MS 430 2/2 Bandi 1805 AL 1814, 17
5 August 1805	Avviso	Deserters	Military Discipline	LIBR/MS 430 2/2 Bandi 1805 AL 1814, 18
5 August 1805	Bando	Unripened fruit	Consumer Protection	LIBR/MS 430 2/2 Bandi 1805 AL 1814, 19
19 August 1805	Avviso	Prize money	Distribution of Prize	LIBR/MS 430 2/2 Bandi 1805 AL 1814, 20
2 September 1805	Bando	Deserters	Military Discipline	LIBR/MS 430 2/2 Bandi 1805 AL 1814, 21

5.1. Reconstruction

Introduction

As we have seen, in Chapter 2, the Maltese uprising against the French, in 1798, which had been followed by two years during which the French garrison had been besieged on land and sea, had severely disrupted the administration and the economy of the Island. At the date of the capitulation, the Island's economy was in a state of collapse. The export of cotton to Spain, which generated about £500,000 per annum, had been impossible during the blockade.[3] Much of the Island's traditional revenue had been lost when, in 1792, the French confiscated the assets of the Order in France. There was little economic activity, because the shops in Valletta had been either destroyed or looted; the bank had been plundered; and the merchant and fishing fleets of Valletta smashed. The wherewithal to re-build the infra structure depended, in part, upon the British taxpayer and, otherwise, upon the gradual recovery of the economy. A significant backlog of public works accrued before the problems could be fully resolved. Re-construction work continued whilst Coleridge was on the Island.

The question of road maintenance was one of the first problems that confronted Coleridge in his new public appointment, since he was only eleven days into his office when his first Bando, as Public Secretary, was issued. Its purpose was to minimise future damage to the highways arising from the use of certain types of wheels.

Roads

Some evidence of the significant investment made in the repair and maintenance of the highways, at this period, survives. In his annual financial report upon the affairs of the Island, for the year 1803-1804,[4] Ball warned Camden that significant sums would have to be spent, not only in repairing the roads in the countryside but also upon the continuing street repairs in Valletta. As matters turned out, he was right to do so because the financial statement for the following year, 1804-1805, revealed that the Island's continuing deficit was, in part, attributed to the cost of restoring the roads and other infrastructure; indeed, Ball considered the road reconstruction

---

3   Hardman, 535.
4   Ball to Camden, 10 September 1804, Kew, CO 158/9/59.

programme to be one of the heaviest financial burdens of government.[5]

A number of methods, apart from regulating the design of cart wheels, were employed to keep the road network in good condition. The administration used conscript labour, including French and Spanish prisoners of war, to work upon road maintenance.[6] There is some, slight evidence, in his Notebook entry of 23 January 1805, that Coleridge might have visited them on or about this date.[7] He was, later, to record that the POWs were "shamefully" treated on Malta.[8] This adverse judgement could easily have been influenced by what he witnessed of the men labouring at such arduous work, although it must not be forgotten that one of the victims of the anti-Semitic violence, whom a crowd was invited to stone, was also a French prisoner.[9]

The use of these prisoners to reduce labour costs must have been attractive, given the limited resources otherwise available, to meet the significant arrears of work. Perhaps, for this reason, the POW labour force was about to be expanded by Maltese convicts. Ball and Coleridge were, in effect, about to experiment with a type of community service programme. The Bando of 22 March 1805[10] (regulation of spirits) was to stipulate that, although certain offences were punishable by fine, those who either could not or would not pay their fine could either be sentenced to a term of imprisonment or six months community service engaged upon public works. But the administration recognised that these methods, by themselves, would be insufficient. In effect, these were simply measures to treat the symptoms of abuse. More had to be done to reduce the expense, to government, arising from unnecessary damage to the surface of the roads.

Ball's parallel strategy, which Coleridge's first Bando of 29 January 1805[11] implemented, was aimed at minimising the need for costly repairs. The Administration had identified the use of studded wheels as a major and avoidable cause of damage to the road surface. Unless Ball abolished their use, the only alternative would be to repair the damage they caused,

---

5   Ball to E. Cook (Under-Secretary), 1 March 1806, Kew, CO 158/11 no folio reference – Revenue & Expenditure of Malta & Gozo, 25 July 1804-24 July 1805. Ball reported that very considerable sums had been expended on roads without specifying the amounts spent.

6   Sultana, 274.

7   *CN* 2, 2412.

8   To Robert Southey, circa 24 December 1809, *CL* 3, 265.

9   See Public Order and Crime, below.

10   NLM LIBR/MS 430 2/2 Bandi 1805 AL 1814, 4.

11   NLM LIBR/MS 430 1/2 Bandi 1790 AL 1805, 2.

which would have meant raising additional revenue by taxes or duties. In a constitutional sense, this latter policy choice might have been possible. In the days of the Order of St John, wheels had, indeed, been taxed for the repair of streets and roads, and once the work had been completed the tax had was no longer levied. This precedent meant that *ad hoc* taxation for the maintenance of the highways was not a "new" tax, and so it fell within the terms of the Maltese constitution.[12]

Political reasons probably explain Ball's reluctance to levy hypothecated road taxes. A burdensome and, possibly, unpopular tax on wine was about to be promulgated, and Ball fully understood the risks to his policy of retaining Malta if his government lost favour with the inhabitants.[13] As we shall see below, any increase in taxation would have to be carefully managed. Legislation exacting two new imposts, each imposed within a few weeks of the other would be courting trouble. If Ball appeared to resort, too readily, to tax-raising it might spark renewed calls from the Nationalists for a representative assembly such as the *Consiglio Popolare*[14]. Moreover, if the harmful wheels were prohibited instead, and the roads less easily damaged, he no doubt reasoned that an unpopular road tax would not be necessary.

However, if this was his assessment, it was unduly optimistic. The thorny question of how to fund the communications network was not fully resolved by either this or any other of the early British administrations. When the Royal Commission reported in 1812,[15] it acknowledged that the repair of streets and roads continued to remain an item of heavy expenditure; but it shared Ball's preference to address the matter by means other than taxation. The Commission's recommendation was that prisoners, who might otherwise have been sentenced to servitude on the galleys, should instead be required to maintain the roads as a community service. This was so, in part, because the sentence of time in the galleys was an obvious anachronism, this form of punishment having fallen into disuse. This signalled an approval of the community service ideas employed by Ball in 1805.

---

12   The question whether the constitution precluded new taxes was a particularly vexed one. It is considered in the theme concerning taxation at 5.3, below.
13   See generally Chapter 2 and the taxation theme at 5.3, below.
14   As the Royal Commission acknowledged in 1812: Kew, CO 158/19.
15   Ibid.

Bando 29 January 1805[16] – Regulating Studded Wheels

Coleridge pursued three distinct strategies to limit the damage to the surface of the highways. These strategies are of interest because they suggest that there were significant political constraints upon the use of regulation and, in particular, constraints upon the employment of sanctions under the criminal law. They also reveal something of Coleridge's inexperience as an administrator.

Firstly, the Bando required that wheels should be made to a pattern supplied by, or on behalf of, the government to the wheelwrights. Craftsman who made wheels to any alternative design would commit a criminal offence for which they would become liable to a fine of twenty *oncie* for each offence, upon conviction.

Secondly, and as a separate offence, the Bando prohibited the *construction* (as opposed to the *use*) of wheels that had iron nails or studs protruding from the rims since these damaged the surface of the highways. Failure to comply with this regulation also constituted an offence punishable by a fine as above.

The final strategy adopted was to exhort the majority of vehicle owners to fit and use the approved wheels even if their existing wheels had only recently been fitted. Intriguingly, the continued use of studded wheels by members of the public was not punishable. This decision is interesting because, if the major cause of damage to the highways was the use of studded wheels, we would expect any instrument deploying the criminal law to include penalties, such as a fine, to enforce the removal of studded wheels from use. That this was not done reveals a concession to practical politics that forced Coleridge into an alternative strategy.

Rather than using criminal penalties against a potentially large number of Maltese, he instead resorted to a reasoned appeal to their self-interest. He argued that journeys in carts without studded wheels would be more comfortable; the carts and wheels would have a longer life since the jolts caused by the studs would, necessarily, cease; the goods carried would be less liable to damage; and the beasts drawing the carts would not tire so quickly. To drive home this final argument, he resorted to the laws of physics by asserting that the studs operate against the moving force and so a greater effort is required to draw carts fitted with studded wheels than

---

16   NLM LIBR/MS 430 1/2 Bandi 1790 AL 1805, 356; 431 II/3, 50.

would be the case otherwise.

Depending upon how successful this exhortation to the owners may have been – and much might have depended upon the cost and convenience of wheel replacement (as much as on the reasons Coleridge expressed) – the restriction of criminal sanctions to the manufacturing process suggests that the Bando was really aiming at a long-term strategy. It would take time before new vehicles were produced according to the new design. Short term gains in reducing the damage to the road surfaces depended upon early, but voluntary, compliance in having studded wheels upon existing vehicles replaced.

The reluctance to enforce a prohibition upon the use of studded wheels was, probably, perceived to be necessary for pragmatic, political reasons. Mandatory wheel replacement would put a majority of the citizens to significant expense and risk unpopularity. It is unclear whether the craft capacity of the Island could achieve a rapid replacement of the old, harmful wheels; and the criminalisation of a potentially large number of people, including, perhaps, the less affluent who would be unable to afford to replace their wheels, would be unpopular. It would tend to frustrate the overriding British policy designed to secure the support of the Maltese for the British administration. There is evidence that Coleridge succeeded in limiting political damage because the restrictions on wheels did not feature in the litany of complaints, made in 1805, about Ball's administration.[17]

However, Coleridge's failure to impose a criminal offence for the continued use of the wheels is also interesting because it reveals something of his inexperience and lack of confidence as an administrator. It reveals his uncertainty as to whether his reasoned appeal, to the self-interest of the Maltese owners, would succeed in persuading them to alter their behaviour. Had most of them complied voluntarily the number of recalcitrant owners who retained the studded wheels would be quite small. This means that, if his reasoned appeal succeeded, the political objections to using the criminal law to punish those who did not make the change of wheel would have been less powerful because there would have been fewer offenders to bring to court and less resistance to the new policy. Coleridge, as an inexperienced public official, can be seen to experiment with persuasion, and he was, evidently, not confident that his explanation and appeal, no matter how objectively reasoned, would secure the goal he intended.

---

17   *Memorial and Petition of the Maltese* (unsigned and undated): Kew, CO 158/10/151 (1805).

Certainty

Legislation normally informs a society, or a class of the population, of the conduct that is required of it or, alternatively, that certain conduct is prohibited. The behaviour that is either permitted or prohibited must be clearly established so that law-abiding individuals can go about their business without risking a penalty. This is not possible if the law is unclear.

The drafting of Coleridge's first Bando suffers from certain interpretational problems.

Firstly, it was enacted so that the craftsmen should only make wheels according to the pattern supplied to them. Presumably, although the Bando does not make this clear, no craftsman would have been liable for making wheels according to other designs until the pattern had been supplied to him.

Secondly, it was enacted so that it would be an offence to depart from the pattern. A separate offence was the manufacture of a wheel with nails that protruded from the rim.

It can be objected that the second offence was redundant since the obligation to construct wheels according to the government's approved pattern would, obviously, mean that the wheels would not have protruding nails. This also reveals Coleridge's inexperience as a legal draftsman.

The fine of twenty *oncie* was imposed on craftsman "for each offence". It can be asked whether the construction of a wheel with protruding nails is one or two offences? Is it an offence contrary to the requirement to manufacture according to the pattern (offence 1) and a further and separate offence to have protruding nails (offence 2)? This is unclear and is further evidence of lay draftsmanship.

Enforcement

The experience of any legal system is that a law that is not enforced is almost worthless. However, legislators do not always address this question by providing an adequately-resourced enforcement mechanism that will prove effective in identifying and prosecuting offences. The effectiveness of public-enforcement bodies can be compromised if they suffer from under-funding, a lack of zealous, efficient staff, poor management or a lack of political or public support.

On Malta at this period, the absence of an organised police force limited

Calesse

9. The presence of studded wheels on this Calesse suggests that Coleridge's Bando
had not fully succeeded by the late 1830's. Lithograph by C. de Brocktorff
[1838]

the scope for the detection of offences. Coleridge's Bando sought to avoid
this potential pitfall since the inhabitants were, in effect, recruited to
perform the work of detection and evidence gathering. He achieved this
by invoking the aid of self-interested informants who were to be rewarded
with one half of the fine to which an offender would become liable upon
conviction. Whilst minimising a public burden – that of detecting the
offences – it nevertheless created a conflict of interest since the informant,
who might easily be a witness, had a pecuniary interest in a conviction. As
we discuss in Chapter 6, this is also a matter in which we find Coleridge
having to set aside his own published opinions to pursue goals set for him.

As we shall see, there is evidence that the Maltese were reluctant to
inform upon their fellow citizens. Co-operation with the authorities, in their
law enforcement activities, seems to have been problematic. A financial
inducement to inform and give evidence may have been the only possible
means of encouraging individuals to inform against their neighbours, and,
even then, the required flow of information was not guaranteed.[18] But this
was not all. Whilst the prosecutorial decision, in any given case, remained
one for the public authorities, which would provide some control upon
the activities of informants who were obviously malicious or vexatious, it

18   As the two Public Notices and the Proclamation concerning desertions from
the Royal Malta Regiment revealed: see the military discipline theme, below.

would not necessarily prevent all cases of injustice that might arise from untrue or exaggerated witness statements.

Proclamation of 8 March 1805[19] – the Excise Duties on Liquor and Wine

Re-construction policies were also a feature of the later Bando of 8 March 1805. This concerned the re-introduction of an excise duty on liquor and wine. In order to make the tax more acceptable to the Maltese, Coleridge identified some of the purposes for which the revenue was to be raised. These included the reconstruction of the economy and certain infra-structure. Charitable institutions that were engaged in constructing buildings to be enjoyed by the public were identified as beneficiaries of public funding, no doubt because their work had popular support amongst the devout Maltese. This Proclamation is, however, more fully considered elsewhere.[20]

5.2. Distribution of Prize

Introduction

In 1801, the British reversed their policy and decided not to award Maltese military personnel a share of the prize money arising from the capture of Valletta. This had, naturally, become a lingering cause of friction between the British and the Maltese. Following the intervention of the Secretary of State, there was a further *volte face*, but problems surrounding the authorised distribution remained unresolved by the time Coleridge held office. As we shall see, the payments occurred in two instalments, the first, in 1803, and the second, under Coleridge's supervision, in 1805. From the Maltese point of view, even the revised terms of the 1805 distribution were disappointing because his Avviso still excluded many individuals from making a claim. Moreover, the British were later to overturn some claims that had been formally recognised as meritorious by Maltese officials. This added fuel to other grievances, such as the bad bread, trade competition,

---

19   NLM LIBR/MS 430 2/2 Bandi 1805 AL 1814, 2.
20   See the taxation theme, below.

and the complaints over civil and political rights. Thus, the issue of prize money, which was, no doubt, intended to earn political capital and reward loyalty, added to the difficult political context that Ball and Coleridge had to administer.

Promises

A brief account of how the British and their allies acquired Malta by means of a naval blockade and the landward siege of Valletta has been offered in Chapter 2 and Appendix 2. After Valletta eventually fell to the allied armies, Maltese military personnel were led to believe that they would be given a share in the bounty to be distributed to the victorious armies. To implement this, Major-General Pigot ordered Captain Ball (as he then was) to prepare a list of the Maltese military, of all ranks, who could qualify for reward.[21] However, when he saw the list, Pigot changed his mind, which meant that, in the aftermath of the French capitulation, no prize money was actually paid. Pigot's argument was that it would be difficult to allocate shares according to rank because rank, in the Maltese forces, depended upon social status rather than the number of men commanded.[22] However, the argument overlooked the political damage inflicted by a breach of promise.

Ball, who was fully aware of hostile local sentiment regarding this and other aspects of British conduct both during the campaign and, in particular, in relation to the terms of capitulation,[23] regarded the breach of faith as politically disastrous. He knew that there was also anger that the British had excluded the Maltese from the negotiation of the capitulation – an unwise decision that they would later have good reason to regret; and Pigot's inconsistency would only fuel disillusionment with British occupation thereby making the peaceful, stable and long-term government of Malta problematic. Ball wrote to Dundas, the Secretary of State for War and the

21   NAM LIBR A22 PS09 Maltese Corps Serving at the Surrender of Malta on 4 September 1800. The list names 2506 individual officers and men whom Captain Ball identified as potentially eligible to claim.
22   Captain Ball's list, ibid., recorded, for example, that the colonel of Birchicarra (sic) battalion commanded 478 officers and men, whilst his counterpart in the Crendi Battalion commanded a mere 25 troops.
23   The Maltese were excluded by the British from the negotiations for capitulation. As a result no provision was made in the Articles of Capitulation for reparations to be paid to those Maltese citizens whose private property had been looted: see Appendix 2.

Colonies, warning of instability and urging that Pigot be overruled.[24]

This letter is particularly interesting because it offers an unguarded insight into the conduct and bravery of the British army on Malta. Ball drew Dundas' attention to the military achievements and hardiness of the Maltese soldiers. His powerful comparison between British conduct and that of the Maltese troops was intended to make the case that the Maltese were *more* deserving of reward than their British allies. Ball did not hesitate to point out that, when the British troops finally arrived to assist the Maltese insurgents, the British withdrew from the most dangerous positions and left them to be defended by the Maltese. The following statement, intended to emphasise the justice of the Maltese claim is revealing:

> Another post was abandoned to the Maltese, because the British troops *deserted from it* to the enemy, and the Maltese, *who were more to be trusted than our own troops*, were the means of preventing our own troops from deserting, and actually arrested one of our own men close to the enemy's works.[25] (Emphasis added).

Not only is this account a powerful and critical assessment of the contribution made by British land forces to the siege of Valletta, it also explains why the Maltese regarded themselves as having liberated themselves, with the British performing only an "auxiliary" role.[26] Ball's openness is also worthy of comment because, at this time, Ball continued to serve as a captain in the Royal Navy (and had, by then, returned to his ship). Coleridge's subsequent, later references to inter-service rivalry may, however, provide an interesting perspective on this apparent frankness.[27]

As stated above, the British government in London eventually acceded to the representations made on behalf of the Maltese. An annotation made in 1803, to Captain Ball's original list of beneficiaries, formally signalled that policy had changed and that Ball (who was by now Civil Commissioner) was to decide upon the entitlements of the individual officers and men.

The Distribution of Prize in 1803-1804

The new policy was first implemented when the Public Secretary, Alexander Macaulay, announced that a sum of £13,916. 13s. 4d was to be distributed

24 Ball to Dundas, 6 March 1801, Hardman, 344-5, Kew, CO 158/10/15.
25 Hardman, 345.
26 See, for example, the 'Humble Representation of the Deputies of Malta and Gozo' in October 1801, English translation, with annotated alterations, Kew, CO158/2/272 ; also Hardman, 410-15.
27 *The Friend*, 1, 544 n. and *Table Talk*, 1, 475, April 1834.

amongst the Maltese who had served in the Maltese battalions. The criteria governing each claim were published in an official Notice (Avviso) dated 3 December 1803.[28] These criteria caused significant popular confusion – perhaps even consternation and dissent – because Maltese *civilians* (as opposed to enlisted troops), who wrongly assumed that they would qualify, fell outside the scheme. To avoid widespread disappointment Macaulay had been forced to clarify the entitlements in a further Notice dated 11 December, 1803,[29] but the damage had already been done. Expectations had been raised, and now the British were seen as having once more frustrated them. As we shall see, Coleridge broadly adopted the criteria of 11 December 1803, but with important refinements in relation to enlisted men that were intended to address some of the perceived injustices. Civilian *franc tireurs* were still excluded.

Controversy

The difficult problem the British encountered was to establish eligibility criteria that would win public confidence without appearing to undermine the rules of war. It will be recalled that there had been a popular uprising against the French, which had, from the Maltese point of view, been supported by the wider community, many of whom had suffered considerably. Not least amongst these had been the citizens of Valletta who had been subjected to the severe privations of the blockade, which caused a large number of casualties. Freedom fighters, some of whom had been captured and shot by the French, had also shown bravery. Some civilians had taken part in the resistance by fulfilling *ad hoc* roles, for example in providing food, shelter or medical aid for soldiers; others may, for a short time, had been in battle and risked their lives. Yet others, including some priests, had performed important political or administrative roles. Some local leaders had served on Ball's Council. Guerrilla forces had also participated in the uprising. These were, according to Macaulay's Avviso, to be satisfied with the honour of having served their country, and could not expect a financial reward.

This blanket denial of entitlement to these individuals seems to have been a major cause of resentment. Even those who had, in the words of the Avviso, "answered the call of the bells" and who went immediately to

---

28   NLM LIBR/MS 430 1/2; Bandi 1790 AL 1805, 321.
29   LIBR/MS 431 1/3 Bandi 1800 AL 1803, 333.

provide assistance to the military were excluded from the bounty. From the British point of view, the distinction between civilians and enlisted troops was probably necessary to avoid the legal and political complexities that might have arisen if the British had been seen to promote irregular forces.[30] But, given the dangers they had encountered, in some cases shoulder to shoulder with the enlisted soldiers, the misunderstood decision to refuse them a share seemed to the Maltese to be arbitrary and harsh.

1803 Criteria

The 1803 rules essentially prescribed two categories of qualifying *enlisted* personnel eligible to present a claim for a share in the Prize. The first category comprised those who had been in "full military service" *at the time of the surrender of the City*.[31] The Notice of 11 December 1803 stated that this group included all battalion commanders, their officers, soldiers, quartermasters, doctors and surgeons, second mates and military chaplains. The claim by soldiers who had served prior to the fall of Valletta but who had left service before 5 September 1800 fell under a second, discretionary, category of entitlements, whilst those who joined at a late stage of the campaign would not have been eligible.

This discretionary category allowed a claim by soldiers who, for legitimate reasons, had not been in service at the date of the surrender, provided that they fulfilled two conditions. The first, and potentially the most restrictive, was that each claimant (or their relatives in the case of the deceased) would have to demonstrate that the soldier in respect of whom the claim was made had "distinguished themselves by their bravery in some venture" *and* that they had either been killed or wounded in combat or had suffered some "involuntary accident" that had prevented their continued military service. In the case of the deceased, their families could present a claim. Those who left service "voluntarily" were excluded.

---

30   Private citizens could only take enemy vessels as lawful prize on the high seas under the authority of "letters of marque", or the express prior authority of the Crown. In the absence of this authority the seizure was liable to be condemned as piracy. Although this legal doctrine could not directly influence the British decision regarding the Valletta prize money, it reveals that the policy of international law supported the use of irregular forces only under the authority of the Crown and subject to the limitations on such action, namely that the legality of the seizure should be tested in a Court of Vice-Admiralty, such as the one the British established in Valletta in 1803.

31   5 September 1800.

The authorities, clearly, had a certain discretion as to what degree of distinction and valour was required. It is not entirely clear whether merely taking part in the military venture – for example taking part in a battle – was, by itself, enough, or whether the claimant had to demonstrate that they had distinguished themselves by exceptional valour. This meant that the various Luogotenente (civil magistrates) could each make their own judgements on the facts of each case with all the attendant risks of arbitrariness or unfairness. This was likely to have been one of the main causes of friction between the disappointed claimants and the authorities.

The second category was obviously intended to make clear that deserters were not to be rewarded.

Role of Luogotenente

The 1803 scheme also made it clear that the Public Secretary was unwilling to interest himself in the minutiae of claims. Macaulay emphasised that the Luogotenente had been especially authorised to resolve the claims, and that the claimants were not to apply to the Secretariat. The problem was that the trust placed in the Luogotenente *ipso facto* removed control over the outcomes of claims from the senior officials of the British administration. This may have been something that the authorities later regretted because the decisions of the Luogotenente did not placate certain disgruntled Maltese.

Although the 1803 Avviso does not make it explicit, the amount actually received by any entitled person would have been determined by their rank in military service. This was another area of policy that Coleridge's Notice re-considered.

Coleridge's "Prize" Avvisi of 8 March 1805[32] and 19 August 1805[33]

In 1805, by which time Coleridge had replaced Macaulay as Public Secretary, the bounty was £22,703.0s.6d.[34] Coleridge issued a Public Notice dated 8 March 1805 to explain how the claims would be managed. This depended upon the category of claimant.

---

32   NLM LIBR/MS 430 2/2 Bandi1805 AL 1814, 3.
33   NLM LIBR/MS 430 2/2 Bandi1805 AL 1814, 20.
34   Caruana, Introduction.

For those who had been successful under the 1803 scheme, the claims would be paid on the spot by the local Luogotenente on 10 March 1805. This was because the claims had, in effect, already been verified in 1803. For undisclosed reasons, the timescale was very short because Coleridge gave just two day's notice to the claimants. Why this was done is unclear, although it suggests that the Administration wanted to act as quickly as possible. Perhaps the urgent action was intended to offset, as quickly as possible, the political fallout from the excise duties, which had been passed into law that same day (8 March 1805). If so, this is suggestive of the nervousness in the Administration at this critical juncture.[35] Sultana suggests that the simultaneous promulgation of these two measures was hardly coincidental;[36] and we can, reasonably, infer that the timing of the announcement of the distribution of Prize was also influenced by pressing public relations concerns.

For other claimants – those "unjustly excluded" in 1803 – there was to be a two stage process. The claimants – in effect *appellants* – were to have their claims re-considered and, if successful, certified by the Luogotenente within one month of 10 March (i.e. until 9 April 1805). After that date, no further avenue of redress was available.[37] Once a claim had been certified, it would mean *prima facie* eligibility for payment. Coleridge issued a further notice, dated 19 August 1805, to inform the successful appellants, whose claims had now been authorised, how to receive payment. As the claimants were to discover, payment was not to be automatic; in other words, the officials of the Secretariat would not honour all certified claims. This would prove to be a further cause of grievances.

Eligibility in 1805

Coleridge re-shaped the eligibility criteria, for the 1805 award, by removing the requirement that the enlisted man must either have been in service at the date of the surrender or have been killed or wounded during a distinguished military service. In his distribution, no distinction was to be drawn between those who had served for a short period of time, but who had left their battalion prior to the surrender, and those who were

---

35   See the discussion of the excise duties in Chapters 2 and 5, particularly, the taxation theme, in Chapter 5 below.
36   Sultana, 300.
37   Although, as mentioned below, the Maltese Constitution gave the Maltese a right to petition the Civil Commissioner sitting in Segnatura about any grievance.

still enlisted on 5 September 1800. This important revision enlarged the categories of enlisted man entitled to make a claim. It removed the injustice of excluding (i) those who had genuine reasons other than being wounded to leave military service before the campaign had concluded, and (ii) those who had suffered disabling wounds who had not shown particularly distinguished bravery during their service. Its real significance was, of course, that it removed much of the discretion from the Luogotenente. A soldier wounded in action would, *ipso facto,* have a good claim to the 1805 instalment without the Luogotenente having to determine what constituted distinguished bravery. Moreover, the Luogotenente could consider claims by others who had neither been in service at the capitulation nor wounded "out".[38]

However, Coleridge also added, somewhat confusingly, that claims could only be paid to those who had been judged worthy of a payment in the 1803 award. This is confusing, since the rules *had* obviously changed. It is either an example of a lack of clarity in drafting or a deliberate attempt to mask a further embarrassing *volte face* in respect of the prize money undertaken in response to public pressure. The essential point, for those interested in Coleridge's work, is that the drafting of the Avviso was not a model of clarity and reveals either a lack of skill or care.

However, Coleridge's intention was not to give the new rules retrospective effect. In other words, whilst every killed or wounded soldier not in service on 5 September 1800 (or those who left the campaign for other good reasons) could claim a share of the second instalment, only those with a distinguished service record could appeal successfully against the refusal to pay them in 1803. In practice, this meant that some wounded soldiers not in service at the capitulation might qualify for a share of the second instalment but not the first. From the Maltese point of view this must have seemed incoherent. Either their service merited a reward or it did not. An entitlement to one instalment but not another was, from their standpoint, simply bizarre.

From the British perspective, there were, probably, reasons to view the matter differently. Coleridge was, probably, unable to undo the damage of the 1803 rules by granting a share of the first instalment to those who had genuine reasons for leaving service before the fall of Valletta. First, the prize money available to meet the 1803 claims had been distributed and, as

---

38   They had to establish that they had left due to some "involuntary accident", which potentially included other reasons than disabling wounds.

we have seen, the finances of the Island in the spring of 1805 were too frail to draw upon money from general public funds. This was the reason for the wine duty enacted that very day. Moreover, there may also have been a reluctance, on Ball's part, to admit that he and Macaulay had made an error of judgement; but this is merely speculation.

Maltese Officials

As in 1803, claimants and appellants alike were required to present themselves to their local Luogotenente with documentary evidence to support either their claims or appeals respectively. These arrangements are worthy of comment because they reveal that, like Ball, Coleridge was generally willing to trust Maltese public officials.[39] They also align with comments Coleridge later ventured in *The Friend*.[40] At this time (March 1805) he clearly had faith that the Luogotenente would make an appropriate assessment of the appeals and would not indulge in arbitrariness or unfairness. This might have been unduly optimistic because, as we shall see, there is some suggestion that the Luogotenente did not assess the appellant's service records as carefully as they should have done. Interestingly, this experience of their collusive or fraudulent conduct did not persuade Coleridge to qualify his remarks upon the wisdom of Ball's policy of relying upon Maltese appointments, which he supported in order to extend British influence.

Amount of Bounty

The 1805 scheme made the further reform that there would only be two levels of award. The distinction between the higher and lower sums awarded was made according to the military rank of the recipient. The first category included officers and non-commissioned officers of the rank of sergeant or above, and, the second, soldiers below those ranks – that is corporals and enlisted soldiers. The Avviso does not disclose the actual

---

39   Although there were exceptions. The Civil Commissioner retained the power to licence premises retailing spirits: see the Bando of 22 March 1805, NLM LIBR/ MS 430 2/2 Bandi 1805 AL 1814, 4, and the consumer protection theme, below. The explanation for this instance may be that Ball was under pressure from the military authorities to prevent ill-discipline amongst the British troops awaiting embarkation.
40   *The Friend*, 2, 569.

sums paid to each grade.

Reasons and Transparency

Coleridge's Avviso of 8 March 1805 infers that the authorities were required to give reasons to disappointed claimants who asked for them. The evidence of this can be located in the final paragraph of the Avviso which states that after 9 April 1805 no request for any reason would be provided.

This is interesting because it means that the Luogotenente were not only required to *have* relevant, lawful, reasons for reaching their decisions, but that these had to be communicated to a disappointed claimant who requested an explanation. This was most likely to arise in the case of the appellants because the Luogotenente had the power to grant or withhold the certificates according to the evidence of service records presented to them.

By imposing this duty of transparency, Coleridge recognised a value in open government and administrative candour. Generally, administrators understand that if reasons are given it is more likely that these would not only have been properly thought out but that they would withstand public scrutiny. The Luogotenente would have to make sure that each case was properly assessed, and this would give assurance to the claimants that their claim had been properly considered and that the appropriate rules had been duly applied. This would help in avoiding any possible perception of unfairness or arbitrariness. In other words, Coleridge seems to have understood that the giving of reasons made decisions more acceptable by emphasising their rationality. He clearly hoped that a properly reasoned refusal would extinguish some of the anger that surrounded the 1803 bounty.

The resulting exposure of any faults in the decision-making process could also underpin a right of appeal, although in the case of the 1803 appellants and the 1805 claimants this would be only to the *Segnatura*.

Appeals and the Controversial Administration of Claims

As mentioned above, the second of Coleridge's "prize" Avvisi, dated 19 August 1805, invited the successful appellants (who were, by then, in possession of "certified" claims) to attend the Secretariat, between 22 and

29 August 1805, to collect their share of the 1803 distribution, after which no further claim would be met. The critical burden was that the claimants had to present their certificates when making a claim. This was an obvious safeguard, but the reliance upon the certificate, to identify the genuine claims, seems to have failed.

This is so because certain appellants whose appeals had been upheld and certified by the Luogotenente, in March 1805, were later turned away by officials at the Public Secretary's office, perhaps even by Coleridge himself (although Ball was blamed). Clearly, the British were not convinced that the certification process had worked as it should have done. The refusal of certified claims caused significant anger, and was used as further ammunition to undermine Ball. The refusals provoked a flurry of angry petitions that were heard by the *Segnatgura* on 29 August 1805. These were mostly claims brought by civilians who had taken part in the uprising in the Maltese countryside. All twenty-one petitions were rejected, although another petition that was heard a few days later was successful.[41]

The politically-sensitive allegations, that Ball (or Coleridge) was denying claims certified to be meritorious, emerged in an anonymous letter of complaint about Ball's administration that was sent to Eton, Ball's main political rival, who forwarded it to the Secretary of State in 1806. It contains a significant passage relating to the Prize distributions: "They (the Maltese) complain of his (i.e. Ball) having under false pretences taken from the meritorious certificates of their services during the siege".[42]

The reference by the complainant to "false pretences" is particularly suggestive of a decision that resulted from an abuse of power. This was a damaging allegation. It was a matter that the Secretary of State took up with Ball who, eventually, denied that he had acted improperly; but there seems little doubt that some Maltese were frustrated, as the petitions to the *Segnatura* revealed.[43]

The reasons why the Administration did not honour some of the certificates is unclear. One possibility is that either the Public Secretary or his staff suspected collusion between the Luogotenente and the claimant. If so, this does resonate with other administrative contexts (such as the military bounty) where some Maltese cynically attempted to make the most

---

41   See NAM LIBR 43/11, *Registro de memoriali decretati da sua Excellenza il Sig. Cavalier Alessandro Ball Regio Commissionario Civile di Sua Maestà Britannica*, vol. N.
42   Anonymous letter passed by Eton to Windham enclosed in a letter dated 11 October 1806, Kew, CO 158/12/ no folio reference.
43   Ball's rebuttal survives: Ball to Windham, 28 February 1807 Kew, CO 158/13/64.

of every opportunity to obtain money from the British. Similar suspicions later surrounded the Università. Whatever the reason, the adverse decisions in relation to the controversial certificates caused political damage.

Appeals and the 1805 Instalment

Coleridge's Notice did not allow for an appeal by any person who was unjustly refused their share of the second, 1805, bounty. Appellate rights were only given to those unjustly excluded from the 1803 award. The failure to provide a similar right in 1805 is puzzling. Coleridge must have been confident that the decisions of the Luogotenente could not be controversial; after all, they were, in most cases, simply paying money to individuals whose claims to the first instalment had been officially recognised in 1803 and this recognition triggered the entitlement to the 1805 award. However, Coleridge clearly overlooked the possibility that problems might arise when the certificates were presented to the Secretariat for payment. He may, also, have overlooked the likelihood that the 1805 award would re-ignite resentment of those denied in 1803. These numerous individuals could be predicted to re-state their grievances; and this is what, indeed, occurred.

However, in Coleridge's defence it can be argued that an explicit right of appeal was not strictly necessary. Coleridge knew very well that any aggrieved individual would petition the Civil Commissioner via the *Segnatura* and this was the avenue that the disgruntled Maltese vigorously pursued.

Further Grievances

As matters turned out, a torrent of petitions from dissatisfied claimants went up to the *Segnatura* for further adjudication. Dozens of these cases fell to be decided after 22 March 1805; and some were still being presented as late as mid May 1805. Most were summarily rejected.[44] The significant number of unsuccessful petitions signalled that, in a number of ways, Coleridge's revised scheme had not succeeded. Very large numbers of Maltese remained dissatisfied; and his desire to get the matter resolved quickly (evident in the rule providing for only two days to present a claim) had also backfired. The

---

44   Some were referred to other officials better placed to determine their merits: see e.g., Michele and Francesco Pivano's cases which were referred to the Governor of Gozo on 22 March 1805, and Rosa Abela case, she was referred to her Luogotenente on 2 April 1805: see NAM LIBR 43/11 above n. 41.

final cases were being adjudicated almost at the moment when the anti-Semitic disturbances erupted, which suggests that the administration had not fully resolved the grievances of the disappointed claimants before the next problem followed upon its heels.

But, even those cases were not the end of the matter because, as we have seen, further petitions were stimulated by the denial of certified claims in late August 1805, which meant that the grievances over the prize money simmered for almost six months from the date of Coleridge's Avviso of 8 March 1805.

Conclusion

The question of rewarding the Maltese with a share of the bounty had been incompetently handled from the moment Pigot reneged on a promise to make a payment. Once that decision had been overruled, the 1803 scheme had failed to win the support of the Maltese. Coleridge, later, found himself charged with addressing problems that were not of his own making and, of course, turning the tide of hostile public opinion.

Coleridge perhaps achieved as much as he could within the political constraints within which he found himself. His insistences that the decisions of the Luogotenente should be fully reasoned and that the reasons should be communicated to those who asked for them reveal Coleridge's concern for transparency and open government. It introduced into practical politics some of the qualities of Ball's administration, and, not least, the emphasis upon rational, evidence-led decision-making that Coleridge most admired.[45]

Coleridge's reforms were not well drafted, because the criteria were not always as clearly expressed as he might have intended. Moreover, they were not sufficiently bold to cure the political damage. Perhaps Coleridge should not be blamed for this outcome because Ball, rather than Coleridge, would have been the final decision-maker, albeit that Coleridge would have been consulted.

The very large numbers of disgruntled Maltese who took their cases to the *Segnatura* meant that the administration had not won the argument. Since almost all petitions were, unsurprisingly, rejected by Ball it is evident that a significant number of those who took part in the uprising resented their treatment. The rejection of claims, which they saw as justified, meant that a

---

45   *The Friend*, 2, 552.

large number of Maltese continued to feel anger against and betrayal by the British. In summary, the initiative, intended in part, to deflect criticism of the excise duties, was exploited by Maltese nationalists to inflame dissent and widen support for the broader agenda of having Ball removed from office. The episode was critical in undermining confidence in the British administration at a challenging time. The importance of this should not be overlooked because it is part of the difficult political environment that Coleridge had to address in his careful efforts to win back public support.

5.3. Taxation[46]

Introduction

As we have described, the timing of the distribution of prize money was intended to deflect criticism from the Administration at a time when it had decided to increase taxation. There were many political and some legal reasons why the British administration, reluctantly, imposed excise duties when other preferences, such as cost-cutting, had been exhausted. The political reasons for Ball's hesitation were rooted in internal dangers to Malta, as a new British possession, if the Government became unpopular; and legal objections arose because of the, perceived, constraints of the Maltese Constitution. These restraints – albeit weak ones – were buttressed by a significant, but ill-defined, formal promise that had been made to Maltese people in 1801 by the first British Civil Commissioner.[47] Two of Coleridge's Bandi are either concerned with or shaped by the politics of taxation.

As we have earlier described, Coleridge's first Bando of 29 January 1805[48] was imposed to reduce the need for costly repairs to the highway. By preventing the damage caused by the studded wheels, and by requiring

---

46   In what follows we are principally concerned with the imposition of excise duties. In so far as a "tax" is imposed on a transaction, and a "duty" on goods, a "tax" can be distinguished from a "duty". However, that distinction was not applicable in Malta under the Constitution in force in 1798 and therefore in what follows there is no legal significance between a tax and a duty and so the terms can be used interchangeably.
47   See e.g. the Proclamation of 15 July 1801, NLM LIBR/MS 430 1/2; Bandi 1790 AL 1805, 204.
48   NLM LIBR/MS 430 1/2 Bandi 1790 AL 1805.

new wheels to be made according to an approved pattern, less damage would be done and (at least in the long term) the expenditure on highways could be reduced. This Bando was, thus, concerned with reducing the demand for publicly-funded expenditure. The Bando of 8 March 1805[49] was concerned with raising funds from direct taxation.

Ball's Political Agenda

By the spring of 1805 Ball had recognised that increased taxation was necessary if the Island's financial deficit was to be eliminated. He had already, formally, assured ministers that achieving a balanced budget was possible; and his financial strategy gave him confidence that this would shortly be achieved.[50] He had observed a significant improvement in economic conditions, evidenced by rising wages and increased private wealth, which meant that some increased taxation would not, unduly, suppress demand.[51]

Ball's despatches to London reveal that the proposed duties underpinned his ambition that the Island should be retained as a British possession. When added to the revenue that Ball expected to generate, by speculating upon grain, he forecast that the duties would remedy the Island's financial deficit and, thus, make Malta a more attractive proposition to British ministers.[52]

We have described elsewhere[53] the economic strait–jacket into which Ball's enthusiasm for Malta placed him. If British ministers were to be persuaded to retain it as a possession of the Crown, the Island could not be

---

49   LIBR/MS 430 2/2 Bandi 1805 AL 1814, 2.
50   Ball's Memorandum to Dundas of 26 December 1800, Kew, CO 158/1/12-25, assured ministers that Malta, if retained as British possession, would not be a burden on the Imperial power. This hardened into a political expectation as Hobart's Instructions to Cameron dated 14 May 1801 make clear: see Hardman, 350, 355: "Under the head of expenditure I have only to state His Majesty's expectation that the revenue will be found fully adequate to defray all charges of the Civil Government (as well as other listed expenses)". In 1805 Ball continued to assure ministers that a balanced budget would be achieved: see e.g. Ball to Camden, 19 April 1805, Kew, CO 158/10/125.
51   Ibid, 131: the "general distress" caused by the economic collapse of 1800 "has already ceased". The rising demand for labour and an increase in wages, in his judgement, permitted an increase in taxation.
52   He estimated that the duty on wine and spirits would raise a surplus (after the sums for the relief of bank depositors and the increased salaries of public servants) of £6,000 per annum: Ball to Camden, 19 April 1805, above n. 50.
53   See Chapter 2.

a burden on the British taxpayer – as ministers repeatedly made clear.[54] On the other hand, the British, in their continuation strategy, which necessarily meant generous public expenditure, had encouraged Maltese expectations of benign welfarism. These highly-expensive policies were problematic because the confiscation of the assets of the Order of St John, in 1792, and the resulting collapse of the Island's revenues, meant that the Island's public expenditure could not be sustained without additional sources of revenue. In addition, the damaged infrastructure, the enormous costs of repairs (for example to the roads and public buildings), the cost of unemployment and a collapsed economy, all placed burdens upon the State in the years after 1800.

Thus, in the Proclamation of 8 March 1805 Coleridge re-introduced an excise duty on the importation of wines and imposed a further new excise duty on spirits.[55] When taken with the projected profits accruing to government from the grain monopoly, these duties were expected to generate sufficient funds to produce a balanced budget.

The Political and Constitutional Problems of Taxation

Although wine dealers had been liable to pay excise duty on wine imports under the *ancien regime*,[56] Ball was known to be extremely nervous about the imposition of *new* duties, (in this case on spirits) not least because their likely unpopularity would lead to a collapse in confidence in British rule. This political priority collided, however, with the British Imperial imperative that the Island should not impose continuing burdens upon the British taxpayer.

Regular taxation was almost unknown to the Maltese (who had been accustomed to *ad hoc* taxes designed to raise funds for particular, identified, purposes, including the repair of the road network).[57] Every Grandmaster had taken office subject to an oath not to impose new taxes, which was perceived by the British civil government as having created a constitutional

---

54   See Cameron's *Instructions* of 14 May 1801, Hardman, 350, and, more generally, Chapter 2, above.

55   This was actually a re-introduction of the wine tax because the Jurats of the Università had failed to collect it from about 1802-1803 following some confusion about the status of Malta as free port. See Macaulay to Camden, 25 January 1804, Kew, CO 158/8/111.

56   See De Bono.

57   The tax would no longer be levied once its purpose had been achieved: see Report of Royal Commission of 1812, Kew, CO 158/19.

right, in the Maltese, not to be regularly taxed.[58] To their eventual consternation, the British had, unwittingly, reinforced this inconvenient constitutional entitlement by their own actions. This had occurred in the famous Proclamation of 15 July 1801,[59] in which the new British civil administration had promised to respect the rights, property and freedom of the Maltese. When taken with the other aspects of the Maltese system, this was thought to require that the British uphold a constitutional restriction upon the powers of the government to impose new, permanent, taxes.[60] However, as we have described, it is unlikely that these constitutional restraints could have been judicially enforced,[61] although this weakness seems not to have been discussed within the British administration.

As said, in so far as the Proclamation imposed a duty on imported wine, Coleridge and Ball could present an argument for the constitutional legitimacy of their action, because there had been a precedent for placing a duty on wine in the time of the Order of St John. Less certain, was the duty to be imposed on spirits.

As his despatches to London reveal, Ball was aware of this problem and would, naturally, have been nervous about it.[62] Despite this, he had no alternative to increasing taxation. Even if Chapman's corn mission were fully successful, only two thirds of the income required would be raised.[63] Of course, the mission eventually failed, but, in March 1805, Ball was still able to assume that it would generate the projected surplus to supplement the general revenues of government.

Early 1805 was, thus, a critical period in the life of Ball's administration. Ball had to increase taxation, but he knew that the risks of appearing to renege on a promise to the Maltese would exacerbate a situation that was becoming inflammable.[64] This explains why Coleridge was forced to make

---

58   See Ball to Camden, above n. 50.
59   NLM LIBR/MS 430 ½.
60   See the Report of the Royal Commission, 1812, Kew, CO 158/19.
61   See Chapter 3.
62   See e.g. Ball to Cooke, 3 February 1805, Kew, CO 158/10/128.
63   As described in Chapter 2, Thornton reported that the mission resulted in the greatest loss that the Università had sustained. Thornton, Kew, CO 163/33. Ball's forecast of an estimated profit of £20,000 on the 40,000 salms of wheat to be purchased in the Black Sea area can be found in Ball to Cooke, 16 September 1804, Kew, CO 158/9.
64   It should not be forgotten that within a few weeks, significant numbers of Maltese rose up against the Jews. Their wrath was also directed against the British and their immigration policies because the demonstration of two thousand angry Maltese processed to the seat of government in Valletta.

the political case for the need to raise revenue by enumerating various classes of deserving beneficiaries who would receive government aid by virtue of the new duties. Their needs were, thus, held up by the British to make the case for the new duties. But the British agenda was much wider than their needs, and if this were known, the Maltese were less likely to accept the new duty.

Persuading the Maltese

It is important to emphasise just how important Coleridge's propaganda was in persuading the Maltese to accept the excise duties. Coleridge drafted the Proclamation with considerable astuteness, clearly responsive to the sensitive context of the measure. He and Ball had, clearly, determined that the popularity of the identified beneficiaries, which Coleridge would emphasise, and the unpopularity of alternative policies, would, together, make a persuasive political case for the new tax.

As in Coleridge's first Bando, the unusual efforts undertaken to give reasons for the decision are interesting. In essence, Coleridge's technique was to over-play one of Ball's subordinate motives for introducing the duties, and, for political reasons, entirely suppress the dominant motive. He was to suggest to the Maltese that additional revenue was necessary to provide for certain identified deserving causes (and no others). In other words, he was suggesting that Ball sought to achieve *increases* in public spending. In contrast, the Civil Commissioner's true priority was to impose the new taxes to help him meet *existing* expenditure.[65] This was so because the duties were planned to raise about £10,000 per annum[66] – more than would be required to fund the explicitly stated aims of assisting the poor families, raising public sector salaries and so on. The difference, between what was represented to the Maltese and what was intended by government, is significant; and the priority given to the latter partly explains why there were no binding commitments to fund the deserving causes. The claims of

65   Albeit that he would also endeavour to make provision for the deserving causes. Nevertheless, these represent almost a footnote in his strategy: Ball to Cooke, above n. 62.

66   This sum can be deduced from Ball's prediction that, when combined with the £20,000 from the corn speculation, the total revenue raised would be £30,000: see Ball to Camden, 19 April 1805, Kew, above n. 50, 134. Ball failed to offer a firm commitment to raise this sum (i.e. £10,000) from the new duties presumably because, as the Proclamation of 8 March 1805, conceded, he was unsure how great the resulting revenue would be.

the British Treasury would come first.

This deliberate and careful obfuscation reveals something about Coleridge's controversial approach to the business of practical politics. He can be seen to have collaborated with Ball in ensuring that public goods could be delivered outside of the constitutional framework. Even if the Maltese constitutional norms were judicially unenforceable *vis a vis* the Civil Commissioner, they nonetheless existed and they prescribed the constitutionally-permitted boundaries of governmental action. In other words, Coleridge seems to have been compelled by Ball to accept that adherence to the Rule of Law was not always in the public interest and that government could sometimes only succeed if it was prepared to do what was expedient, even if it were unconstitutional.

Such conduct also reveals the extent to which Ball's government felt justified in pursuing a controversial conception of the public interest notwithstanding legal and constitutional impediments. Had Ball respected the legal (albeit unenforceable) limitations upon his administration's powers, he would have been compelled to inform London that the Island's deficit could only be resolved with the continuing support of the British taxpayer. This would have been a disaster for his reputation, not least because London's (mis)understanding of the financial state of the Island had originated in Ball's own Memorandum of 26 December 1800.[67]

Moreover, the Proclamation of 8 March 1805 revealed how far he and Coleridge were prepared to go to fulfil Ball's obligations to Camden, the Secretary of State. This was one of the morally-complex challenges that practical politics presented to Coleridge. As we shall see in Chapter 6, the outcome in this instrument marks a very different approach from that he advocated, so powerfully, in his political journalism in England. It raised questions about the moral legitimacy of governmental action, which, for Coleridge, now became a troublesome dilemma revealed to us in his private *Notebooks*.[68]

Further Propaganda

The preamble to the wine Proclamation impressed upon the Maltese the Civil Commissioner's concern for the well-being of the inhabitants; and it served to remind them of the costly policies Ball has pursued to secure their

---

67   Ball to Dundas, Kew, CO 158/1/12-25; See further, Chapter 2.
68   See e.g. *CN* 2, 2412 and *CN* 2, 2413.

welfare. Coleridge recalled the reform of the courts, the continuing public works projects, the revival of the institutions such as the *Monte di Pietà*, the hospitals, almshouses, the orphanage and the monthly payments under the welfare scheme for the relief of poverty.

Coleridge emphasised that the raising of revenue was not a matter of choice but of necessity. Ball, he explained, had been confronted by alternative means of achieving this: either to raise the cost of grain supplied by the Università, or to impose this excise duty. Some officials, including Eton, had favoured raising the price of grain in order to replace the lost capital.[69] No doubt, Ball wanted to court popularity by signalling to the inhabitants that he had not chosen to tax a staple foodstuff. The moral justification for placing duties on alcohol consumption was more easily understood because Ball could be seen to be discouraging a vice, as well as burdening the drinking habits of foreigners in preference to those of the Maltese.[70]

Coleridge stated that, subject to sufficient revenue becoming available, the intended spending priorities were: the alleviation of the financial hardship of certain private individuals whose income had been reduced, following the appropriation by the French of the capital they had deposited in the Bank of the Università; the increase in salary of deserving civil servants; and financial aid to the charitable institutions (which included the hospitals, the orphanage, and the Office of the Grand Almoner) giving priority to those institutions that were constructing publicly useful buildings. Coleridge also emphasised that the economic incentive, established by the duties, was an incentive to alter behaviour, most notably the reduction of excessive alcohol consumption.[71] As we shall see, alcohol-fuelled violence, especially in the taverns, was causing disquiet on Malta, and had attracted other interventions from the British authorities.[72] Controlling abuse of spirits was also high on Ball's agenda.

For good measure, this list was reinforced by exploiting the simmering

69   Eton to Sullivan, Kew, CO 158/2/308.
70   Each of these policy goals was favoured by the Royal Commission: Kew, CO 158/19.
71   Because of the political and legal sensitivity of this measure, Ball had consulted widely prior to its introduction, including the Commander in Chief of British forces (Major-General Villettes), "the field officers" and the Chief Physician of the Medical Staff. We might expect their viewpoints to emphasise the importance of reducing alcohol consumption. See Ball to Camden above n. 50, 133-4.
72   E.g. a Bando of 18 October 1802, NLM LIBR/MS 430 1/2; Bandi 1790 AL 1805, 273 to restrain the abuse of pointed or sharp weapons often used in violent assaults. See generally, the consumer protection theme, below.

dislike of foreigners on the Island[73] who, as Coleridge seemed eager to point out, would be the most likely to bear, indirectly through consequential retail price increases, the burden of the new duties. It is typical of Coleridge that he appealed to reason in this way; but the explicit exploitation of the Maltese attitude to foreigners is a concern. Its explicit "targeting" of the duties, borne most heavily by foreigners, might have unwittingly suggested an official policy that foreigners were somehow less deserving than the Maltese. If so, Coleridge's language in this Bando may, unintentionally, have provided an unfortunate context given the anti-Semitic unrest that broke out in May 1805.[74]

Protecting Poor Families and Raising Salaries

Pre-eminent amongst the deserving causes that Coleridge identified, and given the most emphasis in the Proclamation, was the protection of certain poor families.

The issue, in this instance, was that the assets of the Università, including the capital sums placed on deposit by the inhabitants, had been looted and carried off by the French during their occupation. This had given rise to a major grievance amongst the Maltese because of an unfortunate gesture by the British military.

The problem originated in the exclusion of Maltese officers from the negotiations for the French surrender almost five years earlier.[75] The Maltese had understood that the French had offered hostages as a security to ensure that the sums taken from the Università, and elsewhere, would be reimbursed. The British military, who were, perhaps, concerned with upholding military customs, failed to make any provision for this in the

---

73   It is unlikely that Coleridge would have regarded the few English persons on the Island as "foreigners", although it is possible that, from the Maltese perspective, the English might have been growing as unpopular as some other nationalities. There is some evidence for this in a letter in which it was stated: "...the Maltese begin to hate the English..." from Borg to Eton, 30 May 1806, Kew, CO 158/12/no folio reference. Maltese and English alike were, for some purposes, officially regarded as British subjects after September 1800: see the Treaty with the Dey of Algiers, 19 March 1801.

74   See further Public Order and Crime, below.

75   The arrangements for the capitulation gave rise to a long term grievance amongst the Maltese: see the Petition of the Maltese to His Majesty King George III, 10 July 1811: Hardman, 509-511, and a more detailed account is offered by the Marchese di Testaferrata to Earl Bathurst (undated), January 1812, Hardman, 512, esp. 513 and also the Report of the Royal Commission, Kew, CO 158/19.

surrender articles. The French officers were allowed to leave Malta with their "private property" (some of it looted from the Maltese) which was, conveniently, carried to French ports on British transports.[76] This regrettable miscalculation resulted in financial misery for a number of Maltese who lived off the interest paid on the capital that they had deposited in the Università. For those dependent upon these interest payments, the economic bedrock of their lives had been destroyed. The Maltese naturally blamed the British administration for the negligence of their military.

We can also note, *en passant*, that a further consequence of this theft had been that the Maltese, after 1800, were no longer prepared to invest their remaining savings in the Bank of the Università. Ball had been compelled to obtain funds from the British Treasury to underwrite it. Whilst this was a necessary step, it was not sufficient to restore the *status quo, ante* the French invasion. The Bank had to be able to draw upon the private capital of the Island, which meant that risk-averse potential depositors had to be assured that their funds would be safe.

The British had underwritten the Bank by investing about £100,000 to restore its credit,[77] and by 1804 it was considered possible to invite the deposit of new private capital. On 7 March 1804 Ball issued a Public Notice authorising the Bank to receive deposits and authorising the payment of interest of 3% thereon.[78] This initiative succeeded in attracting deposits in excess of 925,000 *scudi*[79] repayable on demand. Interest was paid on these deposits until 20 March 1805 at which time the interest on them was declared to have ceased.

---

76   Although by Article 5 of the Articles of Capitulation the French Generals had given an undertaking that the property in question (which was not to be searched) did not contain any "public or private property": Hardman, 320. A similar arrangement was later to be agreed in the notorious Convention of Cintra, 1808. Under its terms, the French carried looted property away from Portugal on British ships after their defeat at the Battle of Vimeiro. The controversial Convention drew much criticism in Britain, not least from William Wordsworth who famously produced a critical pamphlet on the subject (Wordsworth W, Concerning the Convention of Cintra, London: Longman, Hurst, Rees and Orme, 1809). Unlike the French in Valletta, who were surrendering a fortress, the defeated French army under General Juno enjoyed a weaker bargaining position. The conduct of the British responsible for the Convention (including Arthur Wellesley, later the Duke of Wellington) was investigated at an official inquiry, but all concerned were formally exonerated.

77   See Eton to Sullivan, Kew, CO 158/2/308.

78   Thornton, above n. 63, and Chapter 2, Kew, CO 163/33/25-6. Appendix 9 of Thornton's Report contains a translation into English of the text of the Avviso that was signed by Alexander Macaulay.

79   Ibid.

This was, of course, aimed at attracting new investment. It did nothing to address the plight of those whose capital had been taken by the French.

Ball had received petitions requesting him to take steps to deal equitably with the affected individuals and, eventually, had little choice but to alleviate their distress. However, as we have seen, there may be more than a hint of opportunism in Coleridge's Proclamation. Both Ball and Coleridge were prepared to deploy the justice of the claims of the poor (and those of other good causes) to persuade the Maltese to accept the excise duties – and, thus, the increased retail price rises – that would raise significantly more revenue than the meeting of these claims would require.

The poor families were not, of course, the only intended beneficiaries. Ball took the opportunity to use some of the revenue raised for other (presumably popular) public purposes. As we have seen, public sector salaries were so low that some, albeit not many, employees boosted their income by diverting public funds, or as Maitland, the first British Governor called it, by drawing "unfair perquisites".[80] Ball had identified low salaries as a problem and now wished to provide targeted salary increases to "deserving" public employees. As we have seen, this included, in 1805, salary incentives for the President of the hospitals.[81]

Increasing public sector pay was a necessary reform, but it seems that the strategy was not vigorously pursued at an operational level because the problem of low pay, particularly amongst the more numerous junior staff (and the illegitimate "perquisites") was left to Maitland to address in 1814. Money continued to be diverted, and false entries made in the accounts. Inadequate remuneration may have been one reason for this corruption. Certainly, it remained an issue during Ball's administration: and the failure to use the money raised by the wine duty to solve this problem reveals the extent to which Ball had his eye on the priority of placating British ministers by reducing the Island's deficit.

The Operation of the Duties

The duties on wine and spirits were a tax on *importation*, rather than

---

80   Maitland to Bathurst, 24 October 1814, Kew, CO 158/25/209, et seq., in which he reports that the salaries of junior staff had been much too low. He added that this problem had been so grave that it had been impossible for them to exist without fees or "unfair perquisites". He accordingly raised their remuneration.

81   Significantly, this only amounted to £71 19s 6d per annum: see Macaulay to Ball, 10 September 1804, Kew, CO 158/9/51.

consumption. This meant that the home-produced wine and spirits would not be subject to duty, which signalled that it could achieve a competitive advantage over imported products. This economic policy may have been intended to extend the benefits of a reviving economy from Valletta to the rural areas – wine production having increased during and since the days of the Order.

In relation to the duty on spirits, the Proclamation imposed a duty levied according to volume, which was, thus, a tax on consumption. As we shall see, this was consonant with Ball's policy of regulating the consumption of spirits, not least to prevent drunken violence by British soldiers.

The Proclamation imposed a duty of six *tari* per barrel on all wine, regardless of its nature or quality, and thirty *tari* per barrel on spirits, the duty to be collected by the Università. Since there were no exemptions from the duty, it was a relatively simple tax to administer. The penalty for evasion was the confiscation of the entire quantity of wine or spirits on which the duty had not been paid.

The Proclamation was careful to avoid commitments as to the detailed manner in which funds would be allocated. Ostensibly, this was so because the Administration was not in a position to forecast how much additional expenditure could be afforded until it was clear what revenue would be raised. At one level, this is unsurprising. It would have been highly unusual for any Administration to commit itself, in advance, to how money raised from taxation would be spent. But, as we have seen, Ball would have wanted to give himself a means of avoiding apparent commitments to future, additional, spending in order to disguise the problem that the revenue was needed to meet existing spending requirements. To have made binding commitments of significant, additional, expenditure would have frustrated this ultimate and overarching goal. If the Island was to remain a British possession, giving it a dominant military and commercial position in the central and eastern Mediterranean, the current account deficit had to be eliminated.

Outcomes

Although ultimately effective in raising revenue, the wine duty Proclamation proved to be controversial and problematic. The principal concern was that the instrument created wider expectations than those that the British were prepared to honour. This problem began an unresolved controversy that was to last into the twentieth century. The refusal to meet these expectations is further suggestive of the extent to which Ball's true agenda prioritised British rather than Maltese concerns.

It will be recalled that the private investors in the Università were not the only ones to lose significant sums as a result of the French predations. The religious institutions, such as the convents, had also lost their deposits and other property. They had formerly received interest at a rate of 3% on their deposits, but this had ceased.[82] Coleridge provided as follows:

> His Excellency therefore wishes to advise, that it is his intention is to pay all *individual owners of capital* tied up in the bank of the above mentioned university, interest on their money at the rate of thirty tarì for every hundred. (Emphasis added).

In contrast, the religious foundations were only given a vague promise that help would be forthcoming – when it could be afforded. Coleridge made this clear as follows:

> As soon as he is able, His Excellency shall not neglect to give the necessary help to places of worship, and to religious foundations.

This careful language, as well as subsequent events, revealed that Ball was not concerned with assuming a British responsibility for making restitution to all those who had suffered loss at the hands of the French; apart from addressing the deficit, his subordinate policy was essentially to moderate individual hardship.

However, the religious institutions were, subsequently, to argue that by paying interest on the capital, the British had acknowledged the debt owed to all those, including themselves, who had formerly had capital deposited in the Bank. The 1812 Royal Commission had also concluded that, by its conduct, Britain had assumed responsibility for a large debt, so the charitable institutions' case was not completely unsupported.[83]

Their case was not, however, to succeed. By the terms of a Treaty of 25 April 1818, the French were to be compelled to compensate British subjects who had suffered loss as a result of their actions. The private individuals amongst the Maltese, who had been amongst the first victims of the War, eventually received compensation, but this entitlement did not extend to the Maltese religious institutions. These were compelled to pursue their claims by diplomatic means, arguing, unsuccessfully, that the responsibility

---

82   See Eton to Sullivan, above n. 77, 308 et seq.
83   Kew, CO 158/19.

to make restitution lay with the British government.[84] The funds lost were never recovered.

Conclusion

Ball's general approach to tax policy was vindicated by the Report of the Royal Commission in 1812.[85] It concurred in the view that any reversal of policy, so as to impose taxes (by which it meant those which did not have popular support), would have caused distrust and, worse still, would have led to renewed calls for a representative assembly constituted as a *Consiglio Popolare*. It had concluded that Ball had succeeded in winning popular support for the measures he introduced, and this, in part, reflects Coleridge's skilled manipulation of government information.

Table 2:
Revenue raised by the duties imposed by the Proclamation of 8 March 1805

From	To	Revenue to Università (scudi)
25 July 1804	24 July 1805	48,107/10/7
25 July 1805	24 July 1806	109, 805/11/7
24 July 1806	24 July 1807	99,620/6/1
25 July 1807	31 December 1807	22,650/1/10
1 January 1808	31 December 1808	124,264/6/11
1 January 1809	25 October 1809	111, 823/5/6
26 October 1809	31 December 1809	21,374/6/14
1 January 1810	12 May 1810	31, 750/5/0
13 May 1810	31 December 1810	81,082/11/6
1 January 1811	31 December 1811	155, 939/10/1
Total		**806, 420/3/3**

Source: *Report to His Excellency the Governor on the Accounts of the University of Valletta from 4th September 1800-31st December 1814* by W. Thornton dated 12 July 1816, Kew, CO 163/33

---

84   Bonnici.
85   Ibid.

5.4. Public Order and Crime

The Problem of Crime and Public Order on Malta 1800-1806[86]

The crime rate, whether against persons or property, appears to have increased from the onset of British rule in 1800. As early as 3 December 1800, Major-General Pigot's administration[87] issued a Proclamation targeting "vagabonds" and "layabouts",[88] which meant persons without visible or verifiable legitimate means of support. These people were to be placed under supervision, questioned about their means and (if they lacked an income) given a maximum period in which to find employment. Should they not have succeeded in this, they risked permanent exile. If this Proclamation had been strictly enforced, exile must have been the fate of many unfortunate Maltese because the economy, at this time, was in ruins: unemployment, hunger, poverty and associated problems were evidence of a major social and economic crisis – as Coleridge later recalled in *The Friend*.[89] However, it can be noted that, at this time (1800-1801), the authorities seem to have attributed the rising number of thefts to idle Maltese rather than to immigrants.

Immigration increased and, with it, the competition for scarce jobs during the economic slump that followed the liberation. Maltese resentment was made worse by the belief, amongst the foreigners, that they were not subject to Maltese law. Alexander Macaulay, in his capacity as Public Secretary, intervened to clarify their obligations in a Public Notice dated 23 July 1801.[90] This was intended to make clear that foreigners were subject to Maltese jurisdiction and would be punished for offences committed on the Island.

The steps taken by the administration to address the crime rate did not fully succeed and, by 1805, the number of offences, particularly offences

---

86   See generally, Galea.
87   Major-General Pigot was in charge of a military administration of Malta from 5 September 1800 until 14 May 1801 when Charles Cameron, the first Civil Commissioner, was appointed.
88   NLM LIBR/MS 430 1/2; Bandi 1790 AL 1805, 156.
89   *The Friend*, 1, 567; see also Chapter 2.
90   NLM LIBR/MS 430 1/2; Bandi 1790 AL 1805, 205.

against property, seems to have been causing discontent.[91] Along with other accusations concerning the effectiveness of Ball's administration, the crime rate was used by Ball's political opponents, including William Eton, in an attempt to undermine ministerial confidence in Ball as the Civil Commissioner.[92] Ball was forced to respond to these accusations in a detailed defence of his government.[93]

The most commonly-committed offences seem to have been burglaries, and robberies,[94] including highway robbery. Offenders seem either to have operated individually or in gangs, often perpetrating their crime in urban areas, where there more lucrative opportunities. After the offence, they would flee to the countryside.

There is evidence that offences against the person were also common. The use of weapons in alcohol-related violence, in the taverns, was a significant problem which the administration was required to address. The authorities issued a Bando, 18 October 1802, to reinforce the prohibition in the Code de Rohan against the carrying of sharp weapons.[95] This measure also prohibited shopkeepers from serving wine to persons carrying knives or having sharp weapons in their possession.

Ball's report to the Secretary of State, on the crime rate, is comprised, mainly, of assertions unsubstantiated by statistics.[96] However, he did include some limited, but revealing, information that is corroborated by Coleridge's Bandi and Avvisi. For example, Ball's report revealed that, under British rule, there had been only five murders amongst the civil

---

91   See Eton to Windham, 11 October 1806, Kew, CO 158/12 (no folio reference) and note the references to "frequent robberies" and "frequent murders" in Borg to Eton, 30 May 1806, Kew, CO 158/12/no folio reference. See also Ball to Windham, 28 February 1807, Kew, CO 158/13/53.

92   See Windham to Ball, 6 January 1807, quoted in Hardman, 499. and Eton to Windham, 11 October 1806, Kew, CO 158/12 (no folio reference).

93   Ball to Windham, 28 February 1807, Kew, CO 158/13/9 et seq.

94   This was conceded by Ball to Windham although with the caveat that by 1807 no similar offence had been committed for "some months": ibid at 83. An interesting case involving robbery and homicide came before the Segnatura on 1 June 1805 when four petitioners unsuccessfully sought to have their sentences of exile reduced. An interesting feature of this case was that it involved a claim for sanctuary, and one of the grounds for the petition was that the Curia Romana had not delivered its verdict on the status of the sanctuary. Thus the case touched upon the relationship between the civil and ecclesiastic authorities: *Registro de memoriali decretati da sua Excellenza il Sig. Cavalier Alessandro Ball Regio Commissionario Civile di Sua Maestà Britannica*, NAM LIBR 43/11 vol N.

95   NLM LIBR/MS 430 1/2; Bandi 1790 AL 1805,273. *Code Du Rohan*, translated by Lydia Davis, Book 5 Item 2, II.

96   Ball to Windham, above n. 93.

population. However, the conviction rate seems to have been poor because, according to Ball, the police had difficulty in obtaining sufficient evidence to sustain prosecutions.[97] Ball revealed that only one offender had actually been hanged for murder (in 1802).[98]

Ball's hint at community solidarity, in sheltering offenders from the British authorities, provides an illuminating context to Borg's accusation that offenders were, too frequently, remaining undetected and unpunished.[99] A serious issue seems to have been the use, by Maltese suspects, of sanctuary to evade apprehension and trial. This drew explicit adverse comment from the Royal Commission of 1812.[100] As we shall see below, there were other instances of "a code of silence"; and the possibility of witness intimidation cannot be ruled out. The fact that rewards had to be offered to informers implicitly recognised a lack of voluntary support for aiding the authorities in upholding the rule of law.[101]

Immigration and Crime

After the British took possession of Malta the population began to increase. This was a consequence both of increased immigration and decreased emigration. Galea,[102] who focused on the crime problem during Cameron's administration (1801-1802), linked the deteriorating crime rate, during this early period, to significant immigration; indeed, it is evident that the Maltese made this connection for themselves and quickly adopted a jaundiced attitude towards foreigners.[103] Immigrants were widely

---

97   Even where the identity of the offender was known, it was still possible to evade capture. This could only have been possible with local support. For example when Giovanni Vasallo, a shop worker, ran off after fatally stabbing a soldier outside a wine shop in Valletta on 30 September 1805 he was never caught despite the offer of a reward: http://website.lineone.net/~stephaniebidmead/chapter567.htm consulted 17 January 2007.

98   The conduct of the public execution reflected badly on the Administration. This was so because the public had been allowed to end the suffering of the offender by shooting him during the execution by hanging. Accidentally or otherwise, shots fired from the crowd hit both the executioner and his assistant killing the former and wounding the latter. See Ball to Windham, above n. 93 at 83.

99   Borg to Eton, 30 May 1806, Kew, CO 158/12/no folio reference.

100 Kew, CO 158/19/ 24-28.

101 See below and note the evidence in the Avviso of 25 May 1805 that Borg, who intervened to save a perceived Jew from severe injury, seems not to have informed on the aggressors. See also Chapter 6.

102 Ibid.

103 It is unlikely that in this early period (1800-1802) there was much antipathy to-

perceived as selfish opportunists who came to the Island for motives of personal gain.[104] Immigration and crime, thus, became closely intertwined political issues.

Most immigration strategies are formulated to take account of two dominant, although not necessarily coterminous, considerations: the first is the country's labour or commercial needs; the second is security. Each of these may have become an issue on Malta. Increasing wage rates, which became an issue in 1805, suggest a shortage of labour that continued immigration might have alleviated.[105] By that date, public disturbances, and the deep suspicion of foreigners amongst the Maltese, had already forced policy-makers to adopt less liberal policies. Although immigration was not prevented altogether, it was subject to ever-tighter controls. Coleridge's Proclamation of 21 June 1805 was merely the latest in a series of interventions described below. Security had also become a major, and possibly the dominant, concern by the summer of 1805.

The benefits of immigration tend not to be evenly distributed. Most immigrants are low-skilled or unskilled workers whose presence often drives down the wages of similarly low-skilled domestic workers. They also increase the pool of labour thereby making competition for scarce jobs more intense. However, these trends operate to the advantage of those who can most benefit from the decreased cost of labour, such as businesses relying on unskilled or low-skilled labour. Low-skilled workers in the destination state, who can often compete on price only by taking lower wages, represent the most obvious group who lose out because of immigration. Ball's evidence may suggest that this was very much the issue on Malta. He stated, in a despatch to Windham, that the disturbances that took place against the Jews, in May 1805, were perpetrated by the "lower orders" of Maltese society.[106] Other evidence corroborates this. As we shall see, it was shop workers who acted, in concert, to abuse the Jew, Di Biaggii, on the afternoon of 18 May 1805. And, although poorly articulated, their concern can be read as signalling a fear of the threat that the Jews posed to them in their capacity as shop workers or artisans.

After 1805, as the economy improved, complaints by the Maltese about the inflationary consequences of a rising population became yet another

---

wards the British, although attitudes may have hardened by 1806: see Borg to Eton, 30 May 1806, Kew, CO 158/12/no folio reference.

104   Royal Commission of 1812, Kew, CO 158/19.

105   See Chapter 2.

106   Above n. 93.

grievance against the new immigrants.[107] Shortage of accommodation, and rising prices in particular, attracted adverse comment.[108] This combustible mixture, of economic pressures, crime and a suspicion about the motives of many foreigners, resulted in severe social friction with which the administration, including Coleridge, urgently had to engage, not least when violence erupted against Jews. Deeply embedded anti-Semitism led to what Coleridge was to describe as a "persecution" of the Jews in May 1805.[109]

Official Action to Regulate Foreigners

By 1802 we can see a subtle shift in policy in the official attitude towards foreigners (other than the British). From this time, official action targeted foreigners, whether or not they were guilty of crime. The inference was, of course, that the Administration now shared the popular view that foreign visitors should be treated with suspicion.

The Bando of 24 March 1802 stipulated that foreigners resident in hotels or houses had to report and be registered within twenty-four hours of arrival. It also required innkeepers, and others giving rooms to foreigners, to report, to government, their dealings with those foreigners.[110] Any failure to comply was to be met with the draconian sanction of the innkeeper in question losing his or her licence. These measures were supplemented by a Proclamation of 4 May 1803 which required all foreigners to state their profession, and the reason for their stay on the Island, when they registered.[111] This was intended to weed out the "ne'er do wells" and exclude those who had no means of support.

This filtering and monitoring of foreigners suggested a cautionary approach, which might have reinforced some of the anxieties amongst the Maltese. But the British were not willing to allow this hostility to threaten the maintenance of law and order, for the authorities also acted to *protect* foreigners admitted to Malta. Of course, officials fully understood that commerce had to be promoted if the Island was to prosper and this meant interaction with neighbouring states. *Bona fide* foreigners, present on the

---

107 Ball to Camden, 19 April 1805, Kew, CO 158/10/123, 131: the "general distress" caused by the economic collapse of 1800 "has already ceased". He noted that there was a demand for labour and an increase in wages.
108 Royal Commission of 1812, Kew, CO 158/19.
109 See below.
110 NLM LIBR/MS 430 1/2; Bandi 1790 AL 1805, 239.
111 NLM LIBR/MS 430 1/2; Bandi 1790 AL 1805, 285.

Island, had to be protected from any arbitrary "insults" and vigilantism committed on the Maltese streets. Cameron had issued a Proclamation of 5 October 1801 forbidding such "insults" to Turkish merchants and their families.[112] Even so, the local antagonism to foreigners was not eradicated;[113] and in 1805 its particular focus was the commercially-vibrant Jewish community.

Ball's despatches to London on the subject of law and order were, of course, designedly reassuring. He was eager to impress upon ministers that the crime and public order problems in Valletta were no greater that might have been expected in any British port city: but, he conceded that "bad characters" were always attracted to sea ports.[114] By 1805 the trade focused on the port area was recognised as the motor of economic revival bringing much needed prosperity to the Island. This increasing affluence was, probably, a magnet for more "bad characters" to travel to the Island.

By 1804-1805 the Maltese concern about immigration seems to have subtly shifted from the threat of crime to the problems caused by increased rivalry in trade. Immigration, of course, brought new skills to Malta; but it also brought increased competition for the local traders. Ball explicitly mentioned this in that part of his report to Windham dealing with the anti-Semitic disturbances. [115]

The Administration was aware of the benefits that would arise from immigration. Amongst the indirect benefits was the increased "tax take", which increased public revenue. But this is not all because there are indications, in his Proclamations, that Coleridge was prepared to exploit, for British purposes, the Maltese dislike of foreigners in order to win support for certain unpalatable measures. As we have described, he explicitly stated that the excise duties, introduced in the Bando of 8 March 1805,[116] would be a duty paid predominantly by "foreigners" because it mainly affected their drinking habits rather than those of the Maltese. The fact that foreigners paid more would have been particularly satisfying to the Maltese – as

112 NLM LIBR/MS 430 1/2; Bandi 1790 AL 1805, 219.
113 Antagonism remained a feature of Maltese society by the time the Royal Commissioners reported in 1812: Kew, CO 158/19. By that date, the British seemed willing exploit it by shifting the tax burden towards foreigners rather than Maltese, thereby achieving popularity as well as increased revenue – a process that Coleridge had begun in his wine duty Bando of 8 March 1805, see taxation theme, above.
114 Ball to Windham above n. 93 at 53.
115 Ball to Windham, above n. 93.
116 NLM LIBR/MS 430 2/2 Bandi 1805 AL 1814 f.2.

Coleridge well knew; and he did not hesitate to curry favour with the Maltese by pointing out that the Administration was enacting, indirectly, discriminatory measures that would harm Maltese interests much less than those of the foreigners. This is suggestive of some confused thinking about the best means of promoting effective community relations. We can only speculate as to whether Coleridge might have altered his public-relations spin on this tax had he known that the "insurrection" against the Jews would take place a little over two months later.

Constitutional Principles: Public Order and Crime

The role of the Civil Commissioner in the operation of the criminal justice system on Malta is particularly controversial. At issue is the question of what influence he might have exercised over the punishments imposed in criminal trials. If he intervened in the criminal process it would raise controversial questions about the fairness of the trial, and of the independence of the judiciary, notwithstanding that the Maltese Constitution permitted such interventions.

According to a general theory concerning the separation of powers, the punishment appropriate to a particular offence should be a matter for the courts – to be decided according to the law rather than the official determination of the Executive. It implies the making of a prior law, an adjudication, the finding of guilt and the handing down, by a judge, of a penalty of a nature and severity that falls within legally-prescribed limits. Bureaucratic sentencing, outside the judicial process, violates these fundamental principles.

Under the Maltese Constitution, as we have seen, the principle of the separation of powers was entirely disregarded. The Constitution conferred upon the Civil Commissioner almost unlimited autocratic powers.[117] The judiciary was not independent; and the Civil Commissioner exercising his powers in the *Segnatura* could overturn or set aside judicial decisions.[118] Like the Grandmasters, the Civil Commissioner was the supreme magistrate and had the liberty to interfere in the criminal process. Grandmasters regularly intervened in the sentencing process.

The British had undertaken to perpetuate the Maltese constitutional

---

117 See Hardman, 6.
118 The Royal Commission report offers an account of the Civil Commissioner's Constitutional powers: Kew, CO 158/19. These powers included reversing the decrees of the Tribunals.

system: continuation was the central bulwark of Ball's administrative strategy. Even so, this need not necessarily have *compelled* Ball to interfere in the judicial process. In other words, he could have exercised a self-imposed restraint so as to import into Malta a *de facto* respect for fundamental constitutional values with a view to raising the standard of government.[119]

However, Coleridge's Bandi and Avvisi, as well as other primary materials, reveal that these rule of law principles were not applied on Malta during this period and this will be examined below.

The failure to respect the separation of powers in the imposition of sentences, as evidenced in some of Coleridge's Avvisi, is of interest given the emphasis he had placed upon respecting the doctrine in his earlier political journalism. The concentration of power in the hands of the French Consul was, he had argued, the fatal flaw in the French Constitution of December 1799. This is important because Coleridge did not see the separation of powers as a British principle, but as a universal one.[120] However, in his role as Public Secretary, Coleridge failed to persuade the Civil Commissioner to confine governmental action within the constitutional values that he (Coleridge) had earlier advocated; indeed, his later writing, in *The Friend*, approved of Ball's actions.[121]

We shall first consider the Avviso concerning extortion and then the Avvisi issued after the anti-Semitic disturbances before looking at other measures concerned with immigration and public security.

The Avviso of 1 March 1805[122] – Extortion

Public Notices announcing convictions were issued where there was a particular public interest in drawing attention to the offence and the punishment imposed. This Notice gave community-wide publicity to an important conviction of a named individual, Matteo Sacco, for extortion. It also contained an explicit warning that the public should be wary of Sacco following his release from gaol. But as we shall discover, the additional motive for the instrument was that it allowed Coleridge to portray the

---

119 Coleridge might have made these arguments although, if he did, the evidence is now lost. The above is subject to the important caveat that constitutional values were under strain in Britain following the suspension of habeas corpus and the Act of Indemnity 1801 (see Chapter 1).

120 The separation of powers is not a defining characteristic of the British Constitution.

121 *The Friend*, 1, 544.

122 NLM LIBR/MS 430 2/2 Bandi 1805 AL 1814, 1.

Government as benign and responsive.

The Public Secretary's decision to issue a Notice to inform the general public of the offender's conviction would, by itself, damage the latter's reputation. In providing the further *explicit* exhortation, that the inhabitants should be wary of him, suggests an official intention to ostracise the offender. According to one view, this can be seen as an example of Ball's role as *parens patriae* ("father Ball"); by drawing the attention of the inhabitants to a corrupt rogue (who might try to re-offend in the future) Ball was protecting the Maltese from becoming his next victims. However, the effect of this warning, can be also seen as a further penalty over and above the punishment determined by the court. This is so because Coleridge's warning would naturally tend to isolate the offender. Depending on the response of his fellow citizens, this might actually be more damaging to him than his term of imprisonment and the obligation to repay thirty *scudi*. It implied little faith in Sacco's rehabilitation. However, the Notice did recognise the importance of corrective justice by requiring the offender to restore to the victim the sum extorted. There was, as Coleridge understood, an important principle of equality and rectification at issue here, namely that at Miccallef's (the victim's) expense, Sacco had unlawfully acquired a gain that he should be required to restore to Miccallef.

Sacco was imprisoned until the sum of thirty *scudi*, that he had extorted from Micallef, had been repaid. The obvious difficulty created by this punishment is that, whilst incarcerated, Sacco could not earn money. In the case of a poor offender without savings this could make repayment (and thus release) impossible. We do not know if Sacco faced this difficulty.

The major reason why Coleridge decided to issue the Notice was that it provided an opportunity to repair some of the damage to Ball's reputation, with the Maltese public described in Chapter 2. Since the offence related to a demand for money to procure from government a benefit, namely a recission of an order placing the victim in exile, he assured the inhabitants that they could petition the Civil Commissioner directly without incurring the expense of unnecessary (and dishonest) intermediaries. This affirmed the commitment made by Charles Cameron in the Proclamation, addressed to the Maltese Nation, in which he conveyed not only the "paternal care and affection" of the King for the Maltese people but also promised that: "(m)y door shall be open to all; I will hear everyone's plea; I shall be ready to render justice…".[123] Coleridge clearly felt it necessary to associate Ball with

---

123 See the Proclamation of 15 July 1801, Hardman, 358-9. W. Eton's account is

this commitment. As we shall discuss in Chapter 6, this was a key component of Coleridge's strategy to re-build Ball's public reputation following a series of damaging decisions, not least the summary exile of a Maltese who had presented a petition to the *Segnatura*.[124] Coleridge's Notice of 1 March 1805 reveals that the authorities knew that Ball's conduct in the summary exile case, allowed Nationalists to condemn what they portrayed as his "despotic scourge" and "thundering vengeance" – a ruthlessness which, they alleged, had not even been possible under the worst of the Grandmasters. As we shall see, Coleridge's assurances were the Administration's riposte and a direct appeal to the public to place confidence in British prerogative justice.

5.4.1. The Anti-Semitic Disturbances

The Avvisi Concerning the Anti-Semitic Disturbances

We are now concerned with the Public Notices that were issued as a consequence of criminal behaviour connected with the unrest against the Jews. These matters were amongst the most difficult that the Civil Commissioner encountered during Coleridge's period in office. A detailed examination, based on records not previously available, shows a series of actions demonstrating the difficulties of reconciling the priorities of government with the need to uphold the rule of law. It also reveals Coleridge's use of government information in securing the dominant strategic goal of a stable society under British rule.

Context

Jewish immigration was resented by sections of Maltese society. Agitators keen to foment violence, exploited fear and distrust. The history of the Jews on Malta at this time is revealing. Ball reported, in 1807, that under the Order of St John, Jews had been excluded from residing freely on Malta,[125] and Jewish visitors were subject to restrictions.[126] This stance

---

revealing. He stated that the Maltese petitioners risked punishment if they showed the "least freedom in remonstrating" Eton, vol. IV, 145 et seq. Fear of inviting the ire of the Civil Commissioner must have been a disincentive to use the Segnatura, and hence a reason why intermediaries such as Sacco had come to the fore.
124 These were outlined in Chapter 2.
125 Almost the only Jews on the Islands during the government of the Order were captive slaves or others who concealed their faith.
126 *The Edict of Expulsion* signed in Palermo on 18 June 1492 excluded Jews from Malta after that date.

was thought to have encouraged the popular view amongst the Maltese that Jewish immigration would be harmful to the public interest. This restrictive official policy on Jewish immigration was reversed under the British administration. One of the causes for the first migration was the outbreak, in Gibraltar in the autumn of 1804, of yellow fever. This caused an unknown, but significant, number of the Jewish community there to emigrate to Malta.[127] Under British rule, Jewish immigrants were, thus, permitted to enter and settle on the Island; and these immigrants were, eventually, to prosper. But their early reception was troubled.

The differences were partly cultural and partly economic, and each of these was inter-related. The reliance of the Maltese on the welfare systems of the Knights had produced a dependency culture. However, the Jewish immigrants of 1804 were of a different and more independent, enterprising outlook. Following their arrival they had set up their own businesses that competed with Maltese shopkeepers and others, particularly in Valletta. [128]

This new competition made the British policy reversal unpopular amongst those economically threatened by it. Jewish entrepreneurs had a notable reputation for commercial acumen, which made some Maltese, with vested interests, antagonistic to the new settlers. It will be recalled that, at this time (spring 1805), the Island's economy was only just beginning to recover from the severe economic collapse that had followed the blockade.[129] Any immigration policy likely to prejudice individual prosperity would have been particularly sensitive. It is also likely that the particular concern amongst the Maltese business community also implied a less well-defined popular prejudice, against the Jews, amongst the ordinary Maltese. This was capable of leading to violence. Mobs, that were prone to assault their victims, were operating on Malta – as Coleridge's Avviso of 25 May 1805[130] indicates. Such was the anti-Semitic hysteria that merely calling someone a Jew could lead to that victim becoming subject to violence. As we shall see, any <u>unpopular</u> or suspected person was at risk of assault even if they were

127 See Kew, CO 158/10/3; also Ball to Windham, above n. 93 at 67 in which he referred to the immigration in the following terms: "In the autumn of 1804....*many* persons of the Jewish persuasion took refuge on Malta". (Emphasis added). It is possible that they arrived with a convoy under the protection of a Captain Mundy of the Hydra on 14 October 1804.
128 Ball became aware of the jealousies that began to emerge between the Maltese and Jewish communities: above n. 93 at 67-8 where he refers to the "...fear amongst the Maltese that the Jews would divide amongst themselves the advantages of trade".
129 Above Chapter 2.
130 LIBR/MS 430 2/2 Bandi 1805 AL 1814, 9.

not Jewish; in other words, labelling someone as a Jew, could be used as a pretext to incite violence against any member of the community. Although Jews were targeted some unpopular gentiles were also at risk.

The Events of May 1805

Coleridge's *Notebooks* contains two entries on this important subject. The first of these records states, "Latter end of May-&c-THE JEWS!",[131] and the second, probably written some weeks later, records, "Saturday 18 May 1805-Valetta (sic)-the persecution of the Jews commenced".[132] A further Notebook entry records a massacre of Jews in Algiers that took place on Saturday, 29 June 1805, a day that became known within Jewish circles as the "Black Sabbath".[133] Referring to the mob violence in Algiers, Coleridge recorded "more than an hundred of that unhappy race massacred- their Bodies burnt".[134] This reveals that, in the early summer of 1805, racist violence against the Jews was not confined to Malta, although the immediate causes of the two instances of violence were different in each case.

Contrary to Ball's intention to downplay the insurrection,[135] there is ample evidence that the authorities were alarmed by it. Ball admitted that some of the most significant disturbances were orchestrated by a number of agitators who went from place to place, such as the taverns and shops, repeating the ancient blood libel that the Jews had abducted children to sacrifice in their religious rites.[136] This is corroborated by court records. As we shall discover, one of the convicted offenders, Andrea Borg, had begun a rumour that Jews were prowling around looking for children to kill. No children had been reported missing, which suggests that the slanders

---

131   *CN* 2, 2594.

132   *CN* 2, 2646.

133   *CN* 2,2668. The riots and murder followed the assassination of Naftali Buchnach or Busnach. Coleridge, who recorded that the assassination took place on 27 June 1805, spelt the name Bushnak: *CN* 2, 2668.

134   *CN* 2, 2668.

135   Above n. 93 at 67-8.

136   Ibid. The accusations made by the anti-Semites amongst the Maltese resonated with a version of the ancient blood libel levelled at the Jews. The defamation may have originated in the legend created by Thomas of Monmouth in 'The Life and Passion of St William the Martyr of Norwich' completed in 1173. The charge levelled is normally that Jews kill an innocent Christian infant, usually male, so that the blood can be mixed with their unleavened bread at Passover. For an account of this origin of the libel, see Jacobs; also Anderson, and further Bennett. A general study of the nature, origins history and influence of this blood-libel in whipping up anti Semitic hysteria see Dundes.

clearly resonated with some members of a resentful population who were, in the absence of hard facts, pre-disposed to display racist behaviour. [137]

The evidence of what took place 18-19 May 1805 is not altogether clear. However, in an unsigned and undated letter (a copy of which may have been sent to the British Prime Minister) an anonymous individual alleged that a mob of about two thousand Maltese assembled in Valletta and then "dispersed without doing any mischief".[138] Ball's delayed response did not offer a firm denial.[139] Instead, he described how the jealousies of tradespersons and others had led to problems for some of the Jews who were accosted by the demonstrators. This seems to be a reference to the events described below that took place in St Paul's Street, Valletta, on 18 May 1805.

The low-level public disorder in St Paul's Street cannot fully explain the haste and severity with which the authorities acted, so it is likely that a more dangerous demonstration of hostility had, indeed, taken place. Moreover, one of Coleridge's Avvisi refers to a physical assault against an individual, believed to be a Jew, which, it alleged, took place in Mdina. The authorities clearly believed that outbreaks of violent disorder were spreading across the Island. Ball's refusal to deny this, in his report to the Secretary of State (delayed until 1807 when he was forced to respond to allegations made against his administration), is also suggestive. However, as we shall see below, the Avviso in question misreported, and in some ways exaggerated, the events that actually took place in Mdina.

We also have Coleridge's subsequent testimony which suggests a threat of widespread and serious violence. In *The Friend* he described the anti-Semitic disturbances as a "difficult emergency".[140] In an unpublished letter of 1820, written to a Jewish friend, he described his own role in preventing "an intended Massacre". He claimed to have read to Dr Borg Oliviero, the Chief Justice, Chapter 11 of Paul's letter to the Romans in order to emphasise shared human values.[141] Coleridge's later accounts suggested that the authorities believed that the insurrection might have become more widespread and even more serious. As it was, they responded with rapid

---

137 NAM 92/04 1805 box 1.
138 The relevant part is as follows: "That in the beginning of June 1805 (sic) there was a tumult of 2000 persons in Valletta who however dispersed without doing any mischief". Eton passed this information to Windham in a letter dated 11 October 1806, CO 158/12 (no folio reference).
139 See Ball to Windham above n. 93 at 67.
140 *The Friend*, 1, 544.
141 *CN* 2, 2646n; "I also am an Israelite".

and severe punishments to quell that possibility – in other words to nip trouble in the bud.

Official action on Malta, to stamp out anti-Semitic violence, included two denunciatory Avvisi of 22[142] and 25 May 1805.[143] These notified the population of the severity of punishments meted out. As we shall see, there is evidence that Ball himself intervened to ensure that these exemplary and exceptionally draconian punishments were imposed. He was obviously prepared to regard the command in the Royal Instructions of 14 May 1801 to indulge "the prejudices of the inhabitants" as having been overridden by the just claims of the Jewish population to the protection of their lives and property.

But this is not to conclude that Ball ignored the Royal Instructions of 14 May 1801. He made some concessions to what Coleridge publicly acknowledged as the anti-immigration prejudices of the Maltese – a phrase which recalls the very words of the Instructions.[144] This resulted in a Proclamation dated 21 June 1805 that imposed even more restrictive controls upon foreigners.[145] When taken with the evidence of the Royal Commission of 1812 that there was still hostility to foreigners on the Island, this flurry of domestic measures qualifies the impression, created by Ball in 1807, that the problem of social friction leading to anti-Semitic violence was short lived.[146]

As we shall see below, an Avviso, dated (Wednesday) 22 May 1805, announced the first convictions (fig. 10). Its date reveals how promptly the authorities responded to the unrest because, in only a few days, they had identified and located the culprits (Andrea Borg, Hasciach and Bonello), tried them, punished them and then drafted and promulgated the Avviso. The further Avviso, on Saturday 25 May 1805, which discloses weekend working, also corroborates the argument that officials had identified an emergency requiring timely action. Ball's portrayal of an unrattled State is unconvincing. The absence of Notebook entries for ten days after 14 May

142 NLM LIBR/MS 430 2/2 Bandi 1805 AL 1814, 8.
143 NLM LIBR/MS 430 2/2 Bandi 1805 AL 1814, 9. The date of issue was 25 May 1805, not March 25 1805 as claimed by Kathleen Coburn: *CN* 2 (Notes), 2594.
144 In the Notice of 25 May 1805 Coleridge acknowledged the existence of a "popular prejudice" against the Jews.
145 Although Coleridge omitted to define "foreigners": NLM LIBR/MS 430 2/2 Bandi 1805 AL 1814 f14.
146 Above n. 93 although when Ball refers to the "whole affair" he seems to be referring exclusively to the riot rather than the underlying social problem. Even so it creates an impression which, whilst politically convenient, might not have been strictly accurate.

AVVISO

SI fa noto che Giovanni Hasciach della Città Pinto, Andrea Borg, ed il Ragazzo Saverio Bonello della
Cospicua sono frustati, e poi saran mandati in esilio
per avere inventato e sparso vane voci, le quali di-
sturbarono la tranquillità degli Abitanti; Ed è de-
terminazione di S. E. di trattare nella medesima gui-
sa tutti Coloro che si scopriranno Autori o Complici
in simili dicerie, o che anche per semplice conver-
sazione ne avran fatto il racconto, o che infine trovan-
dosi presenti a siffatti racconti non avran cercato di
disingannare gli Ascoltanti, e di farne inteso il Tribunale della Gran Corte della Valletta.

　　Trattandosi d'una cosa che riguarda la quiete
pubblica, scopo principale della Società civile, niun
grado o condizione di Persone, e neppure l'istessa
età minore esenterà veruno dal rigore del castigo.

　　　　Segreteria del Governo li 22. Maggio 1805.

　　　S. T. Coleridge Seg. Pub. del Commiss. Regio.

10. The Avviso of 22nd May 1805 announcing the convictions of Borg, Hasciach
and Bonello.

1805 is also suggestive that Coleridge was preoccupied by official business
connected with the disturbances.

Disturbances in Valletta, Saturday 18 May 1805

We can now question, in more detail, why the anti-Semitic allegations spread
by Andrea Borg, Hasciach and Bonello did not explain all that took place
on the afternoon of Saturday 18 May 1805 – the day the violence erupted.
Surviving witness evidence shows that the disturbances arose as a result of
more than one cause. This corroborates Ball's account of the participation
of the trades-people, who seemed to have felt that their livelihoods were
threatened by the Jews.

　　In the late afternoon of 18 May 1805, in St Paul's Street, Valletta, a Jew, known as Di Biaggii, was verbally abused by a group of boys. He had gone with a local man, Gauci, to inform the police (the Viscount).[147] Di Biaggii and Gauci intended to return to the scene with the Viscount to remonstrate with the boys and warn them so that they should did not repeat their misbehaviour. However, the delinquents had fled by the time the three men returned to St Paul's Street. Unfortunately, the incident was not over because a group of local shopkeepers and passers-by gathered. Amongst them, a youth called Paolo Catania, the son of a shoemaker, further insulted Di Biaggii, by asking him, "Do you still want to crap on our heads".[148] The words spoken were corroborated by another witness.[149]

Whilst the true meaning of this insult can obviously be contested, one possible reading suggests that the aggressor was concerned that the Jews had achieved some threatening and dominant position. Had Paolo Catania been primarily concerned about possible child abduction then this anger would, almost certainly, have been expressed in other ways.

The group of hostile Maltese then reprimanded Gauci for having assisted Di Biaggii. A fight ensued in which Gauci was assaulted before making his escape pursued by "many people". Presumably Di Biaggii also fled. It is indicative of the strength of opinion that any Maltese who assisted Jews were also likely to be attacked.

Disturbances outside Valletta 18-21 May 1805.

Elsewhere in the four cities, rumours were being spread that Jews were attacking Maltese victims. Conspicua seems to have been something of a "hot spot". Andrea Borg admitted under interrogation that, whilst intoxicated, he had spread a rumour that Jews were searching for children to kill. Moreover, during the night of 18-19 May 1805, he allegedly entered a shop and asserted, to those inside it, that a Jew living in Conspicua had thrown a vase of flowers out of a window at him. Neither assertion was true; and Andrea Borg claimed, when questioned on 21 May 1805, that he had committed these acts simply because he was drunk and for no other reason.[150]

Other witnesses gave evidence of further trouble. On Sunday 19 May 1805, at *Rappello di Coradino* on the road out of Conspicua, Nicolas Zammit

---

147 As he was required to do under the terms of the *Code de Rohan*.
148 NAM 92/04 1805, 21 May 1805.
149 Statement of Joseph Pizzuto, ibid.
150 Andrea Borg's statement, 21 May 1805 NAM 92/04, 1805, box 1.

and another man encountered a twelve year old boy who was walking some distance behind two foreigners. The boy reported that the foreigners were Jews who had tried to harm him. Zammit also gave hearsay evidence that his wife had told him that a Jew had threatened one of their friends, and that he had reported this to the local Luogotenente.[151] The authorities at first suspected Bonello (below) but the witness was certain that he was not the boy in question, following an identity parade.[152] The conclusion, that other boys must, therefore, have been involved, naturally made the situation worse from the authorities' point of view.

Saverio Bonello (also a twelve year old boy) was a resident of Conspicua who had been arrested. He had falsely accused unknown persons of threats made against him; but he gave contradictory evidence. At first he stated that *three* men, believed to be Jews, had run aggressively towards him whilst he was fishing. He then described how he had been compelled to flee from the *four* men (*sic*) to escape.

As we discuss below, Fortunata Tagliana also incited racist violence against a French prisoner of war at Notabile (Mdina), so the disturbances were not confined to the four cities. Her offence took place during the evening of 21 May 1805.

Borg and Bonello must have been tried and convicted the same day that their statements had been taken, 21 May 1805, or , if not, no later than the following day, because this was the date on which Coleridge announced the convictions and sentences. This alacrity, especially when taken with what we know about Coleridge's vast workload, again suggests a sense of urgency on the part of the authorities.

The Public Notice of 22 May 1805

This Avviso notified the public of the punishment inflicted on three named individuals, Andrea Borg, Giovanni Hasciach and Saverio Bonello for having originated and spread the malicious anti-Semitic rumours. The notice announced that the offenders had been whipped and were shortly to be sent into exile. The petitions discussed below suggest that each of them was exiled to Gozo.

The Notice raises a number of constitutional and other issues. Firstly, the text suggested the offenders were sentenced as a result of the decision

---

151 Ibid.
152 Ibid.

of the Civil Commissioner rather than a court of law, which, if true, would provide a strong example of the absence of a separation of powers in Maltese law. It would raise important questions about the right to a fair trial in Malta. Secondly, the Avviso does not record the offence of which they were convicted, and the question can be asked whether rumour-spreading was an offence known to the law. This engages the principle that no-one can be punished except for breach of an existing law: *nulle peona sine lege.* Thirdly, because the punishment was not in accordance with that prescribed for the offence under the Code de Rohan, there is a further controversy about respect for the rule of law under British rule. Finally, there is a concern about the separation of powers.

Punishment by Law?

In any stable and peaceful society the state has a *prima facie* monopoly on the use of force. This is acceptable provided its coercive powers are exercised in the circumstances which the law allows and the punishments inflicted do not exceed those permitted by law. The rule of law thus requires that legitimate punishment can only be imposed in accordance with existing publicly-disclosed laws – in other words when an individual has committed behaviour that is legally proscribed.

The requirement that official action should conform to existing legal rules is concerned with legitimacy and is, thus, a founding principle of the rule of law. It is a fundamental violation of the rule of law if the conduct punished is merely something of which the authorities disapprove but which violates no legal rule. Civil rights would cease to have any force if officials could punish any behaviour which caused them inconvenience or which they disliked. There would simply be no limit to the circumstances in which individuals could be punished.

Moreover, in a system that conforms to these standards, the authorities cannot simply declare that henceforward certain conduct will be proscribed. Constitutionally-mandated processes must be followed before new legal rules can be established. New laws must be duly passed.

The first question concerning Coleridge's Notice is that it is silent on whether the convictions followed from a prosecution and judgment of a criminal court in accordance with an existing law. This is an important matter because the adjudication of legal rights is a matter for an independent judiciary that is not required to abide by the directions of politicians. In this case the internal evidence from the Avviso, when taken in isolation, suggests that this was not fulfilled. The actor, explicitly named by Coleridge, in the criminal process was the Civil Commissioner. Coleridge recorded:

> His Excellency is determined to treat in the same manner all others who are discovered to have started, or who have been complicit in similar [i.e. anti-Semitic] gossip.

The impression created is that the accused were convicted and punished by Ball himself. In contrast, Ball's report to Windham in 1807 emphasised that criminal liability, in cases arising from the persecution of the Jews, was determined by the judicial process: "some of the most guilty amongst the men", he reported, "were tried, convicted and punished".[153] The more likely conclusion is, therefore, that these men were indeed *tried* before a criminal court. As we shall see, the determination of the appropriate *punishments* was a different matter.

Code de Rohan

As far as the relevant law was concerned, Code de Rohan contained provisions against "slanderous publications'[154], and it is likely that the court decided that this provision governed the conduct of the accused in this case. The punishments imposed on these defendants, which were deliberately severe (whipping and exile) are, however, controversial.

As we shall see below, in the case of *female* offenders, the Code de Rohan permitted a number of possibilities to be considered. These were either internal exile (to the "villages" or to Gozo) or overseas exile "outside the Dominion"; but no similar provision existed in the case of male offenders. The prescribed punishment for males convicted of spreading slanderous publications[155] was that they

> shall incur the penalty of ten years, or even life in the galleys. .... If for some reason they are unable to row in the galleys, they must be punished with the whip, and must then serve on public works for the rest of their life, or for ten years, depending upon the seriousness of the offence.[156]

Punishment by the whip *and* the imposition of life-time exile was, in the case of the male offender, outside the scope of the Code (if, as we assume,

---

153 Above n. 93 at 67-8.
154 Book 5 item 3, no 5.
155 See para. VII.
156 Book 5, item 3, no 5.

the charges brought related to "slanderous publications").[157] This suggests two possible conclusions. The first is that the sentences were unlawful in so far as the court exceeded its authority under the Code de Rohan; or, alternatively, that the Civil Commissioner had exercised his recognised constitutional authority and intervened in the judicial process so as to increase the sentences.

Ball's Role

Of the two possibilities, the latter (i.e. Ball's intervention) is the only one that would conform to the Maltese Constitution, albeit inconsistently with the rule of law. In his report to Windham in 1807, Ball, significantly, revealed how the criminal justice system worked. The information he disclosed allows us to infer that he at least claimed a power to interfere in the outcome of cases. The critical passage is as follows:

> In all criminal cases, in particular, the whole proceedings are laid before me as soon as the trials are finished; and where … there appears any difficulty in the case, it has been my practice to take the opinion of an English barrister, (who, Ball reported, gave advice upholding the judge in all but one case).[158]

In 1805, the Maltese petitioned the Crown for certain constitutional reforms.[159] The petition, *inter alia,* sought relief from the Civil Commissioner's power to sentence in criminal cases. In a forceful passage it requested that: "..the sentence (of the court) may be mitigated *but not augmented by the Civil Commissioner* and that those sentences may be pronounced in open court *and not first submitted to the Civil Commissioner".* (Emphasis added)

The evidence of the Avviso suggests that in the cases of Andrea Borg, Hasciach and Bonello, Ball exercised his power to determine the sentence, for, in translation, it will be recalled that Coleridge recorded that: "His Excellency is determined to treat in the same manner all others who … [offend]". Thus, Coleridge identified the Civil Commissioner rather than the court as the actor responsible for punishments in all other cases.

But that is not all because there is other evidence that the criminal

---

157 Contrary to para. V of Part III of the Code.
158 Ball to Windham above n. 93 at 51. The use of the word "upholding" also implies that Ball's exercised a superior, reviewing role in the hierarchy of courts because his decision to "uphold" the decision (taken on the advice of the English barrister) implies a power to over-turn.
159 Memorial and Petition of the Maltese (unsigned and undated): Kew, CO 158/10/151 (1805).

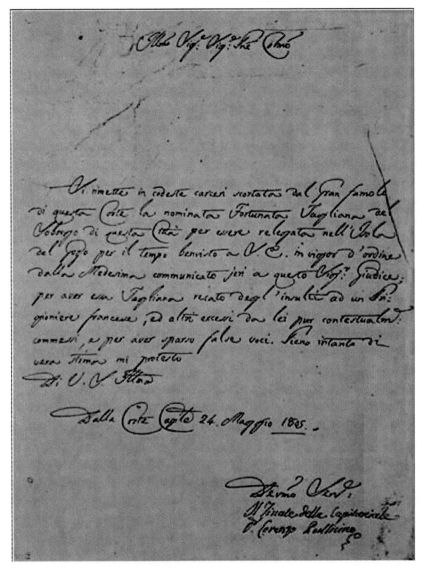

11. The letter from the official of the Corte Capitanale which reveals that the Civil Commissioner had instructed the judge to sentence Fortunata Tagliana to exile in Gozo.

judges acted on Ball's instructions in sentencing these particular offenders. This evidence relates to a subsequent trial which also arose from the anti-Semitic disturbances (the Fortunata Tagliana trial, the outcomes of which are considered below). In that case an official recorded: "This (punishment) is in line with the *order given yesterday by His Excellency to the Judge*".

(Emphasis added – see fig. 11).

Ball's undoubted interference in the Tagliana trial is likely to explain the punishments in the trials of Borg, Hasciach and Bonello. As said, within the terms of the autocratic Maltese Constitution, this was not unconstitutional behaviour, but it is further evidence of a legal system that signally failed to meet what today we should regard as the minimum standards of fairness. It also revealed Ball's double standards.

In *The Friend*, Coleridge portrayed how, when he was in command of a ship, Ball was a just law-giver. British seaman under his command were entitled to be punished according to the Articles of War in order to avoid "arbitrary" decision making.[160] This meant that punishments under his command were only inflicted in accordance with rules that had been publicly declared in advance; and Ball's officers had no discretion to vary the prescribed punishments. Above all, it reveals that their commander understood that justice could only be achieved through a system rooted in the rule of law – punishment according to rules known in advance – and the principle of a fair trial. Thus, it speaks volumes that Maltese civilians were not always treated according to these "fairness" standards. "Justice" in their case was embodied in the will of their governor who punished them according to undisclosed standards that were notably inconsistent with, and which prevailed over, the published laws.

Thus the evidence suggests that notwithstanding Coleridge's awareness of the importance of maintaining the separation of powers for the preservation of civil liberties – the observance of which by the British (Imperial) Government he had insisted upon in his journalism – Coleridge was either unable or unwilling to persuade the Civil Commissioner to show restraint by allowing the courts to determine the penalty without interference.

In fairness, Ball might have felt that intervention was permitted under the terms of the Royal Instructions, dated 14 May 1801,[161] that explicitly required him to continue the system of executive intervention that applied under the Grandmasters.[162] However, whilst the Maltese Constitution (and thus the Royal Instructions) might have *permitted* Ball to direct the judges, it

---

160   *The Friend*, 1, 169-70.
161   See Hardman, 350 et seq.
162   The relevant part of the Instructions dated 14 May 1801 stated: "You will therefore understand that the administration of justice and police is, as nearly as circumstances will permit, to continue to be exercised in conformity to the Laws, and Institutions of the antient Government of the Order of St John".

was not a requirement that he do so in any or every criminal case. In other words, he might have shown restraint in order to uphold the fundamental values of fairness and the rule of law that he recognised and had practised during his naval service. The circumstances of these cases suggests that Ball *chose* to intervene to augment the punishments in ways that he had denied himself and his officers whilst at sea. Thus, the outcomes of cases were, arguably, tainted by the Civil Commissioner's political sentiment that repressive measures were necessary in order to maintain law and order. When Coleridge later complained of the sordid nature of politics[163] he may have had this example in mind.

The Avviso of 22 May 1805 and New Offences

There is also evidence in the Notice that Coleridge purported to *extend* Article V of the Code de Rohan so as to criminalise certain anti-social behaviour arising from the disturbances. This strategy was intended to punish, firstly, those individuals who repeated the false rumours and, secondly, those who were present during the relation of such rumours, who either did nothing to "undeceive" the listeners, or did not inform the Tribunal of the Grand Court.[164] Thus, the Notice purported to announce an extension of the criminal law.

As we have explained, the principle of *nulle peone sine lege* requires that an individual be punished according to an *existing* law. Since Coleridge's Avviso, a Public Notice, was not a law-making instrument, it was incapable of making the necessary reform – that required a Bando. The mere announcement of a new offence, by Notice, amounted to the Administration punishing conduct of which it disapproved.

Coleridge's apparent willingness to have individuals punished without a legal justification for the punishment is a surprising lapse given his awareness of these fundamental constitutional values. Thus, we have

---

163 See Chapter 1, pages 43 and 44.
164 This arguably extended Para. V of Part III of the *Code de Rohan*, which states: "Anybody who invents or composes slanderous publications, or who sticks up posters containing libellous, abusive or offensive material, shall incur the penalty of ten years, or even life in the galleys. All their advisors, composers, supporters, participants and people who fixed up the posters will suffer the same penalty". It is not obvious that these words unambiguously impose a duty on persons hearing false rumours to "undeceive" other listeners who happen to be present. Just one objection to Coleridge's interpretation is that to be a "participant" the person would arguably have to spread the rumour, not merely hear it spoken in conversation.

further evidence that, in his official capacity, Coleridge was not able to practise or respect the constitutional morality that he espoused in his political writings.

"Malicious Rumours" and "Undeceiving Listeners"

In the Notice, Coleridge described the new offence as one of "spreading malicious rumours" not "maliciously spreading rumours". "Malicious" was intended to be synonymous with "false" or "false and damaging". Since a malicious (false) rumour can be spread unwittingly, a person could be liable for the innocent repeating of information that happened to be false. Thus, the offence, under the Code de Rohan, of spreading malicious rumours was likely to catch more rumour mongers within its net than one that required malicious intent. Moreover, the new offence was not confined within the context of the emergency. It applied to any false story.

However, in relation to the other purported new obligation, to "undeceive" other listeners, evidence of knowledge, on the part of the accused, that the information was false, would be required before a prosecution could succeed.[165]

This Avviso created impossible burdens for individuals because it assumed that those hearing certain information – listening to rumours – would be able to differentiate between fact and falsehood. This was a prerequisite because the obligation to "undeceive" logically arose only when an individual (in the company of others) was confronted by information that they could identify as false. Information conveyed to them which was true clearly did not give rise to any obligation to "undeceive". However, what about information that was actually untrue but which the listeners nonetheless found credible?

The weakness of Coleridge's strategy in this respect was exposed in Ball's 1807 report to the Secretary of State. As Ball understood it, the problem was that a large number of the Maltese were "gullible" to the point that they were prepared to demonstrate against individual Jews as a collective response to invented information that the Jews sacrificed children (when none had been abducted). If Ball's version of events is reliable, it would be a naïve official who believed that the less-educated Maltese could distinguish fact from fiction or rumour from truth.[166]

---

165 Although, as already indicated, no such offence was properly known to the law.

166 Coleridge's assessment was that the ordinary Maltese (the peasantry) suffered

Coleridge's reform placed the Maltese in some jeopardy. If, for example, they heard information in the market place which they believed to be true, but which was, in fact, false, they risked punishment for failing to "undeceive" (although, as we have seen, there was no properly enacted and existing law requiring them to do this) . The only practical way of avoiding that liability would be to decline to listen to any information on sensitive subjects – in this instance any information touching upon the Jewish community. "Listeners" would find this a necessary precaution in order to avoid the risk that information conveyed to them might prove to be untrue.

Before leaving this poorly drafted section of the Avviso it is worth recalling that Coleridge explicitly ordained that minors would be liable to the same penalties as adults for the offences described within it. Given that adults clearly had difficulty in distinguishing fact from fiction (e.g. the belief that Jews sacrificed children), the policy of criminalising children regardless of their age seems harsh and ill-judged. For example, if a child of five unfortunately found itself in the company of adults spreading malicious information, the child would, according to the Avviso, be criminally responsible unless he or she spoke out against the rumour, and informed the Tribunal. Just one objection to this would, of course, be that a young child would neither understand the difference between malicious rumour and truth and, even if they did, they would probably never have heard of a Tribunal let alone been able to access it. If the terms of the Avviso were intended to be applied as literally drafted then such measures would be unjust to the point of fanaticism. If this outcome seems improbable, it is important to recall that Ball banished a twelve year old boy (Bonello) to Gozo for spreading false rumours.

Whilst it can be readily appreciated that the British authorities had a duty to stamp out anti-Semitic violence, the steps taken to do this seem harsh. Bonello's case offers little prospect that the Avviso would have been leniently applied in the case of minors. For this reason, as well as its other unreasonable burdens and its dubious status as a legally effective instrument, it stands out as further evidence that the legal system on Malta fell below the minimum standards of constitutionalism and fairness expected of a more fully developed system infused with the values of the rule of law.

---

from "childish ignorance". *The Friend*, 1, 536.

Aftermath

On 19 June 1805, Maria Bonello, Saverino's [Saverio's] mother, successfully petitioned the Civil Commissioner sitting in the *Segnatura* to have the sentence on her son rescinded. The grounds on which she pleaded for clemency were that the boy, who was then on Gozo, now lived in extreme poverty and went hungry. In short, she argued that he was "deprived of every human comfort". Given that exile had been Ball's preferred punishment for the troublemakers, her chances of success might not have been considered to be encouraging. However, the Civil Commissioner did show clemency to the boy.[167]

Andrea Borg also tried, at first unsuccessfully, to have his sentence overturned. On 29 May 1805, he petitioned Ball, in the *Segnatura*, to rescind the order that he be exiled.[168] Following Ball's rejection of this first petition, he submitted a second on the grounds that he was, by then, starving on Gozo and needed to return home to look after his "poor" mother. These grounds were strikingly similar to those that had won Ball over in Maria Bonello's petition. Moreover, it is interesting that Andrea Borg's second application was made after Maria's had already succeeded. No doubt his advisers sensed that Ball was now more amenable to show mercy. And so it proved because, on 26 June 1805, the Civil Commissioner granted Borg's second application. His act of clemency appears to have been conditional because, on 2 July 1805, Borg's formal retraction of his evidence was read to the assembled crowd in Conspicua.[169] This seems to have been a condition of his returning home to the City. It may also confirm that Conspicua had been a "hot spot" of trouble during the disturbances since retractions do not appear to have been publicly declared elsewhere.

No reason for Ball's *volte face* in these cases is recorded, but it can be speculated that if, by then, the emergency was over (as Ball later claimed[170]) he probably judged that there was no longer a need to make an example of a small boy and a starving man. The danger of widespread violence had passed; and Ball perhaps sensed that there were compelling political reasons for a show of compassion to combat the combustible complaints

---

167 The petition can be found in the National Archive of Malta, NAM 92/04 1805, box 07; and the decision in the case is recorded in NAM LIBR 43/11 vol N.
168 Registro dei Memoriale e Decreti da Sua Excellenza il sig Cavalier Alessandro Ball Regio Commissionario Civile di Sua Maestà Britannica NAM LIBR 43/11 vol N.
169 NAM 92/04 1805 box 1.
170 Ball to Windham, 28 February 1807 above n. 93.

that he was a "despot" whom the Maltese had come to fear.[171]

The Avviso of 25th May 1805[172]

This was the second Public Notice arising from the anti-Semitic disturbances. Here, Coleridge notified the inhabitants of the severe punishment meted out to a named individual, Fortunata Tagliana, who had, according to Coleridge, been convicted of inciting anti-Semitic violence that resulted in an assault, by a gang of assailants, on a French prisoner of war. Surviving court records suggest that she was convicted of "insulting" the Frenchman and spreading malicious rumours.[173] As we shall discover, Coleridge's Notice may have been neither a comprehensive nor accurate account of the facts.

This Public Notice further recorded the financial reward paid by the authorities to another named individual, Francesco Borg, who intervened to rescue the victim.

Unlike the earlier case of the convicted offenders, Andrea Borg, Hasciach and Bonello, there is evidence that Fortunata Tagliana was tried and convicted by the criminal court. However, as we have described, there is unambiguous evidence that the court was acting on the Civil Commissioner's instructions when it imposed the sentence.

The sentence of permanent exile was, no doubt, intended to be an exemplary punishment: Coleridge had already made clear, in the terms of the Public Notice of 22 May 1805, that sentences for the spreading of false rumours would be severe and be imposed regardless of age. However, Fortunata's exile to Gozo is distinguishable from the punishment meted out previously to Andrea Borg, Hasciach and Bonello because hers was within the range of permitted punishments under the Code de Rohan. [174]

The promulgation of the instrument on a Saturday, rather than on a normal working day, lends further credence to the argument that the persecution of the Jews had caused considerable anxiety. The administration clearly believed that the public interest required the earliest possible dissemination of the news of her conviction. In accordance with government orders the Notice was published, and its contents disseminated, the following day, a Sunday.

---

171 See Chapter 2.
172 LIBR/MS 430 2/2 Bandi 1805 AL 1814 f.9.
173 NAM 92/04 1805.
174 Item III, para. VII.

The offences committed by Fortunata Tagliana in Notabile (Mdina) reveal that violent anti-Semitic sentiment had spread beyond Valletta and the three cities (where most of the Jews had settled). It also indicates the intensity of racial hatred: her mere denunciation of the French prisoner of war as Jewish was sufficient to persuade the attackers to pursue him.

Coleridge's Strategy

The Avviso is of particular interest because it revealed Coleridge's approach to significant government information at a time of public emergency. In common with other Avissi it performed an important political function. First, it communicated information that was essentially irrelevant to the purpose of denouncing an attack upon a Frenchman. In particular, it engaged the audience in Fortunata's motive – the cause of her actions – as well as the methods she employed to achieve her ultimate purpose. This important information reveals something of Coleridge's style, which has a narrative quality not usually associated with similar official instruments that were principally concerned to publicise the outcome of a case.

Another important feature of the Notice is that the information it contained is misleading. This may have been deliberate, or simply a consequence of the over-hasty response to what the government saw as a crisis. Certainly, the Notice differed, in important respects, from the witness testimony. Even if Coleridge had access to the court records, the discrepancies, some of which are potentially of great significance, are difficult to explain.

The Notice recorded that Fortunata encouraged the attack because she wished to pursue a grievance with a female neighbour "with whom she was in disagreement". According to Coleridge's text, she did this by inducing others – the "delinquents" – to "beat up" and stone a French prisoner of war who was claimed to be a Jew.

The extensive witness evidence, although not wholly consistent, offered a markedly different account. All witnesses agreed that the Frenchman entered the neighbour's house, accompanied by a blind Maltese man, in order to buy poultry and eggs. The witnesses also agreed that, as the Frenchman was leaving by the front door, Fortunata was on her roof terrace and that she began to call out that a Jew had entered the neighbour's house (the house of Anna Singlia). According to one account, Fortunata, was reported to have accused the supposed Jew (the Frenchman) of doing magic; according to another, of intending to slit the arteries of the inhabitants. Importantly, these accounts also revealed that, as well as calling on her neighbours to attack the Jew, Fortunata came down into the street and threw stones at him. This evidence is particularly important because it altered the criminal nature of her conduct. It is not simply that she incited violence intending it to be perpetrated by others, but rather that she initiated that violence and took part in it herself. This evidence made her offence more serious and perhaps explained why she was exiled for life. It is all the more remarkable that these, critically significant, facts were omitted by Coleridge from his Notice.

But this is not all. According to Coleridge, it was the "delinquents", and not Fortunata, who stoned the French prisoner. However, according to the latter's own testimony, the only stones were thrown by Fortunata. The other assailants merely threatened to punch him. Following Francesco Borg's intervention, he escaped unharmed.

As stated above, Coleridge's Notice explicitly connected the attack on the Frenchman with a disagreement between Fortunata and Anna Singlia. There was a suggestion of a "vendetta". Coleridge's emphasis on this motive was not a casual one. Not only was Fortunata a threat to her fellow citizens, she was also cruel and manipulative. Coleridge inferred that she was so evil that she thought it acceptable to have a third party assaulted simply to cause distress to a neighbour.

However, the "vendetta" was Coleridge's own invention: there is no evidence of it in any of the witness statements. Anti-Semitic sentiment alone caused and motivated Fortunata's behaviour. This was, of course, a most serious matter and, arguably, sufficient to convey his message without embellishment. So why did Coleridge go further and invent the "vendetta"? The answer to this is elusive, but one possibility is that the supposed dispute with the neighbour suggested even greater malevolence because it involved cunning manipulation. In other words, in choosing those particular means of distressing her neighbour, she had been willing to have an unconnected third party stoned. It portrayed even greater Machiavellian ruthlessness. The "vendetta" also created an additional victim from *within* the Maltese community (the neighbour). Did Coleridge feel that this was important to win greater public support for her conviction? Was her anti-Semitic behaviour not enough to secure public revulsion? If so, and Fortunata had to be portrayed as a threat to her "own" community as well as to the Jews, it suggests that anti-Semitic sentiment must, indeed, have been widespread.

The stated purpose of the punishment (exile for life) was to cure Fortunata of her anti-Semitic attitudes. In that sense, its dominant purpose was, ostensibly, rehabilitative; but, somewhat contradictorily, the Notice records that there were no Jews on Gozo; and the possibility of readmission to Maltese society was precluded, unless the exile was rescinded. Despite its stated purpose, the punishment was predominantly designed to remove Fortunata from Malta to protect community relations. The severity of the punishment also revealed an intention to deter others.

The Notice contained certain paradoxes concerning the reward granted to Francesco Borg, who intervened to rescue the Frenchman. The fact that a reward was conferred implies a recognition of exceptional conduct – in this instance the courageous and independent action Borg had undertaken when he intervened to confront, alone, the numerically superior "two or three delinquents" who were (according to Coleridge's version) stoning the victim. The offer of a reward, by itself, commended Borg for his conduct.

Curiously, the Notice continued that the Civil Commissioner was displeased at "having" to reward Borg for doing no more than his civic duty. Moreover, the Notice, somewhat bizarrely, emphasised that this displeasure was even *greater* than that Ball had suffered when having to punish Fortunata for her incitement of violence.

This somewhat astonishing statement was, perhaps, designed to be a standard-setting measure. Perhaps it was intended to remind society that intervention to prevent assault is a normal civic duty. If so, the strategy seems clear: Ball and Coleridge intended to encourage individuals to act on their own initiative either to prevent or to restrain any further anti-Semitic violence. However, the manner in which this was achieved, in particular by the grudging statement concerning the reward, cannot have acted as an incentive to others to confront those actually using, or prepared to use, violence against Jews.

The conclusion, that the reward was reluctantly granted, is reinforced by the emphasis Coleridge placed on reserving rewards for cases of greater merit. It is possible to ask what cases might be more meritorious? After all, according to Coleridge's account, Borg was depicted as having moral and physical courage to intervene against a gang who were stoning an innocent victim. The impression created is that the gang might have turned upon him, so Borg had showed conspicuous bravery to save, from serious harm, a member of an unpopular minority.

However, the facts were not as Coleridge would have the Maltese believe, and the suggestion is that Coleridge knew this. Borg made no claim to intervene in a stoning; and the victim, the Frenchman, testified that the group of assailants merely *threatened* to punch him, and that he escaped *uninjured*. This places Coleridge's remarks about reserving financial rewards for more meritorious conduct into context. A conclusion to be drawn from this might be that Borg was not rewarded for any outstanding courage in confronting a dangerous mob, but rather to signal an appropriate official approval of those who challenged the "popular prejudice" of anti-Semitism.

The Public Notice is also of interest for its obvious omission. It does not record what punishment, if any, was meted out to those whom Coleridge alleged perpetrated the alleged assault upon the Frenchman. The Avviso is also conspicuously vague as to whether there were two or three attackers (the witness evidence is not). The impression Coleridge created was that the "delinquents" were never identified and that they ultimately escaped justice.

In fact, the witness evidence is clear. It identified and named all those who pursued the Frenchman, which meant that the authorities would have had no difficulty in apprehending them had they wished to do so. The reason they were not arrested is that their conduct was not sufficiently serious to justify prosecution. Apart from Fortunata's conduct, a blow was threatened, but none was actually inflicted. It was Fortunata who was the most serious offender: she incited violence; she initiated and took part in it herself. In fact, she was the only individual who threw stones at the victim. This must have been the reason why she alone was prosecuted. Coleridge again misrepresented the facts.

Are the inconsistencies the result of the haste with which the Notice was prepared and promulgated? Did Coleridge resort to invention to ensure Maltese support for Fortunata's conviction? If so, why not refer to the stoning that she alone perpetrated? These are difficult questions. Certainly, it would seem to be the case, that Coleridge knew more of the factual background than the Notice, in its terms, revealed, and that Coleridge may well have manipulated information to further the government's purpose in portraying anti-Semites, such as Fortunata, as malicious individuals who acted not to only harm unpopular Jews but also their fellow Maltese. Coleridge used information to reinforce the appropriate conclusion that it was in the interests of all inhabitants to suppress anti-Semitism. Whether Coleridge deliberately misled the inhabitants is open to speculation. If he did not deliberately mislead then the conclusion must be that either he or his staff did not take sufficient care to ensure the accuracy of the information he communicated.

5.4.2. Immigration and the Detection of Crime

Proclamation of 21 June 1805 – Immigration and Crime[175]

This Proclamation was aimed, on the one hand, at the regulation of immigration and the presence of foreigners on the islands, and, on the other, the registration of vehicles and vessels. According to the preamble, the common theme of these two, apparently distinct, policy goals was the reduction of crime.

Contrary to Ball's assertion, in his despatch to Windham,[176] that the insurrection was a matter that was soon forgotten – one that blew over within a few days – it seems likely that the authorities understood that the destabilising social friction resulting from immigration required further official action. The control of immigration had, since 1801, been a matter upon which the civil (rather than the military) authorities could legislate.[177] Even so, the moral basis of the intervention in 1805 is perplexing.

The problem of unemployed foreigners having been forced into crime had been, in the former days of the economic slump, a pressing political issue that justified the early interventions by the authorities; but these new, far-reaching legislative controls on foreigners, including foreigners already present on Malta, (many of whom must have satisfactorily demonstrated their peaceful intentions) requires special justification. This is especially so when much of what took place in May 1805 was a consequence of racist agitation resulting from simmering anti-Semitism. Why did Ball appear to indulge this sentiment?

The first possibility is that, as a pragmatist, Ball might have acted in the belief that this Bando was necessary to preserve public order. We have described evidence that the authorities were more unsettled by what took place than Ball's despatch of 1807 acknowledged; and Coleridge's own evidence suggests that the authorities actually believed that a massacre had narrowly been avoided. Ball might have decided that the new regulations would be a proportionate response to the threat of insurrection; after all, he did not re-instate the former ban on Jews living on Malta. And in Ball's

175 NLM LIBR/MS 430 2/2 Bandi 1805 AL 1814, 14.
176 Above n. 93.
177 Hobart to Cameron, 2 September 1801, Kew, CO 158/1/207 et seq.

defence we must not overlook ministerial directions, which he was bound to follow. He was, it will be recalled, ordered to maintain the popularity of his administration even if this meant indulging the "prejudices" of the Maltese.[178] If Coleridge hesitated at the moral problems posed by policy-making driven by indulging racial prejudices, the business of government may have been thought to make such compromises expedient and even necessary. Thus, the actions of government in the aftermath of the disturbances of May 1805 might have been on Coleridge's mind when he expressed contempt for political morality when he left office.[179]

Coleridge's Bando introduced tighter controls on immigration, more extensive powers to monitor the foreigners present on the Island, and strengthened the power to deport. It was a further step in tightening the regulations to which foreigners had been subjected on the Island since the first Bando on the subject in 1802.[180]

Curiously, Coleridge also used this Bando to introduce new measures concerning other matters. Gigs for hire, carts, ferry boats and fishing vessels had to be registered under a new system thereby ensuring that the authorities could identify them and their owners. This might have served a number of purposes that included crime prevention and detection. Bearing in mind the apparent problems of gaining witness evidence in many cases, Coleridge may have wished to make it easier to identify miscreants. It is unclear why Coleridge decided to bring all these matters within a single Bando.

Immigration and Foreign Visitors

As we have seen, under existing regulations, the authorities had the power to require overseas visitors to state their occupation and the purpose of their visit. This allowed the Administration to exclude persons who had no *bona fide* purpose on the Island, or those who might have been tempted into crime if they had no obvious means of earning their livelihood. Coleridge's Bando allowed the authorities to take even more extensive

---

178 Cameron's Royal Instructions of 14 May 1801 had instructed him as follows: "No alteration should be made in the modes, laws and regulations according to which the civil affairs and the Revenue of the Island have been heretofore managed unless the same shall appear ...to be evidently beneficial and desirable, as to leave no doubt of its expediency or of it being generally acceptable to the wishes, feelings and even *prejudices* of the inhabitants". (Emphasis added).
179 See Chapter 6.
180 NLM LIBR/MS 430 1/2; Bandi 1790 AL 1805, 273.

powers, including the power to limit the numbers of foreigners present on the Island, by means of a permit system, and introducing, for the first time, a maximum duration for the visit.

Significantly, the regulations forced foreigners already present on the Island (including the Jews) to obtain a permit in order to continue residing there. This signalled a recognition that the existing population of immigrants required control, albeit for political reasons.

The rationale of Coleridge's Bando was that immigration and settlement would only be permitted when it served a public interest as identified by the authorities. It offered the public assurance (if nothing more) that the authorities were acting to protect the Maltese from foreign criminals, carpet-baggers, opportunists and or anyone who would disturb the stability of Maltese society.

The Bando introduced a requirement for all overseas visitors to obtain official permission in order to stay on the Island. Those not registered were prevented from obtaining accommodation. As said, it re-iterated the requirement of earlier Bandi (see above) that the grant of permission depended on the overseas visitor satisfying the authorities of the reason for their presence on the Island. However, it introduced a major reform. Even in cases in which the purpose was either innocuous or conducive to the public good, the Maltese authorities now took a further power to determine the maximum limit of the visit. Longer term visits (longer than four months), became a matter for the discretion of the Civil Commissioner. Thus, the Civil Commissioner would have the power to determine which foreigners could reside on Malta.

Before examining the Bando in more detail it is important to state that the instrument does not define who are foreigners and, thus, who might be regulated. Whether, for example, the term "foreigner" included British subjects is unlikely because the Maltese were, in law, British subjects, although this was not publicly admitted by the British during this period.

The Registration System

Every foreigner wishing to remain "for a period of time" on the Island had to obtain a permit. This requirement extended to all foreigners already resident on the Island as well as future immigrants.

Somewhat confusingly, the penalty for non-compliance was inserted into Article 2, which dealt with particular categories of foreign visitor and foreign residents. However, it is likely that Coleridge intended this provision to apply generally, for there was no other provision dealing with penalties for breach. Foreigners without a permit (including existing foreign residents) would be subject to a fine of ten *oncie* and *immediate* deportation. They would, thereafter, be subject to permanent exclusion from the Island. This was a severe penalty. It can readily be understood that the existing foreign residents, already present on Malta in June 1805, must have been extremely anxious to obtain a permit. If this had been refused, the prospect of immediate deportation would, inevitably, have caused hardship especially to those with non-liquid assets on the Island.

The permit system was to be operated by both the President of the Grand Court of Valletta and the Chief of Police, who had, jointly, to sign any permit issued. Where they thought it appropriate to do so, they could consult with the Civil Commissioner.

The involvement of the Chief of Police, in particular, suggests that the authorities were concerned about foreigners who visited Malta with criminal intent. One purpose of the registration scheme was, clearly, to weed out criminal elements before they entered Maltese society. This concern can also be seen in the information that the foreigner was required to provide, which includes his or her *real* name. This provision suggests that foreigners intent on wrongdoing had previously entered the Island using aliases.

The Bando was highly prescriptive in the demands it placed upon the licensing authorities. They were obliged to meet every day, at ten o clock in the morning, to consider the cases of the foreigners who had arrived that day. It is unclear what legal consequences would follow if they failed to meet as required.

The regulations specify, in detail, how two, distinct, registers relating to the foreigner's admission to Malta were to be maintained, one by the President of the Court and the other by the Chief of Police. The information included the identity of the foreigner, and, of course their reason for being present on Malta. It was also noted which documents the authorities had inspected to establish the foreigner's credentials. The form of the entries was also stipulated in precise detail.

Most importantly, the Chief of Police's register was required to record the date on which the foreigner quit the Island and whether the permit had been surrendered. This clearly allowed the authorities to monitor the number of foreigners present on the Island.

The information concerning the date of departure and surrender of the permit had to be communicated "by hand" to the President of the Grand Court. For reasons that are not obvious the regulations did not explicitly require the President to record this "exit" information in his register, although presumably, the President would, naturally, have wished to keep a record of the information he received from the Police.

Limitations on Entry to Malta

In order to obtain a permit, the overseas visitor had to provide the authorities with the information required by the Bando which was recorded in the register as well as on the face of the permit.

Included in this information was, in the words of the Bando, the amount of time that the foreigner "wishes, and is able to remain on the island". This should not be read as allowing the foreigner to determine the length of the permitted stay on the Island – i.e. a duration determined according to his or her wishes. Articles 4 and 7 of the Bando made it clear that the permitted duration of the visit was a matter for the Maltese authorities, and even they did not have unlimited discretion in this respect. Article 4 stipulated that the maximum duration of the permit, in the first instance, could only be two months and was renewable, by the President and Chief of Police, for a period of no more than two further months. Any stay longer than four months was a matter for the Civil Commissioner. This, of course, placed effective control, of settlement on the Island, within British rather than Maltese hands. Clearly, the authorities were unwilling to allow foreigners to take up permanent residence or to operate businesses based on the Island without being able to satisfy the Civil Commissioner that their presence was conducive to the public good.

The reference to the period of time the foreign visitor would be "able" to remain on Malta is perhaps a response to the problems caused when foreigners had arrived on the Island lacking independent means of support. Coleridge was required to ensure that the authorities could enquire into the length of time during which any foreigners could provide for themselves.

The Civil Commissioner's discretion to grant or refuse a (residency) permit, for a visit in excess of four months, was unlimited. He could take into account any information or any suspicion that he considered relevant. The *Registro dei Memoriale e Decreti* provides unambiguous evidence that a more stringent and discriminating approach was being taken with these applications after the coming into force of Coleridge's Bando of June 1805.

Many applications by foreigners for an extended residency (or, alternatively, for naturalisation) were rejected, albeit that some were granted. Those whose applications succeeded were, however, only granted a permit to remain during the Civil Commissioner's pleasure. Removal was possible at any time in his discretion: no right of residency was thus created.[181]

The regulations provided that those foreigners already on Malta, when the registration system came into force, would have to "try" to obtain the necessary permit within eight days. It was not made clear, in the Bando, what would satisfy this obligation. It certainly reveals that not having the permit after the expiry of eight days would not necessarily be an offence provided an attempt had been made to get one. However, the reality was that each foreigner was liable to a fine and deportation if a permit was refused.

The Regulations were obscure in their scope. For practical reasons, not all foreign visitors were required to obtain a permit. Given that a distinction was to be drawn between those who were regulated and those who were not, it became imperative to distinguish between them. The Bando merely states that those wishing to remain "for a period of time" must register and remain in possession of a permit. This is plainly intended to alleviate a burden upon both the foreigner and the Maltese administration by making provision for certain short-term visitors. But it is unclear what duration of visit triggered a requirement to register. This represents a further, obvious, defect in the scheme of regulations. Given the draconian penalties for not obtaining a permit, this lack of clarity might have encouraged many to obtain a permit to safeguard themselves. If so, the problem, with this cautionary approach on the part of visitors, would have been that the administration would have had to process more cases than might have been intended.

Frequent overseas visitors to the Island were required to obtain a permit "immediately after their arrival" or risk a penalty of being fined ten *oncie* and permanent exclusion from the Island.

In common with other Bandi, the fine was to be used to reward informants who offered information about unregistered foreigners. The need for paid informants implicitly acknowledged that incriminating information would not otherwise have been given to the authorities. Given the popular feeling

---

181 See e.g., the application of Diego Decandia, 29 August 1805, in the *Registro dei Memoriale e Decretati* above n. 68. This was subject, of course, to a successful application for naturalisation, such as that presented by Domenico Amadori on 31 August 1805, ibid.

against foreigners, it is unclear why Coleridge doubted the willingness of the Maltese to inform: presumably, unregistered foreigners would have been identified as troublemakers that the Maltese would wish to see deported.

As we have seen, it is clear that the authorities wished to know who was on the Island at any one time because, when they left the Island, the foreigner had to return his permit to the Chief of Police. By the simple method of recording the number of permits issued (and not returned) the authorities intended to know, at any given time, the number of overseas visitors present. Of course, this depended on ensuring that the foreigner would surrender the permit on leaving the Island. Failure to do this was made, under Article 5, a grave matter since the offender would be permanently excluded from the Island. This was a mandatory sentence; there was no discretion to impose a lesser exclusion.

This provision, requiring surrender, also had the effect of removing the permit from circulation, thus preventing it being passed on to a potential wrongdoer who could then claim entry. Doubtless, Coleridge had the unfortunate experience of the "Mediterranean passports" in mind when he drafted this provision.[182]

Unregistered Foreigners

To make it difficult for foreigners to evade the registration system, the new regulations provided that lodgings could not be "given" to an unregistered foreigner, nor any house rented to him. The terms of the Proclamation were particularly harsh because the penalty for an offending landlord was a mandatory life-time exile from Malta. Moreover, this was, from the landlord's viewpoint, an especially draconian measure because a landlord had no defence when he had been shown a false permit. This meant that the risk of deception was borne by landlords. Coleridge's Bando, accordingly, advised landlords to check the authenticity of the permit with the authorities. It seems that proof of having taken this step was the only defence when a landlord unwittingly let a room to an unlicensed foreigner who presented a false permit.

Thus, the regulation placed under the strict control of the authorities, the presence of all but a very few short-term visitors to the Island. They could ascertain, from the number of permits issued, how many foreigners

---

182 Considered below under "Passports".

were on the Island; the registers recorded why each individual was present and how long they were permitted to remain. Permission to remain would, normally, be for a maximum of four months unless the express permission of the Civil Commissioner was obtained. This gave the Maltese some assurance that immigration would potentially be controlled and policed.

Gigs for Hire, Carts, Ferries and Fishing Boats

Coleridge's Bando also created a vehicle and vessel registration scheme for Malta. This involved the keeping of three sets of registers. The first maintained by the President; the second lodged with the Government office but updated by the President; and the third maintained by the local lieutenants of the casals and the fiscal lawyer of the maritime court.

The owners of vessels and vehicles had to obtain a number for their vessel or vehicle from the President of the Court. The number, painted in oil, was then displayed on it. The President was required to stipulate the place where the number had to be displayed. He had to maintain a register of the numbers allocated and in the format required by the regulations (see Reg. 11). The register had to include the name of the proprietors, their country of origin or place of residence. Any sale or transfer was intended to result in a new entry in the register but, in what appears to have been a startling error, Coleridge did not require the sale or transfer to be notified either by the seller or buyer/transferee. Presumably, the authorities discovered this information during their monthly inspections (below). This is interesting because the burden of detecting changes in ownership fell upon the authorities. An alternative system might have required the owners to notify a transfer of ownership, which would have alleviated the burden upon the authorities.

The number was to be reallocated if the vehicle or vessel was destroyed.

Records containing similar information were to be maintained by the local lieutenants in the casals and the fiscal layer of the maritime court. Somewhat surprisingly, the role of the fiscal lawyer of the maritime court was not confined to the registration of vessels. In so far as he had to register the number of gigs for hire and the number of carts, reg 15 treated the fiscal lawyer similarly to the lieutenants of the casals. Presumably, this was intended to create a national register of the carts in addition to the local registers. Each month these office-holders were required to inspect the vehicles/vessels to make sure their numbers were still legible and update the record to reflect changes in ownership etc. The identities of all owners and the condition of the numbers had to be reported monthly to the Government.

A copy of the register kept by the President had to be submitted to the government within one month; and this copy, held by the government, had to be updated regularly thereafter ensuring that it corresponded with the copy maintained by the President.

Drivers and operators were also to be issued with a card showing the number. This, of course, meant that the authorities who stopped a vehicle/ vessel and its driver would have some *prima facie* indication as to whether any suspected vehicle or vessel was being lawfully operated.

A failure to comply either with the registration requirement (the obligation to obtain a number) or to carry the card bearing the number when the vehicle or vessel was in use[183] would result in a fine. This was stipulated to be six *oncie* for a first offence. There was no discretion to impose a lesser penalty.

A second offence would result in the mandatory confiscation of the vehicle or vessel, which was to be sold following its confiscation. There was no express prohibition on its re-acquisition by its offending former owner.

Three *oncie* from the proceeds of sale were to be given to the informant who notified the authorities of the offence – a familiar device in Maltese legislation, and perhaps a measure necessary to encourage reluctant witnesses.

Enforcement Agency

The President of the Grand Court was given responsibility for overseeing the implementation of this Proclamation, as well as a number of others to which Coleridge referred. These included the Proclamation of 3 December 1800 which regulated "layabouts" and "vagabonds"[184] as well as the Proclamation of 12 November 1804 which was concerned with the participation of women in politics. Unfortunately, no record of this latter measure can be found in the archives of the National Library of Malta.

The day to day enforcement activity became the responsibility of the Grand Viscount, or his lieutenant, the *Maestro di Piazza,* as well as various other captains and viscounts. These were essentially officers of the local

---

183   The language of the Bando suggests a wider obligation requiring the card to be carried at all times (regardless of whether the vessel/vehicle was actually in use).
184   NLM LIBR/MS 430 1/2; Bandi 1790 AL 1805, 156.

law enforcement to whom offences had to be reported under the Code de Rohan. We have seen, earlier, how the Jew, Di Biaggii, went to complain to the authorities about the taunts and insults he endured from the boys in St Paul's Street, Valletta. He had gone immediately to the Tribunal and returned to the scene with the Viscount.

Responsibility for enforcing earlier regulations for the highways had already been imposed on the *Maestro*, so, to that extent, this Bando was broadening the jurisdiction of an existing structure concerning the transport system. For example, it was the *Maestro* who enforced powers and duties under the Bando of 29 August 1801,[185] which was concerned with removing street nuisances and obstructions. These new regulations gave further powers in relation to vehicles.

5.5. Corruption

Introduction

The problem of corruption, particularly amongst officials in the various Maltese departments of state, including the Università, has been noted elsewhere.[186] It was an insidious and threatening problem for Ball's strategy of Government since the central goal of British policy was aimed at winning and retaining popular support for his Administration.[187] Corrupt practices threatened to undermine this because, by their very purpose, they were intended to distort the manner in which a public body ought to function when performing its legal and administrative duties. This problem, clearly, had the potential to combine with other causes of disillusionment with the British Administration and, thereby, further undermine public trust in government.

Sufficient evidence survives to reveal suspicions about official behaviour on Malta. For example, the conclusions from Thonton's analysis of the affairs of the Università, between 1800 and 1814, are not convincingly explained by official incompetence alone.[188] The inference is that either theft

---

185 NLM LIBR/MS 430 1/2; Bandi 1790 AL 1805, 213.
186 See Chapter 2 and the taxation theme.
187 It will be recalled that Ball's Instructions were to "attach" the Maltese to British rule: Secretary of State to Ball, 9 June 1802, Kew, FO 49/3/51.
188 Thornton identified "fictitious entries" where the books did not balance. See Thornton, *Report to His Excellency the Governor on the Accounts of the University of Val-*

or other forms of dishonesty were a problem in this department. It seems that Maltese officials illegitimately diverted public money for private purposes in the knowledge that the British Treasury would ultimately replace it. The British had signalled to the Maltese, at the time of Treaty of Amiens in 1802, that British interests would be prioritised even if this meant damaging those of the Maltese. Some Maltese officials – we do not know how many – might have been tempted, in what perhaps came to be regarded as a cynical relationship, to siphon off funds to make the most of the opportunities presented by British rule.[189] Such conduct might well have had the tacit support of a population that, as we shall see, was perhaps not always sympathetic to British goals.[190] So much for theft, what about bribery?

We cannot be certain how deep-rooted attempted bribery had become by the time Coleridge was on the Island, but we do know that Aloisia Caruana's case – the subject of Coleridge's Avviso – was not an isolated one. Ball reported to London, in 1807, that he had banished, to Barbary, two inspectors of the public market each of whom had accepted bribes.[191]

Corruption

Bribery can be regarded as a means to persuade an official not to perform his or her public duty. If it succeeds an individual can attain a priority for their selfish interests that it might not otherwise have obtained, and this can be damaging to the public interest in rational and fair administration. Moreover, if there is a widespread perception that "justice" can be bought and sold, disputes will be resolved outside of the court structure. The State's monopoly on the use of coercive powers would break down: vendetta and vigilantism would replace adjudication.

In some cases, and Coleridge's Avviso deals with one of them, the initiative to depart from formal processes comes from the individual, at other times it comes from the public official. In the latter case, officials illegally demand money, from members of the public, for their services. Because the victims are members of the public, frictional effects are almost

letta from 4ᵗʰ September 1800-31ˢᵗ July 1814, Kew, CO 163/33/9.
189 Such opportunism also extended to ordinary Maltese. See for example Coleridge's Public Notice of 20 June 1805, NLM LIBR/MS 430 2/2 Bandi 1805 AL 1814, 12, which is concerned with civilians profiting by obtaining money by deception under the enlistment system, see the military discipline theme, below.
190 See for example the military discipline theme.
191 Ball to Windham, 28 February 1807, Kew, CO 158/13/91.

inevitable, not least where many individuals cannot afford the price demanded. The case of the corrupt Maltese market inspectors was likely to have fallen into this latter category.

Coleridge's Avviso 14 June 1805[192] – Attempted Bribery

This Notice recounts that Aloisia Caruana was imprisoned for having attempted to bribe the Penal Judge of the Grand Court of Valletta, with an ounce of Sicilian gold, in order to ensure a favourable outcome in her appeal. It seems that she had already been convicted of a criminal offence; and the judge whom she attempted to bribe, one Doctor Vincenzo Caruana Zerafa, had been listed to hear her appeal. There was no suggestion that Zerafa had accepted the payment; it had merely been offered. Presumably, the judge had then taken action to have her punished. Thus, in one sense, the Notice is not simply concerned with announcing the punishment of an offender; it also records the moral integrity of the Maltese judiciary and invites public support for the criminal justice system.[193]

This Avviso had a wider significance because it was issued in the weeks following the anti-Semitic disturbances during which the Administration had interfered in the judicial process to exact a higher sentence for convicted offenders. As we have seen, this interference had caused significant alarm in Malta. It became one of many complaints about Ball's administration that was recounted in a Petition to the Crown. Ball and Coleridge may have issued this Avviso to stress the integrity of the Maltese judiciary and to re-build confidence in it.[194]

Punishment

The sentence imposed on Caruana – an indeterminate but brief incarceration – suggests that her offence was not regarded as particularly heinous. By contrast, the sentence of banishment imposed on the market officials was of a different and altogether more reprehensible character because they

---

192   NLM LIBR/MS 430 2/2 Bandi 1805 AL 1814, 11.
193   The tactic of naming the judge in this instance safeguarded his judicial reputation, but Coleridge might have achieved greater confidence in the judicial system had he not chosen to do so. This would have created a stronger inference that the Maltese judges were incorruptible.
194   See Chapter 2.

had betrayed the trust reposed in their office. The authorities distinguished between the *offering* and *acceptance* of corrupt payments and treated more harshly the abuse of public office by those officials who allowed themselves to *receive* bribes. Even so, an ounce of gold must have represented a significant sum as it is hardly conceivable that Caruana would have attempted to bribe an appeal court judge with a trivial sum of money.

The sentence imposed on the offender raises some interesting questions about the judicial process on Malta in 1805. We have already mentioned that the Notice does not specify the duration of the period for which she would be incarcerated. The formula employed was that she would continue to remain in prison for "several days". The reason why the period of the detention was not stipulated is unclear. One possibility is that Coleridge, deliberately or otherwise, refrained from giving specific information, although it is difficult to imagine why this could be sensitive.

Another possibility is that the sentence to be served was not actually fixed at the start of the sentence and so Coleridge could not include it in the Avviso. Her release date might have depended upon the discretion of the penal authorities, possibly even upon that of Ball himself since he had an absolute discretion to release prisoners.[195] It appears that this prerogative power was exercised in consultation with the Chief Justice or the pro-seggretario, Zammit,[196] and, if so, Coleridge would not have wished, by means of a prior public announcement, to pre-empt their decision in this matter.

Public Relations

It is highly significant that Coleridge recorded that the confiscated property was to be distributed amongst the poor, although this distribution had not taken place at the time the notice was promulgated. Since this information was, essentially, extraneous to the deterrence, it is likely that Coleridge included it for the deliberate reason that he did not wish to miss a valuable public relations opportunity. He had clearly realised that he could use this Avviso to present Ball as he wished to be presented – as a just and kindly governor.

One resentment that endured after the uprising concerned the harsh

---

195 There appears to have been a custom that at Christmas and Easter prisoners might have their sentences reduced, or even that they might be released. See Sultana, 322-3.
196 Sultana, ibid.

sentences that Ball had demanded from the judiciary. As we have described, a boy of twelve was amongst the banished; and Ball had declared that, in future, he would punish minors with an equal severity to adults. This, perhaps, explains why Coleridge emphasised the steps Ball would take to protect the weaker members of society. He would also have wanted to remind the Maltese that Ball was concerned about their economic welfare, since the uprising had, in part, been motivated by fear of renewed poverty resulting from competition in trade. Thus, the Avviso represented an attempt to re-engage with a number of Maltese concerns after the civil disturbances of the previous month. It is another example of an Avviso being used to stimulate public approval of Ball, and it is one of many that served Coleridge's broader political agenda of retaining popular support for British rule.

5.6. Consumer Protection

Introduction

In this section, we shall consider Coleridge's measures to regulate the availability of strong spirits, to impose inspections on wine, to control sales of unripened fruit and to warn of counterfeit coinage.

The purpose of consumer protection laws is to correct market failure. In other words, the legislator will have identified trading practices that require State intervention. This is achieved by making regulations to protect consumers.

Laws are often introduced to safeguard the economic interests of consumers, for example, by prohibiting unfair or deceptive practices or to protect health and safety either by removing dangerous goods and services from the market place or, alternatively, by restricting their availability.[197] Some of Coleridge's Bandi, such as those concerning spirits, also indirectly served public order purposes by reducing alcohol-related crime.

It is important to understand which purpose a law is intended to serve before we can judge the competence and coherence of its drafting. If, for example, its concern was health and safety, we would assess the measure on its potential to remove the dangerous commodity from use. Alternatively,

---

197 As was the case in relation to spirits, where the authorities regulated the quantity available: See further below.

if the measure was intended to prevent shopkeepers confusing customers (as in the case of the unripened fruit in the Bando of 5 August 1805[198]) we would expect the measure to permit consumption, but to regulate the circumstances in which the goods are displayed – e.g. by requiring clear labelling. However, for the reasons set out below, the drafting of Coleridge's consumer-protection measures sometimes suffered from confusion about what evil was to be eradicated.

A preliminary matter of interest is that Coleridge's legislative agenda did not extend beyond correcting certain particular, and quite narrowly defined, examples of market failure. For example, he targeted the sales of unripened fruit, rather than imposing a general duty upon sellers to ensure that *all* food offered for sale was fit for consumption. This suggests that neither Coleridge nor Ball had a broader political ambition to introduce general principles of consumer protection that would apply to all transactions. This is unsurprising at this date in history. The approach to regulation was minimalist, which indicated that policy-makers favoured a conception of the State's role in regulating commerce that promoted freedom of contract – an ideology that normally expected consumers to safeguard their own interests without expecting the state to perform this role for them. Regulations were, thus, reserved for cases that caused particular difficulties.

The hesitation in using criminal penalties is another significant feature of Ball's approach, which was not confined to consumer protection. As we have seen, there was also a notable failure to criminalise the continued use of studded cartwheels even though they damaged the roads.[199] The penal code seems to have been reserved for the most serious abuses, which, naturally, required the making of value judgements. However, where criminal penalties were available they could be mandatory and severe.

5.6.1. The Regulation of Spirits in the Bando of 22 March 1805[200]

Introduction

The British authorities had already identified excessive alcohol consumption

---

198   NLM LIBR/MS 430 2/2 Bandi 1805 AL 1814, 19.

199   See Bando 29 January 1805, which is considered under the reconstruction theme.

200   NLM LIBR/MS 430 2/2 Bandi 1805 AL 1814, 4.

as a policy problem by the time Coleridge drafted the Bando of 22 March 1805. He had already made reference to this in a Bando of 8 March 1805 dealing with the re-imposition of the wine tax. Unlike the later instrument, (22 March) the 8 March 1805 Bando did not have public health protection as its primary purpose. It merely used the Administration's concern over excessive consumption of alcohol as an additional means of making the argument for the re-introduced excise duty. As we have seen, the real purpose was to raise revenue to finance the Island's deficit.[201]

The timing of the controls on alcohol is of critical interest because, in the spring of 1805, a large contingent of British troops had arrived on the Island in readiness for an expedition to defend Sicily. The troops were garrisoned on Malta until November 1805. The potential availability of cheap, low quality, liquor was a problem for the military authorities, who were not only concerned about drunkenness and discipline, but also violence between the garrison and civilians. Alcohol abuse by British troops, and others, had already prompted such earlier Bandi as the instrument of 24 November 1801[202] and a further measure banning alcohol sales to anyone carrying a knife.[203] There were also fatal assaults inside and outside bars.[204]

It is significant that Ball wrote to Camden that Coleridge's Bando of 22 March 1805 had the support of military commanders, including Major-General Villettes, Commander-in-Chief of British land forces on the Island. The Chief medical officer had also welcomed the measure, which Ball emphasised, in his despatch to London, would place stricter controls on the trade in spirits than on wine.[205]

As in other Bandi, there is, thus, strong evidence to suspect that Coleridge's statement of the purposes of the regulations were neither comprehensive nor objective. According to the published text, he chose to emphasise that the planned restrictions would maximise welfare, in particular public health, by limiting the quantity and regulating the quality of the product accessible to the retail market. However, when the law is examined alongside the surviving records of licence applications it is clear

---

201 See taxation theme.
202 NLM LIBR/MS 430 1/2; Bandi 1790 AL 1805, 224. This prohibited the sale of wine, brandy or rum to the English soldiers living in the city of Notabile and Boschetto.
203 Bando, 18 October 1802, NLM LIBR/MS 430 1/2; Bandi 1790 AL 1805, 273.
204 See e.g. the fatal stabbing of a British soldier by a Maltese in September 1805: http://website.lineone.net/~stephaniebidmead/chapter567.htm, consulted 16 December 2008.
205 Ball to Camden, 19 April 1805, Kew, CO 158/10/133-4.

that the purpose of regulation was to make it very difficult for British military personnel to gain access to strong liquor. The publicly-stated (but not comprehensive) reasons for the enactment of the Bando is another example of an appeal to win the consent of the Maltese to a regulatory measure. By presenting it as one designed to ensure their safety and well-being Coleridge was suggesting a congruence between the British and Maltese interests in this matter. As in other instruments, we find Coleridge obfuscating the policies underlying the measure. His opening paragraph might be seen as propaganda or "spin":

> The attention of His Excellency the Royal Commissioner has been drawn to the abuse of spirituous liquors, and to the damaging effect that they have on health. He has therefore, willingly undertaken the task of trying to find a way to limit this problem and with this aim in mind he proposes the following decrees, and orders their strict observance.

Regulation of the Supply Chain

Coleridge decided to reject the use of a price mechanism to limit demand for spirits. Price alone would not achieve the various public-policy goals that Coleridge wished to pursue. He brought under the control of the State the entire system for the import, manufacture, distillation, distribution and sale of spirits. These extensive layers of controls were seen to be necessary to achieve a number of further goals, including preventing low quality, even dangerous, spirits entering the market;[206] preventing undesirable persons importing, manufacturing or distributing liquor; reducing the quantities produced; regulating the premises entitled to sell alcohol; regulating those approved to sell spirits to the troops.

The Bando is a labyrinthine and complex instrument lacking in both clarity and legal certainty. It has many of the hallmarks of inexperienced authorship.

Coleridge drafted a sophisticated regulatory system that would bring the entire supply chain of spirits under the control of the authorities. Importers, distillers, manufacturers, wholesalers, distributors and retailers are all regulated in different ways. His special concerns were to regulate the quality and quantity of spirits sold and especially to control the retail trade. As we shall see, these activities were the focus of criminal penalties (in contrast to unlicensed wholesaling that was not).

---

206 It is noteworthy that the inspector was the Chief Physician.

The production of spirits was placed under a particularly restrictive regime. First, the distillation of wine to produce brandy was separately regulated (see reg 4) and required a special licence from the President of the Grand Court. The authorities were clearly concerned to control the amount of distilled spirits entering the market place because Coleridge required the licence to state the maximum amount permitted to be distilled. Presumably, the authorities wished to know what quantities were available to be purchased. Moreover, if fewer establishments were licensed than previously, the product could become more scarce which would encourage the price to rise. This could be expected to reduce demand for it and so further restrict consumption.

Other manufacturers had to obtain their licence by way of a special decree from the Civil Commissioner. A surety of fifty *oncie* had to be provided, which was probably intended to prevent back-street or small-scale operations. Surviving records suggest that applicants were required to apply to the Civil Commissioner in the *Segnatura*.[207]

Importers, wholesalers, distributors and even retailers were required to have a licence, issued by the President of the Grand Court of Valletta, for their activities, which would identify them as the licensed person by virtue of regulation 1. Any person even *receiving* spirits would require a licence. Thus, any person taking delivery of spirits fell within the licensing system. What is more, shopkeepers, innkeepers and publicans could only trade with an additional "special decree" from the Civil Commissioner.

The number of persons eligible for a licence was limited, presumably to prevent the proliferation of persons engaged in the trade. The fewer persons who operated within it, the more easily abuse could be detected. Under regulation 3 licences to import, unload or take delivery of spirits were restricted either to those who were already licensed to *produce* spirits or, alternatively, to apothecaries. This meant that wholesalers who would either have to be licensed apothecaries or licensed manufacturers.

But Coleridge was not content that each wholesale distributor should have a licence. He wanted to ensure that no unregulated sales were made by wholesalers selling to unlicensed or shady operators, that is, persons outside the regulated supply chain. To make sure of this he made it an offence for a wholesaler to sell to anyone other than a licensed retailer.

---

207 NAM 92/04 1805. For example, Giuseppe Camilleri was granted a licence to run a bar (tavola) on 3 March 1801.

Retail Outlets

Coleridge particularly wanted to control the retail outlets. In addition to the licence from the President of the Grand Court, innkeepers, publicans and even shopkeepers also had to possess and an additional "special decree" from the Civil Commissioner. They also had to be well known and of good repute – a requirement intended to deter back-street and shady dealers. In deciding whether to grant this licence the Civil Commissioner was required to consult with the President of the Court. This reveals that Ball did not wish the licensing of the retail chain to fall under the exclusive control of Maltese judicial administrators, but, nonetheless, wished to obtain their advice.

Military and Wine

There were special regulations for retail sales in the four cities and Vilhena and for sales to military personnel. Within these districts, the retailers were obliged (under reg 9) to specialise, and, thus, to decide whether to sell either wine *or* spirits. This restriction did not apply elsewhere on Malta. This is unsurprising because the four cities would be an obvious destination for troops seeking rest and relaxation. But this is not all because a special licence had to be acquired to sell spirits to soldiers. Producers of spirits,[208] confectioners, and shopkeepers, as well as the owners of cafés, inns and taverns were eligible to apply for special authority which, if granted, would permit them to sell spirits to soldiers.

In practice, very few retailers succeeded in their applications. The surviving records reveal that when retailers applied for their wine or spirits licences, these were almost always granted subject to a standard condition that *spirits* could not be sold to either soldiers or sailors.[209] The standard condition was only omitted if the retailer merely wanted to sell *wine* to the military.[210]

---

208 Coleridge would seem to have overlooked the foregoing provision that prevented manufacturers from selling other than to licensed retailers – i.e. precluding direct sales to the public.

209 The condition also required the licensee to observe all other provisions of the Bando.

210 See e.g. Rovario Farrugia's application (wine only), 5 April 1805. The terms of this and the other licences can be seen in NAM LIBR 43/11: *Registro de memoriali decretati da sua Excellenza il Sig. Cavalier Alessandro Ball Regio Commissionario Civile di Sua Maestà Britannica*, vol. N. The first of many applications was presented on 2

Coleridge required the shops, inns and taverns that were licensed to sell wine or spirits to soldiers to display a sign on their doors. Of course, within the four cities they could only sell either wine *or* spirits, and the sign would indicate which beverage could be supplied to soldiers. This saved the retailers from having to refuse troops – possibly drunken troops – who entered their premises and demanded alcohol of a type they were not licensed to sell. The signs must have been intended to remove this potential flashpoint.

The Licensing Authorities

Identifying the authority responsible for the licensing the various activities was far from straightforward and was suggestive of Coleridge's lack of expertise and possibly his lack of attention to detail.

In the case of importers, distributors and anyone taking delivery of spirituous liquor, the responsible licensing agency was the President of the Grand Court of Valletta. This judicial officer had the power to grant licences, at his discretion, "wherever required". The Regulations failed to state any eligibility criteria for the licence, so Coleridge must have intended that anyone who applied for a licence should receive one. This suggests that the authorities simply wanted to know who was engaged in the regulated activities.

It is less clear who had the power to grant a licence to sell spirits to soldiers, although it can be inferred that it was the Civil Commissioner. Nonetheless, Coleridge ought to have made this explicit.

The Civil Commissioner was the relevant authority in the case of manufacturers of spirits (other than those distilling spirits from wine). He was not explicitly restricted in the factors he could take into account in reaching his decision whether to grant or refuse a licence, except that he had to inform and consult the President of the Grand Court who might, in practice, have provided advice as to the suitability of an applicant.

Producers were to be "held to account" for the quantity of liquor imported, manufactured or distilled. This was a strictly-regulated matter so that those who obtained their special decree from the Civil Commissioner would discover that the maximum quantity they could produce and sell would be regulated.

Presumably, a licensee could, subsequently, apply to the court to have

---

April 1805.

the amount imported manufactured or distilled varied if opportunities increased but this was not made clear, nor was it clear upon what criteria the maximum amount was to be determined. Presumably, the purpose of any upper-limit was to control the appropriate maximum volume of spirits available for sale on Malta.

Record Keeping

Coleridge used the licensing system to keep track of those engaged in the import, manufacture, distribution and sale of liquor. Licences awarded to importers, distillers (from wine), wholesalers and distributors had to be entered in a register, maintained by the President of the Grand Court, which was available for inspection at the Tribunal of the Grand Court. Like the wholesalers, the retailers also had to present themselves to the President of the Grand Court so that their licences could be registered. It is unclear what purpose this served. If it was to reinforce the provision that a shopkeeper or innkeeper or tavern keeper had to be of good repute, it seems ill-conceived. If the President had reason to doubt the reputation of those before him when they presented themselves, it would appear to have been too late for him to intervene because, by then, they had their licences from the Civil Commissioner.

The manufacturer's licence, granted by way of special decree by the Civil Commissioner, was not explicitly required to be entered into the Register, although it may have been Coleridge's intention that comprehensive records be maintained. Certainly, the Civil Commissioner, in exercising his powers, had to notify the President of the Court and one probable reason for this – which Coleridge did not make clear – was that the President should know, for record keeping purposes, which persons had been granted a producer's licence by the Civil Commissioner.

The register was to be open to inspection "whenever required" at the Tribunal of the Grand Court. The interpretive ambiguity surrounding this is obvious and begs the question whether there were restrictions upon the conditions of access. Did this regulation mean unrestricted public access? Did the legislator intend to make it available to any curious member of the public? The regulation was also silent on the times during which inspection was possible. Coleridge chose to leave these matters to be decided by the administrators, and ultimately, the courts.

A failure to maintain the register or a failure to permit access to it was a breach of public duty, but it is not stipulated as a criminal offence.

Manufacturers also had to keep business records of all sales made, to ensure that they were not exceeding the permitted maximum. The records would also allow the authorities to monitor to whom sales were made and, thus, to oversee the supply chain.

Inspections and Quality

There must have been problems with the quality of liquor sold on Malta because one of the key regulations that Coleridge introduced required quality controls. The Chief Physician had to certify that the spirits intended for sale were of a satisfactory quality. All liquor produced on the Island was subject to this inspection, and it was an offence to sell it without the appropriate certificate of approval. This is consistent with Coleridge's preamble which states that the authorities were concerned about the effect of spirits on the health of the population. No doubt, it would also have been of concern to the military commanders who were, of course, concerned to maintain the efficiency of the armed forces.

Penalties

The Bando was highly selective about which activities it sought to criminalise. It is revealing that most, but not all, of the new offences were aimed at breaches of the regulations concerned with retailing. Interestingly, the Bando contained twelve articles, of which only the breach of articles six to eleven carry criminal penalties. For example, it was not an offence to trade, as a wholesaler or distributor of spirits, without a licence. It is unclear whether this was an oversight on Coleridge's part.

Similarly, a producer who manufactured spirits without a licence (i.e. a licence granted by special decree from the Civil Commissioner) committed no offence. However, such a person would have been required to forfeit the surety of fifty *oncie* deposited with the Treasury.

The Bando created various offences. It became an offence to operate as an unlicensed shopkeeper, innkeeper or tavern keeper or for retailers within the four cities to sell both wine and spirits, or to sell spirits to soldiers without a special licence. It was also an offence for them not to display the required notice on their doors. Also liable to a criminal penalty was conduct exceeding the upper limits on the amount of liquor permitted to be imported, distilled or manufactured. Similarly, the producers would be liable if they sold spirits without a prior inspection by the Chief Physician.

The Bando stipulated the penalties for offenders. The standard punishments were severe. There was a mandatory, fixed, penalty of fifty *oncie* payable to the Treasury. Failure to pay would lead either to imprisonment or compulsory public service. In addition, the offender would, permanently, lose their right to continue in business. Presumably, this could be achieved by the simple expedient of removing their licence following conviction, although this would not seem to be the intended process. Thus, a forfeiture of the business would appear to be the result of a judicial act (conviction), rather than an administrative one (removal of the licence).

Inspections of Wine – the Avviso of 22 March 1805[211]

An Avviso of 22 March 1805, issued on the same day as the Bando regulating spirits, was intended to reinforce an existing custom requiring the pre-sale inspection of wine by State officials. A further customary power allowed officials to adjudicate on the quality of wine in case of disputes. The purpose of this customary scheme was to prevent the consumption of poor quality wines that would be injurious of public health.

In this brief Avviso Coleridge warned that the officials accompanied by the Chief Physician would, in future, conduct random inspections of shops and warehouses belonging to wine merchants. The Notice reminded them of the State's role in this respect and emphasised that the "Royal Commissioner" (sic) was anxious not to have to punish offenders. This was clearly intended to give the merchants advance notice of enhanced-enforcement activity with the inference that they should remove inferior, and, thus, illegal products immediately so as to avoid infraction.

The Avviso stated that wine of insufficient quality would be confiscated. Presumably, this was the customary penalty, and Coleridge's Avviso merely re-stated this. If confiscation was a new penalty, falling outside the scope of the custom, it ought to have been enacted within a Bando rather than introduced, administratively, by means of an Avviso. This was necessary to avoid offending the principle of *nulle poena sine lege* – that there should be no punishment that is not imposed in accordance with an existing law.

---

211 LIBR/MS 430 2/2 Bandi 1805 AL 1814, 6.

Unripened Fruit: the Bando of 5 August 1805[212]

The retailing of unripened fruit had been the subject of earlier legislation which had been brought into effect prior to Coleridge's arrival on the Island. In a Bando of 13 May 1803,[213] the British administration had imposed a general prohibition on the *sale* of unripened fruit. Although this was of universal effect, binding everyone on the Island, its primary focus was, for obvious reasons, the activities of shopkeepers and allotment-holders. The purpose of this law was to remove unripened fruit from the market place. For reasons that remain unclear, the authorities obviously regarded the prevention of sales as a serious matter of public concern. It seems that by 1805 the Maltese had discovered means of circumventing the earlier law.

Coleridge's law revealed that the mischief, at which the 1803 Bando was aimed, cannot have been fully addressed by the prohibition on sales alone. The difficulty seems to have been in the drafting of the 1803 Bando which emphasised the sale of unripened fruit as the trigger of criminal liability. This created a loophole because proving a contract of sale was a requirement for a successful prosecution. Advertising, display or offering for sale were all activities that the 1803 Bando failed to penalise. The requirement for the contract of sale caused two problems. Firstly, there would have to have been a victim, that is to say a consumer, who had actually bought unripened fruit from the seller before the seller could have been convicted of an offence. As we have seen, victims were not always eager to give evidence. Secondly, the 1803 measure failed as a preventative measure – it was not primarily designed directly to prevent such sales but to punish them once they had occurred.

A further loophole arose because the acquisition of the fruit by other means than sale would not have been unlawful. Although we do not know what evasive measures were employed, any transfer of unripened fruit from seller to buyer, in the absence of a contract of sale, would have been lawful.

This means that the litmus test for the 1805 law was whether it successfully avoided the need for a "victim" and eliminated the possibilities of evasion. But, to answer this question, it is important to understand what the purposes of regulation were, and the curious drafting renders any conclusions on this tentative and problematic.

Coleridge's aims were somewhat obscure because it is unclear whether

212 NLM LIBR/MS 430 2/2 Bandi 1805 AL 1814, 19.
213 No Bando of this date can be discovered in the National Library of Malta.

he wanted to remove unripened fruit from the market place or merely to make sure that traders did not confuse buyers in the way they displayed their products.

When considered along with the Bando of 1803, Coleridge's Bando results in a scheme comprising both contractual and pre-contractual elements of regulation. As we have seen, the 1803 Bando was a prohibition on the *selling* of unripened fruit (i.e. a contractual restraint); the 1805 Bando extends this prohibition, controlling pre-contractual behaviour by eliminating certain, *but not all*, displays of unripened fruit. The lack of a general prohibition of the display of such fruit is confusing if the purpose was to remove the product from the market place, why did Coleridge not simply prevent the sale and display of unripened fruit? If it was permitted to display it, why was it not permitted to sell it?

Confusingly, the illegal behaviour comprised the display of unripened fruit "next to other saleable goods". This strongly suggests that Coleridge's intention was to prevent sellers confusing their customers by mixing ripened and unripened fruit or by displaying them side by side. Displaying unripened fruit separate from other fruit was not illegal (although selling it would have been).

This means that, because Coleridge's Bando did not altogether remove unripened fruit from the market place, the law still failed to rectify a major weakness of the Bando of 1803. This may imply some uncertainty about the true purpose of the later Bando. In particular, the transfer and consumption of unripened fruit, in certain circumstances, remained lawful. For example, unripened fruit could have been offered as a gift. This means that Coleridge's law would not have been sufficiently robust to eradicate all possible evasive practices.

It is, however, clear that the targeting of pre-contractual behaviour (certain types of display) would have made prosecution more straightforward, since the need to prove a contract of sale would have been removed. It also avoided the need for a "victim". In particular, it would have not have been necessary for the buyer to give evidence. This is, perhaps, the real purpose of the Bando which seems to provide further evidence that Maltese made reluctant witnesses.[214] We must be careful not to place more importance upon this slight evidence than it warrants, but it may hint at an uncooperative public either sceptical about the benefits of enforcing laws such as these or simply too afraid to give evidence against their neighbours

---

214 See the Public Order and Crime theme above.

on a small island.

The drafting of the enactment is interesting. The first issue is that there is no definition either of "fruit" or of "ripeness". In the case of "fruit", is a botanical definition to be applied, or one understood by the reasonable person? Opinions may vary, for example, on whether tomato is a fruit or a vegetable; similarly strawberries and rhubarb may be regarded for some purposes as "fruit" although scientifically they might be classed as vegetables.

Similarly, whether fruit was "unripe" within the meaning of the Bando was not defined. It would, presumably, have been a question of fact for the criminal court. This would entail an assessment of its colour, flavour and texture. These would have to have been optimal in fruit judged to be ripe. Whether the fruit was ready for harvest might also have been a relevant factor, but not a decisive one because fruit can be harvested when not fully ripe.

Penalties

The Bando of 1805 stated that the penalties it enacted were *in addition* to those available under the 1803 Bando.

The additional penalties were severe and mandatory. There was no judicial discretion to impose a lesser sentence, for example, by taking into account any mitigating circumstances, or other considerations that might affect the justice of the case. This, perhaps, reveals the *dirigiste* instincts of the British administration *vis a vis* the Maltese courts, in so far as they wanted to control the outcome of cases following conviction. This is a matter considered further in Chapter 6.

The penalties are not without their controversies and, indeed, certain obscurities.

The additional penalties were to be imposed regardless of how much unripened fruit was displayed. As mentioned, there was no discretion to impose a more lenient penalty for less serious cases, nor power to impose a higher sentence for repeat offenders.[215]

The various mandatory punishments were to be imposed according to the seller's activities. They included a life-time ban on the "right to run a shop", or, in the case of an agriculturalist who did not own land, a life-

---

215 No doubt the possibility of a life-time ban was intended to prevent re-offending, but see further below.

time ban on the right to work a plot of land. These measures seem to have been intended to remove, from the offender, the opportunity to retail unripened food in the future. Offending landowners, as opposed to those who worked the land, seem to have been treated more leniently. In their case, the mandatory sentence was one month's imprisonment at their own expense, after which they could resume cultivation and then retail their produce. The reason for the distinction between the criminal responsibility of owners and workers is obscure.

Notwithstanding the severity of these punishments, there remained means by which convicted offenders could, in future, become involved in the retail supply of foodstuffs. Under the two Bandi, when taken together, a convicted shopkeeper could not be prevented from *owning* a shop, only from running it. Employing a manager, or other staff, would still have been possible. Similarly, an agriculturalist (not being an owner of land) could be deprived of his right to work a plot of land, but not it seems, to own other land which might be leased to a tenant. Perhaps the reason in this case was that the produce would, normally, belong to the tenant rather than the landlord.

The convicted land*owner*, once released from serving a term one month's imprisonment, could return to work the land.

An obscurity concerns the case of the convicted agriculturalists (who did not own land). Did Coleridge intend the prohibition to be a life-time ban on working the land *personally*? As drafted, the Bando seems to have permitted a convicted farm tenant to employ workers to work the land on his behalf, in which case the produce of the land would be owned and controlled by the convicted individual. This may be an oversight on Coleridge's part.

The concern, that convicted landowners, condemned to a term of one month's penal servitude, should meet the expenses of their incarceration, was no doubt intended to increase the severity of the penalty. It might also suggest a concern to minimise, so far as was possible, the burden upon the public revenue. Ball was, at this time, heavily engaged in the corn speculation designed to raise significant funds for the general revenues of the Island. The pressing financial constraints upon government, as well as the political pressure to balance the budget, must have been very much to the fore during this period.[216]

---

216 See Chapter 2.

Conclusion

The Bando is of interest because of its apparent temerity. It stops far short of creating a general scheme for consumer protection. It does not, for example, bring into law a general requirement that fruit sold must be fit for purpose. Instead, like the companion measure of 1803, it was narrowly focused upon one type of produce (unripened fruit) and regulated only one type of their display (display next to other saleable goods). It suggests a highly cautious approach, to the regulation of the free market, in the public interest. Regulation seems to have been *ad hoc*, relatively unsystematic and a response to particular problems as they arose.

If it was designed as a health and safety measure it would have been of limited success because the Bando did not preclude the acquisition of unripened fruit by means other than sale. If it was designed to avoid the confusion of the consumer where ripened and unripened fruit were mixed or placed closely together, it suffers from over-reach because it rendered illegal certain displays where no confusion could occur – for example where unripened fruit was displayed next to other saleable goods of a completely different type.

The small but significant advance it enacted was that it removed the need for a victim, since sellers displaying goods in a prohibited manner would be liable to a criminal penalty. No proof of sale was necessary.

The Bando must have been difficult both to interpret and to apply since it lacked a clear definition of the produce falling under its regulation. It also suffered from significant obscurities in relation to the penalties it imposed.

5.6.2. The Avviso 12 June 1805[217]

Aim

The purpose of this Avviso was to draw attention to counterfeit coinage in circulation. It also imposed certain obligations on those who received or came across false money.

Analysis

The Avviso warned that false money was often, but not exclusively, found

217 LIBR/MS 430 2/2 Bandi 1805 AL 1814, 10.

in the form of silver one-*scudi* coins imprinted with the image of the former Grandmaster Rohan (sic) (Emmanoel de Rohan, 69th Grandmaster of the Order of St John, 1775-1797). Coleridge misspelt his name.

Although the Avviso indicated that forged coins were not confined to one-*scudi* pieces, it did not alert the population to what other types of false money might be in circulation. To that extent, this omission would weaken the usefulness of the Notice.

The Avviso also created obligations on those to whom false coins were passed or were attempted to be passed. These were stated to be as follows:

> Should anybody come across such a coin, he shall be obliged to deliver it at once to the Tribunal, or to the local lieutenant, indicating who gave it to him, or tried to give it to him, so that he may be brought to justice.

The recipient's primary obligation was to inform either the Luogotentente (i.e. the local village magistrate) or the Tribunal of the identity of the person who passed or who attempted to pass the coin. This had a number of purposes. This was a necessary safeguard to protect the innocent who might, otherwise, have been found in possession of false money and wrongly accused.

But this is not all because the Notice also made clear that the purpose of gaining information about the identity of the passers of false money was to gather evidence for intended prosecution. The obligation to notify one of the named authorities not only acted as a safeguard for the innocent receiver of forged money but also had the further purpose of making them become an informant against those persons responsible for passing or attempting to pass false coins. Thus, a person who, innocently, accepted a false coin could expect to find themselves not only explaining to the authorities how they came across it, but also informing against the person who passed the coin. This might be expected to extend to giving evidence against them in court.

From the point of view of the Administration, this coercive strategy would have seemed a useful and effective one, likely to expose the forgers, since anyone knowingly in possession of a false coin would have been obliged to come forward. Those who chanced to receive false coins and who might well have found themselves in a moral dilemma might, however, have viewed this course with less enthusiasm. Should they avoid becoming an informant, by not declaring their possession of the false coin, and run the risk of prosecution themselves if it were discovered? Or should they obey the requirements of the Public Notice and hand it in and identify the person who passed it to them. The latter course would clearly run the risk of possible retribution and vengeance from the forgers.

No doubt, the authorities believed that the affected Maltese who received forged money would resolve this difficulty by coming forward. As we have seen, the use of Maltese as informants against wrongdoers amongst their fellow citizens was a commonly-employed strategy in the *Bandi* and *Avvisi*, and so a requirement not only familiar to but also accepted by the Maltese.

However, the Notice contained an obvious logical flaw in relation to the requirement that the false coin be delivered up. It stated:

> Should anybody come across such a coin, he shall be obliged to deliver it at once to the Tribunal, or to the local lieutenant, indicating who gave it to him, or tried to give it to him, so that he may be brought to justice.

Anyone coming across a false coin was required to deliver it to the authorities immediately, naming the person who gave it to him or who "tried to give it to him". In the latter instance, where a culprit had tried to pass a false coin to an intended recipient, but the latter had not accepted it, the intended recipient was, obviously, unable to deliver the coin up to the authorities.

5.7. Regulation of Trade

The Purpose of the Notice

Coleridge issued two Public Notices on 22 March 1805.[218] The one with which we are presently concerned was intended to promote the cotton industry, whilst the other, which we considered in the "consumer protection" section, governed inspections of wine.[219] The purpose of the cotton *Avviso* was to reinforce the existing controls on the production of cotton. As we shall see, the Order of St John had, formerly, legislated to ensure the quality of the product, and Coleridge intervened to maintain the standard. His Notice reminded the population that disobedience of the existing regulations, which prohibited the manufacture of cotton otherwise than with seeds or

---

218 This was a busy time for Coleridge because he also issued was also a significant and detailed *Bando* regulating spirits on that day: LIBR/MS 430 2/2 Bandi 1805 AL 1814 f.4.

219 See NLM LIBR/MS 430 2/2 Bandi 1805 AL 1814 f.5 (cotton); ibid. f.6 (inspections of wine). For a study of the cotton trade, see generally Debono from which much of what follows is derived.

with wool, was an offence.

The Cotton Trade

The central role that cotton production and manufacture had played in Malta was considered in Chapter 2.

When Coleridge was on the Island, the cotton industry, and, thus, the livelihoods of as much as half of the population, had come under severe strain. Moreover, the industry was in a state of transition.[220] Hard-pressed producers were, at first, tempted to compromise quality to boost profits. This tactic was not new: regulatory intervention had been necessary, as early as 1777, to ensure that producers were not tempted to increase their short-term profits by producing inferior cotton – mixing it with cheaper alternatives.[221] Although improving, the economic and international situation had clearly tempted Maltese producers to revert to their former cost-cutting techniques, in particular by spinning cotton in ways prohibited by Maltese law.

Coleridge intervened to halt this, in order to maintain the legally-required standards. This was a timely, and appropriate, intervention to ensure that the product retained its market appeal. Increasingly, the Maltese producers had to add value to the product, which they could now only sell, within the domestic market, by weaving it into cloth.

The finished product was increasingly sold to foreigners (mainly British) who were now present on the Island in larger numbers. In the spring of 1805, for example, a large number of British troops, under the command of Lieutenant-General Sir James Craig, had arrived in readiness for an expedition to Naples. As demand for finished goods rose, so the number of looms on the Island also increased. The Island's prosperity, which the export ban had seriously threatened, began to improve when rising wages began to take effect.

An Avviso not a Bando

Coleridge's Notice announced an "order" of the Civil Commissioner purporting to alter the punishments for the "extract[ion of] cotton not <u>manufactured</u> with seeds or with wool, without a specific licence". As the

---

220 Debono.
221 See the Proclamation of 1777 regulating the production of Gozitan cotton and preventing its mixture with foreign cotton: NLM LIBR/MS Bandi 1772-1779, 429.

Notice made clear, the offence had already been enacted in Maltese law; Coleridge merely announced an increased punishment for offenders. The question raised by this is whether it was constitutionally appropriate for Coleridge simply to announce this new punishment in a Public Notice rather than legislate to introduce it by means of a Bando? The principle of *nulle poena sine lege*, which requires that legitimate punishment can only be imposed in accordance with existing, publicly-disclosed laws, is particularly at issue. Coleridge's drafting suggests that either he did not fully appreciate these rule of law values or, if he did, he was not able to persuade the Civil Commissioner to respect them.

Further Issues

The newly prescribed sentence was to be a one month's term of imprisonment. The Maltese criminal court was not entrusted with a discretion to impose an alternative sentence which, as we have seen in other instances, meant that it could not take into account mitigating circumstances and so impose a lesser term or a fine. In addition to the jail term, the offender would have all illegally-cultivated cotton confiscated.

The enforcement strategy was similar to that found in other measures creating criminal offences, which also relied heavily upon information supplied by informants. The controversial nature of this strategy will be considered in Chapter 6. As in other instruments,[222] the informants were encouraged to give information by the promise of financial gain. One quarter of the cotton confiscated was to be given by the offender, to the informant, as a reward for information given. It is unclear what legal consequences would follow from a refusal to comply. Moreover, if the purpose was to keep the poor-quality cotton out of the market place, the requirement for the offender to give one quarter of it to the informant would have been counter-productive. An obvious alternative, which might better have fulfilled the public interest, would have been to offer a reward for information.

It is somewhat perplexing to discover that this responsibility, to hand over the informant's share, lay with the offender rather than a court official. If literally interpreted, the Notice seems clear on this point: "… furthermore, [the offender] shall suffer the confiscation of all the cotton grown illegally,

---

222 See e.g. the Bandi of 29 January 1805/MS 430 1/2 Bandi 1790 AL 1805 f.356; 431 II/3, 50, and 21 June 1805, LIBR/MS 430 2/2 Bandi 1805 AL 1814, 13.

one-quarter of which he must hand over to the informant". (Emphasis added).

Since the entire illegal crop was to be confiscated, it would seem more logical for the informant to be given his reward by the authorities rather than the offender. However, Coleridge's preferred solution apparently compelled the offender and informant to have contact. At the very least, this could have been unpleasant. In a extreme case it could have been dangerous since the offender would have the opportunity to exact revenge upon the informant who had given information to the authorities. More problematically, from the authorities' viewpoint, the unpleasant process was likely to have been a disincentive for the informant to co-operate in a prosecution. Coleridge's approach would appear to give rise to substantial practical difficulties. As a relatively early example of his legal drafting, it is, perhaps, evidence of Coleridge's inexperience and a lack of familiarity with Maltese behaviour.

The instrument does not explicitly stipulate that the informant was to be rewarded only where information led to conviction. Nevertheless, this must have been the intended meaning since the informant received a share of the cotton that the court ordered confiscated. It is an elementary consequence that a confiscation order could only be made after a conviction. An informant would, therefore, receive nothing if the accused were acquitted, despite having run the risk of giving information to the authorities and, as would have been likely, having given evidence in open court.

Finally, the Notice offered a public undertaking from the Civil Commissioner that, should it be in the public interest to do so, and the crop for the current season proved to be plentiful, licences for the extraction of cotton would be granted to ensure plentiful supply of the raw material for the inhabitants earning their livelihood from cotton spinning.

This is a highly contingent promise and it is evident that the judgement about where the public interest lay and consideration of the state of the crop, would be made by the Civil Commissioner in his discretion. It will be recalled that a decision that the Civil Commissioner reached in his discretion could not be challenged in the Maltese courts.

This part of the notice only had effect in the 1805 season and would have lapsed thereafter. This meant that no representation about future government behaviour had been made in respect the following seasons.

5.8. The Harbours

The Avviso of 9 March 1805[223] – Mooring Rope

In this brief Avviso, Coleridge acted to safeguard navigation in the Grand Harbour. The safe passage of shipping both to and from Valletta was, naturally, a matter upon which Malta's prosperity and security depended, not least because the Island had to import food and serve as a base for vessels of the Royal Navy (fig. 12). Maintaining the channels for safe navigation was, pre-eminently, a matter of governmental concern.

Harbour matters fell within Coleridge's supervisory remit, and reports seem to have been produced in considerable quantity. His private *Notebooks* record them as one of the vicissitudes of office, which produced a pang of guilt when he considered using them as tapers. An entry of February 1805 records, "I am almost ashamed to confess to myself what pulling back of Heart I feel whenever I wish to light a candle or kindle a fire with a Hospital or Harbour Report and what a cumulus lie upon my Table, I am not able to conjecture what use they can ever be…"[224] A nocturnal entry of Sunday 12 May 1805 records that harbour reports were spread out on a table at the Treasury, which suggests that they had not been filed at the end of the working day.[225]

This Avviso drew to public attention, the steps that the authorities had taken to warn shipping of a small area of shallow water that had been discovered in a dangerous place near the entrance to the Grand Harbour close to Fort St Elmo. To warn navigators, a thick rope had been attached to an anchor that had been sunk onto the seabed. The floating rope was intended to alert shipping to the danger.

It seems that the purpose of the rope was not immediately obvious to navigators, and that some Maltese were using it either to tie up their boats or for other unspecified purposes. As a result, the anchor was being dragged away from the site of the danger, and the warning, thereby, rendered useless.

Coleridge issued the Avviso to explain, to the inhabitants, the reason for placing a rope and anchor in the harbour, and indicated to them where this device could be located (presumably to avoid confusion with

223 NLM LIBR/MS 431 2/3 Bandi 1804-1808, 97.
224 *CN* 2, 2446. With considerable prescience, he recognised that what might appear to him to be useless might be invaluable to others.
225 *CN* 2, 2583.

12. The Naval Arsenal in the Grand Harbour, Valletta. Lith. by C. de Brocktorff [1838].

genuine mooring ropes). No punishment was fixed for misusing the rope. However, the Avviso warned that anyone who did abuse the rope would be greeted "by rifle shots" for which they would only have themselves to blame. Presumably, the garrison of the Fort had been ordered to open fire upon anyone misusing the rope, although this is not made clear in the instrument. Whether these shots were intended to be warning shots or the use of deadly force is also unclear. If the latter, it suggests that the authorities were exasperated by the behaviour of harbour users. Even so, lethal force would seem to have been a disproportionate response.

The Avviso of 21 June 1805[226] – Licensing of Ferryboats in the Grand Harbour

This Notice served a number of purposes connected with the licensing and night-time operation of ferryboats in the Grand Harbour. It also clarified the existing regulatory scheme in response to a turf war between the Lieutenants of the Cities of Vittoriosa, Senglea and Cospicua (fig. 13) concerning their respective jurisdictions and their entitlement to receive the small dock charges paid by the night-time ferryboat operators. This Notice accompanied a more wide-ranging Proclamation, also issued on 21 June 1805, which, as we have seen, ordered that the ferryboats (and others)

226   NLM LIBR/MS 430 2/2 Bandi 1805 AL 1814,13.

had to be registered and display a registration number.[227] The registration requirement applied regardless of when the ferryboats operated.

In this instance, Coleridge's notice made it clear that the authority responsible for licensing the night-time ferry boat operators was the Lieutenant of Vittoriosa, but "ordered" that the dock revenues flowing from their operation should be divided equally between the respective districts.

Licensing Scheme

He also ordered that the Lieutenant of Vittoriosa could only grant a night-permit to boatmen of whose honesty he was "convinced". This was obviously intended to remove the "fly by night" operator. However, it is interesting that Coleridge's public protection policy did not extend to regulating the safety of the vessel, which ought to have been a critical concern had the measure been primarily for the protection of the public.[228] The inference is that there was no problem with badly maintained vessels operating at night in the Grand Harbour.

State Liability

Coleridge also provided that the Lieutenant who negligently granted a licence might also be liable for damages to any third party suffering loss as a result of the illegal behaviour by a licensed operator. Presumably, Coleridge meant that the Lieutenant would be responsible for loss resulting from the illegal actions of dishonest operators. This is interesting because it reveals that a claim for damages would lie against the public authority for the negligent exercise of the licensing power.

The usual defendant in third party claims arising from a maritime accident would be the ferryboat operator who was responsible for causing the loss. However, the ferry boat operator might not be as "valuable" a defendant as a public authority. Because the damage that might result from a maritime accident could be significant, it could readily exceed the resources of the defendant personally to meet the potential liability. The Notice, therefore, provided that a victim of a maritime accident, who sustained loss, could, in certain circumstances, bring a claim against the licensing authority. In other words, the effect of the measure was to make

---

227   NLM LIBR/MS 430 2/2 Bandi 1805 AL 1814 ,14, see the Public Order and Crime theme, above.
228   Although a Bando might have been necessary to achieve this.

13. The Grand Harbour from Valletta towards Fort St Angelo and Vittoriosa.
Kalkara creek lies to the left of the Fort whereas Dockyard creek lies to the
right. The British naval dockyard first operated from the latter.

the State the insurer against loss caused by dishonest operators where the
Lieutenant had issued a licence without having made proper enquiries into
the honesty of the operator.

It is an interesting and puzzling question why "honesty" rather than
reasonable competency was made the appropriate medium whereby
compensation could be granted. One possibility is that Coleridge wanted
to restrict liability to cases where the administration was at fault. He may
have felt that a failure to inquire into an applicant's honesty would be a
straightforward surrogate measure for fault. But this is open to the obvious
criticism that fault lies in any negligent operation of the licensing power:
Coleridge need not have restricted the regulations to cases where dishonest
operators slipped through the regulatory net. Unqualified operators should
also have triggered state liability.

The result, in practice, of this emphasis upon dishonesty would have
been somewhat arbitrary. Losses caused by incompetent (honest) operators
would not fall upon the State, whereas those dishonest operators who were
negligently licensed would. The transfer of risk lacks a clear rationale.

Thus, Coleridge's policy was unclear. A more properly-developed
scheme would have emphasised the competence of the operator and the
safety of a vessel operating at night, which this Notice conspicuously failed
to do.

5.9. Passports

Introduction

The maritime trade conducted by Maltese vessels was fundamental to the wealth and security of the islands, not least because the Maltese were reliant upon imported food supplies. The proximity of the piratical Barbary states posed a threat to navigation. Maltese ship owners wanted to ensure that the protection of the Royal Navy was available to them and, as we shall discover, Sicilian and Neapolitan masters sought similar protection.

Vessels, whether British or Maltese, trading from Maltese ports were required to sail under a pass that was issued by the Public Secretary's office. This pass was normally valid for one voyage to an identified port. Once the vessel returned to Malta, the pass was to be handed back to Government and was available to be issued to another master. Given the small tonnage of the vessels of this period, sea journeys for the import of food and other goods were frequent. A significant part of Coleridge's official role thus involved the issue of passports. Following ministerial intervention, he issued a Notice, on 25 June 1805,[229] to regulate entitlement to British protection on the high seas. The Notice is also of interest because it reveals Coleridge's broader political agenda in boosting Ball's reputation with the Maltese

Authority for Passports

From the outset of British rule, the subject of passports had, for a variety of reasons, been a vexed and controversial matter. The first problem had been an internal dispute as to who had responsibility for their issue. The later, and more embarrassing problem for the British, was whether the Civil Commissioner had acted lawfully when issuing passports to foreign ships' masters. Ball's policies had given rise to a serious international incident, and even the risk of war.

Identifying the appropriate authority responsible for the issue of passports was, at first, controversial within the demarcation dispute that erupted when the civil administration was split from the military. As we have seen, the appointment of Charles Cameron as Civil Commissioner in May 1801 marked the beginning of British civil administration on

---

229 Avviso, 23 June 1805 (date of 23 crossed out and 25 substituted) LIBR/MS 430 2/2 Bandi 1805 AL 1814, 15.

Malta. The civil authorities, which naturally did not have any authority over military affairs, were directed, by the terms of the Royal Instructions of 14 May 1801,[230] to work closely with the military. In other respects, the Instructions were obscure, and this soon resulted in the important functional dispute between Major-General Pigot and Civil Commissioner Cameron. Responsibility for a number of centrally-important issues was disputed, including the role of the military in the promulgation of new laws, the control of the police in Valletta,[231] the admission of foreigners and, importantly in the present context, the issue of British passports.[232] It fell to Lord Hobart to resolve the *impasse*. He decided that each of these matters would fall within the jurisdiction of the civil authority.[233] On the subject of passports, his lordship explicitly instructed that "All passports except to officers holding military commissions ... should proceed from the Civil Commissioner, and shall be signed by the Secretary of Government".[234] Thus it was that, when in office, Coleridge had to assume the burdensome task of issuing passports to intending overseas travellers.[235]

Entitlement to a Passport

The question of who was entitled to British protection had also become controversial. Prior to Coleridge's arrival on Malta, a serious diplomatic incident had arisen over the unlawful issue of British passports to foreigners. The aftermath of this furore was still in progress when Coleridge served as Public Secretary; indeed, he was involved, along with others, in the re-alignment of policy and the limiting of the damage done. The events that gave rise to this incident could be traced to the time French-occupied Valletta surrendered to the British in September 1800.

International Incident

As we have described in, Chapter 2, the purpose of the siege of Valletta, and the blockade of the Island, was to starve the French garrison, besieged in

230 Kew, CO 158/1/ 53 et seq.
231 Pigot to Cameron, 2 July 1801, Kew, CO 158/1/119.
232 Ibid.
233 Hobart to Cameron, 2 September 1801, Kew, CO 158/1/207.
234 Hobart to Cameron, ibid., 209.
235 Although the text of the Avviso of 25 June 1805 (below) suggests that entitlement was determined by a decision of the Tribunal, not Coleridge, which must have eased his administrative burden.

Valletta, into submission. The very object of the strategy was, thus, to run down the food supplies. Naturally, at the moment when collapse occurred there would be a starving populace. As matters unfolded, there was but eight days stock of grain in Valletta when the French capitulated.

The urgent crisis[236] could only be solved by importing grain, but the problem was that the French had destroyed the Maltese vessels to use them for firewood. In this, emergency, the new British administration had to turn to Neapolitan and Sicilian vessels to import grain to feed the population.[237] When the Sicilian and Neapolitan owners demanded the protection of the British Crown to protect their vessels against the piracy of the Dey of Algiers, Ball acquiesced since, in his view, the emergency justified it. It was important to ensure that the food supplies carried in these vessels reached an Island desperate for food and incapable of meeting more than one third of its own requirements. Ball was aware that the predations of the Barbary pirates[238] were a notable hazard given the widespread shortage of grain in the Mediterranean between 1799 and 1806, which would have made the cargo highly prized. The security of the Island, as well as that of the crews depended upon the safe completion of the voyages – not least by avoiding their capture by pirates either for ransom or for sale as slaves.

Ball, therefore, instructed Alexander Macaulay, Coleridge's predecessor, to issue passes, valid for one sea voyage, to foreign nationals.[239] Although Ball seems to have been made a scapegoat for this unlawful act, he later claimed that Lords Keith and Nelson also issued passes to Neapolitan Masters. Ball's defence was that this was a policy of last resort agreed with and implemented by the most senior military commanders in the region.[240] Ball's further argument was that the vessels would be crewed by the Maltese and, thus, would fall within the spirit of international law.

---

236 It might be asked why a stock of grain had not been brought into the Island in readiness for the surrender. The absence of such preparations suggests either a lack of forward planning or the suddenness of the French collapse.

237 As Coleridge described in the text of the preamble to this Avviso of 25 June 1805, LIBR/MS 430 2/2 Bandi 1805 AL 1814, 15.

238 The term "Barbary States" refers to the territory between seaports of Tangiers and Tripoli. Britain and other nations trading in the Mediterranean paid the Dey tribute in order to ensure the safe passage of British vessels. The purpose of the Treaty, of 19 March 1801, was to extend this protection to the Maltese.

239 Sultana, 9.

240 Ball to Cartwright, 9 September 1805, Kew, CO 158/10/239, 240.

The Legal Context

Shortly after Malta fell into British hands a Treaty, dated 19 March 1801, had been concluded between the Dey of Algiers and the British Government. This ended, as far as the Maltese masters were concerned, the threat from pirate ships of the Dey. Maltese vessels were no longer liable to be captured and their crews held in captivity as slaves. The Treaty, eventually, secured the release of Maltese prisoners held by the Dey, and it prevented further attacks on Maltese ships.[241] However, the Dey had not undertaken to restrict his activities in relation to Neapolitan and Sicilian ships and a state of war continued to exist between these States and the Divan. This is important for what follows.

The Capture and Imprisonment of Maltese Crews

Unfortunately for Ball, four Sicilian[242] vessels, bearing Ball's passports, were captured by cruisers of the Dey in 1803, and their crews, including Maltese citizens, imprisoned for ransom, in Algiers. The official British response was a belated *volte face* concerning passports. Despite private misgivings that he, formally, expressed in writing to Ball,[243] Macaulay promptly issued an Avviso, on 28 October 1803,[244] regulating the issue of passports to make sure that they were only issued to those with entitlement, namely British subjects (including the Maltese). The preamble indicated that the authorities were already aware of "abuses" whereby passports were being unlawfully used by foreigners. Of course, by 1803, Ball was able to ascertain that the Island had sufficiently recovered to enable the Maltese to import grain and other foodstuffs on their own behalf. Merchant capacity

241 An Avviso of 5 February 1803 announced the release of one hundred and sixty-four Maltese prisoners from Constantinople: NLM LIBR/MS 430 1/2; Bandi 1790 AL 1805, 175.
242 Sultana, 165. We may also note the seizure of Neapolitan vessels used to transport supplies to the Islands during the siege: Ball to Cartwright, 9 September 1805, Kew, CO 158/10/239, 240 where it was revealed that the Sicilian and Neapolitan captives, as well as Maltese slaves, were still being detained. Dr Moncrieff to Ball, 13 October 1805, Kew, CO 158/10/247 et seq. referred to negotiations for the release of Sicilians. He reported that the Maltese slaves had been released. Ball to Castlereagh, 26 December 1805, Kew, CO 158/10/227 revealed that negotiations had not yet been concluded.
243 Ball to Cooke, 21 July 1805, Kew, CO 158/10/187, 191. This was, according to Ball, the only occasion on which Macaulay formally dissented from Ball's policies.
244 NLM LIBR 431/1 Bandi 1800 AL 1803, 309.

had increased, given the arrival of vessels that had been purchased with the aid of British funds, and the 1801 Treaty meant that navigation was, as far as Maltese vessels were concerned, reasonably safe. Thus, the practice of issuing passports to foreign vessels ceased.[245] Even so, Ball was nervous. As late as 1803 he ordered that any master whose vessel encountered interference, from cruisers of the Dey, should report the incident to the Public Secretary.[246] Moreover, there was still a problem with the passports in circulation amongst the foreign owners; and the crisis caused by the capture of the Maltese crews remained unresolved.

The British decided to test the will of the Dey. In January 1804 Nelson appeared off Algiers with seven ships of the line in an effort to persuade the Dey to release the Maltese prisoners and pay compensation for the seized vessels but the Dey refused to co-operate because, he argued, the British had not been entitled, under the terms of the Treaty of 1801, to issue passports to his enemies, the Sicilian Masters.[247] Nelson left empty handed. Although Ball wanted to treat the seizure of the Sicilian vessels as an act of war, Nelson held the unequivocal opinion that British passports did not entitle the Sicilians to British protection.[248] British ministers sided with Nelson and open warfare was avoided.

The Secretary of State, Lord Camden, decided to adopt a compromising stance and to pursue better diplomatic relations with the Dey. He shared Nelson's conviction that Ball had acted unlawfully in granting passports to persons not entitled to them.[249] Ball, in effect, suffered a reprimand for his original policy. Hereafter, he was to be supplied with new, "Mediterranean" passports under the instruction that they were only to be granted to British subjects including Maltese owners. Neither the Sicilians nor the Neapolitans were to be entitled to them.

Nonetheless, a significant number of the "old" passes remained in circulation because the owners of Sicilian vessels had refused to surrender them to Macaulay. Coleridge's Notice of 25 June 1805 even suggested that there were other kinds of evasions intended to continue British protection for foreign vessels. These included applications made under false credentials, or deviations from the named port of destination, or even "sham" sales. The

---

245 See also Ball to Cooke, 21 July 1805, Kew, CO 158/10/187.
246 The Avviso of 22 October 1803, NLM LIBR/MS 430, Bandi 1790 AL 1805, 314.
247 Sultana, 20, 24 and 155.
248 Sultana, 165.
249 Sultana, 256. Interestingly, a dispatch from Ball to Cartwright implicated Lords Nelson and Keith in the issue of the "emergency" passports: Ball to Cartwright, 9 September 1805, Kew, CO 158/10.

latter were arrangements under which Sicilians and others had purported to sell their vessels to Maltese owners, (thereby entitling them to British protection) whilst, in fact, retaining ownership. These passports had to be called in as soon as the new, Mediterranean, passes arrived. By March 1805[250] Ball was still awaiting the arrival of the new passports that had been despatched from the Lords Commissioners of the Admiralty in London. Coleridge's Notice of 25 June 1805 reveals that they had reached the Island by that date.

The Notice of 25 June 1805 – Passports

In this Notice Coleridge recalled many of the events surrounding the problematic passports, including the reasons why Ball had been compelled to issue them after the surrender. He described how Macaulay had issued a proclamation, in October 1803, explaining that no further passports would be issued. Naturally, as Coleridge explained, this had not addressed the problem of the passports that were still, fraudulently, in circulation. Coleridge's Notice thus cancelled all the existing passports and required intending travellers to obtain one of the new Mediterranean passports. The effect, for those holding the "old " passports, was significant because Coleridge warned that these would no longer guarantee British protection. He reminded them that the Dey would not restrain his ships from capturing and enslaving Maltese crews aboard vessels that were not entitled to the passports they were carrying. Ball, he added, would not take any steps to secure their release if this misfortune befell them.

It is interesting that Coleridge cancelled the "old" passports with immediate effect (i.e. on 25 June 1805), but the Notice was not published until the following day, 26 June. It is not known whether this resulted in any hardship.

Analysis

This Notice shares a similar narrative style to the Notice of 25 May 1805, announcing the conviction and sentence of Fortunata Tagliana.[251] In each of these instruments, Coleridge included significantly more information than was necessary in order to announce the outcomes of an administrative

250 Sultana, 305; see also Camden to Ball, Kew, 27 March 1805, Kew, CO 159/3/161.
251 NLM LIBR/MS 430 2/2 Bandi 1805 AL 1814, 9. See the Public Order and Crime theme, above.

decision. Had he not been concerned with a broader political agenda then some very limited factual information would have sufficed. In relation to the passports, this information was straightforward and could have been briefly stated – the existing passports were cancelled and would no longer entitle the holders to British protection. Anyone who disregarded this would be at risk of capture. Finally, he might have stated that new Mediterranean passports should be obtained by those intending to travel overseas. It is, however, of central interest that Coleridge went beyond this minimum so as to recount, in some detail, the history of the events which made the latest intervention of the authorities necessary. More importantly, he offered some explanation of the reasons underpinning official decision-making. Why was this additional material included?

Coleridge's major objective was to vindicate Ball's actions which, as we have seen, had been both contentious and unlawful. Coleridge's wider objective was to deflect criticism for what might, otherwise, have been attacked as a serious misjudgement and to restore his superior's credibility. In this Notice, Coleridge entered the realm of the propagandist, deftly shaping the government's message. Damaging information was suppressed, and the effect was deliberately misleading, not least because Ball was presented as the benign actor who was the sole decision-maker. Ball's political weakness was also disguised.

The manipulation of information began early in the text with the proffered excuse that, when Ball had given passports to foreign nationals, he had acted from the highest of motives in solving the crisis following the capitulation and, at all times, for the benefit of the public.[252] This was given some prominence by Coleridge to avoid inconvenient conclusions about the illegality of past governmental action. Coleridge faithfully portrayed Ball's defence, of necessity, in the face of the criticism arrayed against him and, by implication, Coleridge was arguing that the Civil Commissioner had shown courage in putting the welfare of the Maltese above his own career even if it meant breaching international law by offering passports to foreigners.

> Given the lack of our own national ships, and the urgent need to assist the transport of goods, His Excellency was obliged, in those early days following the surrender of these cities, to distribute certificates which promised British Protection to various foreign vessels. The governors of the Barbary states

---

252 Ball was now prepared to be open with his superiors about his decision: Ball to E. Cooke, 21 July 1805, Kew, CO 158/10/ 93.

agreed to respect this measure, which was dictated by the necessity of the situation.

This passage also disclosed something of Coleridge's own engagement with morality and law in governmental action. His appeal to a superior moral order revealed that Coleridge had been forced to confront the predicament that arises when just and pragmatic solutions collide with legal norms. Coleridge's intellectual engagement with public life had already revealed the need to develop a conception of morally-just administration. He had, earlier, considered whether government could ever, legitimately, use expediency to vindicate its departure from positive laws. An undated Notebook entry, of late January 1805, witnessed Coleridge reflecting upon the "'betwixt and between" of positive law & the dictates of right reason" in the work of the Court of Vice-Admiralty.[253]

The essential premise of Coleridge's vindication of Ball, in the public notice of 25 June 1805, was that a responsible, benign, government cannot always deliver good and effective administration within the formal constraints of the Rule of Law, and that public action can be justified even if a departure from positive legal norms is required, to achieve an important public benefit.

Coleridge's text continued by laying the blame for the policy failure at the door of foreigners (persons neither English nor Maltese) who "abused" the system even to the extent of making dishonest, false, sales to disguise the true ownership of their vessels. It was these dishonest foreigners who had destroyed Ball's necessary system and Coleridge was unambiguous about where the Maltese should lay the blame.

The juxtaposition of the dishonest, selfish foreigner with the courageous and selfless Civil Commissioner was a particular feature of Coleridge's technique. Coleridge was, of course, tapping, once more, into the Maltese suspicion of "foreigners", for political ends. Only a few days earlier he had issued the Bando enacting new laws subjecting foreigners on the Island to much stricter controls and the passports Avviso reinforced the government's message that these people were suspect opportunists. The aim was, of course, to win sympathy for Ball. He had done his best to feed the inhabitants, and, in return, he had been duped and embarrassed by untrustworthy, scheming, foreigners. It was a message that Coleridge must have believed the public would accept.

Throughout Coleridge's text, Ball was presented as a benign actor

---

253 *CN* 2, 2413.

controlling events. Naturally, Coleridge would not have mentioned that the political decision in this matter had been removed from Ball's hands. It was an obvious obfuscation, but one for which Coleridge can hardly be blamed. Similarly, the suggestion that the Dey and his spies had merely become "suspicious" about vessels bearing the old passports. The Dey's actions went beyond merely suspecting impropriety: he had used force. No mention was made about Maltese crews who had already been captured and whose release Ball was struggling (so far unsuccessfully) to achieve. But the danger that the Sicilian vessels faced was the true reason why Coleridge warned them of the risk of capture. Coleridge chose not to reinforce his message by revealing the truth about the hostages because it would have disclosed British weakness and would damage prestige. Even Nelson's squadron had not been able to rescue captured Maltese crews, which meant that Ball would be politically and militarily powerless to intervene successfully against a recalcitrant Dey if yet more individuals fell into his hands. Coleridge disguised this impotence by suggesting that Ball did not intend to intervene to save law-breakers from captivity. The careful use of language implied an act of free will.

Negotiations, to have Maltese crews released and returned to Malta, succeeded in October 1805.[254] However, the Neapolitan captives had still not been released by the end of the year, although Ball continued to express optimism that their release could be obtained.[255]

5.10. Military Discipline

Introduction

In the aftermath of the capitulation of the French occupation forces in 1800, a military government, under Major-General Pigot, had been created to administer both the civil and military affairs of the islands. As we have seen, this arrangement was unpopular with the Maltese and, as soon as the risks to British long-term interests had been understood by the Secretary of State, the civil and military functions were separated. Cameron's appointment as

254 Dr Moncrieff to Ball, 13 October 1805, Kew, CO 158/10/247 et seq.
255 Ball to Castlereagh, 26 December 1805, Kew, CO 158/10/227. He referred in this despatch to Neapolitan holders of British passports still held by the Dey of Algiers. They had been in captivity since the time Ball had had to use foreign vessels to supply the Island.

the first Civil Commissioner, in May 1801, resulted from this policy shift, which placed the responsibility for "civil" affairs under his jurisdiction. Pigot retained control of the military.

In practice, this, apparently, straightforward demarcation had been obfuscated in the Royal Instructions, resulting in intractable disputes between Cameron and Pigot. As we described in Chapter 3, the responsibility for policing and for passports had each given rise to disagreement.

By the time Coleridge held public office, Pigot had been replaced by Major-General Villettes. However, the working relationship between Ball and Villettes may also have been strained. Lord Windham eventually received an allegation from a Maltese agitator, Vincenzo Borg, that Villettes and Ball were not in "harmony".[256] Sultana has also concluded that in the summer of 1805 there was tension between the military and civilian authorities,[257] and the most likely causes of friction were the requests from the military that the civil government take the unpopular measures necessary to ensure military efficiency. Although the evidence in Coleridge's Bandi and Avvisi suggests some close co-operation, the text of these instruments, by itself, does not reveal how willingly this assistance was offered, or what arguments may have preceded the promulgation of the desired measures.

In 1805, the major problem was that civilian behaviour, such as the abuse of the enlistment system and the sheltering of deserters, could only be remedied with the aid of the civilian authorities, (because, *ex hypothesi*, the military usually had no jurisdiction over the conduct of Maltese civilians). The army expected the civil administration to deal with these sensitive and difficult problems. Coleridge's Bandi and Avvisi reveal that Ball had agreed, although, in the case of the fugitives, it would require some political sensitivity if Ball were to avoid the resentment of an unsympathetic civil population.

Plans to Recruit

Following the British decision not to implement the Treaty of Amiens 1802, the Neapolitan and Sicilian troops who had served alongside their British counterparts, in the liberation of Malta, were expelled. As a consequence, the British military authorities became concerned at a shortage of

---

256 Borg to Windham, 30 May 1806, *British National Archive*, Kew, CO 158/12 no folio reference.
257 Sultana, 347.

manpower. The British garrison (which was also required to defend Gozo) comprised only the Royal Artillery, the 20th (East Devonshire), the 27th (Inniskilling), 35th (Dorsetshire) and 61st (South Gloucestershire) regiments, with a combined strength of about 3,800 enlisted troops.[258] The authorities decided that a regiment of Maltese infantry should be raised. However, the terms under which they would serve were controversial. One reason for this was the proposal to merge two corps of Maltese militia (then under the command of Maltese officers) into one Regiment. This was to be placed under the command of British officers. There had been an exchange between Ball and Lord Camden concerning the terms of service. Ball, in a memorandum drafted by Coleridge, had proposed an alternative plan. He advocated that the new Regiment should be placed under the command of aristocratic Maltese – a proposal that was fully consistent with Ball's general staffing policy.[259] However, Camden had insisted that British officers rather than the local nobility should command the corps.

The Royal Regiment of Malta

The Royal Regiment of Malta was created in December 1804 and Villettes appointed its Colonel.[260] Coleridge was, later, to allege that the merger of the local militia into the new Corps took place merely to give Villettes, who had influential friends in the War Office, the command of a regiment and for no other reason.[261] Coleridge also, somewhat forcefully, expressed qualms about the moral legitimacy of recruiting fifteen hundred soldiers to serve in any part of the Empire not least because of the relatively tiny population of Malta.[262]

Recruitment began in earnest in March of the following year, with the intention that the unit would take part in an expedition, under the command of Lieutenant-General Sir James Craig, to Naples.[263] As we shall

---

258 1804: See http://website.lineone.net/~stephaniebidmead/chapter567.htm, consulted 5 January 2007.
259 Ball's staffing policy is described in Chapter 2. For Coleridge's involvement in policy discussion, see: to Robert Southey, circa 24 December 1809 *CL* 3, 265.
260 See generally, http://website.lineone.net/~stephaniebidmead/ "A History of the British Army in Malta". Consulted 5 January 2007.
261 To Robert Southey, circa 24 December 1809, *CL* 3, 265.
262 To Robert Southey, ibid. This decision was, he argued, "*cruel*" and "*shameful*" (emphasis in the original).
263 Eight thousand British troops were sent to Malta in readiness for the campaign in 1805: Camden to Ball, 29 March 1805, Kew, CO 159/3/170. Part of the Kingdom of the Two Sicilies had been occupied by the French when they entered Naples. See

see below, there were soon problems with desertions. Action to recapture fugitives was urgently required lest the Regiment should not be available for its planned deployment. In fact, the expedition eventually sailed without the Royal Regiment of Malta, in November 1805, because the corps, (its strength no doubt still depleted by the unresolved desertions) had not yet achieved combat readiness.[264]

To stimulate recruitment, the Maltese were offered a bounty of ten guineas to enlist for general service for an unlimited period or seven guineas for seven year's general service. By May 1805 these payments had attracted three hundred and sixty-seven new recruits, which rose to a total of four hundred and fifty two months later.[265] However, as Coleridge's Avviso of 20 June 1805[266] (Abuse of the enlistment money) revealed, some civilians were abusing the bounty system by taking the enlistment money and using it without any intention of submitting to military service.

In the end, the Royal Regiment was not placed on the strength of the British army until 1807, which is, perhaps, suggestive of the difficulties caused by the desertions and the impact upon recruitment of the unpopularity of the decision to require general service.

Desertions

A widely-debated question concerned the terms of service and, in particular, where the Royal Regiment could be required to serve.[267] The thorny issue was whether Maltese troops were only to be deployed in the defence of Malta – which was acceptable to the Maltese themselves, because most of them then in service had come from the local militia – or whether they were to be recruited for (unpopular) general service anywhere within the Empire. Ball, who had been aware that the Maltese would not readily assent to general overseas service, had strongly resisted any policy to send them overseas other than as a garrison force.[268] Coleridge later expressed

generally, on the proposed offensive strategy in the Mediterranean, Holland et al. Sicily was eventually occupied by British forces for eight years after January 1806.
264 Rather surprisingly, Coleridge later claimed to know little about the Regiment on the grounds that he had left the Island before the Regiment embarked on its mission: to Robert Southey, circa 24 December 1809, *CL* 3, 265.
265 Above n. 260.
266 NLM LIBR/MS 430 2/2 Bandi 1805 AL 1814, 12.
267 Sultana, 231, 318-9.
268 Ball to Camden, 22 April, 1805, Kew, CO 158/10/ 151. Coleridge also claimed to have written a memorandum on the subject on behalf of the Civil Commissioner: To Robert Southey, circa 24 December 1809, below n. 271.

his support for Ball's preferences in this matter arguing that the decision to require general service had been "cruel".[269] The Secretary of State was not to be moved: he had already determined that "general service" – with all that entailed – would be required.[270]

In a letter to Southey, written when the Regiment was blamed for the loss of Capri in 1808, Coleridge criticised the ministerial decisions that had, in effect, overruled Ball. Coleridge argued that the Maltese troops, the large majority of whom were married, would have fought bravely if fighting at home; but, he remarked that they could not be expected to fight abroad where their interests were not at issue.[271]

As Sultana indicated, Coleridge had altered his views on some of these issues. Coleridge had earlier argued that soldiers fight better away from home.[272] This *volte face* may indicate the extent to which Coleridge had assimilated the views of the Maltese "establishment", in particular those of the Civil Commissioner.

Thus, the signal that the British sent was that they were willing to use the Maltese as warriors in any British cause. Locally, this was both resented and feared. As a consequence, in 1805, troops were deserting the regiment in significant numbers and disappearing into the countryside.

A likely reason for the resistance to overseas service in the British army was that it recalled past experience, which made the Maltese fearful. Many of their friends and relatives had been forced to serve in the French Revolutionary army, with fateful consequences. Long after he had relinquished his public office in Malta, Coleridge, recalling first-hand information from a "survivor", recounted how, in 1798, Napoleon had addressed the Maltese regiment and invited them to serve with him in the expedition to Egypt. Napoleon had appealed to them to add "glory" to their "freedom" and to share the "immortal wreaths of fame".[273] Not one of the Maltese volunteered, whereupon the survivor recounted that the Maltese were surrounded by a French regiment and forcibly taken to troop ships for embarkation.

Their reluctance to serve Napoleon may, of course, have been symptomatic of a reluctance to serve in the military of the French invader:

---

269 To Robert Southey, above n. 12.
270 See above n. 268, where Ball makes reference to and quotes from the Secretary of State's earlier letter to him dated 13 February 1805.
271 To Robert Southey, circa 24 December 1809, *CL* 3, 265.
272 Sultana, 326.
273 *The Friend*, 1, 258.

but this possible interpretation can be contested. Napoleon was only on Malta for a brief period (9-14 June 1798) at which time the French were still perceived as liberators. The more likely explanation of these events is that the Maltese were simply reluctant to risk their lives in an imperial cause that did not serve their interests. The wisdom of this distrust was subsequently born out when the fate of the Maltese conscripts was revealed.

Coleridge's account, in *The Friend,* alleged that the unfortunate Maltese had been placed in front of French soldiers, not only as shields but also to prevent desertion.[274] Whatever the truth behind these assertions, there is no doubt that the British administration on Malta was fully aware of the casualties that the Maltese suffered. Macaulay had reported to Ball, in January 1804, that of the eight thousand Maltese men conscripted by the French army for Egyptian service, few returned.[275] Such a recent disaster can hardly have been an inducement to the Maltese to serve in the armed forces of another imperially-ambitious State.

Thus, the British insistence upon terms of service that were unacceptable to the Maltese was the immediate, and perhaps unsympathetic, cause of the significant desertions from the regiment with which Coleridge had to deal.

As a first step, Coleridge issued Avvisi making public the Civil Commissioner's insistence that the population should seek out the deserters.[276] At this stage, the intention was to motivate potential informants by offering a reward for information leading to arrest. But, in addition, and somewhat controversially, the first Avviso also warned that punishments would be imposed on those who assisted the deserters. It is not clear whether aiding them was an offence contrary to existing Maltese law, so this threat was constitutionally controversial. The second Notice (5 August 1805)[277] purported to clarify existing laws in order to deny the fugitives sustenance. When these Avvisi failed to persuade the Maltese, Coleridge, with more than a hint of desperation, resorted to legislation imposing new criminal penalties. The problem of desertion was, however, unresolved by the time he left the Island in September 1805.

Desertion was not, however, the only problem the British encountered. Maltese civilians were taking the bounty proffered for enlistment and then refusing to serve. This was also a problem Coleridge had to deal with and we shall consider this problem first.

---

274 Ibid., 259.
275 Macaulay to Ball, 25 January 1804, Kew, CO 158/8/19.
276 Avviso, 15 July 1805, NLM LIBR/MS 430 2/2 Bandi 1805 AL 1814, 17.
277 NLM LIBR/MS 430 2/2 Bandi 1805 AL 1814,18.

The Avviso of 20 June 1805[278] – Enlistment Money

The recruitment campaign, which began in March 1805, soon ran into unexpected difficulties. On 20 June 1805 Coleridge was forced to issue a public notice condemning the fraudulent practice by which civilian men, who pretended to be interested in enlistment, accepted the enlistment money only to use it as an interest free loan with which to gamble. Having accepted the bounty, they would, unlawfully, refuse to proceed with enlistment. Of course, they hoped to escape enlistment by repaying the bounty and the required penalty, but this depended, of course, on having won their bets.

To combat this opportunism, Coleridge announced a more vigorous enforcement, of the existing regulations, available under the articles of War. This scheme employed a "cooling off period" after the payment of the bounty. An intending soldier had to be taken before an official or magistrate and sworn in; but under the articles of War this process was not to take place earlier than twenty-four hours and not later than forty-eight hours after receiving payment. In other words, the articles of War enabled an individual who had second thoughts about military service to repay the enlistment money together with a ten *scudi* penalty and, thereby, avoid enlistment without committing an offence.

The restriction that Coleridge imposed was that the repayment of the enlistment money and the ten *scudi* penalty had to occur within twenty-four hours of the enlistment money having been accepted. This meant that the unsuccessful gambler would have little opportunity to recoup the lost stake and win the ten *scudi* necessary to escape military service.

The problem with this restriction is that it appears to contradict other terms of the articles of War, notably the earlier provision that the cooling-off period could be as long as forty-eight hours. The internal consistency of the Regulations is problematic.

The Avviso of 15 July 1805[279] – Deserters

Large-scale desertions were a problem for the authorities that were not confined to the Royal Regiment of Malta. Surviving witness testimony reveals that desertions of up to twenty men at a time were taking place during July 1805 – the foreign soldiers of the Corsican regiment bribing

278   NLM LIBR/MS 430 2/2 Bandi 1805 AL 1814,12.
279   Avviso 15th July 1805, NLM LIBR/MS 430 2/2 Bandi 1805 AL 1814, 17.

Maltese boat owners to take them overseas.[280]

Coleridge's Public Notice of 15 July 1805 was intended to secure the recapture of fugitives from the Royal Regiment of Malta. Normally, desertion would have been a matter exclusively for the military but, as mentioned above, civilians, who were usually beyond the reach of the military jurisdiction, were assisting the soldiers, and so the matter was passed to the Public Secretary. The Avviso gave formal notice that those who aided the deserters would be severely punished.

The (successful) desertions were to continue throughout the summer, which reveals that the authorities had great difficulty in eradicating the support networks which made evasion possible. As we have seen, the total strength of the Regiment increased by a mere eighty three men in the two months from May to July 1805, despite the offer of a very tempting bounty. Although it is unclear whether these limited numbers included those who had now deserted, the statistics suggest slow progress in building and maintaining the fighting strength of the Corps. If these enlistments did include some or all of the now deserted troops then the actual numbers available for service would have been significantly fewer than the nominal strength. The reaction of the authorities suggests that British policy was being seriously undermined.

Coleridge's text was carefully constructed. The deliberate intention was to suggest to the civilian inhabitants that the fugitives were armed, dangerous and desperate, which implied that it was in everyone's interest to get the men back to barracks as soon as possible. He also claimed that the fugitives were causing a disturbance to the population. However, if these disturbances ever took place, it is possible to be sceptical about the scale of the threat suggested. The evidence from the various Bandi and Avvisi is that family and friends, who had no wish to see "their" soldiers sent overseas to risk their lives in the service of a foreign power, actively supported the fugitives. If the absconders really had been isolated, threatening and aggressive we can surmise that they would soon have been turned over to the military, not least because the authorities had promised a reward to informants for information leading to arrest.

The facts speak for themselves. The confinement of the deserters on a small island upon which they would, inevitably, have been pursued, with some determination, by the military authorities, reveals that they had support from friends. In the intense heat of summer, they would quickly

---

280 NAM 92/04 1805.

have been forced to obtain water. Since there are no rivers on the Island, their supply problems, in the absence of civilian aid, would have been insurmountable. If it occurred at all, the disturbance to which the Avviso refers may have been isolated attempts to obtain supplies from unwilling property owners; but there is no convincing evidence of widespread threatening behaviour of a kind that would destroy public sympathy for their plight. As said, the portrayal of the fugitives as armed and dangerous may have been little more than a concoction of the authorities designed to whip up public anxiety. If so, it is possible to interpret the language of this Avviso (15 July 1805) as another example of Coleridge's propaganda. And it failed. In the Bando of 2 September 1805,[281] Coleridge was eventually forced to concede that "hospitality" in rural areas had been offered to the deserters. This admission is revealing.

Constitutional Issues

Constitutionally, the Avviso of 15 July 1805 was controversial because it purported to announce that the offering of assistance to any deserter, or failing to inform the authorities of their whereabouts, would lead to "severe" punishment. It also purported to impose new duties: the Maltese were required to make all efforts to discover the whereabouts of the deserters (and inform on them).

It is not a Bando and thus could not, by itself, alter Maltese law. Moreover, there is no reference in the text of the Notice to an already existing law that would entitle the authorities to do impose a lawful punishment; indeed, we can be reasonably certain that no such law existed because Coleridge was compelled to promulgate a measure creating new offences in the Bando dated 2 September 1805. As we describe,[282] it is a violation of the Rule of Law and, in particular, of the principle *nulle poena sine lege*, if conduct of which the administration merely disapproves can be subjected to punishment. Punishment can only take place in accordance with the law.

The Avviso of 5 August 1805[283] – Provisions for Deserters

The Notice of 15 July 1805 plainly failed in its purpose. On 5 August 1805,

---

281 NLM LIBR/MS 430 2/2 Bandi 1805 AL 1814, 21.
282 See Chapter 6.
283 LIBR/MS 430 2/2 Bandi 1805 AL 1814, 18.

Coleridge was compelled to issue a further Notice that sought to prevent the supply of provisions to the deserters as a way of denying them the means of subsisting outside the military system. This Notice of 5 August 1805, by "reminding" the public of the terms of a Proclamation of 3 April 1801,[284] targeted a particular form of "help" – ostensibly the purchase of goods by soldiers and, in particular, bread. When taken together with Coleridge's earlier instrument (Notice of 15 July 1805) the authorities can be seen to have pursued a strategy to deny the deserters both shelter and sustenance, whether donated or sold; in other words, the civil authorities wished to starve the soldiers back to barracks.

The political sensitivity of the problem and, in particular, the desire to avoid resentment, was revealed by Coleridge's statement in the August Avviso that the Civil Commissioner wished the population to be aware of the laws so as to avoid the need to inflict punishments. As elsewhere,[285] Coleridge did not miss this opportunity to present the Civil Commissioner as a benevolent Governor who made efforts to educate the population about the measure rather than punishing them for its contravention. This was pursued, no doubt, to boost Ball's public image at a difficult time when there must have been some friction between the authorities and the communities in which the deserters had (successfully) taken refuge.

Coleridge's Avviso of 5 August 1805 was not an overtly law-making measure: Coleridge appears to have thought (or at least claimed to believe) that he was merely reinforcing prohibitions already enacted in the Proclamation of 3 April 1801. However, for reasons that are not clear, Coleridge whether deliberately or otherwise, fundamentally misstated the meaning of the 1801 Proclamation.

In translation, the 1801 Proclamation states:

> In order to prevent any further abuses, His Excellency orders that anyone who dares to *buy* any goods from a soldier should be punished not only by the loss of both the purchased article and the money which he paid, but also by a fine decided by the Grand Court, which will be fixed depending upon the type and circumstances of the offence committed. (Emphasis added).

Thus, the 1801 Proclamation criminalised purchases *from* military personnel ("soldiers") whereas Coleridge, incorrectly, stated that the measure prevented any purchase *by* soldiers.[286] The explanation for this

---

284 NAM LIBR 431 1/3 Bandi 1800 AL 1803, 69.
285 See Chapter 6.
286 The Proclamation of 1801 prevented soldiers selling arms and other military equipment to civilians.

error is elusive. One possibility is that Coleridge did not investigate the language of the Law of 1801, for himself.[287] If he did examine it, he may have misunderstood the original Italian, or had it misrepresented to him by an official. His Notice suggests that this official may have been Ball himself since he attributed the mistaken belief, about the significance of the 1801 Proclamation, to Ball.

However, the alternative possibility is that Coleridge deliberately misstated the law so that it, conveniently, appeared to criminalise sales to soldiers. In other words, the misconstruction of the 1801 Proclamation may have been deliberate in order to appear to furnish the Administration with the necessary legal norm that enabled them to block supplies to deserters.[288] Whichever is the proper explanation, it is undoubtedly true that Coleridge's Avviso misstated the legal powers available to the Administration.

However, it is highly doubtful that any Maltese would have been taken in by this tactic, because soldiers regularly and, uncontroversially, bought goods from the public, including goods made from the locally-produced cotton, for which they were the major customers in 1805.[289] Moreover, Coleridge had recently issued a Proclamation which regulated the sale of spirits to soldiers,[290] so Coleridge's Notice of 5 August 1805 was manifestly inaccurate and would have fooled no-one. From the Maltese perspective, the pretence that sales to soldiers had been illegal since 1801 was simply foolish and preposterous. Thus, Coleridge's thin ruse must have seemed rather desperate. It is, however, suggestive of the extreme anxiety experienced by the British administration. The ridiculous tactic may have contributed to the loss of public confidence that eventually led to Ball's administration being caricatured and lampooned on the streets.[291]

It should also be emphasised that the purported extension to the criminal law (i.e. the attempt to criminalise sales to soldiers) raised legal and constitutional complexities. Any attempted prosecution would not only violate the fundamental principle of *nulle poena sine lege*, but would also result in an acquittal, since no offence known to the law would have been committed by a person selling goods to a deserter.

---

287 In his *Notebooks* Coleridge recognised that failing to look at the available evidence was "Imprudence": *CN* 2, 2439.

288 It needs to be emphasised that this could only be effective as a public relations exercise; it could not change the law.

289 See the regulation of trade theme discussed in Chapter 5.

290 Proclamation of 22 March 1805, discussed under the consumer protection theme, above.

291 Borg to Eton, 23 July 1806, Kew, CO 158/12, no folio reference.

In summary, one revealing conclusion is possible: the glaring failure to have due regard to the Proclamation of 1801 meant that Coleridge's Notice of 5 August 1805 fell below the standards of good and efficient government. Its suggestion, that sales to soldiers had been prohibited since 1801, was ludicrous and the measure represents an ill-prepared and ill-judged instrument that could only have damaging consequences for the reputation of Ball's government.

Bando of 2 September 1805[292] – Assisting Deserters

Unsurprisingly, the second instrument failed to curb the spate of desertions, which, by early September, remained, "frequent". Coleridge's final step, indeed his final Bando on Malta, was to introduce a new law punishing civilians for assisting deserters. Thus, the Proclamation of 2 September 1805 rendered liable to a criminal penalty persons offering shelter or other support to soldiers who had deserted the Royal Malta Regiment. This step must have been necessary to redress the earlier bureaucratic bungling.

The prohibition in the Bando of 2 September 1805 was an inclusive one forbidding the inhabitants from giving either shelter or assistance to any deserters. The penalty for breach of this injunction was a fine the amount of which was to be determined by the Tribunal.

It is highly unusual in Coleridge's Bandi that no mandatory fine was created for these offences: in this case the fine to be ascertained by the judiciary with the direction that all the circumstances of the case and, in particular, the identities and, presumably, the relationships of the people involved, should be taken into account. Mitigating circumstances could, thus, be submitted in an attempt to win leniency, and the judges would have been obliged to hear such submissions before passing sentence. This signalled that Coleridge recognised the conflicting loyalties that some families might have encountered. For example, wives who hid their husbands, or children who were found to have taken food to their fathers, might have been more leniently treated. The direction to the judges, to take all circumstances into account, signals an official concern with justice rather than merely with punishment. These considerations were, no doubt, intended to reduce the antipathy towards the administration that the decision, to order overseas military service (which had sparked the desertions), had caused.

This democratising technique, of leaving punishment to be determined

292 LIBR/MS 430 2/2 Bandi 1805 AL 1814, 21.

by the Maltese (through their judiciary), contrasted with some other legislative measures we have examined. As we have seen, the stipulation of a mandatory penalty is normal in Coleridge's legislation, thereby removing discretion from the local judges.

Conclusion

In these laws and public notices we, once again, encounter Coleridge dealing with a difficult administrative problem that went to the heart of British strategic interests in Malta. British unpopularity could threaten long-term possession of the Island, and so the problems surrounding the relationship between civilians and military had to be handled with sensitivity.

As the summer progressed there was rising official anxiety that the Royal Regiment of Malta was not combat ready and this was not the only regiment afflicted with large-scale desertions, as embarkation and combat drew closer. The measures taken to capture the deserters show more than a hint of desperation. In particular, the Notice of 5 August 1805 seems to have been hastily drawn up and incompetently drafted. Its assertion, that an earlier law penalised sales to soldiers and had done so since 1801, was, plainly, ridiculous. We cannot know whether Coleridge was ordered to attempt this ruse or whether it merely resulted from a mistake, either by Coleridge himself or his advisers. Whatever the explanation for this dangerous misrepresentation, the Notice of 5 August 1805 is a revealing example of the standards of public administration at a time when the civil authorities were clearly under urgent and unrelenting political pressure from the military. The unwise decision to issue it can only have damaged the public reputation of the government.

Once the need to enact a properly-framed law had been understood, Coleridge issued the Bando of 2 September 1805. By this date, Coleridge realised ,and had to admit, that the deserters had public sympathy. It is only at this point that we can identify a change in strategy. The decision to confer discretionary sentencing powers upon the Maltese judiciary suggests a more compromising stance and a more emphatic concern with justice. Coleridge understood the problem of divided loyalty and wanted to ensure that Maltese judges were sensitive to this when sentencing.

6. An Assessment of the Proclamations and Public Notices

Introduction

The purpose of this chapter is to examine Coleridge's achievements in the Proclamations (Bandi) and Public Notices (Avvisi). Firstly, we shall consider Coleridge's manipulative use of government information. Secondly, we shall consider the consonance of these instruments with his earlier journalism and with the requirements of the rule of law, such as publicity, comprehensibility and the use of discretion. We shall also examine some of their common features, such as the use of informants, and the criminal penalties imposed. The chapter concludes with an assessment of the extent to which Coleridge's laws were influenced by wartime conditions.

A Conflict of Interest

Coleridge held office on Malta at a moment in history when British colonial policy had undergone a significant and complex shift. At the close of the eighteenth century, Britain had lost confidence in the wisdom of exporting its legal, political and cultural values and superimposing them on overseas territories.[1] As Coleridge was to discover, one consequence of the new model of colonial government, which continued the constitutional arrangements of the former sovereign in conquered territories, was that British colonial governments were forced to administer colonies within a legal and political framework very different from that which existed in Britain.[2] Politicians were, inevitably, compelled to determine whether civil society should be

1   Generally, see Manning.
2   For a general introduction to the geopolitical context, see Rapport.

governed within the framework of local positive laws and values or whether, as Burke had suggested in the notorious impeachment of Hastings, the former Governor of Bengal, justice, in public affairs, should be understood as a matter of conscience – in effect, that empire should be an ethically informed project presided over by a progressive and liberal metropolitan state.[3] Government in Malta was, therefore, predicated upon assumptions about difference, namely that the Maltese legal and constitutional system could be worked effectively without a need for close conformity with the standards that were required by the English common law. How Coleridge responded to this challenge is of compelling interest. As we have seen in Chapter 1, his early journalism displayed an awareness of the importance of the rule of law. Importantly, he regarded this as embodying universal standards. How the Bandi and Avvisi, promulgated by him, conformed to these standards deserves consideration which is given in this chapter. But first, we shall consider Coleridge's propaganda role in seeking to establish the legitimacy of British rule on Malta.

As we have described, in Chapter 2, a large number of government policies were flawed either in conception or execution. The orchestrated complaints of the nationalists, although motivated by a desire to have Ball recalled, were not all without substance. Grievances simmered over breaches of perceived promises, to share prize money, after the fall of Valletta – the *Segnatura* was, consequently, flooded with complaining petitions; there had been a harsh crackdown after the anti-Semitic disturbances, in which Ball had interfered with the judicial process, to impose exemplary sentences which went beyond the criminal Code; free speech had been suppressed; taxes had been levied, notwithstanding a formal pledge to uphold a Maltese system that did not permit regular taxation; crime rates were high and witnesses were not coming forward to give evidence; the community supported deserters from the military who feared being sent on overseas service; bread was formally declared to be only fit for hogs, and so it went on. One of Ball's detractors noted that Ball's administration was lampooned for incompetence. Of course, this correspondent was politically motivated, with an axe to grind, but the frustration he recorded is likely to have been substantially true. Any argument that, in 1805, Ball was still enjoying the reputation and esteem he had won during his first administration is simply unconvincing.[4] There was discontent amongst the Maltese which had led

3   Marshall (ed.), vol 5; Ahmed, 28.
4   Cf. Staines.

to protests on the streets of Valletta. Even in London, ministers hesitated to have full confidence in him.[5] Ball had, as it were, suffered a steep slump in his popularity, albeit, as matters turned out, a temporary one.

Ball's unpopularity in 1805-1806 mattered because, given his autocratic powers, he was a powerful emblem of British rule since all governmental action was taken in his name. All the major policy decisions were taken by him and communicated in his name (as Coleridge emphasised in *The Friend*).[6] Coleridge's task was of strategic significance. He used government information to try to make Ball and his administration popular; and in doing so he was attempting to dispel the notion that Britain's Civil Commissioner was just another, autocratic, alien power whose presence on the Island was merely as exploitative and, as some alleged, more tyrannical, a rule than under the worst of the Grandmasters. Coleridge had to craft government information in order to suggest that British rule was perceived as benign, legitimate, and founded upon a supposed concurrence of British and Maltese interests.

Coleridge as Advocate for the Legitimacy of British Rule

The concept of legitimacy offers a solution to a political problem governing the relationship between power and obedience. It thus governs the relationship between those governing and those being governed. Legitimacy also sustains legal credibility and contributes to the justification for political action. A system of government can be regarded as legitimate if it responds to widely accepted social needs and preferences. This is so because government involves the direction of public affairs in order to advance the common good. As we have seen, for pragmatic British politicians, achieving and maintaining legitimacy was essential to the stable long-term government of an overseas possession with a unique constitutional, political and social structure.

The problem for colonial administrators was that a structural fissure lay at the heart of the colonial project: the inherent conflict of interest between the colonial territory and the Imperial power. The dominant strategic

---

5   See Chapter 2.
6   *The Friend*, 2, 552-4.

function of colonial government on Malta was to control the territory as a secure military base, which, from the British point of view, meant that all governmental power was to be retained under British control. This strategic policy conflicted with, for example, the political aspiration of the Maltese to share governmental power. Political dissent was vigorously suppressed, together with Maltese civil and political rights (e.g. the right to a fair trial).

Coleridge seems to have realised that the legitimacy and popularity of Ball's administration depended upon achieving a recognised congruence between the values of the British civil administration, its policies and those of the wider Maltese social system. The Civil Commissioner's instructions required Ball to win the hearts and minds of the Maltese – to "attach" them to British rule. This meant that upholding the public reputation of the administration was, necessarily, a strategically-significant endeavour. In Ball's opinion, Coleridge had clearly understood that information could be used as a powerful policy instrument.[7]

In the absence of other mechanisms, designed to elicit Maltese popular opinion before a law was introduced, the measure itself could sometimes furnish a useful means for the *ex post facto* persuasion of those regulated. Coleridge's instruments were not merely rules; they were also explanations, justifications and, sometimes, even ingratiations aimed at securing political support not only for obedience to the measure, but, ultimately, for British rule. They are exercises in government communication intended to win public support, influence Maltese opinion and alter behaviour. But they are not uncontroversial because the manner in which consent was invited, the partial nature of the information, how it was selected and presented, and above all, the underlying motivation of government, pose ethical questions about Coleridge's actions.

Ethics

We must not overlook Coleridge's function as a senior British official. Naturally, he would be required to favour and emphasise the British perspective and British interests. He could hardly be expected to be indifferent towards British policy goals, indeed, he was required to act as an advocate for them. But did Coleridge's behaviour go beyond the reasonable, even if zealous, advocacy of Ball's policies? Did he provide information that

7   In September 1805 Ball had sought to retain Coleridge's services for the government and he emphasised the role Coleridge could play as a propagandist and political journalist (see Chapter 1).

was strictly truthful in content, but was, nonetheless, intended to mislead?[8] Many students of his work might consider that he was, at the very least, highly selective in the information that he disclosed. More troubling was that some of the information he communicated was inaccurate, possibly designedly so. Some statements seem to have been deliberately misleading; others may (according to a more generous interpretation) have been merely careless or incompetent.

In principle, there is a fundamental distinction between information that is honest, comprehensive, fair and accurate and information that is biased, incomplete, or intended to mislead. This distinction lies at the heart of integrity in public office. Thus, how Coleridge deployed government information is important to an understanding of his experience of ethics in public administration. The record does not disclose the highest standards in public office and this illuminates Coleridge's dilemmas in reconciling himself to the demands of practical politics.

There is ample evidence that Coleridge was aware of the morally-complex nature of the public office he had assumed. His Notebook entries reveal that this analysis began whilst he still held office. Within a few days of his appointment as Public Secretary, he was already asking the fundamental question, "Wherein is Prudence distinguishable from Goodness (or Virtue) – and how are they both nevertheless one and indivisible" (emphasis in original).[9] This was Coleridge's central dilemma. His experience of public office, and reflections upon it, eventually led him to reject a utilitarian conception of political morality. Governmental action should not merely be concerned with the consequences of a political decision but also with the impulses that directed and motivated it. A concern with actions and consequences should not make government indifferent to considerations of morality. Coleridge concluded that these "inward" motives contributed the essence of morality to the outward expression of public policy.[10]

For Coleridge, writing after his Malta period, an exclusively empirical justification of public action was not the appropriate standard by which governmental decisions should be judged. This is made clear in his conclusions concerning the British policy that led to the Treaty of Amiens 1802. From the British point of view, the terms of the Treaty had been hugely

---

8   For a discussion of ethics in modern governmental communication see Yeung.
9   *CN* 2, 2412, 23 January 1805.
10   *The Friend*, 1, 314. It is revealing that in his Notebook Coleridge had interested himself in the relationship between positive law and "the dictates of right reason = inter Jus et aequitatem". *CN* 2, 2413.

advantageous because they brought an end to the costly hostilities with France. For the sake of our peace, Malta would be sacrificed. In particular, the Maltese were to be forced to accept the return of the despotic Order of St John. This would mean not only that the archipelago would fall under French influence, but that it would also expose the Maltese people (who had rebelled against their former French occupiers) to the risk of reprisals.[11] Coleridge's experience of framing Bandi and Avvisi raise similar problems and are also likely to have been in his mind when he later rejected utilitarian principles. We can surmise that it was his disappointment with the ethical standards of colonial administration that led him, upon his return to England, to express such powerful condemnations of the "wickedness" of colonial government.[12] Fairness, truthfulness, accuracy, objectivity and comprehensiveness, in government communication, would have been of concern to Coleridge.

Ball as an Icon of British Values

Coleridge's major task was to restore public confidence in Ball. He had to re-create a mythology of Ball as a wise, caring and selfless public official in order to re-connect with the tide of popularity, earned during the Maltese Uprising (1799-1800), that had led Ball to become known amongst them as "father Ball".[13] Since legislative judicial and executive power was concentrated in Ball's office, Ball was the high-profile embodiment of British values. The Bandi and Avvisi, could be used to promote this. For Coleridge, the Civil Commissioner needed to be not only a mere office-holder but also an icon. This was an integral part of retaining Maltese confidence in the administration. Thus, Coleridge lost no opportunity to present his superior as having a virtuous and prelatic concern for his people. When he warned the inhabitants about the circulation of counterfeit coinage he was careful to attribute kindly and paternal concern to Ball:

> [The Civil Commissioner] wishes to avert the Public of this so that everybody is properly informed, and may then make every possible effort not to be tricked.[14]

He also strove to counter the stentorian and autocratic public image

---

11   Coleridge concluded that the Treaty besmirched British national honour: *The Friend*, 1, 571.
12   To Daniel Stuart, 22 August 1806 *CL* 2, 1178.
13   *The Friend*, 1, 555.
14   (1774) 1 Cowp. 204, 209; 98 ER 1045, 1048.

that Ball was acquiring by suggesting that Ball did not have a monopoly on wisdom. The opening passage of his first Bando is interesting because it represents Ball as "hoping" that he had exhausted all policy options in maintaining the roads – a formula which hints, to the Maltese, of a sense of self-doubt and which, thus, projects Ball's humanity:

> Given the great benefits to be gained from having a road network which is maintained in a good condition, His Excellency the Royal Commissioner wishes to relay to the Public *his hope that, in seeking to obtain this important objective, he does not neglect any of the ways in which it may be achieved* (Emphasis added)[15]

There are also appeals to the Civil Commissioner's "duty" to the governed, and to his inexhaustible selflessness. These can be seen as direct responses to the fault-line underpinning the colonial relationship which was first made so evident to the Maltese after the Treaty of Amiens, and which Ball had revived by his actions in the early part of 1805. In *The Friend*, Coleridge revealed an awareness of the damage that the Treaty had caused to relations between Malta and Britain when the latter had pursued its selfish interests at the expense of the former. In an effort to counter this damage, His Excellency was depicted as working tirelessly for public causes.[16] Coleridge was, therefore, to suggest a close nexus between British and Maltese policy; indeed that Ball would work tirelessly for their "happiness"[17] – a formula which Coleridge understood would suggest giving precedence to their preferences rather than others. It inferred that Maltese interests had been, and would continue to be, prioritised.

Devotion and Selflessness

Coleridge carefully associated Ball with a moral order to counter the Maltese opinion that Ball was merely an oppressive instrument of selfish British colonial ambitions. Religious imagery was deliberately employed because it would strike a powerful cord with the pious Maltese. In the Bando imposing the duty on wine and spirits,[18] Coleridge emphasised Ball's "sacred duty" and stressed that the Commissioner worked tirelessly for the happiness of the Maltese people.

---

15   Bando, 29 January 1805, NLM /MS 430 1/2 Bandi 1790 AL 1805, 356; 431 II/3, 50.
16   *The Friend*, 1, 571; Bando 8 March 1805 NLM LIBR/MS 430 2/2 Bandi 1805 AL 1814, 2.
17   Bando, 8 March 1805, ibid.
18   Ibid. See further below.

This inexhaustible, selfless devotion had been emphasised a few days earlier in an Avviso of 1 March 1805 when Coleridge represented that, "His Excellency devotes all his time to helping public matters".[19] This Avviso had, ostensibly, been issued merely to notify the public of the conviction of one Sacco for extortion. Had Coleridge confined himself to that subject alone the reference to Ball's devotion would have been quite superfluous. Its inclusion reveals that Coleridge was seizing each opportunity to boost Ball's image. The idea of Ball's devotion was clearly a point that Coleridge felt deserved repetition, which invites the suspicion that he knew that, at this moment in Maltese history, the population needed to be convinced.

The repression of political free speech, particularly the banishment of the petitioner before the *Segnatura* who requested political reform, was a shocking event for the Maltese, and was featured as a major grievance later presented in a Petition to the Crown. The Maltese nationalists, thereafter, felt disenfranchised and powerless, because political speech seems to have been relegated to the streets. The anti-Semitic demonstrations in Valletta and the lampooning, in graffiti, of Ball's administration, suggest that the old avenues, by which autocratic power was managed, had been closed by the British. The Maltese were, no longer, prepared to risk banishment by approaching the Civil Commissioner with their political concerns.

Such was the breakdown in trust that, Coleridge had to respond. He seems to have seized the first opportunity he could. The Avviso of 1 March 1805 was used to emphasise Ball's commitment to open and consultative government. The Civil Commissioner, Coleridge declared, "is always ready to listen to petitions from anybody". Thus, although the Avviso was, ostensibly, a minor announcement about a named individual who had been imprisoned for extortion, its true significance was central to the government's wider political agenda, not only in regaining public trust in Ball, but also the constitutional role of the *Segnatura* as a mechanism by which individual complaints could be heard in safety and addressed by government

Criminal Penalties

The Bandi and Avvisi reveal the reluctance of the British to use the criminal law in cases where official action against widespread law-breaking would

---

19   In fact, this approach is an extension of a style that can be found in earlier British Bandi produced under the hand of Alexander Macaulay in which there are references to the wish of His Excellency to "govern wisely".

antagonise Maltese public opinion and provoke dissent. We have described, in Chapter 5, how Ball would have preferred to endure the politically embarrassing cost of repairing the roads rather than use criminal penalties to ensure that damaging wheels (used by the majority of Maltese) were removed from use (even though the damage they caused was expensive to repair). This reluctance is all the more evident given the extremely difficult budgetary crisis and the cost of maintaining the road network, which might, otherwise, have been reduced substantially and quickly. In fact, it is an indication of Ball's political weakness: he simply dared not risk prosecutions of large numbers of Maltese, not least the poorer members of society, who would have been forced either to buy new wheels or face a fine. Coleridge's language suggested a merciful, paternal care, in so far as the kindly voice behind the Avviso (ostensibly Ball's) is concerned, to guide citizens as to their duties rather than allowing them to offend and be punished. This is a theme that emerged in many of Coleridge's Notices. The Avviso of 22 March 1805 employed a similar strategy. Here Coleridge stated:

> Given that he cares as much about the protection of trade as he does about the merchants themselves, His Excellency the Royal Commissioner is very much hoping to avoid the necessity of punishing anybody, or of making anybody suffer [a penalty].

The Avviso of 14 June 1805 revealed that Coleridge was willing to repeat the political message:

> ... His Excellency...believed it necessary to use this notice to avert the Public of this case, hoping that it shall serve as an example to avoid similar punishments in the future.

Coleridge clearly considered it consistent with the desired public image, of the kindly "father Ball", that the latter could, somewhat patronisingly, remind the populace of their duties so that they could comply with the law and avoid getting into trouble. Thus the Avviso of 25 May 1805, following the anti-Semitic disturbances, closes with:

> Now that the senseless pleasure in inventing malicious slander has stopped, and the people have realised their own foolishness, and how damaging their credulity can be, His Excellency hopes that the nation shall again enjoy its former peace, regardless of those who are envious of its happiness. There should therefore be no more need to punish anybody...

The emphasis on Ball's stated unwillingness to punish is a careful response to the concerns which were later to emerge in the Petition of the

Maltese to the British Crown in 1805. It will be recalled that this cited Ball's "thundering vengeance" and "despotic scourge" – which imply the opposite of restraint.[20] We do not know whether Ball was aware of the Petition, but there is a hint that Coleridge understood the scepticism that existed amongst the Maltese. In the Avviso of 5 August 1805, Coleridge seemed to acknowledge that Ball's public reputation had been severely damaged by his use of criminal punishments (and the power of banishment). As in the other instances, he reiterated the Civil Commissioner's distaste for punishment. However in this instrument, Coleridge conceded, frankly, that Ball's claims to restraint required "proof", without which there would be lingering doubts about the Commissioner. The Avviso included the words "[the] ...proof of his desire to prevent, rather than to punish crimes".

Ball as War Leader

Another technique was to depict Ball as the Maltese had first known him – a decisive military commander. Coleridge carefully emphasised the priority that Ball accorded to the safety of the Maltese and his personal sacrifice in prioritising their interests. Coleridge claimed that Ball was willing to take these steps notwithstanding the interests of his own career and reputation. In summary, Ball, selflessly, pursued Maltese interests even to the point of breaching the international legal order. Nothing would stand in the way of his duty to his people.

The Avviso in question concerned passports. As we have seen, in Chapter 5, Coleridge, effectively, appealed to the Maltese to revive Ball's earlier image, as an heroic and successful war leader, by using the narrative about Ball's courage in securing food for a starving population. Ball was presented as an heroic war leader who took serious personal risks to protect the Maltese (for which they should be grateful). In rather stentorian tones Coleridge reinforced this image by pronouncing that Ball would not assist those who chose to defy him. He was presented as a strong, courageous and selfless protector of the Maltese, but also as a leader who demanded obedience.

Political Advocacy

Apart from promoting Ball's public reputation, Coleridge had to win

---

20   *Memorial and Petition of the Maltese* (unsigned and undated): Kew, CO 158/10/151.

the political argument for each measure he announced. In other words, Coleridge was required to convince the Maltese of the case for each new law that Ball introduced. In this way, the project to win back trust in the Civil Commissioner was buttressed by more explicit reasoning within the instruments themselves. Each strategy was intended to suggest the congruence of Maltese and British purposes and values. Coleridge's task, essentially, embraced an endeavour to make this obvious and more convincing to the Maltese.

If Coleridge's motive was to win *ex post facto* popular consent for a measure, it is disappointing that, at times, he did not refrain from some dubious practices to get it. There are numerous difficulties with his use of government information. Many of the policies, which Coleridge was advocating, were introduced for more than one reason. Amongst the various motives, some may have been represented as primary or dominant and others as subordinate. In other words, had the subordinate motives not been present, the measure in question would still have been introduced.

Moreover, when all the reasons underpinning a policy are taken into account it is apparent that some (whether dominant or subordinate) would have been more palatable to the Maltese than others. As we shall see, Coleridge suppressed the unpopular reasons, which are often the dominant reasons, and over-emphasised those that were subordinate yet more popular. This was done to avoid betraying an obvious lack of correspondence between Maltese and British interests. If the true reasons for a policy had become publicly acknowledged, it would have undermined the legitimacy of British rule; Coleridge recognised the need to obfuscate the true purposes of measures which predominantly benefited Imperial interests.

This is not simply because the use of information involved inappropriate emphasis and a lack of objectivity. Some measures contained statements of fact there were simply untrue. As we have seen, we do not know whether this was a deliberate and dishonest attempt to mislead the Maltese, but if it was not, the error was certainly convenient and served policy goals. Thus as we shall see, Coleridge and Ball did not always furnish information that was honest, comprehensive, fair and accurate.

Fairness and Accuracy

Coleridge's first Bando of 29 January 1805[21], which regulated the manufacture

---

21   NLM LIBR/MS 430 2/2 Bandi 1790 AL 1805, 356; 431, II/3, 50.

of cart wheels, included significant justificatory (and exhortatory) material. This was because Ball refused to punish the continued use of certain detrimental wheels, and, therefore, Coleridge had to persuade the Maltese to abandon them voluntarily. Here Coleridge was concerned to show the Maltese that their self-interest aligned perfectly with the interests of the British administration. However, the measure was a fair and accurate statement of policy.

Incomprehensive Information

The Bando of 22 March 1805,[22] which regulated spirits, was different. There, we witnessed Coleridge deploying information which was not comprehensive and doing so with an inappropriate emphasis. His stated reason for the Bando was that regulation of alcohol was necessary to safeguard health. This message would, of course, have fortified the desired image of Ball as a paternal, beneficent lawgiver. However, we have suggested that the dominant motive behind this instrument was the urgent need to address military discipline and community safety given the presence on the Island of eight thousand troops of the expeditionary force. This is not altogether surprising. Had the measure been more accurately depicted, it might have alarmed the population and caused resentment towards the troops on the Island.

A similar issue concerning emphasis and comprehensiveness arose in relation to the excise duty on wine. Here the major reason underpinning the enactment of the duty, reducing Malta's financial subsidy from the British Treasury, would, if publicly known, highlight the structural conflict in colonial rule. In other words, policies such as this, designed to serve British interests, *ipso facto* burdened the Maltese by transferring wealth from Malta to Britain. Coleridge and Ball were, naturally, concerned that this information should not enter the public domain. As we have seen, Coleridge emphasised that the revenue raised would fund additional spending. This was undoubtedly true, but incomplete. The significant omission was misleading – that the majority of the funds raised would be devoted to addressing the deficit and funding existing expenditure. Coleridge's selective use of information helped maintain the fiction that the legislation exclusively served Maltese concerns – the deserving causes – and that the Bando of 8 March 1805 was imposed for the benefit of the

---

22   NLM LIBR/MS 430 2/2 Bandi 1805 AL 1814, 4.

Maltese people. Far from achieving a genuine legitimacy, Coleridge seems to have been compelled to co-operate in manipulative behaviour.

The Bando of 8 March 1805 also revealed other disquieting strategies because it disclosed Coleridge's apparent willingness to exploit Maltese racist sentiment where it served British imperial purposes. He deliberately assured the Maltese that the re-introduced excise duty would be indirectly discriminatory against (unpopular) foreigners, since it was they, and not the Maltese, who comprised the largest group of consumers of wine. The hypocrisy of this propaganda would be revealed within a few months when the Administration was forced to inflict exemplary punishments upon anti-Semites such as Tagliana, Borg, Hasciach and Bonello. Ball and Coleridge were, then, quick to seize the moral high ground by declaring Ball's displeasure about rewarding a courageous Maltese who had, supposedly, prevented the stoning of a victim. The point Ball wished to make, at that moment, was that standing up for the dignity and civil rights of foreigners was a civic duty and not an act that deserved a pecuniary reward. The striking language used in this later Avviso implied that all persons had a moral obligation to protect foreigners. The double standard is glaring.

Even more concern, about manipulation and concealment, can be raised regarding the instruments concerned with the recapture of the army deserters. Coleridge had portrayed the enlisted men as a threat to community safety. The aim was to encourage informants to betray the whereabouts of the missing soldiers to the authorities. To promote his message he had adopted an alarmist tone by proclaiming that the men were "...now armed and roaming the countryside, disturbing the population".

As he must have known, the deserters had only been successful in evading capture because they had the support of family and friends who did not wish their relatives to be sent on overseas service. The suggestion that the deserters were a danger to public safety was demonstrably fictitious. Moreover, this episode also raised other controversies about Coleridge's approach. One particular issue is that the Public Notice of 5 August 1805[23] contained information that was objectively false.

As we have seen, Coleridge, whether deliberately or carelessly mis-described the effect of a Proclamation of 1801, in order to suggest that those inhabitants who sold goods to deserters would be liable to punishment. His strategy at this time was to force the community to withdraw basic supplies from the deserters and starve them back to barracks. To do this he

---

23   NLM LIBR/MS 430 2/2 Bandi 1805 AL 1814, 19.

made unambiguous representations to the Maltese about the criminal law on harbouring, and aiding and abetting the deserters. That must have had a chilling effect upon those selling food to the deserters. However, his public statement that those selling bread to soldiers risked prosecution under the law of 1801 was simply nonsense.

As we have seen, this was not the only bizarre instrument promulgated on that day: the unripened fruit Bando[24] was also problematic. Even if the convenient misstatement was the result of negligence rather than a deliberate intention to deceive, it is an inescapable conclusion that Ball's civil service did not invariably attain the highest standards in public administration. Was Coleridge so ill and exhausted that his effectiveness in office was impaired? Was he simply beyond caring? As the troops' embarkation date drew nearer, was he under such pressure from Ball and the military that he and they felt justified in making any false statement that might assist in the recapture of the men? If it was, indeed, a deliberate deception, it was clearly desperate and even dangerous because the Proclamation of 1801 was a public record. Once the truth about the earlier instrument was realised, the falsehood would have been publicly revealed. Significant public damage to the integrity and reputation of Ball's administration must have resulted.

But this is not the only instance in which Coleridge's published texts raise concerns about accuracy and a possible lack of truthfulness. In the Avviso of 25 May 1805, which announced the exile of Fortunata Tagliana, Coleridge emphasised that her purpose in orchestrating an attack on a suspected Jew was to harm her neighbour, with whom she had a grievance. This was inaccurate. There are at least two possible explanations for this. The first is that Coleridge was not fully briefed: events were moving at such a pace that he may not have seen the witness statements. If that was so then the inaccuracies were explained by, and lent credence to, the British view of the events as a dangerous emergency.

An alternative possibility was that the inaccuracies were deliberate and helped Coleridge's to control the Administration's message. As we have seen, the emphasis upon Fortunata's vendetta with her neighbour may have been politically convenient because it portrayed her as a threat to the Maltese community as well as the Jews. Coleridge seems to have depicted her conduct in a way that was intended to justify, in Maltese eyes, the severe punishment that she received at Ball's direction.

---

24   NLM LIBR/MS 430 2/2 Bandi 1805 AL 1814, 19.

Conclusion: Propaganda?

Arriving at unambiguous conclusions about Coleridge's work is a complex task. Modern conceptions of an impartial and professional civil service were, of course, inapplicable in Malta at that time. In particular, the obligation, contained in the modern Civil Service Code, to maintain integrity, impartiality and honesty, was for the future. The purpose of the twenty-first-century propriety conventions is to make sure that information should be used for government and not for party purposes. This normative framework delineating the modern boundary between legitimate use of information for explanatory purposes and its illegitimate use for party propaganda purposes had not been developed. And even if it had existed in 1805, it would not have been applicable in the context in which Coleridge worked.

It must be recalled that Coleridge was not appointed to be impartial, independent and judicially-minded. Nor was he a civil servant who lacked a political role. He was a salaried politician/administrator and a senior member of an administration required to prioritise the strategic interest of the British Empire. His superior, the Civil Commissioner, was bound, by the Royal Instructions, to pursue the dominant strategic goals set for him by the Secretary of State in London. Pre-eminent amongst these was to make his administration popular. No guidance was offered as to how this popularity was to be achieved, nor were limits set on the tactics to be employed. Coleridge had to work within this political structure to serve the goals prescribed for him. What the Bandi and Avvisi so often reveal is the limited freedom of action Coleridge had to implement laws that conformed to standards he had advocated in his political journalism. Thus, in public office, because he was responsible to Ball, and subservient to the goals of British policy, he was not always able to introduce, into practical politics, the ethical and constitutional values for which he had earlier argued.

That said, not all the techniques employed in Coleridge's Bandi and Avvisi are controversial. Some of the instruments are simply explanatory. Examples include the Bando of 29 January 1805 (which appeals to self-interest to avoid damage to the roads) and the Avviso of 1 March 1805 to the extent that it merely reminds the population about the constitutional right of petition.

In a different category are his instruments which use carefully crafted language to present Ball in a positive light – to boost Ball's public image.

"Spin" that merely amounts to placing policies and actors in a positive, favourable light is commonly accepted even in modern government communication. It does not necessarily offend the modern propriety conventions, even if it does lack objectivity. Misleading information, by contrast, raises ethical questions. Because Coleridge's texts were congruent with, and directed by the overriding policy to attach the Maltese to British rule, Ball's constitutional position made him an emblem of that rule and an embodiment of its values. It was necessary to make him popular in order to make the government popular.

However, Coleridge's use of information went beyond merely presenting information in a positive light – he communicated incomplete information. A political choice was made as to what information to reveal and what to withhold. Whilst the content, of all of the limited information eventually communicated, might have been true, the effect, when judged in the light of what was omitted, meant that the instrument was calculated to mislead the inhabitants. In the examples given above, Coleridge can be seen as advocating the government's viewpoint rather than merely explaining policy. He was seeking to alter Maltese behaviour for politically-sensitive reasons that could not be disclosed. Coleridge's purpose was polemical in the sense that it revealed partisan and selective advocacy for the policy introduced. The intention in these instruments was clearly to delude the population. The Maltese consent that he aimed to secure was neither properly informed nor genuine.

In yet more extreme instances, the information he communicated was inaccurate and possibly even untruthful. Here Maltese opinion was manipulated in ways that demonstrated an attempt to change opinion or alter behaviour regardless of the means necessary to achieve it. It is in this context that Coleridge's work is most problematic. We encounter this tactic where the stakes were at their highest, for example in relation to the new excise duties and the recapture of the deserters. We can be less confident about Coleridge's motive in the case of the deserters, although certainly the administration was at its wits end having failed by all other means to recapture them. Either there was a deliberate intention to deceive the Maltese about the criminal law (that selling food to soldiers was punishable behaviour) or Coleridge made an avoidable but careless mistake. This latter possibility, if it was true, means that Coleridge was simply negligent. If so, it would be consistent with his exhaustion and low morale in the late summer of 1805.

Undoubtedly, Coleridge was troubled by his experience in government. A political actor, concerned with developing a theory of principled governmental action would, naturally, have had qualms about the ways in which information had been used to shape opinion, alter behaviour and secure an apparent consent to British rule. The private admission that he now knew "by heart the awkward & wicked machinery, by which all our affairs abroad are carried on"[25] in part derives from his experiences of drafting and promulgating the Bandi and Avvisi.

6.1. Constitutional Questions

Introduction

Coleridge's struggle, to maintain the legitimacy and acceptability as well as the interests of British rule, caused him to seek justifications for departures from constitutional norms that he might, otherwise, have been disposed to defend. In his political and journalistic writings, published in the years prior to embarking for Malta, there is evidence of an interest in constitutional government, which was based upon assumptions about the rule of law and the separation of powers through balanced government. The question raised by an analysis of the Bandi and Avvisi is whether such assumptions, expressed from the critical perspective of the journalist-commentator, could survive and be adhered to whilst holding public office, given the consultative role he had and the reliance placed upon his opinion, by the Civil Commissioner?

The Morning Post

Coleridge's understanding of constitutional doctrine, some years prior to his going to Malta, is revealed through his work as political leader-writer, special parliamentary correspondent[26] and critic for *The Morning Post* – a paper generally unsympathetic to the government. Important issues he commented upon included, for example, the introduction of the French constitution, 1799, which placed power in the hands of Napoleon,[27] and

---

25   To Daniel Stuart, 22 August 1806, *CL* 2, 1178.
26   See Erdman.
27   *EOT*, 31-57.

Addington's ministry and the peace policy, 1801-1802.[28]

As we saw, in Chapter 1, these writings included a sustained attack upon the French constitution. It will be recalled that the grounds were, in particular, that power was to be vested in the Chief Magistrate (Napoleon) without adequate restraint. A constitutional theory can be inferred from this attack. It looks for the separation of powers and a system of "checks and counterpoises"[29] to include (though must not be based upon) popular representative institutions. Coleridge noted that the formal constraint on power in the French constitution lay with the people but it was, for Coleridge, a bogus, abstract, democracy which, in practice, excluded the poor and whose influence was easily avoided by elites.[30] But Coleridge did not uphold universal suffrage and direct democracy. He stood for a system where the popular will could be a factor in limiting executive power and providing political energy but a factor that was itself to be limited by the constitutionally decisive and conserving role of property interests.[31] The French constitution created a system of democracy, which, on the face of it, because it was indirect, was preferable to universal franchise. Upon examination, however, the popular institutions and the system of choosing representatives turned out to be bogus "ornamental outworks of military despotism"[32] because, in the end, the real benefits of indirect popular influence upon government were lost. It was the executive, and its creatures, which, in the final stage, were to select the members of the national assembly. Thus Coleridge, at this time, accepted the importance of having ways for all citizens to express their interests politically, but not in a way that was decisive. Stability and good government depended on maintaining property interests in the political system as the predominant check on the executive. These articles also made it clear that Coleridge was alive to the difference between appearance and reality; contrasting the justificatory language, in which power was exercised, with its reality. These perspectives can be compared with his defence, in Malta, of a system devoid of any representative institutions, as well as the justificatory and rhetorical role he performed in the drafting of some of the Bandi and Avvisi.

---

28   *EOT*, 276-311.
29   *EOT*, 57.
30   "a mere trick of French politeness", *EOT*, 48.
31   "We are fortunate enough to live in a country in which, for all its defects, the national character is made up, though in different quantities, by all these three principles, the influence of a Court, the popular spirit, and the predominance of property". Ibid.
32   *EOT*, 53.

From these constitutional writings, a strong belief in the principle of political liberty can be inferred. In passages from *The Morning Post* articles of December 1801 and March 1802, for example, Coleridge's objections to emergency measures, such as Pitt's suspension of H*abeas Corpus*, come over as strong and principled in the sense that suspending *Habeas Corpus* and other measures was wrong in principle and could not be justified even in times of emergency. Some of the old groupings in opposition to Pitt were now allied to Addington and, in government, they reintroduced some of Pitt's measures.[33] In Coleridge's view, this was an over-reaction to the weak French threat.[34] However, this was not the crucial point. Coleridge implied that the existence of a threat was not a sufficient justification. Liberty is a constitutional principle that is to be defended against the executive claims that public emergencies justify its limitation.[35] It is this principled confidence in opposing emergency powers that was, perhaps, most strongly challenged by his government experiences in Malta.[36]

The Morning Post Principles and the Maltese Constitution

Coleridge might have looked upon the Maltese constitution with some consternation. Our discussion in Chapter 3 reveals how, in vesting supreme autocratic powers in the Grandmasters (and, later, the Civil Commissioners) the constitutional system did not embody contemporary conceptions of limited government. As we have seen, the power of the Civil Commissioner was unrestrained: he could pass laws on any subject matter, could appoint to any public post, and could overturn the decisions of the courts. There was no independent judiciary, the Civil Commissioners were not answerable to the Maltese courts for their decisions (although the English courts, through legal fictions, could and did obtain jurisdiction), and directions to the judiciary about criminal punishment in particular cases could be issued under the instructions of the Civil Commissioner. We have seen how, in at least one case arising from the insurrection against

33   *EOT*, 305.
34   "it had mistaken a bull-frog for a bull", *EOT*, 279.
35   *EOT*, 284, where Coleridge acknowledges the courage of those who opposed Pitt's oppressive laws and, even in "the trying hour", persisted in acknowledging and proclaiming "the divinity of [liberty's] mission".
36   See also the discussion of Coleridge's apparent acceptance of the need for informants, below.

the Jews, Ball directed the criminal judge to impose a more severe sentence than that permitted under the Code de Rohan. This may have been action that lay within his powers, but it established beyond doubt that the Maltese, unlike their fellow British citizens, would not benefit from an independent judiciary, for their civil justice system was firmly under political control and direction.

However, it is highly significant that such conduct breached Ball's own standards of justice (as well as Coleridge's). As we have seen, when writing retrospectively in *The Friend*,[37] Coleridge presented Ball as a model law-giver. We have already described how, as a naval commander, Ball published a code of disciplinary offences, along with the prescribed punishments, formally set out, in advance, for each type of military offence. No officer was permitted to depart from the published rules when inflicting a punishment. Thus, Ball linked justice with certainty and punishment only took place in accordance with published norms. In setting this standard of adjudication he had wished to avoid the perception that punishments were arbitrary, or that they could be varied.

This makes a surprising and controversial contrast with Ball as Civil Commissioner. In this office, Ball lapsed into a system where "justice" was merely the will of the governor, and where published norms could be ignored if he thought circumstances merited it. For example, there is good evidence that he was willing, if the occasion demanded, to impose penalties beyond those allowed in the Code de Rohan without going through the processes of changing the law.[38] Thus, the Maltese were not treated in accordance with standards of fairness extended to Royal Navy crews. The significance of this is all the greater when it is recalled that the crews were under military discipline in war time. Even this emergency did not, in Ball's opinion, justify a departure from minimum standards of fairness for British seamen.

However, this standard of adjudication was not to be applied to the civilians of Malta, and the decision relating to Borg, Hasciach and Bonello speaks volumes about Ball's true approach to government. It reveals to us how even the civil justice system was recruited to serve imperial purposes[39].

Thus, Coleridge's account of Ball as a naval commander, in *The Friend*, which he related in order to depict Ball's approach to civil government, is not only seriously misleading, but also a particularly striking example of

---

37   *The Friend*, 1, 169-70.
38   See Chapter 5.4: Public Order and Crime.
39   Ibid.

Coleridge continuing the propagandist role he developed in Malta even after he had left the Island and was reflecting retrospectively upon his experiences there.

In fact, the evidence of Coleridge's response to what happened on Malta is difficult to interpret and is not straightforward. As we have seen, his later private correspondence suggested profound disquiet about governmental practices on the Island. It would reflect his struggle between his preference for principled governmental action and a system capable of responding to all contingencies – the darker world of practical politics. But he also refers to the "wisdom" of action, a likely reference to the anti-Semitic uprising which Ball dealt with by taking apparently unlawful actions. Coleridge's choice of words suggest his agreement with the policies pursued and his support for action that lay outside the prescribed normative framework.

Coleridge's apparent willingness to support, in Malta, the political direction of the judicial process, as well as his stout defence of Ball's unlawful policy of granting passports to foreigners, does not sit happily alongside his fierce and, by implication, principled criticism of, for example, the re-suspension of *Habeas Corpus* by Addington's administration, mentioned above. Coleridge seems to have accepted in Malta something he apparently rejected in London, that a government's perception of emergency could justify restricting liberty and limiting the normal processes of law. The reasons are not clear: could it have been an early expression of support for British colonial power that allowed him to advocate disproportionate and pre-emptive force by the British, in order to retain unimportant overseas territories,[40] or was it an acceptance that the subject Maltese were less deserving of constitutional morality than other British subjects? There is no clear explanation. Perhaps the most likely explanation is a proto-Machiavellian acceptance, based upon experience, of the moral compromises required for effective government.

6.2. Coleridge's Laws and the Rule of Law

The General Principle

The rule of law implies that a person should be legally (as distinct from

40   *The Friend*, 1, 298 et seq.

morally) bound only by the law and not by the discretionary judgements of officials if made without legal authority. It is not enough for a public official to act in pursuit of his or her conception of the public interest. Actions must be capable of being authorised under rules of law; and it is to the judges, and the judges alone, that the identification of those social rules which count as legal rules and which are to be the necessary and sufficient guides to official conduct, is entrusted.

By the twenty-first century, the rule of law had, become a complex body of open-textured obligations and values.[41] Even in the eighteenth century the general idea of the rule of law was accepted as an important constitutional value.[42] Douglas Hay,[43] for example, suggests that the idea of law was central to the ideology of Georgian England by which the rule of property was sustained.

Though an important legitimating principle, the rule of law had not, in the early nineteenth century, been given the developed and particularised theoretical exposition that it currently (in the twenty-first century) enjoys. Nevertheless, Dicey's assertion of the "rule or supremacy of law",[44] a late nineteenth-century abstraction from constitutional history, contrasts the rule of law with arbitrary government. The underlying idea is that one of the weapons against arbitrariness is to authorise government only on the basis of legal rules ultimately determined by an independent judiciary.[45] At the very least, this is a formal constraint upon the exercise of power. The Coleridge Bandi exemplify some interesting tensions with this simple idea

---

41   See, for example, the survey of the rule of law in the twentieth century by G. Marshall, in Bogdanor, 56-7; "open texture" (following the definitions of H.L.A. Hart, *The Concept of Law*, 2nd Ed. (Oxford: Clarendon Press, 1994), Chapter VII/I: pp 124-36) implies a core meaning (that government is entitled to act only if authorised by a rule, whatever its content, identified by the courts as a rule of law) and a penumbra of extended meanings and glosses which are attached to the term in different contexts through which procedural and substantive content to the term is added.

42   See Van Caenegen, 17-21, outlining a series of political and intellectual processes beginning in the early thirteenth century. In England the classic authority for the subordination of government to law as laid down by an independent judiciary is Entick v Carrington (1765), 19 *Howell's State Trials* 1029 (see Chapter 2). Thompson, 263, referring to Douglas Hay's researches accepts that "law assumed unusual pre-eminence[in Eighteenth Century England]...[it was the] central legitimising ideology...England is saturated with the notion of law...Royal absolutism was placed behind a high hedge of law".

43   D. Hay, 'Property, Authority and the Criminal Law', 17-64.

44   Dicey, 107.

45   E.g. Entick v Carrington (1765), 19; *Howelll's State Trials* 1029.

of the rule of law

Rules and Discretion

The opposition of the rule of law with arbitrary government means that legal rules should be appropriately specific about the powers granted to public officials and the offences for which punishment can be imposed. The rule of law is challenged by legal rules which grant indeterminate, personal discretion to officials. If the rule of law means governance on the basis of rules, it should mean that the point and bite of the rules should be precise enough to both limit the administrator and to be followed by the citizen.

One of the noticeable characteristics about the Coleridge Bandi is that they are remarkably different in terms of the degree of official discretion that they allow. The usual approach is a wide-ranging discretion, such as the discretion of the court over the way in which the wine trade was licensed.[46] In contrast, many of the criminal sentences imposed were fixed, with no judicial discretion to vary them. Most of them do not have any leeway for adjusting the penalty to the degree of wrongdoing by the defendant or to his or her circumstances. Today, such automatic punishments raise serious difficulties (under the European Convention of Human Rights, for example) but even in the eighteenth century, common law judges would have resisted this restriction of their discretion.

In contrast, in terms of the procedural detail they laid down, it is striking how detailed some Bandi appeared to be. The best example is in the Bando of 21 June 1805.[47] This imposed a duty on foreigners to register with the courts. Apparently, as a matter of legal obligation, it required the President of the Court and the Chief of Police to meet every morning; and the time of meeting was expressly stipulated to be 10 o' clock. The names of the permitted foreigners were then to be entered into a book which the officials had to carry. The required entries recorded the names of permitted foreigners, and the dates when they left the Island. But this was not all because the Bando continued that this and other information was to be placed on the same page but separated by a margin. The following extract illustrates the minutiae of state control:

> They should make clear notes in the margin of all observations relating to the person, to the reason for their arrival and residence on the island, and

46   Bando of 22nd March 1805, NLM LIBR/MS 430 2/2 Bandi 1805 AL 1814, 2.
47   NLM LIBR/MS 430 2/2 Bandi 1805 AL 1814,14.

to the permit granted as a result, and they should provide details of the documents examined. Then, in a separate column, but on the same page, the Chief of Police should note in the above mentioned book the departure of the foreigner, and whether or not he gave back his permit.

Similarly prescriptive regulation characterised the vehicle and vessel registration scheme. The President had to keep a register of carts, gigs, ferry boats and fishing boats; the Administration also interested itself in the details of how the entries were recorded. The Bando specified that each boat or vehicle was to entered on a separate page. This extraordinary concern for detail is itself a challenge to the rule of law since, by its elimination of discretion and flexibility, it creates a legal duty that is not a practicable reality to put into effect. Any failure to meet these detailed requirements and, presumably, the absence of remedy thereto, would bring the law into disrepute.[48]

Comprehensible

If behaviour is to be governed by law, it must follow that the laws must be "followable". At the very least, their requirements must be comprehensible and capable of being acted upon.[49] Coleridge's laws, however, contain a number of provisions that fail the test of comprehensibility. It is impossible to tell, with any degree of certainty, sufficient to guide conduct, what is required or is prohibited by the instrument.

An Avviso of 22 March 1805[50] is an example. It announces that random quality inspections of wine will be carried out. First, it is an Avviso and, as such, was not a law amending instrument. If that had been the intention, a Bando was the appropriate instrument. An Avviso merely indicated how the laws were to be applied in particular situations. However, the text of this Avviso did not refer to any law that was being applied; rather it referred to "a well known and long-established custom" of inspection. Such a reference did not meet a requirement of certainty. Matters get worse because the point of the Avviso was to announce not only that a regime of inspections will begin, but also to threaten the confiscation of bad wine

48 In the absence of any requirement for notification, it is also quite unclear from the Bando how the authorities would become aware of the sale or transfer of a registered vehicle or vessel.
49 This requirement is treated here as a logical requirement of legal rules aiming to govern behaviour. It is not historically specific. The idea has, of course, been given a full theoretical exposition in the twentieth century by Lon Fuller (see Fuller).
50 NLM LIBR/MS 430 2/2 Bandi 1805 AL 1814, 6.

which failed the inspection. The Avviso also referred to the Commissioner's (His Excellency's) desire not to "punish" anyone. Again, it is quite unclear what, if any, authority the Commissioner, or, indeed, a court, would have to exact punishment. So, we have here a notice which fails the rule of law test in two ways. Firstly, it fails the publicity test in the sense that, unless it is itself a legal act, it fails to identify the law which authorises the actions being proposed (see below). Secondly, it fails the certainty test in that it makes no clear distinction between criminal and civil law.

Similar issues arise in connection with the Avviso of 22 May 1805[51] concerning the punishment of Borg, Hasciach and Bonello for spreading false rumours. The Notice threatened severe punishment for certain individuals who did not "undeceive" listeners to false rumours. It is not possible to infer the existence of a criminal offence. There is no way of knowing objectively under what conditions a rumour may have been false, so as to trigger the duty to inform; nor any indication of how a false rumour was established. The concern is that wide, discretionary power, to impose punitive sanctions, was created for the benefit of the executive, but in a way that was, in effect, uncontrollable by the courts.

A similar problem arose in relation to the threat to punish those who did not hand in counterfeit coins.[52] No references were made to the legal basis of any offence and the duty imposed was not specified, for example, in terms of the state of mind and the degree of knowledge that was necessary to justify a punishment. On the face of it the Avviso was an exercise of arbitrary power.

Even where the Avvisi were merely bureaucratic measures making arrangements for how claims against the Administration were to be settled, clarity was sometimes lacking. An example is the Avviso of 8 March 1805[53] dealing with distribution of prize money still outstanding from the surrender of Valletta in 1800. Coleridge included in the distribution those whose claims had not been settled in an earlier distribution of 1803. Nothing in the Avviso made it clear how these claims were to be resolved, nor what evidence had to be produced.[54]

Thus, any legal analysis of "Coleridge's laws" cannot but be struck by these lapses of clarity, certainty and authority that characterise some of the Bandi and Avvisi. Obligations were apparently imposed which were quite

51   NLM LIBR/MS 430 2/2 Bandi 1805 AL 1814, 8.
52   Avviso, 12 June 1805, NLM LIBR/MS 430 2/2 Bandi 1805 AL 1814, 10.
53   Avviso, 8 March 1805, NLM LIBR/MS 430 2/2 Bandi 1805 AL 1814, 3.
54   Avviso, 19 August 1805, NLM LIBR/MS 430 2/2 Bandi 1805 AL 1814, 20.

unclear in their particular application and which (regarding certain Avvisi) did not disclose the legal authority by which they were authorised.

Publicity

If "law" represents the principle of governance on the basis of rules, then publicity and promulgation are two of the necessary conditions for law's authority. In other words, the law must be communicated to those to whom it applies. Enforcement is also at issue because all citizens are assumed to know the law and ignorance of the law does not provide an excuse. Such principles would not only be unreasonable but also ineffectual if there was not some form of process by which laws are publicised. Publicity is, thus, part of the process of legitimation.

Coleridge's laws were announced and displayed in local ceremonies which took place in customary locations in the four cities and Floriana, and in some instances, at farmhouses in rural areas. Annotation at the bottom of each instrument recorded that the ceremony of promulgation had taken place. This recorded how and when the instrument in question was brought to the attention of the public and the means used, such as the beating of drums or the playing of trumpets. No doubt the fanfare had been intended to draw a crowd to ensure the widest possible dissemination of the information contained in the measures.

An example of the annotations relating to publication is as follows:

> Today [date] it has been read, published and displayed in the usual places of these four cities and Floriana, to the sound of trumpets and in the presence of a great number of people.[55]

It seems that there were no legally-mandatory procedural requirements governing either the publication ceremonies or even a mandatory requirement to record that they had taken place. The annotations and the events they described appear to have had no legal significance other than to place on record the fact that publication in accordance with existing custom and practice had taken place. No legal obligations seem to have been involved. The only reference to any "duty" to record the fact that a ceremony had actually occurred concerned the case of one Avviso (25 May 1805).[56] In this case, a letter "requesting" publication came from the Public Secretary's office. This letter may simply have been a re-enforcement of

---

55 Bando of 8th March 1805, NAM LIBR/MS 430 2/2 Bandi 1805 AL 1814, 2.
56 LIBR/MS 430 2/2 Bandi 1805 AL 1814, 9.

customary practice rather than a constitutional requirement.[57] Interestingly, the absence of annotations as to promulgation is a common feature of earlier Bandi (pre-Coleridgean) and this does not appear to have affected their validity as recognisable and enforceable laws.

During Coleridge's Malta period, the laws and public notices were promulgated in Italian. Although this conformed to established local practice, (and was consonant with the "continuity" strategy) it raised important questions, not least because the majority of the inhabitants spoke the Maltese tongue; indeed, two thirds of them probably spoke no other language. Thus, the laws were published in a language that the majority of those bound by them did not understand. This has been considered in Chapter 4. However, the failure of the British administration to communicate its laws effectively in the language spoken by the majority of its population seems explicable only in the context of its overwhelming desire to continue, in so far as was possible, the laws and customs of the *ancien regime*.

6.3. Enforcement and Forms of Punishment

The Use of Sanctions

We have noted, above, instances in which Ball was reluctant to impose criminal penalties upon the population, hoping instead that a warning Avviso would encourage the inhabitants to comply with the law. Where Coleridge's Bandi and Avvisi did disclose a willingness to compel behaviour under threat of a criminal sanction, the different forms of enforcement, permitted by the Bandi, are an interesting feature of his approach. The Bandi created a range of both positive and negative obligations, which were enforced by a range of penalties, although no clear distinction was made between criminal, civil and administrative penalties.

---

57   See annotation of Avviso 25 May 1805 (LIBR/MS 430 2/2 Bandi 1805 AL 1814, 9) which includes the words: "Today, the 26th May 1805 it has been read and published to the sound of drums as requested by the letter from the Government Offices… "

Capital Punishment

Punishment needed to be lawful. Punishments authorised by the Code de Rohan included capital punishment. This was imposed relatively infrequently and only for the most morally-heinous crimes such as murder committed during a deliberate attack, parricide (execution was then followed by severing the perpetrator's hand, if death had been by the sword, and burning of body and hand) and parent killing (Book 5 item 3). Coleridge's Bandi did not create capital offences. There was, however, one unexplained reference to the danger of being shot. This was in an Avviso of 9 March 1805.[58] As we have described, this concerned the misuse of a critical navigational aid moored in the Harbour. The Avviso explained the purpose of the rope and so removed any excuse a person may have for misuse. The Avviso ended: "and any person who continues to misuse this marker will have only themselves to blame if they are greeted by rifle shots". The implication of this was quite unclear: whether the rifle shots were a punishment or came from sentries seeking to deter unlawful immigration or avoidance of quarantine or from unspecified others. Any legal documents, whether advisory or mandatory, that contain such vague and uncertain threats are open to criticism on those grounds.

Prison

The threat of imprisonment is found in the Coleridge Bandi. The Bando of 22 March 1805[59] created a range of legal obligations in relation to trading in wine and spirits, such as the need to obtain a licence. The penalty was, initially, a fine, but non-payment could lead to imprisonment. The term was not specified, but an alternative (presumably at the discretion of the court) was six months on public works. This was within the lower end of punishments (in the Code, for example, a year on public works was part of the punishment for placing slanderous or abusive placards in public places). Imprisonment of one month was imposed for extracting cotton inappropriately (Avviso of 22 March 1805[60]), one month in prison "at his own expense" if an owner of land sold unripened fruit (Bando of 5 August 1805).[61]

---

58 NLM LIBR /MS 431 2/3 Bandi 1804-1808, 97.
59 NLM LIBR/MS 430 2/2 Bandi 1805 AL 1814, 4.
60 NLM LIBR/MS 430 2/2 Bandi 1805 AL 1814, 5.
61 NLM LIBR/MS 430 2/2 Bandi 1805 AL 1814, 19.

Public Works

Being put to public works is another major punishment in the Code. It could be used for vagabondage or for aggravated brawling, for example. In the Coleridge Bandi it is used once – as a punishment for the non-payment of the fifty *oncie* fine that could be imposed upon unlicensed producers, wholesalers or retailers of unlicensed liquor under the Bando of 22 March 1805.[62]

Fines

Fines are widely used in both the Code de Rohan as well as the Coleridge Bandi. A twenty *oncie* fine could be imposed upon craftsmen who manufactured wheels in a way damaging to roads (29 January 1805[63]); fifty *oncie* had to be paid by sellers of liquor (producers, wholesalers, retailers) who were not licensed under the terms of the Bando of 22 March 1805.[64] A ten *oncie* fine was to be imposed, as well as a deportation order, upon a resident foreigner who failed to obtain a resident permit.[65]

An important characteristic of the system of fines was that the discretion of the sentencing judge to fix the amount was frequently removed. In other words, a fixed fine, rather than a scale, was imposed upon rich and poor alike. There was no attempt at proportionality through equality of burden, nor was the court permitted to take into account the circumstances of the offence, nor of the offender, nor any mitigating circumstances, nor was there judicial discretion to impose a higher sentence than that stipulated, for repeat offenders.

One explanation for not allowing judicial discretion was that the British wished to control the fate of convicted persons rather than leave it to their fellow Maltese. Ball, indeed, exercised his powers under the Maltese constitution to impose higher sentences than those prescribed, where he considered it to be appropriate.[66] Another reason was that a fixed penalty offered certainty. This recalled Ball's approach to punishment whilst he served as a naval captain (discussed above).[67] The Maltese would understand

---

62   NLM LIBR/MS 430 2/2 Bandi 1805 AL 1814, 4.
63   NLM LIBR/MS 430 1/2 Bandi 1790 AL 1805, 356; 431 II/3, 50.
64   NLM LIBR/MS 430 2/2 Bandi 1805 AL 1814, 4.
65   Bando, 21 June 1805, NLM LIBR/MS 430 2/2 Bandi 1805 AL 1814, 14.
66   See the Avviso of 22 May 1805, NLM LIBR/MS 430 2/2 Bandi 1805 AL 1814, 8.
67   Coleridge informs us in *The Friend*, 1, 169-170 that Ball would not allow pre-scribed fixed penalties imposed for disciplinary offences to be varied by any officer,

what would happen to them if they offended and, perhaps, would be less willing to pursue a more lenient sentence through the petitioning process discussed in Chapter 2.

The only exception arose in connection with the army deserters who were still successfully evading capture in September 1805 notwithstanding earlier Avvisi designed to secure their return to barracks. By then it must have been very clear to the authorities that the deserters were calling upon a network of local supporters to assist them. No doubt in many cases these were friends, family and relations. Ball allowed the Maltese judiciary to determine the sentences of those convicted of aiding and abetting the deserters. In pursuance of this decision, Coleridge explicitly directed the judiciary to take into account the identity of those involved, which was, no doubt, a signal to the judges to recognise the conflicting loyalties of the families. Besides, allowing the judiciary this exceptional sentencing discretion distanced the administration from the penalties imposed: this was a Maltese matter. It may also have helped erect a limited *cordon sanitaire* around Ball (and the British military) in respect of a policy that was controversial and unpopular.

Exile

Exile was a draconian punishment in the Code de Rohan that was also used in the Coleridge Bandi. In the Code it could be used against vagabonds, manufacturers of weapons without a licence or aggravated fighting. Delinquent women could be exiled to Gozo. In the Bando of 21 June 1805,[68] exile would be the chosen punishment for a Maltese inhabitant who rented accommodation to a foreigner without a permit. It is arguable that at least some of the uses of exile authorised by the Code are preventative measures which remove hooligans from the country; more fearsome but similar in purpose to the way, in twenty–first-century Britain, a football supporter's order can prevent a person leaving the country or an anti-social behaviour order can limit the places a person can inhabit. In this respect the Royal Commission of 1812,[69] discussing the autocratic powers of the Civil Commissioner, noted that he enjoyed the power of exile "by a simple warrant to that effect". This was understood to be a preventative power since it was available where the perceived safety and tranquillity

including himself as captain.

68   NLM LIBR/MS 430 2/2 Bandi 1805 AL 1814, 14.
69   Royal Commission of 1812, 236.

of Malta so required. An example of this prerogative act was the exile of the petitioner to secure the safety of the islands to which reference was made in the Petition of the Maltese to the British Crown in 1805. The use of exile in the Avvisi of 22 and 25 May 1805[70] (announcing the punishments of Tagliana, Borg, Hasciach and Bonello for spreading false rumours), on the other hand, was clearly a judicial punishment.

Administrative Penalties

If there is uncertainty as to whether a penalty is a criminal punishment or a preventative measure, there is more uncertainty on a range of other enforcement measures which, no doubt, are distinctly disadvantageous to the individuals involved but appear to be administrative penalties. An administrative penalty is one imposed with the aim of ensuring the effectiveness of some regulation or order. It prevents activities continuing which should be properly authorised and, thereby, maintains the effectiveness of the order. The penalty, therefore, engages only with the activity regulated and is distinguished from a punishment in that a punishment is aimed at retribution, deterrence or reform rather than achieving the particular state of affairs aimed at by a regulation.

Thus, the Bando of 22 March 1805 created offences concerning the importation and production of spirits. The punishment for breaking these regulations was a fine of fifty *oncie* and imprisonment for an unspecified period, or six months service on public works if the fine was not paid. In addition, though, the offender could lose his livelihood since he was also made to suffer the "permanent" removal of the right to run a shop or business.

Three such administrative measures were used in a series of trade and consumer protection measures enacted on 22 March 1805. These were the permanent confiscation of wines which failed health inspections;[71] loss of a licence to sell wine on anyone who breached a range of licence conditions;[72] confiscation of illegally grown and unlicensed cotton.[73]

---

70   NLM LIBR/MS 430 2/2 Bandi 1805 AL 1814, 8; NLM LIBR/MS 430 2/2 Bandi 1805 AL 1814, 9.
71   Avviso, 22 March 1805, NLM LIBR/MS 430 2/2 Bandi 1805 AL 1814, 6.
72   Bando, 22 March 1805, NLM LIBR/MS 430 2/2 Bandi 1805 AL 1814, 4.
73   Bando, 22 March 1805, NLM LIBR/MS 430 2/2 Bandi 1805 AL 1814, 5.

Informants

The Bandi and Avvisi attest to the widespread use of rewarded informers to enforce the criminal justice system. In the absence of an organised police force (the modern Malta police force dates from July 1814) one way of seeking to enforce the law was through the use of informers.

However, making the system work clearly presented problems because the Maltese seem to have been reluctant to inform on their fellow citizens. For example, the unenthusiastic public response to informing the authorities about fugitives, or the whereabouts of military deserters, clearly caused official exasperation. Even the need to re-draft the law governing unripened-fruit sales so as to avoid the need for a victim (and thus the need for witness evidence relating to a contract of sale) permits the inference that, on a small island, community solidarity, possibly enforced by witness intimidation, was a difficulty impeding law enforcement.[74] Borg complained to Eton that the high crime rates, especially of robbery, were a problem, and that the assailants went undetected; and a possible explanation for this may have been the reluctance of witnesses and neighbours to come forward.[75] A financial inducement to inform may have been the only possible means of encouraging individuals to give evidence against their neighbours.

Informers were rewarded by being granted a share of the gains achieved by their actions. There was clearly an incentive for bounty hunting with all the issues that can bring with it: e.g. false evidence by the informer and the danger of entrapment. Such concerns do not seem to have entered into the consideration of Coleridge or the Civil Commissioner. Thus, those inhabitants who informed on craftsmen making wheels to a forbidden pattern would receive ten *oncie*, half of the fine (twenty *oncie*); the other half going to the Treasury. Those who informed on those illegally growing cotton would receive one quarter of the confiscated cotton. Those who informed the Civil Commissioner of the hiding places of deserters from the Maltese Regiment would be given a "suitable reward". Ten *scudi* would be paid to a person who informed on a foreigner living illegally.[76]

In some circumstances, Sir Alexander Ball showed himself to be opposed to the informer/reward system. This was not necessarily because of fear

---

74   It is interesting that Gauci was reprimanded by the shop workers for protecting a Jew by helping him to obtain police assistance. This hints at a community prepared to insist on its own standards of behaviour, which may have been standards other than those intended by the British authorities.

75   Borg to Eton, 30 May 1806, Kew, CO 158/12/no folio reference.

76   Bando, 21 June 1805, NLM LIBR/MS 430 2/2 Bandi 1805 AL 1814,14.

that the evidence would be unreliable and the innocent convicted; rather it was the sense that informing was a public duty and should not be further rewarded. He seems to have felt it inappropriate to reward someone for merely fulfilling a civic obligation. In the "Fortunata Tagliana" episode, in particular, it was made clear, through the Avviso of 25 May 1805, that not only was the Civil Commissioner displeased at having to punish Fortunata herself but (according to a literal reading) he was even more displeased at having to reward Francesco Borg, the informant, for doing his normal duty and not acting beyond it. Ball communicated his displeasure at rewarding behaviour that fell within his conception of a normal civil responsibility.

Informing was not always just a voluntary, rewarded, activity. It could also become a legal obligation. In the Avviso of 15 July 1805,[77] severe punishment was promised for those who failed to inform the authorities of the whereabouts of deserters from the Maltese Regiment. Coerced informing was necessary, it seems, because it is most likely that many of the deserters were willingly supported and nurtured by their families. Whipping and exile was threatened for those who did not report to the courts false rumours or who did not try to undeceive those spreading false rumours.[78]

There were some startling contrasts here with Coleridge's views, expressed in 1801, on the use of informants by Pitt and the threatened revival of the practice, by Addington, through the enactment of a Bill of Indemnity. This measure was to indemnify those concerned with detaining political opponents after the suspension of *Habeas Corpus* in 1793.[79] At that time, Coleridge condemned the use of informants in strongly partisan words. It was hardly honourable, likely to lead to alarmism and over-reaction by government, to corruption even, if well motivated,[80] to the entrapment of others and to state crimes immune from prosecution. In Malta, by contrast, he co-operated in the laws requiring the use of informants and their reward and was even prepared to make informing a legal duty.

Coleridge and a Civil Administration at War

To what extent can it be argued that wartime conditions justify and

77   NLM LIBR/MS 430 2/2 Bandi 1805 AL 1814, 17.
78   Avviso, 22 May 1805, NLM LIBR/MS 430 2/2 Bandi 1805 AL 1814, 8.
79   The Bill is said to have "established *espionage* by law" (*EOT*, 1, 284, emphasis in original). The passages referred to are *EOT*, 1, 281-5.
80   "When the authors of acts, like these [Bills of Indemnity] seem inclined to shake hands with freedom, we dread the poisoned gloves of Italy". *EOT*, 1, 284.

explain the constitutionally and legally controversial actions of the British administration on Malta?

Coleridge's own account offers some hints of the strain upon the civil government of a territory at the centre of the Mediterranean theatre of operations. By the summer of 1805 the Island had been filled with troops preparing for an expedition, under Lieutenant-General Sir James Craig, to open a new front in Naples. Recruitment to the Royal Regiment of Malta was expected to provide significantly more troops, but to the embarrassment of the civil authorities who could not persuade Maltese civilians to deliver up the deserters, the unit was by no means at combat readiness despite the approaching date of the offensive. Expectation and nervousness must have been contagious. For Coleridge, the raucous sounds of the increasing military presence had now become a "torture".[81] He was ill, overworked and clearly strained.

However, these were not the only reasons for tension within the civil administration. Ball had gambled the credibility of his administration on the corn mission as a last attempt to fulfil expectations in London that he could balance the Island's budget: but this mission was already going awry. Admiral Lord Nelson was at sea; ever more prizes were being adjudicated in the Vice-Admiralty Court in Valletta; the British had not yet been victorious at Trafalgar and an invasion force, protected by the French fleet, still threatened at home. Maltese dissatisfaction with government was deepening, and there had been, during that spring of 1805, grave public disturbances against the Jews. No doubt, the civil administration was nervous, even to some extent, alarmed. But to what extent did these tensions and uncertainties explain or justify the departures from appropriate legal norms?

Much depended upon the nature of the measure in question. However, it would not be possible either to explain or justify all controversial governmental behaviour by reference to the conflict or a state of emergency. Malta was not, for example, under martial law: the constitution was still in force, the courts still sat and judges and administrators applied Maltese laws. Unlike in England, where the government had enacted special "emergency" powers, removing the right of the subject to challenge, in the courts, their arrest and incarceration, Ball had not felt any need to enact emergency legislation on Malta. It was, therefore, the particular political context, more than fears about the general military situation, which

---

81   *CN* 2, 2614.

informed Ball's strategy for government.[82]

Nevertheless, the political and military issues were complex and often intertwined because Ball's assessment of the value of the Maltese archipelago originated in its military value. It was, indeed, this military agenda that ultimately lay behind many of the policies of the civil government. Ball's immediate problems resulted, as we have seen, from the Secretary of State instructing the Civil Commissioners, in 1801, to achieve Maltese consent to British rule, if necessary by indulging their prejudices. Stability, despite the maintenance of an exclusive British control over Maltese public life, had been the dominant objective. Thus there had been no contradiction between crushing anti-Semitic violence (and punishing other forms of anti-Semitic agitation) whilst also subjecting foreigners to more extensive regulation purely on the grounds of nationality. Similarly, Ball's willingness to banish political opponents was also aimed at removing potentially de-stabilising agitators.

Thus, the major characteristics of Ball's polices, as implemented in Coleridge's Bandi and Avvisi, were not adequately explained as immediate responses to the military conflict, although his ultimate desire to retain Malta as a military base could not be discounted. The war neither explained nor justified many of the departures from appropriate legal or constitutional standards. The internal inconsistency of some of the Bandi and Avvisi, the lack of clarity in their draftsmanship were pre-eminent examples of problems that might well have arisen from Coleridge's authorship in more stable and peaceful times.

Often what was at stake was the identification and pursuit of the "public interest". We frequently found that this "public interest" was coterminous with British interests, and where they conflicted with those of the Maltese, the former were routinely prioritised over the latter. This occurred most significantly in the British refusal to establish the Consiglio Popolare (i.e. the refusal to share power with the Maltese); but this priority was also present in some of the Bandi and Avvisi. Coleridge tried, for example, to persuade the Maltese that the new excise duty had been for additional public spending; as we have seen, it had been to meet the demands of the British Treasury. And the fiasco over the recruitment to the Royal Regiment of Malta had been caused by the decision to disregard the willingness of the Maltese to serve only as a local defence force. In each of these examples, Ball had been responding to the objectives set for him by the Secretary of

---

82   This is more fully explored in Chapters 2 and 3.

State, in the Royal Instructions, and later despatches, rather than any war time emergency.

The one instance in which Ball might have pleaded that a state of emergency existed that justified actions not normally consistent with rule of law standards would have been in relation to the severe punishments imposed upon the anti-Semitic agitators. This argument might have arisen, in particular, in the case of the youth, Bonello, aged twelve, and the increased penalties for his co-defendants. The decision to exile these offenders, when taken with the other terms of the Avviso that reminded the public that children would indeed be treated as harshly as adults, did signal official disquiet and even alarm. But even in these extreme cases Ball would not have claimed to have acted outside the law. If challenged he would have argued that the power to augment a criminal sentence was vested in him under the terms of the Maltese constitution, and that he was not using a perceived emergency as a justification for departing from the Code de Rohan.

Conclusion

In Coleridge's Bandi and Avvisi we have a rich and fruitful insight into the workings of a "colonial" legal system. Pre-eminently the legal system, like the political one, was, ultimately, an instrument of British policy and served British imperial purposes. Maltese interests were vindicated only if they were consistent with those of the Imperial power.

Given the overarching policy of "attaching" the Maltese to British rule, most notably expressed in the "continuation" strategy, this tension was dangerous. If exposed as acting selfishly, the British would lose the support of Maltese public opinion; and the future of the territory as a British possession would be jeopardised. It was a tension that had to be recognised and managed. This required deft political accomplishments, but not necessarily moral integrity. Here must have lain Coleridge's central dilemma.

Coleridge, as acting Public Secretary, was principally responsible for presenting the British administration, and each of the legislative measures it proposed, as benign and designed to protect and benefit Maltese society and its fundamental values. His ability to present the laws as congruent with the interests of Maltese society would have been seen by his fellow officials as crucial to the continued British presence on the Island. Moreover, in these Bandi and Avvisi, Ball was heard, but only through Coleridge's voice. Ball's reputation rested significantly upon Coleridge's skills as a draftsman and propagandist.

Despite his earlier writings upon constitutional morality, we discover, in the Bandi and Avvisi, a more ambiguous and elusive Coleridge. He supported harsh measures against anti-Semites, even children; he disguised, from the Maltese, the reasons why new duties were to be imposed; he proscribed future conduct and announced new punishments without apparent legal justification; he encouraged, even compelled, the use of informers; he obfuscated the important distinction between a Proclamation and a Public Notice; and he launched a sustained public relations campaign to preserve Ball's image as a "father" to "his" people. Some of his drafting was so obscure as to be virtually meaningless; sometimes what he demanded of officials was so unnecessarily demanding that compliance would have been almost impossible. Rule of law values such as *nulle peona sine lege,* and the independence of the judiciary were often outweighed by expediency. Coleridge, not least in his praise of Ball, if not in his expressed support for Ball's polices, was complicit in those acts, even if he was not complacent about them.

But, on the other side of the coin, we also find Coleridge as a skilled propagandist. Whilst he could manipulate public opinion by crude obfuscation, he could also produce powerful moral argument to instil outrage against offences and offenders. Coleridge is both more comfortable and more successful when securing deterrence by argument and reason. In a time of public anxiety about the violence between foreigners and the inhabitants, this was essential opinion forming, and it would have been far more valuable to the British authorities than the levelled muskets of the military garrison. This explains why Ball was, in September 1805, keen to have Coleridge return to Malta as editor of *Il Cartaginese.*[83]

---

83   Wordsworth Trust, Grasmere, manuscript WLMS A. Ball, Alexander, Sir.

Appendix 1.   Translations of the Proclamations and Public Notices

By Dr Lydia Davis

PROCLAMATION

29 January 1805[1]

Given the great benefits to be gained from having a road network which is maintained in a good condition, His Excellency the Royal Commissioner wishes to relay to the Public his hope that, in seeking to obtain this important objective, he does not neglect any of the ways in which it may be achieved.

The type of wheel found on gigs and carts today, constitutes the principle reason behind the deterioration and ruin of the roads. Therefore, His Excellency orders and commands that from now on, all similar wheels must be made to fit a model which will be delivered to all respective craftsmen. Furthermore, he orders that the nails that cover the circumference of the wheel should not stick out from the iron rim. Craftsmen who breach these rules will be ordered to pay a fine of twenty *oncie* for each offence, one half of which will be paid to the treasury, and the other half which will go to the informant.

His Excellency hopes that the majority of those who own gigs and carts will, in light of his wishes and of their own comfort, try to alter the wheels of their vehicles, even if they have only recently been made. One therefore expects from now on, to have the satisfaction of seeing the introduction of

---

1   In each case the date has been added by the present authors for ease of reference

a general system for making wheels that, whilst sparing the streets, will also be of some advantage to the owners of gigs and carts. It is easy to see how, when the large and projecting nail heads give continual jolts to gigs and carts, or to people or goods carried in the vehicles, they damage that same gig or cart even more quickly, and, above all, destroy the iron rims of the wheels, which receive the knocks at first hand. These projecting nail heads cause discomfort to the passenger, damage any goods which are being transported, and exhaust the animals all the more, since they act as numerous points of resistance, working contrary to the moving force.

Government Offices 29 January 1805.

Samuel T. Coleridge, Public Secretary to the Royal Commissioner.

G.N. Zammit - Assistant Secretary.

Today the 1 February 1805 it has been read and published to the sound of drums, and similar notices have been displayed in the usual and customary places of this city… its suburb and in individual farm houses, ut q: p felicem Micalles Bann

PUBLIC NOTICE

1 March 1805

Matteo Sacco of Senglea has been imprisoned for having extorted thirty *scudi* from Ignazio Miccallef of Birchircara, under the pretence of obtaining for him the permission to return from exile. He shall continue to remain in prison until he has repaid the sum extorted. His Excellency hopes that this notice will encourage the Public to be wary of this man in the future, and that it will warn sellers of tobacco, who resemble him, not to dare to scrounge money from the credulous public under the pretence of protection. His Excellency, who devotes all his time to helping public matters, and who is always ready to listen to petitions from anybody, does not see why the offence of promising, or of seeking protection in this way, or in other similar ways, has not entirely ceased.

From the Government Offices 1 March 1805

Samuel T. Coleridge, Public Secretary to the Royal Commissioner.

G.N. Zammit - Assistant Secretary

Today the 2 March 1805, it has been displayed in the usual and customary places of this city and its suburb, ut q: Francesca Ebejer

PUBLIC NOTICE

8 March, 1805

Let all those concerned be informed that next Sunday, 10 March, the appropriate local lieutenants will carry out the distribution of payments due to the Maltese people, which is part of the gift of His Majesty for the actions taken during the surrender of Valletta.

During this distribution, no distinction will be made between Corporals and soldiers, nor between those who served only for a short period of time and those who remained in service right up until the surrender of the city. Neither will there be a distinction made between Sergeants and any other officials above the rank of Corporal. In order to avoid any confusion, the same rules as in previous distributions will be applied and they will only be extended to those who, during other similar payments, have shown themselves to have been worthy of participation in a Royal donation.

The right to participate is also extended to those who can prove on the spot, and with correct documentation, that they have previously been unjustly excluded from participating in a similar event, as set out in the rules adopted for such distributions, and according to the laws established by the notice of 11 December 1803.

Such claimants should submit their appeals within the period of one month beginning on the date mentioned above, 10 March. After this time has elapsed, no appeal or request for any reason will be accepted from anybody.

From the Government Offices 8 March 1805.

Samuel T. Coleridge Public Secretary to the Royal Commissioner

G.N. Zammit - Assistant Secretary

Today the 9 March 1805 it has been displayed...

Ut q. Felicem Micalles Banns

PROCLAMATION

8 March 1805

From the first moment of his ascension to the civil government of this island, His Excellency the Royal Commissioner has esteemed it his sacred duty to occupy himself tirelessly with ways in which to make the inhabitants happy, and how to give assistance to those who have suffered greatest damage during the French invasion, and to those who due to general circumstances were either born or fell into poverty, and to those who, having no means of supporting themselves, apart from some civil employment, base all their hopes for a decent style of living on a monthly honorarium.

The Tribunal has been rearranged as have several public projects. Public works have continued uninterrupted and a monthly distribution of charity has been set up. The Monte di Pietà, the hospitals, homes for the poor, for orphans and for students have been restored. The main area of enthusiasm is currently the Bank of the University of these Four Cities, as His Excellency remains most attentive to the situation of those families who keep all their domestic aspirations alive with the capital that they have invested in this post.

Wishing, therefore, to increase support for so many poor families, and bearing in mind that wines and liquors of the kind usually found in Malta are in general consumed by foreigners, it is hoped that it will be in the public interest to increase the scarcity of these products, as this shall force immoderate drinkers to lower their consumption. It is, therefore, evidently better to generate a small increase in the price of wine and liquor, than to decide to increase the price of grain. His Excellency has also decided to reintroduce the duty that was once paid for the importation of wine, bringing into effect the following orders.

1. From today onwards, anyone wishing to import wine must pay duty of six *tari* per barrel.

2. That this resolution is intended to include all types and quality of wine without any exception.

3. That all types of liquor require duty of thirty *tari* for whatever quantity, corresponding to a measure of one barrel.

4. That no place or person for whatever reason may be, or intend to be exempt from the payment of this duty as set out above.

5. That the exaction of such duty should be entrusted to the above

mentioned University.

6. That the penalty of any contravention shall be the confiscation of the entire quantity of wine found to be illegal.

The employment of the money raised by these taxes cannot be detailed before the exact figure is known. His Excellency, therefore, wishes to advise, that it is his intention is to pay all individual owners of capital tied up in the bank of the above mentioned university, interest on their money at the rate of thirty *tarì* for every hundred, without taking into account the interest rate that was agreed at the time of the deposit.

It is, furthermore, the intention of His Excellency to increase the salaries of those employees whom he considers worthy of such a raise, and to give some financial aid to charitable institutions, particularly those which are involved in constructing buildings which will be of benefit to the public.

The first payment of the interest mentioned above will be that of one semester, and will be paid six months after the publication of this proclamation.

As soon as he is able, His Excellency shall not neglect to give the necessary help to places of worship, and to religious foundations.

From the Government Offices March 1805.

S.T. Coleridge Public Secretary to the Royal Commissioner

Dr. G.N. Zammit -Assistant Secretary

Today March 1805 it has been read, published, and displayed in all the usual and customary places of these 4 cities, and Floriana, to the sound of drums and in the presence of several people.

PUBLIC NOTICE

9 March 1805

In the entrance to the Great Port on the side of Sant'Elmo, an area of shallow water has been discovered which, although very small in size, is dangerous nevertheless. In order to warn any ships and boats which may have to pass this point, an anchor has been thrown down, which is attached to a thick cord that can be seen floating.

Some people, however, imagining this marker as being for some other purpose, have misused it, taking it for themselves to use as a mooring berth. By doing this they transport the cable and anchor, and move it away from the correct place, thereby impeding it from doing its job.

In order to prevent this inconvenience, His Excellency has ordered that this public notice should serve to inform the public about the true state of affairs, in such a way that no-one will now be excused, and any person who continues to misuse this marker will have only themselves to blame if they are welcomed by rifle shots.

Government Offices 9 March 1805.

S.T. Coleridge Public Secretary to the Royal Commissioner

Dr. G.N. Zammit - Assistant Secretary

Today the 9 March 1805 it has been fixed in the usual and normal places of these four cities, and Floriana in the presence of several people....

PROCLAMATION

22 March 1805

The attention of His Excellency the Royal Commissioner has been drawn to the abuse of spirituous liquors, and to the damaging effect that they have on health. He has, therefore, willingly undertaken the task of trying to find a way to limit this problem and with this aim in mind he proposes the following decrees, and orders their strict observance.

1. He orders and commands that no-one may import, unload or take delivery of spirituous liquor of any kind without a written license that refers to the person who wishes to receive the goods.

2. That the above mentioned license may be granted whenever required by the President of the Grand Court of Valletta. The President should then make a note of it in the register, which can be opened whenever required in the Tribunal of the Grand Court mentioned above.

3. That as this license deals with alcoholic spirits, it should not be awarded by the above-mentioned President unless done so in moderation to apothecaries, and to those who have a license to produce liquor.

4. That any distillation of wine in order to produce spirits or brandy (acquavita) is strictly forbidden without a special license from the same President, which specifically expresses the quantity to be distilled.

5. That nobody may produce spirituous liquors without having been licensed by a special decree from His Excellency in communication with the Grand Court of Valletta, and without having informed the President of the same Grand Court. In addition, the licensee must have provided a suitable guarantee to pay fifty *oncie* to the treasury in the case of any contravention of the law.

6. That any producer of liquor must be held to account for the quantity of liquor that he was licensed to import, manufacture, or distil. He may not sell any quantity of liquor to any person without first undergoing an inspection to verify the quality of the liquor to be sold. This should be carried out by the Chief-physician, who must certify in writing that the liquor is of sufficient quality so as to pose no risk to health.

7. That once the liquor has been certified as of good quality, the manufacturer may not sell it at retail, or to anyone else except for those who have obtained the necessary license and are authorised to sell it at retail to the Public, heads of family, and people of good character. Every manufacturer is obliged to keep a record of all sales that he makes within

the limits of both this article, and the preceding one.

8. That no shop-keeper, inn-keeper or publican may sell wine or spirits unless he is well-known, of good character, and in possession of the previously mentioned license granted by a decree of His Excellency, in conjunction with the above mentioned Grand Court.

9. That no person within these four cities, and in the Vilhena district shall be licensed to sell, or to display as if for sale, both wine and spirits at the same time, but must choose either one or the other.

10. That on the door of every shop, inn or tavern, there must be a written sign, visible to everybody, which states whether or not the premises is licensed to sell wine and spirits to soldiers. No producer, confectioner, or proprietor of a shop, café, inn or tavern, may sell sprits to soldiers without an express license for this purpose.

11. That whoever is licensed to sell spirituous liquors either resale or wholesale, must present themselves to the President of the Grand Court in order to make a note of it in the register.

12. That any contravention of the preceding articles from number 6 to number 11 should be punished by a fine of fifty *oncie* paid to the treasury. Any non-payment will be punished with imprisonment or six months service on public works. Furthermore, the offender shall suffer the permanent removal of their right to continue in business, or to run a shop.

From the Government Offices 22 March 1805.
S.T. Coleridge Public Secretary of the Royal Commissioner.
Dr G.N. Zammit - Assistant Secretary

Today the 24 March 1805, it has been read and published to the sound of drums, and copies have been displayed in the usual places of this city, its suburb and in individual farmhouses … ut q: per Felicem Miccalles Bann:

PUBLIC NOTICE

22 March 1805

Although the laws of the land forbid the extraction of cotton which is not spun either with seeds, or with wool, his Excellency the Royal Commissioner is, nevertheless, displeased to hear that some people, in the hope of making a profit, are daring to break the law.

Wishing, therefore, to put an end to such incidents, and to punish the audacity of these offenders, he orders that whoever shall dare to extract cotton not manufactured with seeds or with wool, without a specific license, shall be punished with one month's imprisonment, and that furthermore, he shall suffer the confiscation of all the cotton grown illegally, one-quarter of which he must hand over to the informant.

Meanwhile, His Excellency promises to grant some licences for the extraction of a certain amount of cotton if the universal public good so demands, and if this year's crop proves to be plentiful, in such a way that there will be no lack of material for people used to earning a living by spinning cotton.

Government Offices 22 March 1805

S.T. Coleridge Public Secretary to the Royal Commissioner

Dr G.N. Zammit - Assistant Secretary

Today the 24 March 1805 it has been displayed in the usual places of this city and its suburb.

PUBLIC NOTICE

22 March 1805

It is a well known and long-established custom that all wine should be subject to examination by sworn-in officials responsible for food quality and control, both before being sold, and if any doubts are raised as to its quality.

Given that he cares as much about the protection of trade as he does about the merchants themselves, His Excellency the Royal Commissioner is very much hoping to avoid the necessity of punishing anybody, or of making anybody suffer even slightly. He, therefore, wishes to inform all concerned, that from time to time, officials accompanied by the chief physician will carry out random inspections in shops and store houses belonging to wine merchants. Any wine which is found to be of insufficient quality, and therefore damaging to health, will be permanently confiscated.

Government Offices 22 March 1805.

S.T. Coleridge Public Secretary of the Royal Commissioner

Dr. G.N. Zammit Assistant Secretary

Today the 24 March it has been displayed in the usual places of this city and its suburb.

PUBLIC NOTICE

22 May 1805

Let it be known that Giovanni Hasciach from the city of Pinto, Andrea Borg, and the youth Saverio Bonello from Cospicua have been whipped, and will soon be sent into exile for having invented and spread malicious rumours which disturbed the peace of the inhabitants. His Excellency is determined to treat in the same manner all others who are discovered to have started, or who have been complicit in similar gossip. This includes those who have repeated these rumours in normal conversation, and those who, finding themselves present during the relation of such rumours, did not attempt to undeceive the listeners, or to inform the Tribunal of the Grand Court of Valletta.

As this is a situation which regards the peace of the public, the principal aim of any civil society, no status or condition of person, and not even minors, shall be exempt from the severity of the punishment.

Government Offices 22 May 1805.

S.T. Coleridge Public Secretary to the Royal Commissioner

Today the 22 May 1805 it has been displayed in the usual places of this city, and its suburb. Ut q.& ..Felicem Micalles Bann..

PUBLIC NOTICE

25 May 1805

On 22 May this year, Fortunata Tagliana from the Notabile suburb marked out as a Jew one of the French prisoners stationed in the little wood, who had gone into the house of a woman living near her, with whom she was in disagreement. She caused this man to be followed, and he was beaten up and stoned by two or three delinquents who came running after hearing her cries.

Francesco Borg, from the same district, was woken up by the commotion and ran to the area. Far from following the example of the others, he managed to undeceive the pursuers, and by this means he rescued the pursued man.

Fortunata Tagliana has been banished permanently to the island of Gozo, where, having no opportunity to meet any Jews she will be able, with the change in air, to find a cure for her fanaticism.

Francesco Borg has been rewarded with twenty-five *scudi* for his good conduct on this occasion.

His Excellency is disappointed that he has found it necessary to punish Fortunata Tagliana for her attempt to exploit a popular prejudice. He is even more displeased that he has had to reward the act of duty carried out by Francesco Borg, as if it were one of particular merit. Now that the senseless pleasure in inventing malicious slander has stopped, and the people have realised their own foolishness, and how damaging their credulity can be, His Excellency hopes that the nation shall again enjoy its former peace, regardless of those who are envious of its happiness. There should, therefore, be no more need to punish anybody, and rewards will be reserved for those of greater claim and greater merit.

Government Offices 25 May 1805.

S.T. Coleridge Public Secretary to the Royal Commissioner.

Today, the 26 May 1805 it has been read and published to the sound of drums as requested by the letter from the Government Offices... Copies have been displayed in all the usual places of this city and its suburb, and in individual farm houses. Ut q: Felicem Miscalles Bann.....

PUBLIC NOTICE

12 June 1805

His Excellency the Royal Commissioner has learned that there are false coins in circulation, found especially in silver pieces of one *scudo* with the imprint of the Grand Master Rohan. He wishes to avert the Public of this so that everybody is properly informed, and may then make every possible effort not to be tricked. Should anybody come across such a coin, he shall be obliged to deliver it at once to the Tribunal, or to the local lieutenant, indicating who gave it to him, or tried to give it to him, so that he may be brought to justice.

Government Offices 12 June 1805.

S.T. Coleridge Public Secretary to the Royal Commissioner

Today the 13 June 1805 it has been displayed in the usual places....ut q..Philippum Frendo Servum... [illegible]

PUBLIC NOTICE

14 June 1805

Aloisia Caruana has been imprisoned for having dared to offer to Doctor Vincenzo Caruana Zerafa, the Penal Judge of the Grand Court of Valletta, an ounce of Sicilian gold which she hoped would encourage him to look favourably on her appeal. She will continue to remain in prison for several days, and, furthermore, she will suffer the loss of her monetary offering which will be distributed to the poor.

The insult that this woman made to the Tribunal showed her to be clearly of the most offensive opinion, that any difficulties raised in her appeal could be alleviated by the contemptible methods which she tried to use – a belief which certainly deserved the most severe punishment. Given that is the job of His Excellence to instruct each and every person in his duty, he believed it necessary to use this notice to avert the Public of this case, hoping that it shall serve as an example to avoid similar punishments in the future.

Government Offices 14 June 1805.

S.T. Coleridge Public Secretary to the Royal Commissioner

Today the 16 June 1805 it has been displayed in the usual places ut q...Philippum Frenco Servum [illegible]

PUBLIC NOTICE

20 June 1805

The Royal service requests that an end is put to the continual thefts carried out by people who pretend to enrol in the army, take the money and then use it for gambling or for some other underhand scheme, with the hope of being able to return it within the appointed time. It should, therefore, be noted, that the following decree, extracted from the articles of War, otherwise known as Martial law, will in future be fully applied on these islands.

"Whenever any person receives money for enlistment, within the next forty-eight hours, but not sooner than twenty-four hours (unless through his own choice), he must be taken before a magistrate or an official who is appointed to swear in soldiers. Before this official the person will either declare his consent, or else may freely make clear his dissatisfaction at his enlistment. In case of the latter declaration, he must repay the enrolment money, and after making an additional payment of ten *scudi*, he shall be immediately freed from his obligations in the presence of the above-mentioned magistrate or official.

However, if the person indicated above should refuse, or should neglect to repay the above-mentioned money within the aforesaid period of twenty-four hours, this person will be treated as enlisted, and as if he had given his full consent to the appropriate official as laid out in this document.

Government Offices 20 June 1805.

S.T. Coleridge Public Secretary to the Royal Commissioner

Today the 22 June 1805 it has been displayed in the usual places: ut q: Philippum Frendo Servum [illegible]

PUBLIC NOTICE

21 June 1805

His Excellency the Royal Commissioner wishes to clarify various doubts which have been raised regarding the authority of the Lieutenant of Vittoriosa to allow ferry-boats to work at night inside the Grand Port, and also regarding the duties of the night captains with respect to the lieutenants. He therefore orders

1. That the Lieutenant of the City of Vittoriosa should continue to give the usual permission to ferry-boats to work during the night. The customary small dock-charges should be divided up equally between himself, and the two lieutenants of the cities of Senglea and Cospicua, who themselves must remain on the alert for any possible breaches of the law committed by boatmen authorised in this way.

2. That the above mentioned lieutenant of Vittoriosa should only grant the above-mentioned permit to boatmen of whose honesty he is convinced, so that he does not expose himself to being held responsible for any damage which results from the illegal behaviour of anybody to whom, through his own negligence, he has issued a license.

3. Finally, he orders that all night captains should extend the usual courtesies towards all lieutenants, and that together with the people who make up the patrols, they should perform the rounds every night, providing mutual help to one another whenever necessary.

Government Offices 21 June 1805.

S.T. Coleridge Public Secretary to the Royal Commissioner.

Today the 23 June 1805 it has been displayed in the usual places ut q Felicem Micalles Bann [illegible]

PROCLAMATION

21 June 1805

His Excellency the Royal Commissioner, has observed that despite the proclamations issued up until now, which deal with foreigners, carts, boats, and other issues which involve the police, and which have as their objective the preservation of good order and the prevention of crime, he has not yet managed to create a system which is as smooth running and as comprehensive as he would have wished. Therefore, in addition to those regulations already fixed as laws of the land, and to the proclamations already made, he orders

1. That every foreigner wishing to remain for a period of time on these islands must be in possession of a written permit signed by both the President of the Grand Court of Valletta, and by the Chief of Police. The permit should give details of the real name, surname, and home-country of the foreigner, as well as his business, and the amount of time that he wishes, and is able to remain on the island.

2. That every foreigner already resident in these islands must try to obtain the above mentioned permit within eight days. Any foreigners who come and go frequently, should obtain this permit immediately after their arrival, and should they fail to do so, they will be subject to a fine of ten *oncie* and be ordered to depart immediately and prohibited from ever returning. Out of the above mentioned ten *oncie*, ten *scudi* will be paid to the person who informed the Tribunal of the offence, even if he is a minister of the Tribunal himself.

3. That the above mentioned President and Chief of Police, may only award this permit to a foreigner that is able, using the correct documents, to distance himself from any suspicion, and to cite a feasible reason for his entry into this island, and of the need to remain here for some time.

4. That the above mentioned President and Chief of Police may only award this permit for a period of two months, which they may then extend for the same period of time again in one or more instalments as the situation dictates. Should the foreigner wish for permission to reside for longer than four months, he should apply to His Excellency.

5. That any foreigner about to depart must submit his permit to the Chief of Police. In the case of any infringement of this law, he will suffer the penalty of being denied future permission to disembark in these islands.

6. That no inhabitant of any status or condition has permission to give

lodging, or to rent houses to foreigners, either for their use or for others, without having first ensured that the person in question is in possession of the above mentioned permit. In the case of any infringement of this law, the offender shall be sent into exile. No-one shall be exempt from this law, not even those who claim to have been tricked by being shown a permit granted to someone else, as it is easy to obtain the truth of the matter by appealing to the above mentioned President and Chief of Police.

7. That the above mentioned President and Chief of Police, shall meet every day at ten in the morning in the Grand Court of this city Valletta, and there they shall together review the foreigners who have arrived that day. After ten o'clock on the morning of the previous (sic) day, they shall decide whether to grant them permission to remain on the island, and for how long. They should make their decision together, with the participation of His Excellency wherever the circumstances of the case make this necessary.

8. That the above mentioned President of the Grand Court and Chief of Police both carry a book in which they describe in alphabetical order all the travellers who arrive. They should make clear notes in the margin of all observations relating to the person, to the reason for their arrival and residence on the island, and to the permit granted as a result, and they should provide details of the documents examined. Then, in a separate column, but on the same page, the Chief of Police should note in the above mentioned book the departure of the foreigner, and whether or not he gave back his permit. He should then send by hand all the necessary information to the President of the Grand Court, specifying whether or not the above mentioned restitution of the permit was carried out.

9. That all gigs for hire, all carts, all ferry-boats and fishing boats, must display in a visible place, a number painted in oil, which distinguishes them. This number and the place where it should be painted will be assigned by the above mentioned President of the Grand Court, although it must be painted at the expense of the owner of the boat, gig or cart, by any person whom he wishes to employ.

10. That any driver of gigs or carts, and all boatmen, and those who work on fishing boats in place of the proprietor, should preserve the original number which was assigned by the President in the form of a card or parchment, which must always be carried in their pockets.

11. That the above mentioned President should have a register of all the numbers given to carts, gigs for hire, ferry-boats and fishing boats, together with a note of the proprietor, their name, surname, nickname, and home

country or place of residence. One page should be allowed for each number so that in each page it is easy to note all the passengers and all the changes in ownership of the boats, carts and gigs as they happen. Note should also be made if one of the vehicles is destroyed or if it is missing for some reason, and in this case, the vacant number should be reserved for the next boat, cart or gig which has need of one.

12. That in case of infringement of articles nine and ten as stated above, the proprietor of the gig, cart or boat should pay the penalty of six *onze* for the first offence, one half of which should be given to the informant. For the second offence he shall suffer the confiscation of the cart, gig or boat, from the sale of which three *onze* shall be given to the informant. His Excellency desires that the responsibility for the gig, cart, or boat is entirely that of the proprietor, and that the absence of the driver, boatman or sailor, may not be used as an excuse.

13. That the same President is charged with the task of watching over the implementation of this present proclamation, and also of the laws and the proclamations already published with respect to foreigners and to the numbering of gigs, carts and boats. This should also include that section of the proclamation of 3 December 1800, which regards layabouts and vagabonds, and the proclamation of 12 November 1804 which deals with women in politics, and also all the concerns raised in relation to the job of *Maestro di Piazza*.[2] The President should ensure that the Grand Viscount, or his lieutenant, the *Maestro di Piazza*, and the captains and viscounts are on the look out to ensure that these laws are observed. In the case of any infringement of the law on the part of these junior ministers, the President should appeal, as in the past, to the Tribunal of the Great Court of Valletta so that the cases can be dealt with appropriately.

14. That the same President, within the space of one month, must give a copy of the books which he has made as a result of the above mentioned orders, to the Government Office. He should then keep updating the notes held in the office, making sure that he adds any extra information so that these copies correspond exactly to the books which he himself holds.

15. That the fiscal lawyer of the maritime court, and every local lieutenant, is obliged to keep on their person an up-to-date register of the numbers of gigs for hire, and of all the carts in his district which should contain all the notes specified in article 11. Every month he is obliged to identify all

---

2   No record of the Proclamation of 12 November 1804 has been identified in the National Library of Malta. It appears not to have survived.

owners of these gigs and carts, and the condition of their numbers, and he must then make the appropriate written report in the Government offices.

Government Offices 21 June 1805.

S.T. Coleridge Public Secretary to the Royal Commission

Dr. G.N. Zammit - Assistant Secretary

Today the 23 June 1805 it has been read, published and displayed in the usual and customary places of these four cities, Valletta, Senglea, Conspicua and Vittoriosa and in Floriana to the sound of trumpets and in the presence of several people...Salvatore Cortina night-captain of this G.C.

PUBLIC NOTICE

25 June 1805

The attention of His Excellency has been drawn again to the fact that, despite the effective measures which have been implemented at various times in order to deal with the problem, passport-holders have continued to abuse and exploit their rights to hold passports of this island.

Given the lack of our own national ships, and the urgent need to assist the transport of goods, His Excellency was obliged, in those early days following the surrender of these cities, to distribute certificates which promised British Protection to various foreign vessels. The governors of the Barbary states agreed to respect this measure, which was dictated by the necessity of the situation.

Once the abuses began, His Excellency began to wish to deny the validity of the above-mentioned documents. However, as the circumstances mentioned continued to remain the same, he tried to deal with the problem by introducing by-laws and some new restrictions aimed at providing a remedy for the problem. As even these new by-laws then proved to be ineffective, His Excellency had to take the decision not to issue any more passports, nor to promise British protection to any vessels which were not actually Maltese or English. This arrangement was made known to the public with the proclamation of 28 October 1803. Unfortunately, not even this system has been enough to remove every infringement of the law.

It has been discovered that on several occasions, foreigners may have made a false sale of ships to a Maltese subject, an event which has disappointed the Tribunal entrusted with the job of verifying the pertinence of all vessels which require passports.

This discovery has obliged His Excellency to take the decision to deny the usual passports to all vessels, and to order that any authentic English or Maltese vessels of any description must obtain special passports made from parchment, called "passports of the Mediterranean". It is hoped that the surety that will result from the receipt of these passports, will make any abuses of the law stop at once. Therefore, from today onwards, the old-style passports will not guarantee any vessel which leaves from this port.

His Excellency hopes that with such a move, all breaches of the law will stop at once, above all because all those whom it concerns shall be much less willing to take risks. He wishes to inform everyone that the governors of Barberia have become suspicious, and have employed spies everywhere in order to make sure of the authentic and true pertinence of those vessels which travel under the protection of the above mentioned passports. Any foreigners who abuse the law risk not only the loss of their boat and its cargo, but even the possibility of being captured and enslaved. His Excellency does not intend to engage himself in any manner to help those whom he deems to have broken the law in any way.

Government Offices 25 June 1805.

S.T. Coleridge Public Secretary to the Royal Commissioner

Dr G.N. Zammit - Assistant Secretary.

Today the 26 June 1805 it has been displayed in the usual places of this city and its suburb. Ut q. p Felicem Micallese

PUBLIC NOTICE

15 July 1805

Some people enrolled in the Royal Maltese Regiment have deserted, and are now armed and roaming the countryside, disturbing the population.

His Excellency wishes to put a stop to this problem, and, therefore, orders everybody to make all possible effort to discover their hiding places. He promises a suitable reward to whoever shall provide the relevant official with information leading to the arrest of these deserters. In addition, he wishes that any person who provides help for these deserters, or anyone who knows where they are hidden but fails to immediately inform the Tribunal or the appropriate lieutenant, should be severely punished.

Government Offices 15 July 1805.

S.T.Coleridge Public Secretary to the Royal Commissioner

Today the 17 July 1805 it has been displayed in the usual places of this city, its suburb and in individual farm houses. Ut. q; p Mariam Zammit …[illegible]

PUBLIC NOTICE

5 August 1805

His Excellency the Royal Commissioner recognises that, although the proclamation of 3 April 1801 expressly forbids the purchase of any item by soldiers, it is often generally supposed by many people that the purchase of bread is not included in this. As proof of his desire to prevent, rather than to punish crimes, His Excellency has, therefore, ordered that this notice be published, in order to make clear to those who question whether bread and other things are included in the above mentioned prohibition, that the general prohibition on purchasing goods, obviously includes everything.

Government Offices 5 August 1805.

S.T. Coleridge Public Secretary to the Royal Commissioner

Today the 8 August 1805 it has been read and published to the sound of drums and copies have been displayed in the usual places of this city, its suburb and in individual farm houses. ut. que; Felicem Micalles Bann... [illegible]

PROCLAMATION

5 August 1805

Following the proclamation published on 13 May 1803, in which everyone, including the owners of allotments, was prohibited from selling unripened fruit, His Excellency the Royal Commissioner wishes and orders that the above mentioned proclamation is further extended to include those who display unripened fruit of any sort either inside or outside the shop, next to other saleable goods. In addition to the penalty set out in the above mentioned proclamation, the guilty party will suffer the penalty of permanent exclusion from the right to run a shop, or work a plot of land. If they are the actual owner of one or more plots of land, they shall suffer the penalty of one month's imprisonment at their own expense.

Government Offices 5 August 1805.

S.T. Coleridge Public Secretary to the Royal Commissioner

Today the 8 August 1805 it has been read and published to the sound of drums, and copies have been displayed in the usual places of this city, its suburb and in individual farmhouses, ut q p. felicem Micalles Bann...

PUBLIC NOTICE

19 August 1805

It should be noted that next Thursday, 22 August, the distribution will begin in the Government Offices of the payments due to those people who, during the month fixed in the notice of 8 March 1805, applied to obtain their share of the royal donation.

The above mentioned distribution must be finished by the following Thursday, 29 August this year. Consequently, anyone who does not arrive to make a claim during these stated eight days shall lose the payment allocated to him.

In order that no person should show up unnecessarily, it should be noted that people should only apply, if their applications were supported by a statement from a lieutenant or from another similarly responsible official.

Government Offices 19 August 1805.

S.T. Coleridge Public Secretary of the Royal Commissioner.

Today the 21 August it has been read and published to the sound of drums, and copies have been displayed in the usual places of this city, its suburb and in individual farm houses, ut: q Felicem Micalles Bann.

PROCLAMATION

2 September 1805

Desertions by Maltese Soldiers continue to be frequent despite the strenuous measures adopted. This is principally due to the hospitality which these soldiers find in various farm-houses, where they are welcomed, aided and sometimes even assisted with things which, were they to be deprived of, would perhaps dissuade them from deserting, or ensure that it would not be long before they returned to their regiments or were arrested. Given this situation, His Excellence the Royal Commissioner orders that no inhabitant may give shelter or assistance to any of these deserters, under the penalty of being punished with a fine decided by the Tribunal, which should correspond to the circumstances and people involved.

From the Government Offices 2 September 1805.

S.T. Coleridge Public Secretary to the Royal Commissioner

Today the 5 September 1805 it has been read and published to the sound of drums, and copies have been displayed in the usual places of this city, its suburb and in individual farmhouses, ut q: Felicem Micalles Bann...[illegible]

Appendix 2. The British Occupation of Malta

The French Invasion

In June 1798, during the course of the ill-fated expedition to Egypt,[1] French forces invaded Malta. These were met with only limited resistance and the Order quickly surrendered.

By the time of the invasion, the Order had been in serious decline. Firstly, the Maltese regarded it as autocratic and oppressive, not least because it refused to share political power with them. Secondly, in 1792, the French had confiscated its assets, in France, from which it derived significant revenue. This meant that the Island was almost bankrupt.[2] The paternalist welfare policies that we considered, in Chapter 2, were no longer affordable. Within Malta, political support for the continued rule of the Order was in doubt.

On its arrival in Malta, the army of Revolutionary France was seen by many of the Maltese as an army of liberation and they looked forward to enhanced civil and political rights under French government. Many of the knights fled to St Petersburg others, presumably French, accompanied Napoleon to Egypt. After electing the Russian Emperor, Paul I, to be their Grandmaster, the Order came under his protection in the hope that under his influence they could, eventually, be restored to power in Malta. The actions of the occupying French forces soon caused considerable discontent amongst the Maltese people. Their commander, General Claude-Henri

---

1   The expedition was precipitate because the French had not first established maritime supremacy. This was to prove their undoing. A British fleet had been dispatched to the Mediterranean, inter alia, to protect Ireland against a French invasion. French forces had landed in Wales in 1797, which caused considerable alarm, including the "Spy Nosy" affair in which the Home Office placed both Wordsworth and Coleridge under observation. See Holmes, 1989, 159-60.
2   At the outbreak of the Revolution the Order had supported King Louis XVI.

Belgrand de Vaubois, ordered the confiscation of church plate; money was removed from the Maltese treasury and public bank (the Università); the Islanders were taxed. Coleridge reported that men of the Maltese regiments were forced to serve in the French forces in Egypt. He had been informed that they were placed in front of French troops and used as cannon fodder.[3]

The Insurrection

On 2 September 1798, the Maltese, numbering only about three thousand "badly armed" men,[4] rose up against the occupiers. The immediate cause of the revolt may have been the attempted seizure of church property at Rabat. The timing of the popular uprising probably had more to do with the news, which had reached the Island a few days earlier, of the destruction of the French fleet by Lord Nelson's forces at the Battle of Aboukir Bay. The Maltese must now have realised that the British had naval supremacy, and, with the French expeditionary forces stranded in Egypt, the local garrison could not easily be assisted and reinforced – it was, in effect, cut off.

When the uprising broke out, French forces, possibly comprising about seven thousand troops under Vaubois,[5] withdrew into the fortress of Valletta. The fortress was impregnable to attack from the available land forces of their enemies so the withdrawal was consistent with military logic. Safe inside their walls, the French garrison could either make sorties or await relief. The strategy also meant that the burden of feeding the rural population was imposed upon the insurgents.

The Maltese adopted the strategy of siege, placing their forces around the fortress of Valletta on the landward side. However, in the short term, that tactic resulted in a stalemate since they lacked the strength to storm the fortifications, and possessed no heavy weapons with which to demolish the walls. But that was not all. By abandoning the greater part of the Island and its population, the French commander had also reduced the demands upon his food stores. He also removed the Maltese population from Valletta, and the three cities, in order to eke out the food stores available to his forces.[6] The siege, then, could be endured for much longer than had the French

3   CN 2, 2138.
4   Ball to Dundas, 6 March 1801, Kew, CO 158/10/15.
5   Ibid. There are doubts concerning the accuracy of Ball's account because, on 21 December 1798, General Vaubois claimed to have had a mere 3,822 men under arms excluding the sick: Hardman, xxi.
6   Proclama, 15 December 1798, NLM LIBR/MS 430 1 Bandi 1790 AL 1805.

attempted to retain control of the whole Island. It was an astute tactic. In one sense, the Maltese revolt had been counter-productive because, in its absence, the Royal Navy blockade would probably have succeeded in forcing a capitulation by March 1799.[7] This question of tactical effectiveness would have lasting consequences because it was to influence how the narrative of the liberation would be constructed. Whether the British were merely "auxiliaries" to a Maltese effort (and, thus, later wronged the Maltese by excluding them from the articles of surrender), or whether the effective military efforts were exclusively those of the British was a lingering and bitter controversy.

In order to achieve the complete capture of the Island, the Maltese insurgents needed military assistance. This aid was obtained from King Ferdinand IV of the Two Sicilies who had allied himself with Russia, Austria and Great Britain against the French. On 9 September 1798 Maltese deputies also applied to Nelson for his assistance.[8] Nelson responded by ordering four ships of the line, under Portuguese command, to assist the Maltese. He also directed that arms be landed from the British ships "crippled" after sea battle at Aboukir Bay. On 19 February 1799 the Sicilian King formally expressed his agreement that British forces should protect Malta.

Early in the campaign Nelson had replaced the Portuguese naval commander with Captain Alexander Ball (as he then was) of the Alexander, a 74 gun ship of the line. Ball was ordered to pursue the blockade with three other vessels.[9] Nelson later informed the Emperor of Russia that Ball was "an officer not only of the greatest merit, but of the most conciliating manners" and well suited to the task of commanding the squadron of British and Portuguese ships and liaising with the insurgents. Ball, of course, became a significant figure in the early history of British possession of the Island and in Coleridge's accounts of his time on Malta.[10]

Ball was later required to organise the civil government for that part of the Island liberated from the French. Thus, September 1799 saw the beginning of Ball's first period of government of the Island. However, it must

---

7   According to Bosredon Ransijat, President of the French Commission of Government, who was besieged in Valletta: B. Ransijat, *Journal du Siege et Blocus de Malte.* Imp. De Valade, Paris, an. IX, 17 (Journal of the Siege and Blockade of Valletta) quoted in Hardman, 332.

8   After defeating the French at Aboukir Bay Nelson had returned to Sicilian waters to defend the Kingdom of the Two Sicilies against likely French aggression.

9   Terpsichore, Bonne Citoyenne and Incendiary.

10   See generally, *The Friend*, 1; also Kooy, 2003, 441; Kooy, 1999.

be emphasised that in his governmental capacity, he was a representative of the Neapolitan Court, not the British Crown.

Apart from ensuring the administration of civil government in the liberated part of the Island, Ball had to organise the military effort and resolve disputes between the Maltese and their allies. During the prolonged stalemate morale fell, and it was Ball's responsibility to keep up flagging spirits. Ball recounted to Coleridge how onerous he found his diverse and difficult roles.[11]

Nelson's correspondence with Paul I of Russia offered assurances that Britain would make no claim to the Island. British presence on the Island, at this time, always acknowledged King Ferdinand as the legitimate sovereign. Neapolitan troops were deployed against the French during the siege and the Neapolitan flag was ordered to be hoisted on the Island.

By June 1800 the blockade of the Island was causing difficulties for the French garrison. At this crucial moment, Major-General Pigot arrived with two further British regiments. Napoleon must have believed that capitulation was inevitable so he played an astute hand. He seized the opportunity offered to cede Malta to Russia, calculating that this would cause tension between the allies, giving Russia a legitimate claim to Malta *vis-à-vis* Great Britain. This act affected British colonial policy in Malta after 1800 because Britain was forced to regard the governmental arrangements as temporary, pending a final settlement at international level. Formal recognition of this emerged, for example, in the administration of justice that would not be formally vested in His Majesty. No public statements were made asserting that the sovereignty of Malta was vested in Britain. It was only when Russia gave up its claim in 1812 that this policy changed. However, in private and even in some diplomatic exchanges, British officials regarded the Crown as sovereign in Malta after 1800.

The French Surrender

The fortress of Valletta, faced with famine, eventually offered terms of capitulation which were agreed by the British alone and signed on 5 September 1800. It followed negotiations conducted by the English Commanding Officer, Major-General Pigot, without reference either to the Maltese or to the Civil Governor, Captain Ball.[12] Pigot did not sign the

---

11   *The Friend*, 1, 561.
12   Probably because General Vaubois would not have recognised the Maltese in-surgents. Moreover, Ball had been appointed by the King of Naples, and the Con-

articles offered on behalf of His Britannic Majesty *and* his allies.[13] This was a surrender to Britain alone – the Maltese were treated a third parties.

This exclusion from the capitulation caused much bitterness amongst the Maltese.[14] It was not simply a matter of pride that their brothers in arms had appointed themselves as the senior partners in a military alliance, prepared to exclude their fellow combatants from the rituals of victory. The Maltese considered that the British bungled the arrangements under which the French left the Island. Not least amongst these injustices was the failure of the British to accept the French offer of hostages[15] as a guarantee that assets taken from the Università and other public intuitions such as the Monti di Pietà would be compensated. Moreover, the British did not insert any clause in the articles of capitulation indemnifying the private property rights of the Maltese in this respect.[16] Their Maltese allies must have been even more astonished and angry that the British furnished transports to carry the garrison and its spoils to French ports, including money plundered from the Island.

As we shall see, the failure to consult the Maltese and act upon their views contributed to certain unnecessary but intractable political and administrative problems that were instrumental in tainting the first decade of the British administration of the Island. As we have seen, one of Coleridge's most important laws – the Proclamation of 8 March 1805 – was ostensibly introduced to assist those civilians who suffered loss as a result of these events.[17]

The revolutionary Congress of the Maltese was dissolved immediately after the surrender. Ball continued for a brief but highly significant period

gress of the Maltese, neither of which were recognised as legitimate by the French.
13   Article 11 of the *Articles of Capitulation* which explicitly excluded other troops (Appendix to Stoddart CJ's reports, Kew, CO158/91; see also Hardman, 322.
14   According to Coleridge, their feelings had been "insulted", and this "alienated their affections. He emphasised Ball's part in arguing that, as a question of "plain justice", the Maltese should have been included: *The Friend*, 1, 563.
15   Kew, CO 158/19; also Marchese di Testaferrata to Earl Bathurst, January 1812, Hardman, 512.
16   Article 12 did not require the French to furnish compensation. The British agreed to uphold lawful property transactions effected during the occupation. The clause does not require restitution for money and goods taken by the French. Article 12 stated: "All alienations or sales of moveable or immoveable property whatsoever, made by the French government while in possession of Malta, and all transactions between individuals, shall be held inviolable". Answer Art 12 "Granted, as far as they shall be just and lawful".
17   Although as we shall see the Bando had other purposes. See taxation theme, Chapter 5.

(until February 1801) to act as the Civil Governor of the Island. It was in this six month period that he initiated many of the policies that would characterise British administration of Malta. These were driven by his ambition that the Island should remain in British hands, for which it would be necessary to gain the support of the Maltese.

The reasons for Ball's recall, despite his popularity with the Maltese, need to be explained. His presence on the Island had been under the authority of the Neapolitan Crown and tended to suggest its continuing sovereign rights. His presence was, thus, inconsistent with the policy of the British military authorities that would recognise no foreign power as having a claim to the Island. But, there may have also been a more prosaic reason. It seems that his relationship with Pigot was strained;[18] Pigot appears to have wanted to bring the civil administration under his authority and this view was briefly accepted by Whitehall.

Military Government

Rumours had circulated that the British government would adopt a military government following the capitulation. At the time he was preparing to return to his ship, Ball reported to Dundas that the rumours were causing "dissatisfaction" amongst the local population whom he represented as being unanimously in favour of the establishment a civil authority distinct from the military. The Maltese were anxious that under a military government they would be vulnerable to the same oppression that had occurred under the Order of St John. Ball's own opinion, as the former Civil Governor, was that a military governor would not have the opportunity to devote himself properly to civil affairs. Given the strength of feeling locally, Ball urged that the civil and military power be separated.[19]

Although a military government, under Major-General Pigot, was at first installed, its tenure was but a brief one. It was terminated when Charles Cameron was appointed Civil Commissioner on 14 May 1801.

The First Civil Administration

The use of the title "Civil Commissioner" (as opposed to "Governor") was symbolic rather than substantive. It was generally reserved for cases where

18   There is a suggestion of tension in Pigot to Sir Ralph Abercromby, 5 September 1800, quoted in Hardman, 324; see also Pirotta, 53.
19   Ball to Dundas, 6 March 1801, Kew, CO 158/10/15.

some lesser title than "Governor" was appropriate. It did not, necessarily, imply that the office-holder would enjoy fewer powers, but rather that political reasons existed for avoiding the use of the alternative title.[20] In the case of Malta this choice of title was certainly not unconsidered. When Sir Alexander Ball (who succeeded Charles Cameron)[21] requested that he should officially be styled "Governor"[22] his request was denied. It was not until 1813 that a proper, so called, "Governor" was appointed. For internal political reasons, Ball chose to style himself to as the "Royal Commissioner" – a title that he considered had more dignity than the title "Civil Commissioner" and one that emphasised the constitutional relationship between his office and the British Crown.

Malta and the Treaty of Amiens

In March 1801 the Addington Ministry took office in London. Almost immediately it opened negotiations with France to conclude the war. Central to these negotiations was the question of Malta. It was now seen as a strategically-significant Island controlling access to the Levant, to Egypt and, thus, the overland routes to India.

France wanted to see the Order of St John restored so as to ensure that Britain did not retain possession of the Island. In turn, Britain wished to deny Malta to France.

The policy of temporary occupation became obvious in the terms of the Preliminary Treaty of Amiens concluded in October 1801. In this agreement the British government undertook to permit the restoration of the Order of St John to Malta under the protection of Russia. This settlement was acutely unpopular in Malta. Cameron reported to Lord Hobart that a mere rumour of the agreement "has occasioned most violent fermentation" locally.[23] The Maltese remonstrated that, as France had confiscated the French property of the Knights in 1792, in effect, France would have an indirect control of Malta.[24] They were also concerned about possible reprisals against their people.

A deputation was sent to London to remonstrate with the British, but

20   See Roberts-Wray, 306. The actual power conferred was a matter for the Commission and Instructions under which the Governor/Civil Commissioner acted.
21   Cameron was recalled by a despatch of 9 June 1802: Kew, CO 159/3/84.
22   Ball to Windham, 27th August 1806, Kew, CO 158/12/153. Ball made the case for a pay rise and to have his office entitled "Civil Governor".
23   Cameron to Hobart, 23 October 1801, Kew, CO 158/1/335.
24   Hardman, 410-5.

they were arguing against a *fait accompli*. Lord Hobart replied to them, by a letter dated 20 April 1802, that the abandonment of Malta was "an indispensable sacrifice" necessary to secure a general peace.[25] In return for an assurance that the settlement for Malta would include a guarantee of greater political freedom for the Maltese, the deputies were persuaded to accept the restoration of the Order.[26]

This undertaking was reflected in the terms of Article X, of the definitive Treaty of Amiens of 27 March 1802, which was intended to deny Malta both to France and Britain and also to confer greater rights upon the Maltese. The Treaty provided for the restoration of the Order, the neutrality of the Island, the withdrawal of British civil and military authorities, the establishment of a Neapolitan garrison (which was intended to be present only until the Order could raise sufficient forces to garrison the islands[27]) and enhanced political rights for the Maltese, particularly in so far as the Grandmaster of the Order was to be elected from amongst the native Maltese. This was a particularly significant extension of the political rights of the Maltese *vis a vis* the Order.

Russia had not played a part in the negotiation of the Treaty and, subsequently, expressed its discontent at the civil and political guarantees for the Maltese.[28]

Ball's Second Administration 1802-1809.

Ball returned to the islands in July 1802 having succeeded Cameron as Civil Commissioner. He was additionally styled 'minister plenipotentiary to the Order of St John'. His primary task was to implement the Treaty of Amiens.

The restoration of the Order was still deeply opposed by many, if not all, significant opinion in Malta. On 15 June 1802 a Declaration of Rights[29] was issued under the authority of the Congress of the Islands of Malta and Gozo declaring that the 'King of the United Kingdom of Great Britain and Ireland is our Sovereign Lord, and his lawful successors shall, in all times

---

25   Hardman, 424-5.
26   Coleridge condemned the Treaty on moral grounds as an unjust and inhumane instrument that disregarded the national honour of the Maltese: *The Friend*, 1, 571.
27   The Kingdom of the Two Sicilies had effectively become a vassal sate of France. French forces were in central Italy; and there was suspicion that the Neapolitan troops would be indirectly under French control.
28   Hardman, 444-7.
29   Cm 9657 Appendix F; see also Frendo.

to come, be acknowledged as our lawful sovereign'.

The Treaty of Amiens was never implemented (a major dispute was that the British refused to evacuate Malta because of French aggression) and the war with France resumed in May 1803. At that time, Ball was appointed 'Civil Commissioner', and he successfully obtained the removal of Neapolitan troops. Ball continued as Civil Commissioner in this, his second administration, until his death in October 1809. Ball's successor was the military commander, Major-General Hildebrand-Oakes who was himself replaced in 1813 by Sir Thomas Maitland, the first to be described by the British as 'Governor'. Malta then became a colony of the British Empire.

14. Memorial to Sir Alexander Ball, 1757-1809, Lower Barrakka Gardens, Valletta.

References

Ahmed, S., 'The Theatre of the Civilized Self: Edmund Burke and the East India Trials', *Representations*, 2002, 78 (Spring)

Anderson, M.D., *A Saint at Stake: The Strange Death of William of Norwich*, London: Faber & Faber, 1964

Barrell, J., *Imagining the King's Death*, Oxford: Oxford University Press, 2000

Bartolo, P., 'British Colonial Budgeting in Malta: The First Formative Decades 1800-1838', *Melita Historica*, 1, 1980, 8: 1

Bennett, G., 'Towards a Re-Evaluation of the Legend of 'Saint' William of Norwich and its Place in the Blood Libel Legend', 2005, *Folklore*, 1: 16, 119

Blackstone, Sir William, *Commentaries on the Laws of England*, on-line publication, (the Avalon Project): http://avalon.law.yale.edu/subject_menus/blackstone.asp (accessed 8/12/09)

Blaquière, E., *Letters from the Mediterranean: containing a civil and political account of Sicily, Tripoly, Tunis and Malta*, London: Henry Colburn, 1813

Bogdanor, V., *The British Constitution in the Twentieth Century*, Oxford: Oxford University Press (for the British Academy), 2003

Bonnici, A., 'A Debt that was Never Settled', *Melita Historica*, 1988, X, 127

Burwick, F. (ed.), 'Coleridge as Editor: *The Watchman* and *The Friend*', *The Oxford Handbook of Samuel Taylor Coleridge*, Oxford: Oxford University Press, 2009

Caenegen, Van R.C., *An Historical Introduction to Western Constitutional Law*, Cambridge: Cambridge University Press, 1995

Camilleri, J.J., 'Early Government Schools in Malta', *Melita Historica*, 1970, V: 3, 259

Caruana, J.A., *Catalogue of Records of the Public Secretary and Treasurer 1800-1813*, National Malta Archives, Introduction

Chitty, J., *The Prerogatives of the Crown*, London: Butterworths & Son, 1820

Coburn, K., *The Notebooks of Samuel Taylor Coleridge 1804-1808*, New York: Bollingen, 1961

Coleridge, S. T., 'The Friend', in *The Collected Works of Samuel Taylor Coleridge*, general editor Kathleen Coburn, London: Routledge & Kegan Paul, Bollingen Series, 1969

Craig, P., 'Formal and Substantive Conceptions of the Rule of Law: An Analytical Framework', [1997], *Public Law*, 467

Cremona, J., 'The Jury System in Malta', *American Journal of Comparative Law*, 1964, 13/4: 570

— *The Maltese Constitution*, San Gwann, Malta: Publishers Enterprise Group, 1997

Darbishire, H., *The Journals of Dorothy Wordsworth*, Oxford: Oxford University Press, 1958

Davis H, and Hough, B., 'The British Claim to Rule Malta, 1800-1813', *Melita Historica*, 2007, VIV/4: 387-408

Davis, L., *British Travellers and the Rediscovery of Sicily: 16th – 19th Centuries*, unpublished PhD thesis, Nottingham Trent University and Southampton Solent University, 2006

De Quincey, T., *Works II, Recollections of the Lakes and Lake Poets, Coleridge Wordsworth and Southey*, Edinburgh: Adam and Charles Black, 1863

De Selincourt, E., *The Letters of William and Dorothy Wordsworth, 1787-1805*, 2nd edition, revised by Chester L. Shaver, Oxford: Clarendon, 1967

De Vattel, E., *The Law of Nations*, London: G.G. & J. Robinson, 1797

DeBono, J., 'The Chamber of Commerce and the Cotton Trade of Malta in the Eighteenth Century', *Melita Historica*, 1988, X: 1, 27

— 'La Societá delle Scuole Normali della Valletta: A Brief Historical Backdrop', *Melita Historica*, 1996, XII: 1, 47

Dicey, A.V., *Introduction to the Study of the Law of the Constitution*, 8th edition London: Macmillan, 1915; reprinted: Indianapolis: Liberty Classics, 1982

Dundes, A. (ed.), *The Blood Libel Legend: a Casebook in Anti-Semitic Folklore*, London and Madison: Wisconsin, 1991

Erdman, D.V. (ed.), Erdman D. V. (ed.), *Essays on His Times in 'The Morning Post' and 'The Courier'*, in *The Collected Works of Samuel Taylor Coleridge*, volumes, 3: 1-3 (General Editor: Kathleen Coburn), London: Routledge and Kegan Paul, 1978

— 'Coleridge in Lilliput: The Quality of Parliamentary Reporting in 1800, *Communication Monographs*, 1960, 27: 1, 33

Erskine, M., *Constitutional History*, vol. III, 7th edition , London: Longmans Green, 1882

Eton, W., *Authentic Materials for a History of the People of Malta*, London, 1802-07

Frendo, H., (ed.) *Maltese Political Development 1798-1964: A Documentary History*, Malta, 1993

Fuller, Lon. L., *The Morality of Law*, New Haven and London: Yale University Press, 1969

Galea, J., *Some Official Enactments under Early British Rule*, Valletta: Progress Press, 1949

Gittings, R., and Manton, J., *Dorothy Wordsworth*, Oxford: Oxford University Press, 1985

Gregory, D., *Sicily the Insecure Base*, Rutherford: Fairleigh Dickinson University Press, 1988

Griggs, E.L., *Collected Letters of Samuel Taylor Coleridge*, 6 vols., Oxford: Clarendon Press, 1956- 71

Harding, H.W., *Maltese Legal History Under British Rule, 1801-1836*, Malta, 1968

Hardman, W. (ed.), *A History of Malta During the French and British Occupations, 1798-1815*, London: Longmans, Green & Co, 1909

Hay, D. *et al.* (eds), *Albion's Fatal Tree,* New York: Pantheon Books, 1975

Hay, D., 'Property, Authority and the Criminal Law', in Hay, D. *et al.* (eds)

Hesell, N., 'Coleridge and Column Inches' [2005], *Romanticism on the Net:* http://www.erudit.org/revue/ron/2005/v/n40/012457ar.html (accessed on 5/12/09)

Hinsley, F.H., *Sovereignty,* 2nd edition, Cambridge: Cambridge University Press, 1986

Holland Rose, J., Newton, A.P., Benians, E.A. (eds), *The Cambridge History of the British Empire. Vol II: The Growth of the New Empire 1783-1870,* Cambridge: Cambridge University Press, 1940

Holmes, R., *Coleridge: Darker Reflections:* London: Hodder & Staughton, 1998

— *Coleridge: Early Visions,* London: Hodder & Staughton, 1989

Hough, B., and Davis, H., 'Coleridge's Malta', *Coleridge Bulletin* (2007), 29, 81

Jackson, H.J., and Jackson de J. (eds), S.T. Coleridge, *Shorter Works and Fragments,* 2 vols., Princeton: Princeton University Press, 1995

Jacobs, J., 'St William of Norwich', *Jewish Quarterly Review,* 1897, 748

Jenkyns, Sir H., *British Rule and Jurisdiction Beyond the Seas,* Oxford: Clarendon Press, 1902

Knight, W. (ed.), *Journals of Dorothy Wordsworth,* vol. I, London: Macmillan, 1919

Kooy, M.J., 'Coleridge, Malta and the "Life of Ball": How Public Service Shaped "The Friend"', *Wordsworth Circle,* (1999), 30: 102-108

— 'Differences Between Friends: Coleridge, Ball and the Politics of Eulogy', *European Romantic Review,* December 2003

Laferla, A.V., *British Malta,* Valletta: Government Printing Office, 1938

Lefebure, M., *Samuel Taylor Coleridge: A Bondage of Opium,* London: Quartet, 1977

— *The Bondage of Love; a Life of Mrs Samuel Taylor Coleridge,* London: Gollancz, 1986

Leopardi, E.R., '"Bandi" & co. of the XV Century [II]', *Melita Historica,* 1958 II/3: 186

Livingstone Lowes, J., *The Road to Xanadu: A study in the Ways of the Imagination,* 2nd edition (revised), London: Pan Books, 1978

Manning, H. Taft, *British Colonial Government after the American Revolution 1782-1820,* New Haven: Yale University Press, 1933

Marshall, G.,'The Constitution: Theory and Interpretation', in Bogdanor, Chapter 2

Marshall, P.J. (ed.), *The Writings and Speeches of Edmund Burke* (general editor Paul Langford); vol. 5, Oxford: Clarendon Press, 1981

Mizzi, P., *The Grand Masters of Malta 1993,* Malta: Heritage Books, 2000

Muscat, P., *Aspects of Municipal Government in Malta 1720-1780,* unpublished BA Dissertation, University of Malta, 1975

Penn, G., *The Policy and Interest of Great Britain, with respect to Malta, summarily considered,* J. Hatchard: London, 1805

Pirotta, G.A., *The Maltese Public Service 1800-1940: The Administrative Politics of a Micro-State,* Msida, Malta: Mireva, 1996

Purton, V., *A Coleridge Chronology* , London: Macmillan, 1993

Randon, F., 'Civil Commissioner Charles Cameron in Malta', *Melita Historica,* 1995, XI/4: 347

Ransijat, B., *Journal du Siege et Blocus de Malte*, Imp. De Valade, Paris, an. IX

Rapport, M., *Nineteenth-Century Europe*, Basingstoke: Palgrave Macmillan, 2005

Roberts-Wray, Sir K., *Commonwealth and Colonial Law*, London: Stevens, 1966

Royal Commission, *Report of HM Commissioners for Enquiring into the Affairs of Malta*, 1812, Kew, CO 158/19

Sandford, M.E., *Thomas Poole and His Friends*, Macmillan, 1888

Shaffer, E., 'Infernal Dreams in Romantic Art Criticism', *Wordsworth Circle*, 1989, 20, 9

Staines, P., *Essays on Governing Malta 1800-1813*, San Gwann, Malta: Publishers Enterprise Group Ltd, 2008

Sultana, D., *Samuel Taylor Coleridge in Malta and Italy*, Oxford: Blackwell, 1969

Swinfen, D.B., *Imperial Control of Colonial Legislation 1813-1865*, Oxford: Clarendon Press, 1970

Thompson, E.P., *Whigs and Hunters the Origin of the Black Act*, Harmondsworth: Penguin Books, 1990

Thornton, W.H., *Memoir on the Finances of Malta*, Malta, 1836

Thornton, W., *Report to His Excellency the Governor on the Accounts of the University of Valletta from 4th September 1800-31st December 1814*, Kew, CO 163/33, 1816

Uglow, J., *The Lunar Men*, London: Faber and Faber, 2002

Vella, A.P., 'The Cotton Textile Industry in Malta', *Melita Historica*, 1966, IV: 34, 210

Webb, T., 'Coleridge and Robert Emmet: Reading the Text of Irish Revolution', *Irish Studies Review*, (2000), 8/3: 303-324

Wordsworth, W., *Concerning the Convention of Cintra*, London: Longman, Hurst, Rees and Orme, 1809

Yeung, K., 'Regulating Government Communications', (2006), 65, *Cambridge Law Journal*: 53-91

Index

OpenBook Publishers

Open Book Publishers is an independent community interest company set up and run by academics for academics and for readers of academic work. We publish high quality, peer-reviewed monographs, collected volumes and lecture series in the humanities and social sciences.

All Open Book publications are available online to be read free of charge by anyone with access to the internet, allowing our works to be accessible to colleagues, students, and other readers around the world with poor access to research libraries.

Open Book speeds up the whole publishing process from author to reader by applying three recent technological advances: digital medium, the internet and print-on-demand. We thus offer all the advantages of digital texts (speed, searchability, updating, archival material, databases, discussion forums, and links to institutions' websites) together with those of the traditional printed medium.

Works accepted for publication, after the rigorous peer-review process, are published within weeks.

For further information on our publishing enterprise, additional digital material related to our titles or to order our books please visit our website: www.openbookpublishers.com

or contact the Managing Director, Dr. Alessandra Tosi: a.tosi@openbookpublishers.com

Lightning Source UK Ltd.
Milton Keynes UK
13 February 2010

150029UK00001B/26/P